INDEX TO SOUTHERN PERIODICALS

INDEX TO SOUTHERN PERIODICALS

Compiled by

Sam G. Riley

Historical Guides to the World's Periodicals and Newspapers

Greenwood Press

New York • Westport, Connecticut • London

Library of Congress Cataloging-in-Publication Data

Riley, Sam G.
  Index to Southern periodicals.

  (Historical guides to the world's periodicals and
newspapers, ISSN 0742–5538)
  Includes index.
  1. American periodicals—Southern States—Bibliog-
raphy—Union lists.   2. Catalogs, Union—United States.
I. Title.   II. Series.
Z6952.S6R54   1986   015.75′034   85–27232
[PN4893]
ISBN 0–313–24515–0 (lib. bdg. : alk. paper)

Library of Congress Catalog Card Number: 85–27232
ISBN: 0–313–24515–0
ISSN: 0742–5538

First published in 1986

Greenwood Press, Inc.
88 Post Road West
Westport, Connecticut 06881

Printed in the United States of America

The paper used in this book complies with the
Permanent Paper Standard issued by the National
Information Standards Organization (Z39.48–1984).

10 9 8 7 6 5 4 3 2 1

For Heather and Dan

Contents

Acknowledgments

Special thanks are due to Dr. James T. Sabin, Executive Vice President of Greenwood Press, who gave sage advice on the general design of this book. The compiler's gratitude for their patient help is extended to the research librarians at the Library of Congress; the New York Public Library; and the libraries of Duke University, the University of North Carolina, and North Carolina State University; and to the Humanities librarians at Virginia Polytechnic Institute and State University.

Most of all, the compiler thanks the secretarial staff of VPI and SU's Department of Communication Studies: Karen Smith, Bernice Born, and especially Norma Montgomery, for their assistance in word processing. Finally, sincere thanks are given to Professor David L. Sanford of the Department of Communication Studies for his invaluable aid in computer programming and to the VPI and SU College of Arts and Sciences for the grants that allowed the compiler to pursue this three-year project.

INDEX TO SOUTHERN PERIODICALS

Introduction

The most nostalgic and bittersweet of all mass media forms, with the possible exception of old-time radio, is the magazine. America has produced countless thousands of magazines since Andrew Bradford and Benjamin Franklin published the first of their kind, Bradford's *American Magazine* and Franklin's *General Magazine and Historical Chronicle*, in Philadelphia in 1741. A few have lasted for remarkably long periods of time, but the overwhelming majority, like Bradford's and Franklin's, have been ephemeral.

Nowhere has the magazine been more ephemeral than in the American South, which in the 1800s gained the reputation of a magazine boneyard of dashed hopes. During most of that century, magazines were far more "literary" than they are today, and one publisher after another entered the lists, hoping to stimulate Southern letters and give the region its own distinctive periodical literature. One after another, these ventures ended in disappointment, some after a short but respectable run, others immediately after their initial issue failed to attract subscribers or contributors.

Of the roughly 1,800 Southern non-newspaper periodicals identified in this volume as having been founded before 1900, few are remembered today. Only a handful have been written about by historians, literary scholars, communication researchers or anyone else. Even most history professors could probably name few of their titles. For many of these periodicals, no known file remains; most of the others have languished for decades in dusty repose on the shelves of libraries and archives. Few have been preserved on microfilm, with the exception of those included in the excellent effort of University Microfilms. Their American Periodicals Series gives researchers easy access to 88 U.S. periodicals of the 18th century, 923 titles published between 1800 and 1850, and 117 published during the second half of the 19th century. A number of the South's most important 18th and 19th century periodicals have been included in this collection. A few other titles have been put on film by individual libraries, but most have never been filmed, and, due to costs, never will be. A number of the older periodicals, some held in only one or two libraries, are already in advanced stages of decay despite librarians' best efforts to preserve them.

As little remembered as the South's periodicals are, one should pause and reflect on the tremendous investment of talent, effort and money that has gone into them. A case can be made that a region's magazines, whether well supported in their time or not, are a good reflection of its culture. If this is so, then cultural historians have typically overlooked a valuable resource. The compiler hopes that this collection will, in however modest a way, stimulate interest in the use of this region's magazines as a historical resource.

Looking back at magazine publishing in the early South, one is apt to think it a pity that Southerners were so frequently unsupportive, particularly of the region's literary magazines. How sad that so many Southern readers continued subscribing to the older, better established Northeastern magazines instead of the fledgling offerings of their own region. On the other hand, in any given era there are probably more magazines than are really needed. Competition rules, with the strong surviving and the weak giving up publication. The advocate of such a position might also postulate that many magazines are launched with something to say; after a short run, they have often made their point and "fired their best volleys." Writing in Elliott Anderson and Mary Kinzie's *The Little Magazine in America: A Modern Documentary History*, Michael Anania took this position, commenting, "The genius that magazines have shown for graceful dying has not been entirely lost, and it should be cultivated." However one feels on this point, it is likely that magazines will continue being born and will continue dying, with varying degrees of grace, about as frequently as they have in the past.

The compiler began this work and its companion volume, *Magazines of the American South* (Greenwood Press, 1986); with the consumer magazine in mind. It soon became apparent that to exclude the legal and medical journals, religious periodicals, specialized business periodicals, and the like, would give a very incomplete picture of periodical publishing in the South. The decision was then made to be more inclusive than was originally intended; the resulting list of roughly 7,000 periodicals should help dispel the image held by others, notably Northeasterners, of the literary South as a "Sahara of the Bozart," a place of genteel lassitude where men and women do not like to write, or think.

At the project's inception, the compiler's main interest was in the periodicals of the 18th and 19th centuries. A thorough review of the literature revealed that even less has been written about the periodicals of the early 20th century than about those of earlier years, prompting the decision to carry the collection through to the present.

Parameters of the Study

For the purpose of this book and its companion volume, "The South" is defined as the states of the Confederacy--Alabama, Arkansas, Florida, Georgia, Louisiana, Mississippi, North Carolina, South Carolina, Tennessee and Texas, plus Kentucky. Maryland is treated as a Southern state until the Civil War, though in point of fact, magazines with "Southern" in their titles were founded in this state as late as the 1900s. Post-Civil War examples of Baltimore periodicals excluded due to this arbitrary cut-off date are, *Southern Society* (1867-68), *Southern Home Journal* (1867-69), *Southern Magazine* (1868-75), *Southern Medical World* (1889-92), *Southern Farm Magazine* (1893-1908), and *Southern Homeopathic Medical Association Journal* (1918). Only periodicals published in the states listed above are included in this collection.

Also excluded are a number of periodical varieties that may be found in more comprehensive sources such as the *Union List of Serials*: leaflets, looseleaf services, transactions, proceedings, collections, occasional papers, yearbooks, bibliography series, abstracts, brief news bulletins or newsletters, reprint series, conference comments or proceedings, almanacs, reports, handbooks, tracts, and newspapers' magazine sections. The compiler's aim was to include only periodicals of more substance than the ordinary newsletter. Due to the impossibility of examining each of the roughly 7,000 titles listed here, however, it is certain that some newsletters or news bulletins have been listed inadvertently.

The compiler does not feel it necessary to include a full discussion of what constitutes a "magazine," a "periodical," a "journal," or a "review." For such a discussion, the reader is referred to Volume I of Frank Luther Mott's *A History of American Magazines*, pp. 5-9.

Sources of Information Consulted by the Compiler

The compiler's interest in this subject stems from years of teaching journalism and mass media courses in which magazines played a part, and from personal experience in the 1970s working for two Southern regional magazines--as a contributing editor for *Coastal Magazine* of Savannah, Georgia, and as travel editor for *Southern World* of Hilton Head Island, South Carolina.

Standard reference works vital to this project were the *Union List of Serials*, the *Virginia Union List of Serials*, *Ulrich's International Periodicals Directory*, and the *Ayer Directory of Publications*. Of the many other books and articles consulted, the most valuable single source was Frank Luther Mott's five-volume work, *A History of American Magazines*.

Earlier periodical lists consulted were William Burr's *Checklist of American Periodicals, 1741-1800*, Neal Edgar's *A History and Bibliography of American Magazines, 1810-1820*, and eight lists devoted to Southern periodicals:

- Rhoda Coleman Ellison, *A Check List of Alabama Imprints, 1807-1870*

- Bertram Holland Flanders, *Early Georgia Magazines: Literary Periodicals to 1865*

- Gertrude C. Gilmer, *Checklist of Southern Periodicals to 1861*

- Max L. Griffin, "A Bibliography of New Orleans Magazines," *Louisiana Historical Quarterly*

- William Stanley Hoole, *A Check-List and Finding-List of Charleston Periodicals, 1732-1864*

- Frank McLean, "Periodicals Published in the South Before 1880," Ph.D. dissertation

- Kenneth W. Rawings, "Trial List of Titles of Kentucky Newspapers and Periodicals Before 1860," *Kentucky Register*

- "South Carolina Periodicals in the South Caroliniana Library," in James B. Meriwether, ed., *South Carolina Journals and Journalists*

Additional periodicals were located in the card catalogs of the Library of Congress, the New York Public Library, and the libraries of Duke University and the University of North Carolina.

The result of all this collecting is most definitely not a complete list of all the periodicals ever published in the South. Although far more complete than any previous list, it still falls short of being a census. Trying to assemble a complete listing would be almost as difficult as attempting to count the grains of sand on a stretch of beach. Transitory creatures that they normally are, legions of periodicals have come on the scene with little fanfare and have made quick and even more unheralded exits. Any number have never appeared in any of the standard works of reference. The compiler realizes that many titles have slipped through his net, yet is confident that his collection is complete enough to give the reader a representative picture of periodical publishing in this fascinating region of the United States.

Finding the date of a magazine's birth is usually easy enough. Determining its date of cessation, however, is quite another matter. *Ulrich's Directory* contains a special "Cessations" section, but information on ending dates is sketchy even here. When one finds what appears to be a complete file of an old magazine, one is never certain whether the last issue in the collection was actually the magazine's last, or if that particular library simply ceased subscribing. Consequently, this volume contains a great many question marks to indicate uncertain end dates.

Another complication is caused when periodicals change their titles. The primary reasons behind title changes seem to be a desire to better reflect changes in the periodical's statement of "mission," or to respond to changes in the geographic target for its circulation. It is the compiler's impression that religious magazines have been the most prone to title changes, which is possibly an indication of the clergy's faith in the efficacy of words.

Arrangement of Listings

The entry for each periodical is arranged in the following order: title; place or places of publication; dates of publication; any title changes or information on supersessions, absorptions or continuances; and a sample of libraries that hold files of the periodical's back issues.

In showing files, or holdings, the compiler has used *Union List of Serials* abbreviations: DLC for the Library of Congress, NN for the New York Public Library, etc. If a title is widely available to students or researchers on American Periodical Series microfilm, only the designation APS is shown. If the Library of Congress or New York Public Library hold files of a periodical, they are always shown, as these two libraries have the best periodical collections in the nation. For more complete information on holdings for each title, the reader is referred to the *Union List of Serials*, with the caveat that many titles in this volume's listings do not appear in the *Union List*.

The main body of this volume lists periodicals by date of founding, making it easy to study the changing complexion of Southern periodical publishing, from the literary miscellanies of the late 1700s and early 1800s, to the far more specialized magazines and journals of today. In a separate section, periodical titles are listed alphabetically. A third section lists the titles chronologically by state. Periodicals published in more than one state appear in each state's list.

Library abbreviations cited in this volume appear below:

APS   American Periodicals Series Microfilm

ALABAMA

AAP   Auburn University
ABH   Howard College
ABS   Birmingham - Southern College
AMAU   Air University Library
ATT   Tuskegee Institute
AU   University of Alabama
AU-M   University of Alabama Medical Center

ARIZONA

AZ   Arizona State Department of Library and Archives
AzTeS   Arizona State University
AzU   University of Arizona

ARKANSAS

ArU   University of Arkansas
ArU-M   University of Arkansas Medical Center Library

CALIFORNIA

C   California State Library
CCC   Claremont College

CLL   Los Angeles County Law Library
CLOst   College of Osteopathic Physicians and Surgeons (Los Angeles)
CLS   Los Angeles State College
CLSU   University of Southern California
CLU   University of California at Los Angeles
CNoS   San Fernando Valley State College
CPT   California Institute of Technology
CSaT   San Francisco Theological Seminary
CSmH   Henry E. Huntington Library
CSt   Stanford University Libraries
CSt-H   Stanford University-Hoover Institution on War, Revolution and Peace
CSt-L   Stanford University - Lane Medical Library
CStclU   University of Santa Clara
CU   University of California at Berkeley
CU-A   University of California at Davis
CU-M   University of California Medical Center
CU-RiV   University of California at Riverside
CU-SB   University of California at Santa Barbara

COLORADO

CoFS	Colorado State University	DLC	Library of Congress
CoU	University of Colorado	DNAL	United States Agricultural Library
		DNLM	U.S. National Library of Medicine
CONNECTICUT		DNW	U.S. National War College Library
		DP	U.S. Patent Office Library
Ct	Connecticut State Library	DPR	U.S. Public Roads Bureau Library
CtH	Hartford (Ct.) Public Library	DSG	U.S. National Library of Medicine
CtHC	Hartford Seminary Foundation	DSI-M	Smithsonian Institution - National Museum Library
CtHT	Trinity College		
CtU	University of Connecticut		
CtW	Wesleyan University		
CtY	Yale University		
CtY-D	Yale University Divinity School Library	**DELAWARE**	
CtY-E	Yale University Engineering Library	DeU	University of Delaware
CtY-KS	Yale University - Kline Science Library		
CtY-L	Yale University Law Library	**FLORIDA**	
CtY-M	Yale University Medical School Library	F	Florida State Library (Tallahassee)
		FCU	University of Miami
		FCU-L	University of Miami Law Library
		FDS	John B. Stetson University
DISTRICT OF COLUMBIA		FJ	Jacksonville Free Public Library
DA	National Agricultural Library	FM	Miami Public Library
DAL	U.S. Army Library	FMU	University of Miami
DBRE	Bureau of Railway Economics Library	FPY	J. C. Yonge Library (Pensacola)
DBS	U.S. National Bureau of Standards Library	FTS	Florida State University
DCU	Catholic University of America	FTaSU	Florida State University
		FU	University of Florida
DE	U.S. Office of Education Library	FU-HC	University of Florida - J. Hillis Miller Health Center Library
DF	U.S. Bureau of Fisheries Library	FU-L	University of Florida Law Library
DGS	U.S. Geological Survey Library		
DGU	Georgetown University Library		
DGW	George Washington University	**GEORGIA**	
DHEW	U.S. Department of Health, Education and Welfare	G	Georgia State Library (Atlanta)
DHU	Howard University	GA	Atlanta Public Library
DIC	U.S. Interstate Commerce Commission Library	GASU	Georgia State University
DL	U.S. Department of Labor Library	GAT	Georgia Institute of Technology

GDC	Columbia Theological Seminary (Decatur)
GDS	Agnes Scott College
GEU	Emory University
GHi	Georgia Historical Society (Savannah)
GMM	Mercer University
GMW	Wesleyan College
GM1W	Georgia State College for Women
GS	Savannah Public Library
GU	University of Georgia
GU-A	University of Georgia Agricultural Library
GU-L	University of Georgia Law Library

HAWAII

HHS	Hawaiian Sugar Planters Association Experiment Station

ILLINOIS

I	Illinois State Library (Springfield)
IC	Chicago Public Library
ICADA	American Dental Association (Chicago)
ICF	Chicago Natural History Museum
ICHi	Chicago Historical Society
ICJ	John Crerar Library (Chicago)
ICM	Meadville Theological School
ICMILC	Midwest Inter-Library Center (Chicago)
ICN	Newberry Library (Chicago)
ICP	Presbyterian Theological Seminary
ICRL	Center for Research Libraries (Chicago)
ICU	University of Chicago
ICW	Western Society of Engineers (Chicago)
ICarbS	Southern Illinois University
IEG	Garrett Theological Seminary
IEN	Northwestern University
IEN-D	Northwestern University Dental School Library

IEN-M	Northwestern University Medical School Library
IHi	Illinois State Historical Library (Springfield)
INS	Illinois State University
IU	University of Illinois
IU-M	University of Illinois Medical Sciences Library

IOWA

Ia	Iowa State Traveling Library (Des Moines)
IaAS	Iowa State University of Science and Technology
IaU	State University of Iowa
IaU-L	State University of Iowa Law Library

IDAHO

IdU	University of Idaho

INDIANA

In	Indiana State Library (Indianapolis)
InLP	Purdue University
InNd	University of Notre Dame
InU	Indiana University
InU-D	Indiana University School of Dentistry Library

KANSAS

K	Kansas State Library (Topeka)
KHi	Kansas State Historical Society (Topeka)
KMK	Kansas State College of Agriculture and Applied Science
KU	University of Kansas

KENTUCKY

KyBB	Berea College

KyBgW   Western Kentucky
         University
KyL   Louisville Free Public
         Library
KyLF   Filson Club (Louisville)
KyLoS   Southern Baptist
         Theological Seminary
KyLoU   University of Louisville
KyLoU-M University of Louisville
         Medical Library
KyLxCB   College of the Bible
         (Lexington)
KyLxT   Transylvania College
KyU   University of Kentucky
KyU-ASC University of Kentucky
         Agricultural Library
KyU-M   University of Kentucky
         Medical Center

LOUISIANA

LN   New Orleans Public Library
LNHT   Tulane University - Howard
         Tilton Memorial Library
LNL   Loyola University
LNTC   International House -
         Cunningham Library (New
         Orleans)
LNU   University of New Orleans
LNX   Xavier University Library
LU   Louisiana State University
LU-L   Louisiana State University
         Law Library
LU-M   Louisiana State University
         Medical Library
LU-NO   Louisiana State University
         at New Orleans

MARYLAND

MdBE   Enoch Pratt Library
         (Baltimore)
MdBJ   Johns Hopkins University
MdBM   Medical and Chirurgical
         Faculty of the State of
         Maryland
MdBP   Peabody Institute
MdU   University of Maryland
MdU-B   University of Maryland -
         Baltimore

MdU-H   University of Maryland -
         Health Sciences Library

MASSACHUSETTS

M   Massachusetts State Library
         (Boston)
MA   Amherst College
MAA   University of Massachusetts
MB   Boston Public Library
MBAt   Boston Athenaeum
MBA   Congregational Library
         (Boston)
MBCo   Countway Library of
         Medicine
MBM   Boston Medical Library
MBU   Boston University
MBU-M   Boston University School
         of Medicine Library
MCE   Episcopal Theological
         School - John Gordon
         Wright Library
MCM   Massachusetts Institute of
         Technology
MChB   Boston College
MH   Harvard University
MH-AH   Harvard University -
         Andover/Harvard
         Theological Seminary
         Library
MH-BA   Harvard University -
         Graduate School of Business
         Administration Library
MH-Ed   Harvard University
         Graduate School of
         Education Library
MH-G   Harvard University - Gray
         Herbarium Library
MH-L   Harvard University Law
         School Library
MH-P   Harvard University -
         Peabody Museum Library
MH-PA   Harvard University
         Graduate School of Public
         Administration
MH-SD   Harvard University
         Graduate School of Design
MH-Z   Harvard University -
         Museum of Comparative
         Zoology Library
MHi   Massachusetts Historical
         Society
MNS   Smith College
MWA   American Antiquarian
         Society

MICHIGAN

Mi	Michigan State Library (Lansing)
MiD	Detroit Public Library
MiD-B	Detroit Public Library Burton Historical Collection
MiDU	University of Detroit
MiDW	Wayne State University
MiDW-L	Wayne State University Law Library
MiDW-M	Wayne State University Medical Library
MiEM	Michigan State University (East Lansing)
MiU	University of Michigan
MiU-C	University of Michigan - William L. Clements Library
MiU-L	University of Michigan Law Library

MINNESOTA

MNCS	St. John's University
MnHi	Minnesota Historical Society (St. Paul)
MnU	University of Minnesota
MnU-A	University of Minnesota Department of Agriculture Library
MnU-L	University of Minnesota Law Library

MISSISSIPPI

MsAM	Alcorn Agricultural and Mechanical College
MsJS	State Department of Archives and History (Jackson)
MsSM	Mississippi State University
MsU	University of Mississippi

MISSOURI

MoK	Kansas City Public Library
MoKL	Linda Hall Library (Kansas City)
MoRM	University of Missouri School of Mines and Metallurgy
MoS	St. Louis Public Library
MoSB	Missouri Botanical Garden
MoSCS	Concordia Seminary Library
MoSW	Washington University
MoU	University of Missouri

NEBRASKA

NbU	University of Nebraska

NEW HAMPSHIRE

Nh	New Hampshire State Library (Concord)
NhD	Dartmouth College
NhD-BE	Dartmouth College Business Administration and Engineering Library

NEW JERSEY

NjMD	Drew University
NjP	Princeton University
NjPT	Princeton Theological Seminary
NjR	Rutgers University

NEW MEXICO

NmLcU	New Mexico State University
NmU	University of New Mexico

NEW YORK

N	New York State Library (Albany)
NBM	Medical Society of the County of Kings and Academy of Medicine of Brooklyn Library
NBuG	Buffalo and Erie County Public Library
NHC	Colgate University

NHi   New York Historical Society (New York City)
NIC   Cornell University
NIC-A   Cornell University-State Colleges of Agriculture and Economics
NN   New York Public Library
NN-M   New York Public Library - Municipal Reference Library
NNACS   American Cancer Society (New York City)
NNB   Association of the Bar of the City of New York
NNC   Columbia University
NNC-L   Columbia University Law Library
NNC-T   Columbia University Teachers College Library
NNCo   Collectors Club (New York City)
NNCoCi   College of the City of New York
NNE   Engineering Societies Library (New York City)
NNG   General Theological Seminary of the Protestant Episcopal Church
NNHi   New York Historical Society (New York City)
NNJ   Jewish Theological Seminary of America
NNM   American Museum of Natural History (New York City)
NNN   New York Academy of Medicine
NNNAM   New York Academy of Medicine
NNU   New York University Libraries
NNU-D   New York University College of Dentistry
NNU-L   New York University School of Law Library
NNUT   Union Theological Seminary
NPotC   Clarkson College of Technology
NPV   Vassar College
NRAB   American Baptist Historical Society - Samuel Colgate Baptist Historical Library
NRCR   Colgate-Rochester Divinity School
NRE   Eastman Kodak Company (Rochester)
NRU-Mus   University of Rochester - Eastman School of Music
NSoaS   Long Island University

NSU   Syracuse University
NTR   Rensselaer Polytechnic Institute

NORTH CAROLINA

Nc   North Carolina State Library (Raleigh)
NcCU   University of North Carolina at Charlotte
NcD   Duke University
NcD-L   Duke University School of Law Library
NcDurC   North Carolina College
NcGU   University of North Carolina at Greensboro
NcGW   Woman's College of the University of North Carolina
NcGuG   Guilford College
NcMHi   Historical Foundation of Presbyterian and Reformed Churches (Montreat)
NcRS   North Carolina State University
NcU   University of North Carolina
NcU-H   University of North Carolina Division of Health Affairs
NcU-L   University of North Carolina Law School
NcWsW   Wake Forest University

NORTH DAKOTA

NdU   University of North Dakota

OHIO

OC   Public Library of Cincinnati and Hamilton County
OCH   Hebrew Union College
OCHP   Historical and Philosophical Society of Ohio (Cincinnati)
OCL   Lloyd Library and Museum (Cincinnati)
OCU   University of Cincinnati
OCX   Xavier University

OCl	Cleveland Public Library
OC1M	Cleveland Medical Library
OClW	Western Reserve University
OC1WHi	Western Reserve Historical Society
OCo	Columbus Public Library
ODW	Ohio Wesleyan University
OHi	Ohio State Historical Society (Columbus)
OMC	Marietta College
OO	Oberlin College
OOxM	Miami University
OT	Toledo Public Library
OU	Ohio State University
OWC	College of Wooster

OKLAHOMA

OkEP	Phillips University
OkT	Tulsa Public Library
OkTU	University of Tulsa
OkU	University of Oklahoma
OkS	Oklahoma State University

OREGON

OrCA	Oregon State University
OrCS	Oregon State University
OrP	Library Association of Portland
OrU	University of Oregon

PENNSYLVANIA

PBL	Lehigh University
PCA	American Baptist Historical Society (Chester)
PCC	Crozer Theological Seminary
PCaD	Dickinson College
PP	Free Library of Philadelphia
PPAN	Academy of Natural Sciences (Philadelphia)
PPAP	American Philosophical Society (Philadelphia)
PPC	College of Physicians of Philadelphia
PPF	Franklin Institute
PPHi	Historical Society of Pennsylvania (Philadelphia)

PPL	Library Company of Philadelphia
PPi	Carnegie Institute of Technology
PPiM	Mellon Institute Library
PPiU	University of Pittsburgh
PPiU-H	University of Pittsburgh - Maurice and Laura Falk Library of the Health Professions
PPiU-M	University of Pittsburgh - Schools of Dentistry and Medicine
PPP	Philadelphia College of Pharmacy and Science
PPPrHi	Presbyterian Historical Society (Philadelphia)
PSt	Pennsylvania State University
PU	University of Pennsylvania
PU-L	University of Pennsylvania - Biddle Law Library
PU-Mu	University of Pennsylvania - Museum Library
PV-L	Villanova University Law School Library

RHODE ISLAND

RP	Providence Public Library
RPB	Brown University

SOUTH CAROLINA

ScCc	Clemson University
ScClP	Presbyterian College
ScCleU	Clemson University
ScU	University of South Carolina

TENNESSEE

T	Tennessee State Library (Nashville)
TC	Chattanooga Public Library
TCU	University of Chattanooga
TJoS	East Tennessee State College
TKL	Knoxville Public Library System
TMC	Cossitt Reference Library

TMG	Goodwyn Institute
TN	Nashville Public Library
TNF	Fisk University
TNG	George Peabody College for Teachers
TNJ-M	Vanderbilt School of Medicine and Nursing
TNJ-P	George Peabody College for Teachers
TNJ-R	Vanderbilt School of Religion
TNV	Vanderbilt University
TU	University of Tennessee
TU-M	University of Tennessee College of Medicine, Dentistry and Pharmacy

TEXAS

Tx	Texas State Library and Historical Commission (Austin)
TxArU	University of Texas at Arlington
TxCM	Texas A & M University
TxCaW	West Texas State College
TxDa	Dallas Public Library
TxDaM	Southern Methodist University
TxDaM-P	Perkins School of Theology
TxDN	North Texas State College
TxFS	Southwestern Baptist Theological Seminary
TxFTC	Texas Christian University
TxH	Houston Public Library
TxHMC	Texas Medical Center Library (Houston)
TxHP	Texas Research Institute of Mental Sciences Library (Houston)
TxHR	Rice University
TxKT	Texas College of Arts and Industries Library
TxLT	Texas Tech University
TxSaT	Trinity University
TxU	University of Texas
TxU-Hu	University of Texas - Humanities Research Center
TxU-M	University of Texas Medical School
TxWB	Baylor University

UTAH

ULA	Utah State University
UPB	Brigham Young University
UU	University of Utah

VERMONT

VtU	University of Vermont and State Agricultural College

VIRGINIA

VBP	Virginia Polytechnic Institute
VHS	Hampden-Sydney College
VLxW	Washington and Lee University
VR	Richmond Public Library
VRM	Medical College of Virginia
VRT	Union Theological Seminary
VRU	University of Richmond
Vi	Virginia State Library (Richmond)
ViBlbV	Virginia Polytechnic Institute and State University
ViLxW	Washington and Lee University
ViRCU-H	Virginia Commonwealth University
ViRM	Medical College of Virginia
ViRUT	Union Theological Seminary
ViU	University of Virginia
ViU-H	University of Virginia - Health Sciences Library
ViU-L	University of Virginia Law Library
ViU-M	University of Virginia Medical Library
ViW	College of William and Mary

WASHINGTON

Wa	Washington State Library (Olympia)
WaS	Seattle Public Library
WaU	University of Washington
WaU-L	University of Washington Law Library

WEST VIRGINIA

WvU   West Virginia University

WISCONSIN

WHi   State Historical Society of
       Wisconsin
WM   Milwaukee Public Library
WU   University of Wisconsin

WYOMING

WyU   Wyoming University

CANADA

CaAEU   University of Alberta
CaOONL National Library of Canada
        (Ottawa)
CaOONM National Museums of Canada
        (Ottawa)
CaQMAI Arctic Institute of North
        America (Montreal)

Chronological List of Southern Periodicals

*The North Carolina Magazine, or
Universal Intelligencer*,
Newbern, N.C., 1764-1765, APS

Musical Magazine, Cheshire, Conn.;
Baltimore, Md.; Philadelphia,
Pa., 1792-99, APS

Free Universal Magazine,
Baltimore, Md., Sept. 1793 only?
APS

*Monthly Mirror, or, Maryland
Museum*, Baltimore, Md., 1793

Maryland Magazine, Baltimore, Md.,
1794

The Traiteur, Charleston, S.C.,
1795-96

*Maryland Pocket Magazine, or
Elegant Repository of Useful
Knowledge and Entertainment*,
Baltimore, Md., 1796, MH

*South Carolina Weekly Museum, and
Complete Magazine of
Entertainment and Intelligence*,
Charleston, S.C., 1797-98, APS

The Weekly Museum, Baltimore, Md.,
1797, APS

*The General Magazine and
Impartial Review of Knowledge
and Entertainment*, Baltimore,
Md., 1798, APS

The Key, Fredericktown, Md., Jan.
13, 1798-July 14, 1798, APS

The Vigil, Charleston, S.C., 1798,
MBAt, OU, APS

*National Magazine, or, A Political,
Historical, Biographical, and
Literary Repository*. Richmond,
Va., 1799-1800. Continued as
*National Magazine, or, Cabinet
of the U.S.* Washington, D.C.,
APS

The Baltimore Weekly Magazine,
Baltimore, Md., Apr. 26,
1800-May 27, 1801, APS

*Child of Pallas: Devoted Mostly
to the Belles-Lettres*, Baltimore,
Md., 1800-01, APS

*Post-Angel, or, Universal
Entertainment*, Edenton, N.C.,
1800-?

The Press, Richmond, Va., Jan. 6,
1800 (one issue only)

*Farmer's Library, or, Ohio
Intelligencer*, Louisville, Ky.,
1801-08?

*L'Echo du Sud: Moniteur
Francais*, Charleston, S.C., 1801

*Recorder, or, Lady's and
Gentlemen's Miscellany*,
Richmond, Va., 1801-03? MBAt,
WHi

*Toilet. A Weekly Collection of
Literary Pieces, Principally
Designed for the Amusement of
the Ladies*, Charleston, S.C.,
1801, APS

Georgia Analytical Repository,
Savannah, Ga., 1802-03, APS

Charleston Medical Register,
Charleston, S.C., 1803, APS

*The Medley, or, Monthly
Miscellany*, Lexington, Ky.,
1803, APS

*The Sociable Magazine and
Quarterly Intelligencer*,
Charleston, S.C., 1803-04

*The Alethian Critic, or Error
Exposed By An Exhibition of
Truth*, Lexington, Ky., 1804-06,
APS

*The Companion and Weekly
Miscellany*, Baltimore, Md.,
1804-06. Later as *Observer*

*Minerva, or, Lady's and
Gentlemen's Magazine*, Richmond,
Va., 1804, Vi

Amoenitates Graphicae, Richmond,
Va., 1805

*The Monthly Register, Magazine,
and Review of the United
States*, Charleston, S.C.; New
York, N.Y., 1805-07, APS

*The Spirit of the Public Journals,
or, Beauties of the American
Newspapers*, Baltimore, Md.,
1805, APS

Virginia Religious Magazine,
Lexington, Va., 1805-1807, APS

*Charleston Spectator, and Ladies
Literary Port Folio*, Charleston,
S.C., 1806, APS

The Observer, Baltimore, Md.,
1806-07. Supersedes *Companion
and Weekly Miscellany*, APS

*American Gleaner and Virginia
Magazine*, Richmond, Va., 1807,
APS

The Baltimore Magazine, Baltimore,
Md., 1807. Absorbed by *Port
Folio*, Philadelphia., APS

L'Oracle, Francais-American,
Charleston, S.C., 1807

Moonshine, Baltimore, Md., 1807,
APS

The Quiver, Charleston, S.C., 1807,
ScU

Spectacles, Baltimore, Md., 1807,
APS

Religious Repository, Georgetown,
Md., 1808-09, NjP

*The Baltimore Medical and Physical
Recorder*, Baltimore, Md.,
1809-10, APS

Museum, Nashville, Tenn., 1809

The Visitor, Richmond, Va.,
1809-10.

A Magazine, Baltimore, Md.,
September 24, 1810, PPL

*American Law Journal, and
Miscellaneous Repository*,
Baltimore, Md., 1810?

The Emerald, Baltimore, Md.,
1810-11, APS

The Garden, Bardstown, Ky., 1810,
MWA

Journal of Musick, Baltimore, Md.,
1810? APS

Lynchburg Evangelical Magazine,
Lynchburg, Va., 1810-? ViU

The Scourge, Baltimore, Md., May
26-November 24, 1810.

*Baltimore Medical and
Philosophical Lyceum*, Baltimore,
Md., 1811, APS

*The Baltimore Repertory of Papers
on Literary and Other Topics*,
Baltimore, Md., Jan.-June 1811,
APS

Niles' National Register -- See
Niles' Weekly Register

Niles' Weekly Register,
Philadelphia, Pa.; Washington,
D.C.; Baltimore, Md., 1811-1849.
1811-14 as *Weekly Register*.
1837-49 as *Niles National
Register*, APS

The Weekly Register -- See *Niles'
Weekly Register*

*Evangelical Record and Western
Review*, Lexington, Ky., 1812-13,
APS

Hornet's Nest, Murfreesboro, N.C., Oct. 8, 1812-July 22, 1813

The Kentucky Missionary and Theological Magazine, Frankfort, Ky., 1812-14?

Literary Visitor; or Entertaining Miscellany Comprising Meritorious Selections and Original Productions in Prose and Verse. Baltimore, Md., 1812-13, MH

The Monthly Magazine and Literary Journal, Winchester, Va., 1812-13, APS

The Carolina Law Repository, Raleigh, N.C., 1813-16, APS

Christian Observer, Philadelphia, Pa.; Richmond, Va.; Louisville, Ky., 1813-? APS

Gospel Herald, Frankfort, Ky., 1813-?

National Museum and Weekly Gazette, Baltimore, Md., 1813-14, APS

North Carolina Magazine: Political, Historical, and Miscellaneous, _____, N.C., 1813, APS

The Almoner, A Periodical Religious Publication, Lexington, Ky., 1814-15, APS

The Christian Mirror, Charleston, S.C., 1814, APS

Christian Monitor, Richmond, Va., 1815-17, APS

The Layman's Magazine, Martinsburg, Va., 1815-16, APS

The Monthly Visitant, or, Something Old, Alexandria, Va., 1816, APS

The Portico, A Repository of Science and Literature, Baltimore, Md., 1816-18, APS

Baltimore Weekly Magazine, and Ladies Miscellany, Baltimore, Md., May 2-October 2, 1818.

The Castigator, Lexington, Ky., Nov. 1818-?

The Christian Messenger, Baltimore, Md., 1818-19, APS

Evangelical and Literary Magazine -- See *Literary and Evangelical Magazine*

Journal of the Times, Baltimore, Md., September 12, 1818-March 6, 1819, DLC, MB, MWA, MdBJ, N, NcD, NjP

Literary and Evangelical Magazine, Richmond, Va., 1818-25. 1818-20 as *The Virginia Evangelical and Literary Magazine.* 1821-23 as *Evangelical and Literary Magazine*, APS

Robinson's Magazine, A Weekly Repository of Original Papers, and Selections from the English Magazines, Baltimore, Md., 1818-19, APS

The Sunday Visitant, or, Weekly Repository of Christian Knowledge, Charleston, S.C., 1818-19, APS

The Virginia Evangelical and Literary Magazine -- See *Literary and Evangelical Magazine*

Western Monitor and Religious Journal, Knoxville, Tenn., 1818-20? DLC, TKL

The American Farmer, Baltimore, Md., 1819-97, APS

Columbian Telescope and literary compiler, being a miscellaneous repository of literary productions, Alexandria, Va., 1819-20, DLC, MWA, PPHi

Journal of Belles Lettres,
Lexington, Ky., 1819-20, APS

Ladies' Magazine, Savannah, Ga.,
1819, NcD, NjR

Missionary Weekly, Mount Zion,
Ga., 1819-?

Presbyterian Outlook, Richmond,
Va., 1819-?

Red Book, Baltimore, Md., 1819-21,
DLC, CtY

*The Southern Evangelical
Intelligencer,* Charleston, S.C.,
1819-21, NHi, ScU

Western Monitor, Lexington, Ky.,
Jan. 9, 1819-?

*Western Review and Miscellaneous
Magazine,* Lexington, Ky.,
1819-21, APS

*Cohen's Gazette and Lottery
Register,* Baltimore, Md.,
1820-25, APS

Religious and Literary Repository,
Annapolis, Md., 1820, APS

Southern Literary Register,
Columbia, S.C., 1820, ScU

Aeolian Harp, Petersburg, Va.,
April 1821-?

Charleston Catholic Miscellany,
Charleston, S.C., 1821?-?

Christian Index, Washington, D.C.;
Philadelphia, Pa.; Washington,
Penfield, Macon, Atlanta, Ga.,
1821-? As *Columbia Star.*
1827-27; *The Columbian Star and
Christian Index,* 1829-30. Also
as *The Christian Index, and
Baptist Miscellany, Devoted to
the Diffusion of Truth and
Piety*; *The Christian Index and
Southern Baptist*; and *The
Christian Index. The Organ
of the Baptists of Georgia,* APS

*The Christian Index, and Baptist
Miscellany* -- See *Christian
Index*

*The Christian Index and Southern
Baptist* -- See *Christian Index*

Columbia Star -- See *Christian
Index*

*The Columbian Star and Christian
Index* -- See *Christian Index*

Genius of Universal Emancipation,
Mount Pleasant, Ohio;
Greenville, Tenn.; Philadelphia,
Pa.; Baltimore, Md., 1821-39.
Continued as *Genius of
Liberty,* APS

*Masonic Miscellany and Ladies'
Literary Magazine,* Lexington,
Ky., 1821-23, APS

Omnium Gatherum, Charleston, S.C.,
1821, South Carolina Historical
Society.

*Omnium Botherum or, Strictures on
The Omnium Gatherum,*
Charleston, S.C., 1821, South
Carolina Historical Society.

*The Roanoke Religious
Correspondent, or Monthly
Evangelical Visitant,* Danville,
Va., 1821-23, APS

*The Unitarian Miscellany and
Christian Monitor,* Baltimore,
Md., 1821-24, APS

*Western Minerva, or, American
Annals of Knowledge and
Literature,,* Lexington, Ky.,
1821, APS

*Abolition Intelligencer and
Missionary Magazine,*
Shelbyville, Ky., May 1822-Apr.
1823, MB, WHi

Christian Register, Lexington, Ky.,
1822-23, APS

Commercial Bulletin, Price Current and Shipping List, New Orleans, La., July 27, 1822-84. 1822-Mar. 18, 1882 as *New Orleans Price-Current*, DLC, LNHT, NN, NcU

Family Visitor, Richmond, Va., Apr. 6, 1822-39? Absorbed *North Carolina Telegraph*, Feb. 1827. Later as *Family Visitor and Telegraph*, still later as *Southern Religious Telegraph*.

Family Visitor and Telegraph -- See *Family Visitor*

Journal of the Law-School and of the Moot Court attached to it at Needham in Virginia, Richmond, Va., 1822, DLC, N, WaU

New Orleans Price-Current -- See *Commercial Bulletin*

Southern Religious Telegraph -- See *Family Visitor*

The Theological Review and General Repository of Religious and Moral Information, Baltimore, Md., 1822, APS

Unitarian Defendant, Charleston, S.C., 1822, APS

United States Catholic Miscellany, Charleston, S.C., 1822-61, APS

Vaccine Inquirer, Baltimore, Md., 1822-24, APS

Baltimore Philosophical Journal and Review, Baltimore, Md., July 1823, DSG, MdBM, NNN, PPC

Baptist Monitor and Political Compiler, Bloomfield, Ky., 1823-24? KyLoS

Christian Baptist, Buffalo, Va., 1823-1829, APS

Ladies' Literary Bouquet, Baltimore, Md., 1823-24?

Literary Pamphleteer, Paris, Ky., 1823, ICP, PPPrHi

Western Arminian, Huntsville, Ala.; Knoxville, Tenn., 1823-? Ala. Dept. of Archives and History

Charleston Gospel Messenger and Protestant Episcopal Register, Charleston, S.C., 1824-53, APS

Holston Messenger, Knoxville, Tenn., 1824-29, APS

Ladies' Garland, Harper's Ferry, Va., 1824-28, APS

Methodist Protestant Recorder -- See *Mutual Rights and Methodist Protestant*

Methodist Recorder -- See *Mutual Rights and Methodist Protestant*, APS

Microscope, Louisville, Ky.; New Albany, Ind., 1824-25, APS

Mutual Rights and Methodist Protestant, Baltimore, Md., 1824-July 1828, n.s. Jan. 7, 1831-? Later as *Methodist Protestant Recorder*, and as *Methodist Recorder*, DLC, MdBE, NN, NcD

Southern Christian Register, Charleston, S.C., 1824?

Western Luminary, Lexington, Ky., 1824-35, APS

The Album, Charleston, S.C., 1825

The Carolina Journal of Medicine, Science and Agriculture, Charleston, S.C., 1825-26, APS

Christian Advocate, Montgomery, Ala., 1825-?

Encyclopedia, Yorkville, S.C., 1825-26?

Odd Fellows' Magazine, Baltimore, Md., 1825-26, APS

The Wesleyan Journal, Charleston, S.C., 1825-27. Merged into *Christian Advocate*, ABS

Western Recorder, Louisville, Ky., 1825-current, KyL, NcD

Ariel, Natchez, Miss., 1826?

The Christian Messenger, Georgetown, Ky., 1826-44, PPPrHi, TxU, KyLxCB

Evangelical Inquirer, Richmond, Va., 1826-27, TxU

Evangelical Lutheran Intelligencer, Frederick, Md., 1826-31, MdBE, MdBP, PPL

Georgia Reporter and Christian Gazette, Sparta, Ga., 1826

North American Literary and Political Register, Lexington, Ky., 1826?

North Carolina Telegraph, Fayetteville, N.C., Jan. 27, 1826-Feb. 1827. Absorbed by Richmond *Family Visitor*, DLC, NcU, TxU

Patriot, Frankfort, Ky., 1826, DLC, ICU, NcD

Spirit of '76, Frankfort, Ky., 1826, DLC, ICU, MoS, TxU

Western Arminian and Christian Instructor, Knoxville, Tenn., 1826?

Calvinistic Magazine, Abingdon, Va.; Rogersville, Tenn., 1827-31. Superseded by *The Presbyterian Witness*, CtY, DLC, ICU, MWA, NN, TxU

The Charleston Observer, Charleston, S.C., 1827-45. Merged into *The Watchman of the South*, Richmond, Va., in 1845, NcMHi, PPPrHi

Evangelical Museum, Fayetteville, N.C., 1827-28? NcMHi, VRT, KyLoS

North American, or, Weekly Journal of Politics, Science and Literature, Baltimore, Md., 1827, APS

Passe Temps. Macedoine politique et litteraire, New Orleans, La., 1827-29? LNHT

Agreeable Companion, Harrodsburg, Ky., 1828-?

Columbia Register, Washington, D.C.; Baltimore, Md., 1828-29, DLC, NN

Emerald and Baltimore Literary Gazette, Baltimore, Md., 1828-29, APS

The Irishman, Charleston, S.C., 1828-30

Itinerant, or, Wesleyan Methodist Visitor, Baltimore, Md., 1828-31, In, NjMD, ODW

Southern Agriculturist and Register of Rural Affairs -- See *Southern Agriculturist, Horticulturist, and Register of Rural Affairs*

Southern Agriculturist, Horticulturist, and Register of Rural Affairs, Charleston, S.C., 1828-46, v.1-12 as *Southern Agriculturist and Register of Rural Affairs*, 1840 as *Southern Cabinet of Agriculture, Horticulture, Rural and Domestic Economy*, APS

Southern Literary Gazette, Charleston, S.C., 1828-29, APS

Southern Cabinet of Agriculture, Horticulture, Rural and Domestic Economy -- See *Southern Agriculturist, Horticulturist, and Register of Rural Affairs*

The Southern Review, Charleston, S.C., 1828-32, APS

Presbyterian Preacher, Fayetteville, N.C., 1828-? Supersedes *Virginia and North Carolina Presbyterian Preacher*, NcMHi

Religious Herald, Richmond, Va., 1828-1906, DLC, MWA, NN, NcD, VRU, ViU

Transylvania Journal of Medicine and the Associated Sciences, Lexington, Ky., 1828-39, APS

Virginia and North Carolina Presbyterian Preacher, Fayetteville, N.C., Jan.-Dec. 1828? Supersedes *Presbyterian Preacher*, NcMHi, NcU

American Turf Register and Sporting Magazine, Baltimore, Md., 1829-44, APS

The Christian Examiner, Louisville, Ky., 1829-30, MWA

The Gospel Herald, Lexington, Ky., 1829-? IEG, PPPrHi, TKL

Maryland Medical Recorder, Devoted to Medical Science in General, Baltimore, Md., 1829-32, DSG, ICJ, NNN, OC

Medical Friend of the People, Harrodsburg, Ky., 1829-30, DSG, ICU

The Minerva, Baltimore, Md., 1829

Pedobaptist, Danville, Ky., 1829, ICU, NcD, TxU

Pleiades. A Weekly literary gazette, Charleston, S.C., 1829?

Spirit of the Old Dominion, Richmond, Va., May-Oct. 1829? MWA, OCHP

Transylvanian or; Lexington Literary Journal, Lexington, Ky., 1829, ICU, MHi, NN, WHi

Virginia Farmer, Scottsville, Va., 1829?-33?

Virginia Literary Museum and Journal of Belles Lettres, Arts, Sciences, &,c. Charlottesville, Va., 1829-30, APS

Baltimore Monthly Journal of Medicine and Surgery, Baltimore, Md., 1830-31, APS

Baptist Chronicle and Georgetown Literary Register -- See *Baptist Chronicle and Literary Register*

Baptist Chronicle and Literary Register, Georgetown, Ky., 1830-32. v.1, no.1 as *Baptist Herald and Georgetown Literary Register*, v.2-3 as *Baptist Chronicle and Georgetown Literary Register*, DLC, MWA, NHC, PCA

Baptist Herald and Georgetown Literary Register -- See *Baptist Chronicle and Literary Register*

Carolina Law Journal, Columbia, S.C., 1830-31, APS

The College Magazine: A Monthly Miscellany, Charleston, S.C., 1830-?

Cumberland Presbyterian -- See *Religious and Literary Intelligencer*

The Metropolitan, or, Catholic Monthly Magazine, Baltimore, Md., 1830, DCU

The Millennial Harbinger, Bethany, Va., 1830-70. Continues *Christian Baptist*, CtY, DLC, NN, TxU

The Mt. Hope Literary Gazette, Baltimore, Md., 1830

National Magazine, or, Lady's Emporium, Baltimore, Md., 1830-31, APS

Presbyterian Advocate. A monthly magazine conducted by an Association of ministers, Lexington, Ky., 1830. GDC, ICP, TxU, PPPrHi

Presbyterian Herald, Bardstown, Louisville, Ky., 1830-62. Superseded by *True Presbyterian* in Louisville, Ky. 1830-37 as *Western Presbyterian Herald*, 1838-45 as *Protestant and Herald*, DLC, MWA, PPPrHi

Protestant and Herald -- See *Presbyterian Herald*

Religious and Literary Intelligencer, Nashville, Tenn., 1830-31? Superseded by *Revivalist* and *Cumberland Presbyterian*, OOxM, NN, PPPrHi, TxU

Revivalist -- See *Religious and Literary Intelligencer*

Western Presbyterian Herald -- See *Presbyterian Herald*

Young Ladies' Journal of Literature and Science, Baltimore, Md., 1830-31. MH, N

Baltimore Southern Pioneer and Richmond Gospel Visiter, Baltimore, Md., Oct. 1831-July 1835. 1831-Sept. 1834 as *Southern Pioneer and Gospel Visiter*. DLC, N, NcD, Vi, ViU

Georgia Christian Repertory, Macon, Ga., 1831-32

Irishman and Southern Democrat, Charleston, S.C., 1831.

Lutheran Observer and Weekly Religious Visitor, Baltimore, Md., 1831-July 15, 1833; Aug. 24, 1833-Mar. 22, 1834., MWA, PPL

Methodist Protestant, Baltimore, Md., 1831-32, 1835. Supersedes *Mutual Rights and Methodist Protestant*. Superseded by *Methodist Protestant Recorder*. DLC, NN, NcD, TxU

Railroad Advocate, Rogersville, Tenn., July 4, 1831-June 14, 1832, DBRE, DLC, NN

Religious Intelligencer, Georgetown, Ky., 1831-?

Southern Agriculturist, Laurensville, S.C., 1831, 1853-54, 1856, 1871, ScU, NcD

Southern Pioneer and Gospel Visiter -- See *Baltimore Southern Pioneer and Richmond Gospel Visiter*

Tennessee Monthly Museum, Franklin, Tenn., 1831-?

Unitarian Christian, Augusta, Ga., 1831, ICM, MH

Youth's Repertory and Child's Magazine, Charleston, S.C., 1831-?

Baltimore and Richmond Christian Advocate -- See *Richmond Christian Advocate*

Banner of Truth, Lexington, Ky., Nov. 1832-Mar. 1833? KyLxT

Christian Sentinel, Richmond, Va., 1832-36? NcD

Eclectic Institute Journal of Education, Lexington, Ky., 1832-?

Georgia Constitutionalist, Augusta, Ga., 1832?

Harbinger of the Mississippi Valley, Frankfort, Ky., 1832, APS

Occasional Reviews, Charleston, S.C., 1832? MBAt, PPAP, PPHi

Reasoner, Columbia, S.C., 1832

Richmond Christian Advocate,
Richmond, Va., 1832-1939,
*Baltimore and Richmond
Christian Advocate.* United
with *Southern Methodist* to form
Virginia Methodist Advocate,
DLC, NN, NcD, MdBE

Saturday Visitor, Baltimore, Md.,
June 30, 1832-June 14, 1834

Southern Rose, Charleston, S.C.,
1832-39, APS

*Temperance Herald of the
Mississippi Valley*, Lexington,
Ky., 1832-?

Virginia Advocate, Richmond, Va.,
1832-? GEU, NcD, ViU

Western Weekly Review, Franklin,
Tenn., 1832-34?

*Baltimore Medical and Surgical
Journal and Review*, Baltimore,
Md., 1833-34, APS

Baptist Interpreter, Edenton,
Raleigh, N.C., 1833-35.
Continued as *Biblical Recorder*
in Raleigh in 1835, NcD, NcU

The Cosmopolitan: An Occasional,
Charleston, S.C., 1833, CLS

Episcopal Methodist, Baltimore, Md.,
1833.

*Evangelical Lutheran Preacher
and Pastoral Messenger*,
Winchester, Va., May 1833-Apr.
1835, DLC, MWA, N, NcD, Vi, ViU

Farmer's Register, Shellbanks,
Petersburg, Va., 1833-42, APS

Flag of the Union, Tuscaloosa,
Ala., 1833?

Juvenile Missionary Society,
Charleston, S.C., 1833, 1838,
1840, ScU

The Kaleidoscope, Nashville, Tenn.,
1833

The Lexington Literary Journal,
Lexington, Ky., 1833

The Literary Pioneer, Nashville,
Tenn., 1833

Man of Business, New Salem, N.C.,
1833-35, MH-L, MWA, NcU

Southern Evangelist, Montgomery,
Ala., 1833-?

Southern Journal of Education,
Scottsboro, Ga., 1833-?

Western Methodist, Nashville,
Tenn., 1833-36. Merged into
*South Western Christian
Advocate*, MoS

*Western Monthly Magazine and
Literary Journal*, Louisville,
Ky.; Cincinnati, Ohio, 1833-36,
n.s. 1837. Supersedes *Illinois
Monthly Magazine*, CtY, DLC, NN,
NcD

*Advocate for the Testimony of God,
As It Is Written in the Books
of Nature and Revelation* -- See
Apostolic Advocate

Apostolic Advocate, Richmond,
Amelia Co., Va., 1834-39. Also
as *Advocate for the Testimony
of God, As It Is Written in the
Books of Nature and
Revelation.* PPPrHi, TxU, Vi

Baltimore Athenaeum, Baltimore,
Md., June 7, 1834-June 18, 1835?
DLC, MdBE, N

Banner of the Cross, Columbia,
S.C., 1834, ScU

*Le Corsaire Louisianais, feuille
hebdomadaire*, New Orleans, La.,
1834? LNHT

Entra'acte, New Orleans, La., 1834?

The Farmer and Gardener and Live Stock Breeder and Manager, Baltimore, Md., May 9, 1834-Apr. 23, 1839. Continued as the *American Farmer*

The Harbinger, Chapel Hill, N.C., 1834-?

Lutheran Observer and Weekly Literary Religious Visitor, Baltimore, Md., 1834-37?

Magazine of Gardening and Botany, Baltimore, Md., Jan. 1834, DA, MWA

North American Archives of Medical and Surgical Science, Baltimore, Md., 1834-35, APS

The Southern Evangelist, Charleston, S.C., 1834-36, CLS

Southern Literary Messenger, Richmond, Va., 1834-64, APS

Temperance Banner, Penfield, Ga., 1834-?

Tennessee Farmer, Jonesborough, Tenn., 1834-40, APS

Tramontane Magazine, Louisville, Ky., 1834?

Alabama Baptist, Wetumpka, Marion, Ala., 1835-? Moved to Marion in 1838. Superseded by *Alabama Baptist Advocate*

Baltimore Literary and Religious Magazine, Baltimore, Md., 1835-41, APS

Baptist Banner and Western Pioneer -- See *Tennessee Baptist*

Biblical Recorder, Raleigh, N.C., 1835-? Superseded the *Baptist Interpreter*, a monthly, NN, NcD, NcU

Botanic Investigator, Vicksburg, Miss., 1835, DSG, MBM

Church Advocate, Lexington, Ky., 1835-36, TxU

Episcopal Churchnews, Richmond, Va., Jan. 2, 1835-? 1835-Jan. 13, 1952 as *Southern Churchman*. Absorbed *Chronicle, The Magazine of the Protestant Episcopal Church*, DLC, NN, NcD, ViU

Gospel Advocate, Georgetown, Ky., 1835-?

Literary Journal, Richmond, Va., 1835?

Louisiana Recorder -- See *Louisiana Recorder and Literary Gazette*

Louisiana Recorder and Literary Gazette, New Orleans, La., Jan. 3-Oct. 10, 1835, v.1 as *Louisiana Recorder*, DLC

Maryland Colonization Journal, Baltimore, Md., May 1835-May 1861? DLC, MdBE, MdBP, NN

Nashville Baptist, Nashville, Tenn., 1835-39. Consolidated into the *Western Recorder*, 1839.

The Southern Baptist, and General Intelligencer, Charleston, S.C., 1835-36. CLS, MWA, ScU

Southern Board of Foreign Missions, Charleston, S.C., 1835-36, 1839. ScU

Southern Churchman, Richmond, Va., 1835-99, DLC, NN, OO

Southern Churchnews -- See *Episcopal Churchnews*

Southern Literary Journal and Magazine of Arts, Charleston, S.C., 1835-38, APS

Tennessee Baptist, Nashville,
Memphis, Tenn., 1835-39. Merged
with other periodicals in 1839
to form the *Baptist Banner and
Western Pioneer.* Merged with
Baptist Reflector in 1888, ICU,
PCA

Thomsonian Defender, Maryville,
Tenn., 1835-36. DSG

Western Messenger, Louisville?,
Ky.; Cincinnati, Ohio, Apr.
1835-Apr. 1841, CtY, DLC, KyL,
NN

*Western Methodist Preacher; or,
Original Monthly Sermons by
Ministers of the Methodist
Episcopal Church*, Nashville,
Tenn., 1835-36? T

Western Protestant, Bardstown, Ky.,
1835?-38. Merged with
Presbyterian Herald, 1838

Atlanta Christian Advocate,
Atlanta, Ga., 1836-85.
Suspended 1885-92. Revived as
Methodist Advocate Journal,
Chattanooga, later at Athens,
Tenn., 1893-1924.

Bachelor's Button, Mobile,
Tuscaloosa, Ala., 1836-? AU, NN

Christian Advocate-- See
Southwestern Christian Advocate

Christian Preacher, Georgetown,
Ky.; Cincinnati, Ohio, 1836-40,
KyLxCB, OOxM

Christian Reformer, Paris, Tenn.,
Jan.-Dec. 1836? KyLxCB, TNG

Christian Review, Boston, Mass.;
New York, N.Y.; Baltimore, Md.;
Rochester, N.Y., 1836-63.
Merged into *Bibliotheca Sacra*,
CtY, DLC, NN

*Covenant. A Monthly magazine
devoted to the cause of
Odd-Fellowship*, Baltimore, Md.,
1836-47, CU, DLC, NN

*Cumberland Magazine, devoted to
the doctrine and practice of the
C.P. Church*, Nashville, Tenn.,
1836-? NcMHi

*Nashville and Louisville Christian
Advocate* -- See *Southwestern
Christian Advocate*

*Primitive Baptist. A semi-monthly
periodical*, Tarboro, N.C.,
1836-79? NcD, NcU, KyLoS

Southern Christian Herald, Cheraw,
S.C., 1836?

*Southern Medical and Surgical
Journal*, Augusta, Ga., June
1836-Sept. 1839, n.s. Jan.
1845-Oct. 1861, n.s. July
1866-July 1867, CtY-M, DLC,
DSG, GS, NcD, NcU

Southwestern Christian Advocate,
Nashville, Tenn., 1836-? Became
Nashville Christian Advocate,
1846-50, *Nashville and
Louisville Christian Advocate*,
1850-54. *Christian Advocate*
since 1854, DLC, NN, NcD, TNV

*Tennessee Farmer and Southern
Stockman*, Nashville, Tenn.,
1836-1904. Merged into
Southern Agriculturist, DA,
MdBJ

*Universalist Circulating Family
Library*, Baltimore, Md., June
1836-?

Wesleyan Christian Advocate
Atlanta, Ga., 1836-?

American Presbyterian, Nashville,
Tenn., 1837

Catholic Advocate, Louisville, Ky.,
1837-49? DCU

Central Presbyterian, Richmond,
Va., 1837-1908. Continued as
Presbyterian of the South, DLC,
MH, NN, WHi

Christian Panoplist, Versailles, Ky., 1837

La Creole, Gazette des salons, des arts, et des modes, New Orleans, La., 1837-38?

Franklin Farmer. Devoted to science of agriculture, mind, morals and interests, Franklin, Lexington, Ky., 1837-40. Continued as *Kentucky Farmer*, DLC, ICU, RPB

Kentucky Farmer, Frankfort, Ky., 1837-42? 1937-40 as *Franklin Farmer*, DLC, ICU, RPB

Masonic Olive Branch and Literary Portfolio, Fredericksburg, Va., Jan. 2-Sept. 15, 1837, CSmH

Mobile Monitor, Mobile, Ala., 1837-?

Morning Watch. Devoted to religious reformation and the millennial reign of Christ, Evergreen, S.C., 1837-40?

South Carolina Methodist Advocate, _____, S.C., 1837-71, 1878-1952, 1959. ScU

Southern Botanic Journal, Charleston, S.C.; Forsyth, Ga., Feb. 4, 1837-June 1, 1841, DLC, MH-G, NcD, TxU

Southern Christian Advocate, Charleston, Columbia, S.C., 1837-? CtY, DLC, NN, NcD, NcU, ScCc

Southern Post and Literary Aspirant, Macon, Ga., Sept. 9, 1837-42

Southwestern Journal; A Magazine of Science, Literature and Miscellany, Natchez, Miss., Dec. 15, 1837-July 30, 1838, CtY, LNHT, LU, N, TxU

Temperance Banner and Total Abstinence Advocate, Washington, Ga., 1837-38?

Watchman of the South, Richmond, Va., 1837-45? DLC, NjPT

Western Journal of Education, Louisville, Ky., 1837-38?

The Aegis, Louisville, Ky., 1838-? Merged into *The Aegis and Louisville Literary Gazette*

American Museum of Literature and the Arts, Baltimore, Md., 1838-39, APS

Annals of the Propagation of the Faith, Baltimore, Md., 1838-1923. Merged into *Catholic Missions*, CtY, DCU, MiU, NN, NNU

Augusta Mirror. A Semi-Monthly Journal, Devoted to Polite Literature, Useful Intelligence, and the Arts, Augusta, Ga., May 5, 1838-1941. Merged with *Family Companion* of Macon, Feb. 1842., DLC

Baltimore Monument. A Weekly Journal, Devoted to Polite Literature, Science, and the Fine Arts Baltimore, Md., 1838, APS

Baltimore Literary Monument, Baltimore, Md., 1838-39, APS

Collegian, Charlottesville, Va., Oct. 1838-42?

Evangelical Universalist, Macon, Ga., 1838?-40?

Farmers' Advocate and Miscellaneous Reporter, Jamestown, S.C., 1838-43?

Family Visitor, Wetumpka, Ala., 1838-?

Harp, Augusta, Ga., 1838-?

Herald, Augusta, Ga., 1838-?

Loafer's Journal, Wetumpka, Ala., 1838-?

Louisville Journal of Medicine and Surgery, Louisville, Ky., 1838, APS

Louisville Literary News-Letter. Devoted to News, Science, Literature and the Arts Louisville, Ky., Dec. 1, 1838-Nov. 28, 1840., KyU, LU, N, NcU

Mirror. A Semi-monthly Journal, Augusta, Ga., 1838-41

Morning Watch, Evergreen, S.C., 1838, ScU

Old Baptist Banner, Nashville, Murfreesboro, Shelbyville, Tenn., 1838-?

Richmond Lyceum Journal, Richmond, Va., 1838-39, DLC

Virginia Spectator, Charlottesville, Va., Oct. 1838-39? CtY

Western Magazine and Louisville Literary Gazette, Louisville, Ky., 1838-? Merged with *Aegis* to form *Aegis and Louisville Literary Gazette*

American Journal of Dental Science, Baltimore, Md., 1839-53?

American Silk Society, Baltimore, Md., 1839-41, DA, DLC, MB

Journal de la Societe Medicale de la Nouvelle-Orleans, New Orleans, La., 1839, 1859-61?

Journal of American Silk Society and Rural Economist, Baltimore, Md., 1839-40

Maryland Medical and Surgical Journal, and Official Organ of the Medical Department of the Army and Navy of the United States, Baltimore, Md., Oct. 1839-June 1843, DLC, DSG, MdBM, MiU

Miscellaneous Portfolio; or Southern Weekly Magazine of belles-lettres, news, agriculture, science, and art, Maryville, Tenn., 1839-?

Mobile Literary Gazette, Mobile, Ala., 1839-? DLC, MWA

Mountpleasant Silk Culturist and Farmer's Journal, Brandonville, Va., June 1839? NN

Odd Fellows Magazine, Richmond, Va., Apr. 1839-Mar. 1840. CSmH, OCHP, Vi

South Carolina Temperance Advocate, Columbia, S.C., 1838-51?

The Southern Baptist, Charleston, S.C., 1839-47, NcD

The Southern Christian Sentinel, Charleston, S.C., 1839-41, ICU, MWA

Southern Silk Journal; and Farmers' Register, Columbus, Ga., 1839-?

Southron, Tuscaloosa, Ala., Jan.-June, 1839. Supersedes *Southern Literary Journal and Magazine of Arts*, N, AU, NcD

Advance Guard of Democracy, Nashville, Tenn., Apr. 23-Oct. 23, 1840, DLC, IU, T, TxU

Agriculturist, and Journal of the State and County Societies, Nashville, Tenn., 1840-45? DA, ICJ

Baptist Banner and Western Pioneer, Louisville, Ky., 1840-44, OClWHi

Campaign, Frankfort, Ky., 1840-41.

Carolina Planter, Columbia, S.C., 1840-41. Merged into *Farmers' Register*, DLC

The Chinese Advocate, Louisville, Ky., 1840?-?

Christian Publisher, Charlottesville, Va., 1840-43?

Crisis, Richmond, Va., 1840, APS

Cumberland Presbyterian, Nashville, Tenn., 1840, NNU, OO

Farmer's Book; or, Western Maryland Farmer, Frederick, Md., 1840-41, DA, DGS

Farmer's Register, Columbus, Ga., 1840-?

Gallinipper, Mobile, Ala., 1840-? Ala. Dept. of Archives and History

Gazette, Forsyth, Ga., 1840-?

Gleanings of Husbandry, Augusta, Ga., 1840-42

Loco-Foco, Montgomery, Ala., 1840-? Ala. Dept. of Archives and History

Magnolia, or, Southern Appalachian. A literary magazine and monthly review -- See *Southern Ladies' Book; a magazine of literature, science and arts*

Magnolia; or Southern Monthly -- See *Southern Ladies' Book; a magazine of literature, science and arts*

Omnibus. Journal of politique, litteraire et commercial, publiee a la Nouvelle-Orleans trois fois per semaine, it redige par une Societe de Jeunes Gens, New Orleans, La., 1840-41?

Southern Crisis, Marion, Ala., 1840, Ala. Dept. of Archives and History

Southern Baptist Preacher, Washington, Ga., 1840-41?

Southern Ladies' Book; a magazine of literature, science and arts, Macon, Ga.; Charleston, S.C., 1840-43. 1841-42 as *Magnolia; or, Southern Apalachian*, 1842 as *Magnolia; or Southern Monthly*, CtY, DLC, NN, NcU

Spirit of '76, Nashville, Tenn., Mar. 15, 1840-Jan. 20, 1841, DLC, T, TxU

Tennessee State Agriculturist, Nashville, Tenn., 1840-46?

University Magazine, Knoxville, Tenn., 1840-43

Weekly Pilot, Baltimore, Md., 1840-41

Western Journal of Medicine and Surgery, Louisville, Ky., 1840-55, APS

Yeoman, Richmond, Va., Jan. 2-Dec. 25, 1840, CtY, Vi, ViW

Bank Reformer, Petersburg, Va., 1841-42, DLC, Vi

Banner of Peace, Nashville, Tenn., 1841-40?

The Bouquet, Charleston, S.C., 1841-43, ScU

Family Companion and Ladies' Mirror, Macon, Ga., 1841-43, GMM, GMW, NcD

The Guardian, A Family Magazine Devoted to the Cause of Female Education on Christian Principles. Columbia, Tenn., Jan. 1841-Sept./Oct. 1854, n.s.-June 1866? DLC, NcD, T, TN, TxU

Guardian of Health. A Monthly Journal of Domestic Hygiene. Baltimore, Md., Sept. 1841-Aug. 1842, DSG, MdBE, MdBM

Independent Oddfellow, A Monthly Periodical. Richmond, Va., June 1841-May 1845? Ia, NcD, Vi, ViW

Lorgnette, New Orleans, La., 1841-42? MB

Louisiana Law Journal, New Orleans, La., May 1841-April 1842 DLC, TxU, ICU, N, WaU, NNB

Oxford Mercury, Oxford, N.C., 1841-43?

Plaindealer, Nashville, Tenn., 1841?

Plough Boy, Edgefield, S.C., 1841, ScU

Presbyterian Sentinel, Louisville, Ky., 1841-44, PPPrHi

Religious Ark, Athens, Tenn., Sept. 1841-Aug. 1842, NcMHi

Southern Botanico Journal, Forsyth, Ga., 1841-43? As *Southern Botanico-Medical Journal*, 1842-43? MBM

Southern Botanico-Medical Journal -- See *Southern Botanico Journal*

Southern Cabinet, Charleston, S.C., 1841, ScU

Southern Magazine and Monthly Review, Petersburg, Va., Jan.-Feb. 1841, DLC, NcU, Vi, ViU

Southern Planter, Richmond, Va., 1841-1969, APS

Southron, or, Lily of the Valley Devoted to Literature, Instruction, Amusement, Etc. Gallatin, Tex., Jan.-Dec. 1841, CSmH, CtY, LU, MH, T

Temperance Banner, Maysville, Ky., 1841-?

Baltimore Monthly Visitor, Baltimore, Md., 1842, APS

Baltimore Phoenix and Budget, Baltimore, Md., 1842, APS

Banner of Liberty, Richmond, Va., July 1842, DLC

Bantling, Madison, Ga., 1842?

Baptist Exposidor and South-Western Intelligencer, Columbus, Ga., 1842-?

Baptist Preacher, Richmond, Va., 1842-Jan. 1859? v.1-2 as *Virginia Baptist Preacher.* KyLoS, NN, NcD, NcU, Vi, ViU

Bible Advocate, Paris, Tenn., 1842-44

Charivari Louisianais, New Orleans, La., 1842

Chicora, or, Messenger of the South. A Journal of Belles-Lettres and the Fine Arts, and a Weekly Gazette of Science, Education and General Intelligence. Charleston, S.C., July 9-Sept. 24, 1842. Absorbed by *Magnolia, Or Southern Appalachian*, Nov. 1842, NcD

Cincinnati Lancet and Clinic -- See *Western Lancet*

Cincinnati Lancet and Observer -- See *Western Lancet*

Cincinnati Lancet-Clinic -- See *Western Lancet*

Dollar Farmer, Louisville, Ky., July 1842-June 1846, DA, DLC, KyL, KyU

Literary Messenger, Savannah, Ga., 1842-?

Masonic Journal, Augusta, Ga., 1842-?

Masonic Mirror, Maysville, Ky., 1842?-44

Messenger of Glad Tidings, Wetumpka, Ala., 1842-? Later as *Gospel Messenger*

Monthly Miscellany, Monroe County, Tenn., 1842-43.

Orion, or Southern Monthly: A Magazine of Original Literature, Penfield, Ga., 1842-44, APS

Petersburg Quarterly Review, Petersburg, Va., 1842

Le Propagateur Catholique, Journal des Familles, New Orleans, La., 1842-52? LNHT, LU, NcD

Southern Mirror: A Journal of Masonry, Literature and Science. Columbia, Tenn., 1842-Aug. 12, 1843? CSmH, TKL

The Southern Miscellany--a Family Newspaper, Devoted to Literature, The Arts, Science, Agriculture, Mechanics, Education, Foreign and Domestic Intelligence, Humor, etc. Madison, Ga., 1842-46?

The Southern Planter: A Monthly Magazine of Husbandry, Natchez, Washington, Miss., 1842-? DLC

Southern Quarterly Review, New Orleans, La., 1842-57, APS

South-Western Farmer. A weekly journal designed to improve the soil and the mind, Raymond, Miss., 1842-44? DLC

Spirit of the XIX Century, Baltimore, Md., 1842-43, APS

United States Catholic Magazine, Baltimore, Md., 1842-49, as *Religious Cabinet*, 1842; *United States Catholic Magazine and Monthly Review*, 1843, APS

Virginia Baptist Preacher -- See *Baptist Preacher*

Washingtonian, or Total Abstinence Advocate, Augusta, Ga., 1842-45?

Western and Southern Medical Recorder, Lexington, Ky., 1842-43. Merged into *Western Lancet*, later *Lancet-Clinic*, DSG, MBM

Western Lancet, Cincinnati, Ohio; Lexington, Ky. 1842-1916. v.19-39 as *Cincinnati Lancet and Observer*, v.40-55 as *Cincinnati Lancet and Clinic*, v.16-92 as *Cincinnati Lancet-Clinic*, CtY, DLC, ICJ, NN

Western Literary and Historical Magazine, Louisville, Ky., 1842, WHi

Western School Journal, Louisville, Ky., 1842-?

Alabama Temperance, Wetumpka, Ala., 1843-?

L'Album Litteraire: Journal des Jeunes Gens, Amateurs de la Litterature, New Orleans, La., 1843, MWA

Bibliotheca Sacra Dallas, Tex., 1843-current.

Christian Magazine of the South, Columbia, S.C., 1843-49, ScU, Ia

Christian Teacher, Lexington, Paris, Ky., 1843-47, PCA

Economiste, Baton Rouge, La., 1843

Fackel. Literaturblatt zur Forderung Geistiger Freiheit, Baltimore, Md., 1843-65? CtY, DLC, IU, NN

Interpreter. A Semi-monthly journal, devoted to the English, French, Spanish, Italian, and German Languages, Charleston, S.C., 1843-? GEU, MWA

The Pierian, Harrodsburg, Ky., 1843-?

Rambler, Charleston, S.C., Oct. 2, 1843-Mar. 30, 1844, N

Southern Baptist Advocate, Charleston, S.C., 1843-? ScU

Southern Cultivator, Athens, Ga., 1843-1935. Later as *Southern Cultivator and Dixie Farmer*, APS

Southern Educational Journal, Mobile, Ala., 1843-?

Southern Sportsman, New Orleans, La., Mar. 18-June 5, 1843? MB

Youth's Companion, Columbus, Ga., 1843

Whig Banner, Nashville, Tenn., May 13-July 29, 1843, n.s. May 11-Oct. 26, 1844. DLC, TU, TxU

Carolina Magazine, Chapel Hill, Raleigh, N.C., 1844-? Also as *University of North Carolina Magazine*, and as *University Magazine*, ICU, NN, NcGW, NcU, TxU, ViU

Carolina Planter. A Monthly Register for the State and Local Societies. Columbia, S.C., July 1844-June 1845. DLC, ScU

Christian Review. A Monthly Magazine, Nashville, Tenn., 1844-47.

Christian Sun, Suffolk, Va., 1844-62?

Democratic Mentor, Tuscaloosa, Ala., 1844-? Ala. Dept. of Archives and History

Dollar Whig Athens, Ala., 1844-?

Farmers' Gazette, Cheraw, S.C., 1844?

The Floral Wreath and Ladies Monthly Magazine, Charleston, S.C., 1844-Apr. 1846 as *Heriot's Magazine*. Also as *Heriot's Monthly Magazine; Heriot's Monthly Illustrated Magazine, of Science, Literature and Art*; and as *Heriot's Magazine of Science, Literature and Art*.

Freemason, Louisville, Ky., 1844?

Harry of the West, Wetumpka, Ala., 1844-? DLC

Helicon, Marietta, Ga., 1844.

Heriot's Magazine -- See *The Floral Wreath and Ladies Monthly Magazine*

Heriot's Magazine of Science, Literature and Art -- See *The Floral Wreath and Ladies Monthly Magazine*

Heriot's Monthly Illustrated Magazine of Science, Literature and Art -- See *The Floral Wreath and Ladies Monthly Magazine*

Heriot's Monthly Magazine -- See *The Floral Wreath and Ladies Monthly Magazine*

Louisiana State Medical Society Journal New Orleans, La., 1844-current. 1844-45 as *New Orleans Journal of Medicine* 1845-66, 1873-1952 as *New Orleans Medical and Surgical Journal*. Suspended May 1861-July 1866. Nov. 1870-June 1873 not published. DLC, DSG, LNHT, NcD, NN, OC, PPC

New Orleans Journal of Medicine
-- See *Louisiana State Medical
Society Journal*

*New Orleans Medical and Surgical
Journal* -- See *Louisiana State
Medical Society Journal*

Polyglot, Charleston, S.C., 1844-?

Reformer and People's Advocate,
Frederick, Md., Aug.-Oct. 1844

Republic Sentinel, Richmond, Va.,
Mar. 16, 1844-Oct. 30, 1844.

*Southwestern Law Journal and
Reporter*, Nashville, Tenn.,
1844.   MH-L, NNB

*Southwestern Literary Journal and
Monthly Review*, Nashville,
Tenn., 1844-45.   Became
*South-Western Literary Journal
and Monthly Review*.   ICN, Ia,
MdBJ, PPi, WHi

*South-Western Literary Journal
and Monthly Review* -- See
*Southwestern Literary Journal
and Monthly Review*

University Magazine -- See
Carolina Magazine

*University of North Carolina
Magazine* -- See *Carolina
Magazine*

*Arkansas State Temperance
Journal*, Little Rock, Ark.,
1845-?

Campaign Democrat, Louisville,
Ky., 1845-?

The Carolina Baptist, Charleston,
S.C., 1845-46.   LNHT, ScU, NcD

*Christian Intelligencer and
Southern Methodist*, Georgetown,
Ky., 1845?-47?   DLC, KyBgW

Cumberland Presbyterian,
Uniontown, Pa.; Louisville, Ky.,
1845-84.   First published as
Theological Medium.   Later
published as *Cumberland
Presbyterian Quarterly* and
*Cumberland Presbyterian
Review*.   CtY, DLC, NN

*Cumberland Presbyterian
Quarterly* -- See *Cumberland
Presbyterian*

Cumberland Presbyterian Review
-- See *Cumberland Presbyterian*

Franc-Macon Louisianais, New
Orleans, La., 1845-46?   AU

Gospel Messenger, Wetumpka, Ala.,
1845-?   Later as *Universalist
Herald*

Journal of Agriculture,, Baltimore,
Md., 1845-1848

Masonic Mirror, Covington, Ky.,
1845-47?

North Carolina Farmer, Raleigh,
N.C., 1845-50.   ICJ, NcD, ViU

*Reforme.   Politique, Commercial et
Litteraire*, New Orleans, La.,
1845-46?

*Southern and Western Monthly
Magazine and Review*,
Charleston, S.C., 1845 APS

Southern Medical Reformer,
Forsyth, Ga., 1845 DSG, MWA,
NNN

Theological Medium -- See
Cumberland Presbyterian

Western Baptist Review, Frankfort,
Louisville, Ky., 1845-51.   Merged
in 1851 into *Ford's Christian
Repository*, Louisville, then St.
Louis, Mo.   ICU, WHi

Western Continent, Baltimore, Md.,
1845?-48?   DLC, MdBE

Alabama Planter, Mobile, Ala.,
1846-? DLC

Banker's Magazine, New York, N.Y.;
Baltimore, Md., 1846-95. DLC,
NN, NcU, NcD

*Charleston Medical Journal and
Review*, Charleston, S.C.,
1846-50, n.s. Apr. 1873-Jan.
1877, v.1-2 as *Southern Journal
of Medicine and Pharmacy.*
CtY, DSG, NN, NcD, ScU

*DeBow's Review, Agricultural,
Commercial, Industrial Progress
and Resources*, New Orleans,
La., 1846-80, APS

*Evantail. Journal bi-hebdomadaire,
le Jeudi et le Dimanche*, New
Orleans, La., 1846-47?

*Grelot. Journal Politique et
Litteraire*, New Orleans, La.,
1846-?

Historical Collections of Louisiana
-- See *Historical Collections of
Louisiana and Florida,*

*Historical Collections of Louisiana
and Florida*, _____, _____,
1846-75. 1846-53 as *Historical
Collections of Louisiana*, DCU,
DLC, LNHT, WHi

Indian Advocate, Louisville, Ky.,
1846-55? DLC, NN, PCC

Luminary, Atlanta, Ga., 1846-?

*Naturalist and Journal of Natural
History, Agriculture, Education,
and Literature*, Nashville,
Tenn., 1846, CtY, MH-Z, NIC, MH,
TNV

*The Palmetto: A Temperance
Journal*, Charleston, S.C., 1846

Presbyterian Record -- See
Christian Record

Public School Advocate, Houston,
Tex., 1846-47

Revue Louisianaise, New Orleans,
La., 1846-48? LNHT, DLC, MWA,
NjP, TxU, AU

*Southern Baptist Missionary
Journal*, Richmond, Va., 1846-51.
Merged into *Commission; or
Southern Baptist Missionary
Magazine*, DLC, NHC, NcD, PCA,
TxU, Vi, WHi

*The Southern Journal of Medicine
and Pharmacy* -- See *Charleston
Medical Journal and Review*

Taenarion, Satires Periodiques,
New Orleans, La., 1846-47?

*Tennessee Farmer and
Horticulturist*, Nashville, Tenn.,
1846?

Texas Christian Advocate, Dallas,
Tex., 1846, NN, TxU

Camden Miscellany, Camden, S.C.,
1847-?

Christian Journal, Covington, Ky.,
1847-?

Christian Record, Nashville, Tenn.,
1847-Sept. 1851. As
Presbyterian Record, 1847-48.
Merged into *Presbyterian
Herald*, PPPrHi

*Chronique. Journal Politique et
Litteraire*, New Orleans, La.,
1847-49?

Crystal Fount, Baltimore, Md.,
1847-48. DLC, MWA, NN

Examiner, Louisville, Ky., 1847-?

Franklin Patriot, Apalachicola,
Fla., Sept. 16-Oct. 2, 1847, DLC

*Georgia Botanic Journal and
College Sentinel*, Macon, Ga.,
1847-48. Continued as *Southern
Botanico-Medical Reformer.*

Jonesborough Monthly Review,
Jonesborough, Tenn., 1847-49.
June-Oct. 1847 as *Jonesborough
Quarterly Review,* DLC,MoS, TxU

Jonesborough Quarterly Review --
See *Jonesborough Monthly Review*

Magazine of the South, Richmond,
Va., 1847-61?

Methodist Quarterly Review -- See
Methodist Review

Methodist Review, Louisville, Ky.;
Nashville, Tenn., 1847-1930.
Suspended 1862-78. 1847 as
*Quarterly Review of the
Methodist Episcopal Church,
South.* July 1888 as *Southern
Methodist Review.* Oct.
1888-July 1894 as *Quarterly
Review of the Methodist
Episcopal Church, South.*
1894-1902 as *Methodist Review.*
1903-06 as *Methodist Quarterly
Review.* DLC, ICU, NN, TxU

*Monthly Pictorial Rough and
Ready,* Louisville, Ky., 1847-?

*New Orleans Miscellany. A Monthly
Periodical, Devoted to the
Interest of Popular Science and
to the Advancement of Southern
Literature,* New Orleans, La.,
1847-48.

*Portfolio, or, Journal of
Freemasonry and General
Literature,* Nashville, Tenn.,
1847-50. DLC, T, TKL, TNF, TxU

*Quarterly Review of the Methodist
Episcopal Church, South* -- See
Methodist Review

*Radix; or, Virginia Public School
Advocate,* Richmond, Va., 1847.
Continued as *Southern Journal
of Education,* Knoxville, Tenn.,
DE

Rough and Ready, Nashville, Tenn.,
1847?

*Southern Harmony and Musical
Companion,* Spartanburg, S.C.,
1847?

*Southern Lady's Companion. A
monthly periodical devoted to
literature and religion,*
Nashville, Tenn., 1847-54? DLC,
NcU, T, TN, TU, TxU

Southern Medical Reformer,
Petersburg, Va., 1847-48? DSG,
MiU, NNN

Southern Methodist Review -- See
Methodist Review

The Southern Presbyterian,
Milledgeville, Augusta, Atlanta,
Ga.; Charleston, Columbia, S.C.,
1847-1908. United with other
journals to form *Presbyterian
of the South,* DLC, NcD, KyLoS,
NN, ScU, TxU

Southwestern Baptist Chronicle,
New Orleans, La., 1847-66.
Merged into *Christian Index,*
PCA, MWA, KyLoS

Southwestern Medical Advocate,
Memphis, Tenn., 1847, CtY, DSG,
MBM, MiU

Texas Methodist, Dallas, Tex.,
1847-current. Also as *Texas
Methodist/United Methodist
Reporter.* Currently as *United
Methodist Reporter*

Arminian Magazine, Rome, Ga.,
1848-49, TxU, NNHi

Bon Ton, Louisville, Ky., 1848-49?

Christian Magazine, Nashville,
Tenn., 1848-53? GEU, KyLoS

The Christian Mirror, Frankfort,
Midway, Ky., 1848-?

Christian Monitor, Frankfort, Ky.,
1848-?

Chronicle of Western Literature,
Louisville, Ky., 1848-49? DLC,
MWA

Colman's Rural World, Saint Louis,
Mo.; Louisville, Ky., 1848-1916.
1848-1864 as *Valley Farmer.*
Merged into *Journal of
Agriculture,* DLC, ICJ, NN, MoS

Democratic Statesman, Nashville,
Tenn., July 1848-Jan. 1849, WHi

Deutsch-Amerikanische Didaskalia,
Baltimore, Md., 1848, no.1 as
Didaskalia, DLC, IU, NN

Didaskalia -- See
*Deutsche-Amerikanische
Didaskalia*

*Ecclesiastical Reformer. Devoted
to practical piety.* Frankfort,
Harrodsburg, Lexington, Ky.,
1848-52? KyLxT, OMC

*Iris. Devoted to science,
literature, and the arts,
including medical news,*
Richmond, Va., Mar. 1848, CSmH,
MH, T, Vi

*Journal of the South Carolina
Medical Association,* Florence,
S.C., 1848-?

Literary Weekly Gazette, Athens,
Ga., 1848?

Old Zack, Tuscaloosa, Ala., 1848,
Ala. Dept. of Archives and
History

The Owl, Lexington, Va., 1848-49

*Polyglotte. Journal Scientifique
et Litteraire,* New Orleans, La.,
1848?

*Richard's Weekly Gazette--A
Southern Family Journal.
Devoted to Literature, The Arts
and Sciences, and to General
Intelligence,* Athens, Ga.,
1848-50?

Rose-Bud, La Grange, Ga., 1848?

Southern Journal of Education,
Knoxville, Tenn., 1848-50.
Supersedes *Radix,* TKL, TU

*Southern Literary Gazette. An
illustrated weekly journal of
belles-lettres, science, and the
arts,* Athens, Ga.; Charleston,
S.C., 1848-55, GU, NcD, MWA, S,
ScU, TxU

Southern Methodist Pulpit,
Richmond, Va., 1848-52? DLC,
IEG, KyL, LNHT, MoS, NcD, NcU,
NjMD, Tx, TxU, Vi, ViU, OMC

Southwestern School Journal,
Nashville?, Tenn., 1848-49

Tennessee Organ, Nashville, Tenn.,
1848-52? KyLoS

*Turner's Monthly, A Miscellaneous
Journal and Review,* Turnwold
Plantation, Ga., 1848

Valley Farmer -- See *Colman's
Rural World*

*Virginia Historical Register and
Literary Companion,* Richmond,
Va., 1848-53, APS

Western Boatman, Nashville, Tenn.;
Cincinnati, Ohio; Saint Louis,
Mo., 1848-49? Only no.1
published in Tennessee, In,
MWA, NN, OCHP

Alabama Baptist Advocate, Marion,
Ala., 1849-July 1850.
Supersedes *Alabama Baptist*
Superseded by *South Western
Baptist* Ala. Dept. of Archives
and History, KyLoS

Commission, Richmond, Va., 1849-51,
KyLoS

Crystal Fount, Tuscaloosa, Ala.,
1849-52? Ala. Dept. of Archives
and History

*Friend of the Family. Devoted to
literature, science, and art,
The Sons of Temperance, Odd
Fellowship, Masonry, and
general intelligence,* Savannah,
Ga., 1849-51, GMM

Horn of Mirth, Athens, Ga., 1849-50

Jefferson's Monument Magazine,
Charlottesville, Va., 1849-50?
NNHi, ViU, NcD

Kentucky Medical Recorder,
Louisville, Ky., 1849-54, n.s.,
v.2, as *Transylvania Medical
Journal,* N, NNN, ICJ, KyLxT,
MBM, MiU, NBM, NcD, PPC, KyBgW

Madison Family Visitor, Morgan
County, Ga., 1849-53

*Masonic Journal, Devoted to
Masonry, Science and
Literature.* Marietta, Ga.,
1849-52.

Mistletoe, Athens, Ga., 1849, APS

*Moniteur du Sud. Organe des
population Franco-Americaines,*
New Orleans, La., 1849-50?

Monthly Miscellany, Atlanta, Ga.;
Richmond, Va.; New Orleans, La.,
1849-? NcD

Orion, Montgomery, Ala., 1849-?

*Parlor Gazette and Ladies'
Advertiser,* Baltimore, Md.,
1849-?

Red Lion, Turnwold Plantation, Ga.,
1849

*The Schoolfellow: A Magazine for
Girls and Boys.* Athens, Ga.;
Charleston, S.C., 1849-57, MWA,
NN, DLC, MNS, N, NBuG, NNC-T,
NcD, RPB, ViU, GEU, TxDN

*Semaine Litteraire: Revue
Franco-Americaine,* New Orleans,
La., 1849-50? AU, TxU

Social Messenger, Mount Meigs,
Ala., 1849-? Ala. Dept. of
Archives and History

*The Southern and Western Masonic
Miscellany,* Charleston, S.C.,
1849-52, MWA, PPi, TxU, DLC

*Southern Botanico-Medical
Reformer,* Macon, Ga., 1849-51?
Continues *Georgia Botanic
Journal and College Sentinel,*
DSG

Southern Medical Reports, New
Orleans, La., 1849-50, CtY, DLC,
DSG, ICJ, MB, N, TxU

Transylvania Medical Journal --
See *Kentucky Medical Recorder*

True Union, Baltimore, Md.;
Washington, D.C., 1849-61, DLC,
KyLoS, NHC, PCA

Universalist Herald, Notasulga,
Ala.; Atlanta, Ga., 1849-? Ala.
Dept. of Archives and History

University of Virginia Magazine
-- See *Virginia Spectator*

University Magazine -- See
Virginia Spectator

Veillees Louisianaises, New
Orleans, La., 1849

*Violette, revue musicale et
litteraire,* New Orleans, La.,
1849-50? AU

Virginia Spectator,
Charlottesville, Va., 1849-1937.
1849-58 as *University Magazine,*
1858-92 as *Virginia University
Magazine,* 1892-1926 as
*University of Virginia
Magazine,* 1927-29 as *Virginia
Spectator,* 1932-36 as *University
of Virginia Magazine.* TxU,
NcD, ViU, DLC, NN

Virginia University Magazine --
See *Virginia Spectator*

*Wheler's Southern Monthly
Magazine: A Reflex of
Literature and Art*, Athens,
Ga., 1849-50. Supersedes
Mistletoe, NN, NcD, NjR

American Mechanic, Athens, Ga.,
1850

*American Union and Republican
Review*, Jackson, Miss., 1850-51?
DLC, CSmH, T, TxU

Baptist Review, Louisville, Ky.,
1850-?

Catholic Mirror, Baltimore, Md.,
1850-1908, NN, DLC

The Children's Visitor -- See *The
Sunday School Visitor*

*Civil, Military, and Naval Gazette.
Devoted to the interests of the
citizen, soldier, and sailor*,
Annapolis, Md., 1850? NcD, ScU,
DLC

Day Star of Truth, Milledgeville,
Ga., 1850

Delphian Oracle, Georgetown, Ky.,
1850-?

Echo Von New Orleans, New Orleans,
La., 1850?-?

Family Mirror, Carrollton,
Louisville, Ky., 1850-54?

Farmer and Planter Monthly,
Pendleton, Columbia, S.C.,
1850-61, DA, N, ScU

Gem, Milledgeville, Ga., 1850

Kentucky New Era, Louisville, Ky.,
1850-52?

Louisville Examiner, Louisville,
Ky., 1850? MH, MWA, NIC

Methodist, Trenton, Ga., 1850-?

Methodist Monthly, Frankfort, Ky.,
1850-?

Mountain Messenger, Morganton,
Va., 1850-56, KyLoS

*Naturalist. Devoted to Science,
Agriculture, Mechanic Arts,
Education and General
Improvement*, Franklin College,
Tenn., 1850? NcD, MH

New Orleans Christian Advocate,
New Orleans, La., 1850-1926, NN,
WHi, LU, NcD, TxU

Old Guard, Frankfort, Ky., 1850?
WHi, ICU, DLC, KyBgW, KyL, KyU,
OC, OCHP

Reformer, Macon, Ga., 1850?

The Southern Eclectic Magazine,
Charleston, S.C., 1850

Southern Family Journal,
Covington, Ga., 1850-?

Southern Index, Ashborough, N.C.,
1850?

*Southern Lady's Magazine. A
monthly magazine of literature,
art, and science*, Baltimore,
Md., 1850? DLC

Southern Literary Journal,
Oxford, Ga., 1850

Southern Star, Huntsville, Ala.,
1850-?

Southwestern Baptist, Marion,
Montgomery, Tuskegee, Ala.,
1850-65? Continue *Alabama
Baptist Advocate*. Ala. Dept.
of Archives and History, ABH,
KyLoS, NcD

Sunday School Advocate, Athens,
Ga., 1850

The Sunday School Visitor,
Charleston, S.C.; Nashville,
Tenn., 1850-1921. As *The
Children's Visitor*, 1898-1909,
The Visitor, 1909-1921.
Superseded in 1921 by *The
Torchbearer* (for girls), *The
Haversack*, (for boys), and *Our
Young People*, (for older
students) TxU, MWA, NcD

*Whitaker's Magazine: The Rights
of the South*, Charleston, S.C.,
1850-53. Moved to Columbia,
S.C., 1851 as *Whitaker's
Southern Magazine*, DLC, NcD,
GEU, MiDU, RP, ABH

Whitaker's Southern Magazine --
See *Whitaker's Magazine: The
Rights of the South*

Youth's Friend, Augusta, Ga., 1850

*Youth's Gem and 1850 Southern
Cadet*, Macon, Ga., 1850

*Album Louisianais: Revue
Litteraire et Artistique*, New
Orleans, La., 1851

Dental Times and Advertiser,
Baltimore, Md., 1851-52? DSG,
IEN-D, NNN, PU

Evergreen, Ashborough, N.C., 1851?
NcD, T

Flag of the Union, Jackson, Miss.,
1851?

Foreign Mission Journal, Richmond,
Va., 1851-1916, 1851-74 as *Home
and Foreign Journal*, 1895-96
as *Mission Journal of the
Southern Baptist Convention*,
United with *Home Field* to form
Home and Foreign Fields, CtY,
DLC, ICU, NN, NcD, OO, TxU, Vi

Georgia Home Gazette, Augusta,
Ga., 1851-52

Georgia University Magazine,
Athens, Ga., 1851-?

Home and Foreign Journal -- See
Foreign Mission Journal

Hunt's Magazine, _____, Fla.,
1851?

Kentucky Medical Journal -- See
*Kentucky State Medical Society
Transactions*

*Kentucky State Medical Society
Transactions*, Frankfort, Ky.,
1851-1902. Also *Kentucky
Medical Journal*, DLC, DSG, NNN,
TxU-M

Magnolia Magazine, Baton Rouge,
La., 1851-?

Medical Reformer, Memphis, Tenn.,
1851, DSG, TU-M

*Memphis Medical Journal of the
Progressive Medical and
Physical Sciences*, Memphis,
Tenn., 1851-52, CSt-L, DSG

*Mission Journal of the Southern
Baptist Convention* -- See
Foreign Mission Journal

Mississippi Palladium, Holly
Springs, Miss., 1851-52? LNHT,
ViU

*Nashville Journal of Medicine and
Surgery*, Nashville, Tenn.,
1851-1920. Merged into *Medical
Life*, T, DLC, TxU, NN

*New Orleans Monthly Medical
Register*, New Orleans, La.,
1851-53, DSG, MBM, NNN

Parish Visitor, Richmond, Va.,
1851-?

Randolph-Macon Magazine, Ashland,
Va., 1851-?

Soil of the South, Columbus, Ga.,
1851-1857. Merged into
American Cotton Planter, Jan.
1857, DLC, LU, G, MWA, NjP, WHi

Sons of Temperance, Knoxville, Tenn., 1851-52?

Southern Banner, Athens, Ga., Aug. 14, 1851-?

Southern Baptist Messenger, Covington, Ga., 1851-61? NcD, KyLoS

Southern Home Journal, Charleston, S.C., 1851?

Southern Parlor Magazine, Mobile, Ala.; Memphis, Tenn., 1851-56, Ala. Dept. of Archives and History

Southern Repertory and College Review, Emory, Va., 1851-55, DLC, MoS, NcD, PCaD, Vi, ViU

Southern Standard, Charleston, S.C., 1851?

Spirit of the South, Eufaula, Ala., 1851?

Sunny South, Jacksonville, Ala., 1851?

Stethoscope, Richmond, Va., 1851-55. 1851-53 as *Stethoscope and Virginia Medical Gazette.* United with *Virginia Medical and Surgical Journal* to form *Virginia Medical Journal*, later *Maryland and Virginia Medical Journal*, CSt-L, CtY, DLC, MBM, NNN

Stethoscope and Virginia Medical Gazette -- See *Stethoscope*

Bible Advocate, Louisville, Ky., 1852-?

Christian Sunday School Journal, Lexington, Ky., 1852-?

Cultivator, Covington, Ky., 1852-?

East Tennessee Record of Medicine and Surgery, Knoxville, Tenn., 1852-53. Merged into *Southern Journal of the Medical and Physical Sciences*, CSt-L, DSG, ICJ, N, NNN

Farmers' Journal, Bath, N.C., 1852? Continued by *Carolina Cultivator.* DLC, NcD, NcU

Ford's Christian Repository, Louisville, Ky.; Saint Louis, Mo., 1852-1905, DLC, KyU, KyLoS, TxU, NcD

Freedom's Blade. Devoted to the General Interest of the People of Liberty, Raleigh, N.C., Aug. 1852-? NcD

Holston Christian Advocate, Knoxville, Tenn., 1852-53?

Illustrated Family Friend, Columbia, S.C., 1852-?

Ladies' Pearl, Nashville, Tenn.; Saint Louis, Mo., Oct. 1852-Oct. 1860, n.s. Jan. 1867-Mar. 1868, n.s. May 1868-Apr. 1884. Merged into *Electra, A Magazine of Pure Literature*, DLC, NcD, NcU, TMC, TxU

Literary Magnolia, a Southern Family Journal, Richmond, Va., 1852, MWA

Literary Vade Mecum, Buena Vista, Ga., 1852-53

Memphis Medical Recorder, Memphis, Tenn., 1852-58. 1852-53 as *Medical Recorder*, C, CSt-L, DSG, ICJ, NN, NNN, T, TU-M

Memphis, Arkansas, and Quachita Christian Advocate, Memphis, Tenn., 1852

Miscellany and Review, Memphis, Tenn., 1852-?

Mountain Cove Journal and Spiritual Harbinger, Mountain Cove, Va., 1852-53

Parthenian. A Quarterly Magazine, Devoted to Literature, Education, and the Fine Arts Baltimore, Md., Mar. 1852-Sept. 1859, Jan. 1878? DLC, ICN, NN

Southern Lady's Book, New Orleans, La., 1852-53? AU, In, NcD

Southern Magazine, Mobile, Ala.; Memphis, Tenn., 1852-56?

Southern Medical Reformer and Review, Macon, Ga., 1852-60, CtY-M, DSG, CSt-L, MWA, NcD, OCL, PPC

South-Western American, Austin, Tex., 1852?

Southwestern Monthly, Nashville, Tenn., 1852, DLC, ICN, NcD, TN, Vi

Theological Medium and Quarterly Review, Louisville, Ky., 1852-?

Union Medicale de la Louisiane, New Orleans, La., 1852, DSG, MBM, NNN

Weekly News and Southern Literary Gazette, Charleston, S.C., 1852-57, CtY

American Cotton Planter, Montgomery, Ala., 1853-61, DA, GU, NcU, TxU, NcD

American Freemason -- See *American Freemason's Magazine*

American Freemason's Magazine, Louisville, Frankfort, Ky.; New York, N.Y., Apr. 1853-Aug. 1860. v.1 as *Kentucky Freemason*. v.2-3 as *American Freemason*, also as *American Freemason's New Monthly Magazine*, CtY, DLC, NN

American Freemason's New Monthly Magazine -- See *American Freemason's Magazine*

Cotton Plant, Baltimore, Md., 1853

Kentucky Freemason -- See *American Freemason's Magazine*

Kentucky Garland, Covington, Ky., 1853-?

Maryland and Virginia Medical Journal, Baltimore, Md., 1853-61. 1853-55 as *Virginia Medical and Surgical Journal*. 1856-59 as *Virginia Medical Journal*, DLC, ICJ, MBM, NNN, NcD, Vi, ViU, ViW

Memphis Journal of Medicine, Memphis, Tenn.; Holly Springs, Miss., 1853-57, DSG, LNHT

Metropolitan. A monthly magazine devoted to religion, education, literature, and general information, Baltimore, Md., 1853-59, NN, DLC, N

Park's Reform Medical and Family Journal, Lumpkin, Ga., 1853, DSG

People's Medical Gazette, Abbeville, S.C., 1853-54? DSG, NNN, ScU

Roath's Monthly Magazine, Athens, Augusta, Ga., 1853, NcD

The Self Instructor. A Monthly Journal, Devoted to Southern Education, and to the Diffusion of a Knowledge of the Resources and Power of the South, as Represented by the Negro, the Rail and the Press. Charleston, S.C., 1853-54, MH, NcD

Southern Boys and Girls Monthly, Richmond, Ga., 1853-67?

Southern Eclectic. A monthly magazine composed of selections from the leading periodicals of Europe, with original contributions from the pens of Southern writers, Augusta, Ga., 1853-54, DLC, GU, NcD, NcU

Southern Journal of the Medical and Physical Sciences, Knoxville, Nashville, Tenn., 1853-57, DSG, MBM, NNN

Southern School Journal, Columbus, Madison, Macon, Ga., 1853-55, CSt, DE

The Tomahawk, Macon, Ga., 1853

True Baptist, Jackson, Miss., 1853-54? DLC, MWA, NNUT

Virginia Medical and Surgical Journal -- See *Maryland and Virginia Medical Journal*

Virginia Medical Journal -- See *Maryland and Virginia Medical Journal*

The Western Literary Magazine, Louisville, Ky., 1853-?

Arkansas Magazine, Little Rock, Ark., 1854

The College of Charleston Magazine, Charleston, S.C., 1854-55, 1898-99, 1900-1925, 1827-39, CLS, ScU

Coup d'Oeil, New Orleans, La., 1854?

Fly Leaf, Newnan, Ga., 1854

Georgia Baptist, Forsyth, Ga., 1854?

Georgia Blister and Critic, Atlanta, Ga., 1854-55, CSt-L, DSG, MBM, MiU, NNN

Masonic Signet, Atlanta, Ga., 1854-?

New Orleans Medical News and Hospital Gazette, New Orleans, La., 1854-61. Continues *New Orleans Monthly Medical Register*. Continued as *New Orleans Medical Times*, CSt-L, CtY, DSG, ICJ, MBM, NNN

New Orleans Noesis, or, Journal of Intellectual Amusement: Popular Literature, Science, and Arts. New Orleans, La., 1854-? LNHT

Parlor Visitor, Nashville, Tenn., 1854-57? NcD, T, TC, TKL, TxU

Political and Educational Reform in Kentucky, Somerset, Ky., 1854-?

Shaffner's Telegraph Companion. Devoted to the science and art of the Morse American Telegraph, New York, N.Y.; Louisville, Ky., 1854-55, DLC, DP, IU, N, PPi

Southern Episcopalian, Charleston, S.C., 1854-63, MWA, ScU, KyLoS, NcD, TxU, NcU

Southern Military Gazette, Montgomery, Ala.; Atlanta, Ga. 1854-? Moved to Atlanta in 1855, Ala. Dept. of Archives and History

Southern Statesman, Prattsville, Ala., 1854?

Virginia Historical Reporter, Richmond, Va., 1854-60, CtY, DLC, N, NjP

Western Teacher's Advocate, Louisville, Ky., 1854

Zion's Advocate, various Southern towns, Washington, D.C., 1854-1923, DLC

Acacia, Natchez, Miss., 1855-56? MsJS, NcD

Agricultural and Commercial Journal, Nashville, Tenn., 1855-?

American Citizen, Cahaba, Ala., 1855?

Atlanta Medical and Surgical Journal, Atlanta, Ga., 1855-99. Suspended Nov. 1861-April 1866, Sept. 1868-March 1871. Also as *Atlanta Medical Register*. United with *Southern Medical Record* to form *Atlanta Journal-Record of Medicine*, CtY, ICJ, NNN, TxU-M, G, NcD

Atlanta Medical Register -- See *Atlanta Medical and Surgical Journal*

Baptist Watchman, Knoxville, Tenn., 1855-? PCA, NcD, KyLoS

Carolina Cultivator, Raleigh, N.C., 1855-57? LNHT, NcD, NcU, GU

Christian Advocate -- See *Raleigh Christian Advocate*

Dental Eclectic. A Bi-Monthly Journal Devoted to the Interests of the Profession. Knoxville, Tenn., 1855-87, DSG, MBM, NBuG, NNN

Dental Obturator, New Orleans, La., 1855-56, DSG, NNN, PU, MBM, NBM, PU

Family Christian Album, Richmond, Va., 1855-? Ia, NcD, Vi

Farmers' Banner, Nashville, Tenn., 1855-60?

Fountain, Nashville, Tenn., 1855-?

Good Templar, Louisville, Ky., 1855-56?

Gospel Advocate, Nashville, Tenn., 1855?-57? KyL, KyLxT, NN, NcD

Home Circle. A monthly periodical devoted to religion and literature. Nashville, Tenn., 1855-60?

Journal of Education, New Orleans, La., 1855? DE, LNHT

Knight of Jericho, Atlanta, Ga., 1855-?

Lotos, Memphis, Tenn., 1855?-60?

Masonic Signet and Journal, Marietta, Ga., 1855-60, G, GA, NcD

Message, Greensboro, N.C., 1855-?

North Carolina Christian Advocate, Greensboro, Raleigh, N.C., 1855-? Published also as *Christian Advocate*, as *Raleigh Christian Advocate*, NN, NcU

The Oriental and Chinese Advocate, Louisville, Ky., 1855-?

Presbyterian Critic, Baltimore, Md.; Philadelphia, Pa., 1855-56, ICU, IEG, MA

Raleigh Christian Advocate -- See *North Carolina Christian Advocate*

South Carolina Historical and Genealogical Magazine, Charleston, S.C., 1855-59?, 1875?-?, 1900-? CU, DLC, NcU, NjP

Southern Baptist Review and Eclectic, Nashville, Tenn., 1855-61, DLC, NN, NcD

Southern Times, A literary weekly, Montgomery, Ala., 1855

Sunday School Visitor, Nashville, Tenn., 1855-? DLC, GEU, NN, NjMD, TNG

Temperance Times, Montgomery, Ala., 1855

Texas Baptist, Anderson, Tex.,
1855-61, KyLoS, PCA

White's Counterfeit Detector,
Louisville, Ky., 1855-?

Young America, Tuscaloosa, Ala.,
1855-? Ala. Dept. of Archives
and History

American Banner, Nashville, Tenn.,
1856, MBA, NNHi, TxU

*Arator. Devoted to Agriculture
and Its Kindred Arts.* Raleigh,
N.C., 1856-57? N, NcD, NcU, RPB

Christian Union, Atlanta, Augusta,
Ga., Jan.-Dec. 1856, DLC,
KyLxCB

Cic Magazine, Louisville, Ky.,
1856-?

Ciceronian Magazine, Georgetown,
Ky., 1856-? MWA, NcD

*Commission or, Southern Baptist
Missionary Magazine*, Richmond,
Va., 1856-61, PCA

Guigon Quarterly Law Journal,
Richmond, Va., 1856-59? MH-L,
PU-L

Home Journal, Charleston, S.C.,
1856?

Jewish Ledger, New Orleans, La.,
1856-1902. Merged into
American Hebrew. CtY, LNHT,
NN, NNJ, OCH

Kaleidoscope, Petersburg, Va.,
1856-57

Loge d'Opera, New Orleans, La.,
1856-57?

Louisville Review, Louisville, Ky.,
1856. Continues *Western
Journal of Medicine and
Surgery.* United with *Medical
Examiner*, Philadelphia, to form
*North American
Medico-Chirurgical Review*,
CSt-L, DSG, ICJ, MBM, N, NNN

*Monthly Stethoscope and Medical
Reporter*, Richmond, Va.,
1856-57, DLC, DSG, ICJ, NNN

*North Carolina Common School
Journal*, _____, N.C., Sept.
1856-May 1857, NcD, NcU

Principle, New York, N.Y.;
Baltimore, Md., 1856-58? DLC,
NNN, N, NN

Quarterly Law Journal, Richmond,
Va., 1856-59. Continued as
Quarterly Law Review, C, Ct,
DLC, Ia

*Sinai, ein organ fur erkenntniss
und veredlung des Judenthums*,
Baltimore, Md.; Philadelphia,
Pa., 1856-62? CU, MH, NN, NNJ

South Carolina Agriculturist,
Columbia, S.C., 1856? GDC, N,
NcD, ScU

Southern College Magazine,
Florence, Ala., 1856-? Ala.
Dept. of Archives and History

Southern Light, Edgefield, S.C.,
1856, ScU

Southwestern School Journal,
Louisville, Ky., 1856-57

Tennessee Farmer and Mechanic,
Nashville, Tenn., 1856-57,   v.3
as *Southern Homestead*, T, TKL

University Literary Magazine,
University of Virginia,
Charlottesville, Va., 1856-59

Virginia Farmer, Harrisonburg,
Va., Jan.-Dec. 1856, NcMHi

Western Farm Journal, Louisville, Ky., 1856-57? N

Alabama Educational Journal. Devoted to the Cause of Human Progress, Education, Science, Literature, Morality, Montgomery, Ala., 1857, DE

Baptist Family Visitor, Nashville, Tenn., 1857?

Catholic Youth's Magazine, Baltimore, Md., 1857-61, DLC, DCU

Delta, New Orleans, La., 1857?

Educational Journal, Forsyth, Ga., 1857-61? MBAt

Educational Journal, Montgomery, Ala., 1857-58

Educational Journal and Family Monthly, Atlanta, Ga., 1857-?

Harper's Theatrical Bulletin, Nashville, Tenn., 1857-?

Journal of the Elliot Society of Natural History, Charleston, S.C., 1857-58, CLS, NNM, PP, PPAP, S, ScU

Mississippi Baptist, Jackson, Miss., 1857-61, KyLoS, NHC, PCA

Monitor, Baltimore, Md., 1857? CtH, MdBP, CtY, DLC, MdBE, NcD

Olive Branch, Atlanta, Ga., 1857

Parlor Magazine. Devoted to literature, science, and general intelligence, New Orleans, La., 1857? LNHT

Practicien Homeopathique, New Orleans, La., 1857-58?

Russell's Magazine, Charleston, S.C., 1857-60, ICU, LNHT, MWA, DLC, NcD, NN, ScU, Vi, ViU

South, Richmond, Va., 1857-58, CSmH

Southern Aurora, Baton Rouge, La., 1857-?

Southern Citizen, Knoxville, Tenn., 1857-?

Southern Dial. A monthly magazine devoted mainly to a discussion of African slavery and the interests moral, social, and political which it involves, Montgomery, Ala., 1857-Dec. 1, 1858, GU, NcD, CSmH

The South-Western Dollar Weekly, Murfreesboro, Tenn., 1857

Spiritualiste de la Nouvelle-Orleans: echo mensuel, New Orleans, La., 1857-58? LNHT, MH

Aurora. A Southern Literary Magazine, Murfreesboro, Memphis, Tenn., 1858-61?

Catholic Guardian, Louisville, Ky., 1858-62

College Miscellany and Orphan's Advocate, Covington, Ga., 1858-59

DeBow's Weekly Press, New Orleans, La., 1858, DLC

Dental Enterprise, Baltimore, Md., 1858-60? NNN

Diamond, Memphis, Tenn., 1858?

Erskine Collegiate Recorder, Due West, S.C., 1858-60

Georgia Crusader, Penfield, Atlanta, Ga., 1858-61?

Howard College Magazine, Marion, Ala., 1858-? Ala. Dept. of Archives and History

Journal of Medicine, Savannah, Ga., 1858-66

Legislative Union and American,
Nashville, Tenn., 1858-60, MH,
MHi, T, TN, LU

Louisiana Baptist, Mount Lebanon,
La., 1858-69, PCA, KyLoS

*Medical Journal of North
Carolina,* Edenton, Raleigh,
N.C., 1858-90? DSG, NNN, MBM,
NBM, NcD

Nashville Medical Record,
Nashville, Tenn., 1858-61. v.1
as *Nashville Monthly Record of
Medical and Physical Science,*
C, CtY, DSG, NNN

*Nashville Monthly Record of
Medical and Physical Science*
-- See *Nashville Medical Record*

*North Carolina Journal of
Education,* Greensboro, N.C.,
1858-61, CtY, N, NN, NcD, NcU

*North Carolina Planter. Devoted
to Agriculture, Horticulture,
and the Mechanic Arts,* Raleigh,
N.C., 1858-61? CtY, DLC, ICU,
NcD, NcU

North Carolina Presbyterian,
Fayetteville, Wilmington,
Charlotte, N.C., 1858-1931. Also
as *Presbyterian Standard.*
Merged into *Presbyterian of the
South,* DLC, NN, NcD, NcU

*Oglethorpe Medical and Surgical
Journal,* Savannah, Ga., 1858-61,
DSG, MBM, NNN

Presbyterian Standard -- See
North Carolina Presbyterian

*Repository of Religion and
Literature and of Science and
Art,* Indianapolis, Ind.;
Philadelphia, Pa.; Baltimore,
Md., 1858-63. Indianapolis,
1858-60; Philadelphia, 1861;
Baltimore, 1862-63, DHU, MH,
ViU, In

Salem Magazine, _____, N.C., 1858

Savannah Journal of Medicine,
Savannah, Ga., 1858-66.
Suspended 1861-66, DSG, MBM,
NNN

Southern Homestead, Nashville,
Tenn., 1858

Steadman's Magazine, Raleigh,
N.C., 1858?

Temperance Monthly, McMinnville,
Nashville, Tenn., 1858-60? T,
TxU

The Texian Monthly Magazine,
_____, Tex., July 1858-? TxU

Texas Freemason, Ruck, Tex.,
1858-59?

Virginia Baptist, Fredericksburg,
Va., 1858-59? KyLoS

The Weekly Press, New Orleans,
La., 1858-?

*Young's Spirit of South and
Central America. A Chronicle
of the Turf, Field, Sports,
Literature, and the Stage,*
Nashville, Tenn.; Louisville,
Ky., 1858-?

Arkansas Baptist, Little Rock,
Ark., 1859-61, KyLoS, NcD

Baltimore Methodist, Baltimore, Md.,
1859-1928, Later as *Washington
Christian Advocate,* DLC, NN,
NcD

Baptist Banner, Augusta, Ga.,
1859-64, ICU, KyLoS, PCC, OClWHi

Baptist Champion, Macon, Ga.,
1859-60? KyLoS

Children's Friend, Nashville,
Tenn., 1859-73, KyLoS

*Courant. A Southern Literary
Journal.* Columbia, S.C., 1859,
MB, NcD, WHi

Educational Monthly, Louisville, Ky., 1859-60? Contains *Kentucky Family Journal*, DE, ICHi, KyLxT

Educator, Baltimore, Md., 1859,

Family Journal, Baltimore, Md., 1859-60? DLC, MdBE, NcD

Female Student, Louisville, Ky., 1859-60, KyBgW

Harris's Magazine, Louisville, Ky., 1859-60?

Homoion. Organe de la doctrine Hahnemanniene. New Orleans, La., 1859-61?

Kennesaw Gem, Marietta, Ga., 1859

Kentucky Family Journal, Louisville, Ky., 1859-60. Continued as *Educational Monthly*.

Landmark Banner and Cherokee Baptist, Rome, Ga., 1859-61? PCA

Literary Casket, Fayetteville, Ga., 1859-60?

Louisville Medical Gazette, Louisville, Ky., 1859, DSG, MBM, NNN

Masonic Messenger, New Orleans, La., 1859-?

Medical and Literary Weekly, Atlanta, Ga., 1859, NNN, NcD

Monthly Medical News, Louisville, Ky., 1859-60. Jan. 1-Dec. 15, 1859 as *Semi-Monthly Medical News*, CSt, DSG, ICJ, MBM, NNN

North Carolina University Magazine, Chapel Hill, N.C., 1859, ICU, NN, NcU, ViU

The Philidorian, Charleston, S.C., 1859, MH, NjP, OCl, PP

Pipeline & Gas Journal, Dallas, Tex., 1859-current. Formed by merger of *Pipeline Engineer* and *American Gas Journal*

Presbyterian Sentinel, Memphis, Tenn., 1859-60. Merged into *True Witness*, NcMHi, PPPrHi

Progressionist, Newman, Ga., 1859-?

Quodlibetarian, Medfield, Md., 1859-60? MdBE, NNHi

Rural Register, Baltimore, Md., 1859-63? DLC, N, NcU, TxU

Semi-Monthly Medical News -- See *Monthly Medical News*

South Countryman, A Monthly Agricultural, Industrial and Educational Magazine, Marietta, Ga., Jan.-June 1859, MWA, NcD

Southern Field and Fireside, Augusta, Ga., 1859-64, DLC, GEU, GU, TxU, ViU, NBuG, NcU, MWA

Southern Literary Companion, Newman, Ga., 1859-64, MBAt

Southern Musical Advocate and Singer's Friend, Singer's Glen, Va., 1859-69, DLC, NcD, NcU, ViU

Southern Teacher, Montgomery, Ala., 1859-61, CSt, DE, TxU

Tennessee Journal of Education, Richmond, Tenn., 1859-?

Voice of Masonry, Louisville, Ky.; Chicago, Ill., 1859-99, NN

Weekly Magpie, Edgewood, Md., 1859, DLC, MdBE, MdBP

Baptist Correspondent, Marion, Ala., 1860-? Ala. Dept. of Archives and History, KyLoS

Centre College Magazine, Danville, Ky., 1860-?

Champion, Lumpkin, Ga., 1860?

Cherokee Baptist, Atlanta, Ga.,
1860-?

Church Intelligencer, Raleigh,
N.C., 1860-62, 1864-65? DLC,
MH, NcD

*Educational Repository and Family
Monthly*, Atlanta, Ga., 1860-61?
DE, DLC, N

Georgia Citizen Advertiser, Macon,
Ga., 1860

*Georgia Gazette. A literary
quarto.* ____, Ga., 1860-?

*Georgia Literary and Temperance
Crusader*, Atlanta, Ga., 1860-?
NcD

Georgia Weekly, Greenville, Ga.,
1860

Gopher, Waynesboro, Ga., 1860, GEU

*Historical Documents from the Old
Dominion*, Richmond, Va.,
1860-74, DLC, MB, NN, NIC, WHi

Hygienic and Literary Magazine,
Atlanta, Ga., 1860. Continues
Medical and Literary Weekly,
DSG,MiU, NcD

Katholische Volkszeitung,
Baltimore, Md., 1860-1914? DCU,
MNCS

Kentucky Campaign, Frankfort,
Ky., July 25-Oct. 10, 1860, DLC,
KyU

Lita National, Atlanta, Ga., 1860-?

Literary Weekly, Greenville,
Atlanta, Ga., 1860-?

Louisville Medical Journal,
Louisville, Ky., 1860, CSt-L,
DSG, MBM, NNN

Magnolia, Hopkinsville, Ky., 1860-?

*Mercury. Devoted to Polite
Southern Literature.* Raleigh,
N.C., 1860-? NcU

Nicholas Advocate, Carlisle, Ky.,
1860-?

*The Plantation: A Southern
Quarterly Journal*, Eatonton,
Ga., 1860, G, GE, DLC, GU, ICU,
MB, MH, NN, NcD, NjP, PU

Presbyterian Witness, Knoxville,
Tenn., 1860

Quarterly Law Review, Richmond,
Va., 1860-61. Continues
Quarterly Law Journal, C, Ct,
M, N, NIC, NNC

Sky Rocket, Waynesboro, Ga., 1860

Southern Dental Examiner, Atlanta,
Ga., 1860-61, IEN-D, MiU, NNN,
PPiU-M, DSG

Southerner, Hopkinsville, Ky.,
1860-?

The Southern Insurance Journal,
Charleston, S.C., 1860-?

Southern Rural Magazine,
Montgomery, Ala., 1860-?

Spiritualist, Macon, Ga., 1860-?

Temperance Companion, Covington,
Ky., 1860-?

Virginia Farm Journal, Richmond,
Va., 1860?

Virginia Register, Richmond, Va.,
1860? DLC, WM

*Weishampel's Literary and
Religious Magazine*, Baltimore,
Md., 1860-?

Young Lady's Mirror, Auburn,
Ala., 1860-?

Youth's Monthly Magazine,
Nashville, Tenn., 1860-?

Christian Banner, Fredericksburg, Va., Apr. 1861-May 1862?

Danville Quarterly Review, Danville, Ky., 1861-64, APS

Educational Monthly, Greensboro, Ga., 1861?-?

La Renaissance Louisianaise, revue hebdomadaire, politique, scientifique et litteraire, organe des populations Franco-Americaines du sud, New Orleans, La., 1861?-70? LNHT

The Portfolio: Devoted to Truth, Virtue and Temperance, Charleston, S.C., 1861

Soldier's Dime, Rodney, Miss., Dec. 7, 1861-? CtY

The Southern Lutheran, Charleston, S.C., 1861-64, NcD, KyLoS

The Southern Monthly, Memphis, Tenn.; Grenada, Miss., Sept. 1861-May 1862, CtY, DLC, NN, NcD, T

Southern Visitor, Montgomery, Ala., 1861-?

The Volunteers' Friend, New Orleans, La., 1861, LNHT

Children's Friend, Richmond, Va., 1862-64, n.s. 1866-June 1915. Merged into *Onward*, NcD, VRT, Vi

Child's Index, Macon, Ga., 1862-65, AU, ICHi, NcD, NcU

Countryman, Eatonton, Ga., Mar. 4, 1862-May 8, 1866, OClWHi, GEU, LU, NcU, ViU

Evangelical Pulpit, Forsyth, Ga., 1862-? GEU, NcD

Gulf City Home Journal, Mobile, Ala., 1862-? NcD

Magnolia Weekly. A Home journal of literature and general news -- See *Magnolia: A Southern Home Journal*

Magnolia: A Southern Home Journal, Richmond, Va., 1862-64. Also as *Magnolia Weekly. A home journal of literature and general news*, DLC, NcU

National Advocate, New Orleans, La., 1862?

New South, Port Royal, S.C., 1862-64? CtY, MB, IHi

Southern Christian Advocate, Augusta, Ga., 1862

Southern Illustrated News, Richmond, Va., 1862-65, DLC, NcU, ViU

Telegram, Baltimore, Md., 1862-1915

True Presbyterian, Louisville, Ky., 1862-64, ICU, DLC, MWA, MiU-C, NcMHi

Army and Navy Herald, Macon, Ga., 1863-65

Army and Navy Messenger, Petersburg, Va., May 1, 1863-?

Bohemian, Richmond, Va., 1863, DLC, MB, MBAt, OClWHi

Bugle-Horn of Liberty, Griffin, Ga., 1863, DLC

Children's Guide, Macon, Ga., 1863-Feb. 1865?

Children's Index, Macon, Ga., Nov. 1863-Apr. 1865? AU, NcD, NcU

Confederate Spirit and Knapsack of Fun, Mobile, Ala., Oct.? 1863-?

Illustrated Mercury, Raleigh, N.C., 1863-64

Record, Richmond, Va., June 18-Dec. 10, 1863. Merged into *The Age*.

Sanitary Reporter, Louisville, Ky., May 15, 1863-Aug. 15, 1865, DLC, KyU, NN

Soldiers' Friend, Atlanta, Ga., 1863-64, OClWHi, ICN

Soldiers' Visitor, Richmond Va., Oct. 1, 1863?-Apr. 1, 1865? CSt-H, MWA

Southern Confederacy, Atlanta, Ga., 1863-?

Southern Punch, Richmond, Va., 1863-64? DLC, ICN

Age: Southern Eclectic Magazine, Richmond, Va., 1864-65, MB, RP, CSmH, OClWHi, PPHi

Army and Navy Crisis, Mobile, Ala., July 9, 1864-?

Confederate States Medical and Surgical Journal, Richmond, Va., 1864-65, DLC, NcD, NNN

Maryland School Journal, Hagerstown, Md., 1864-65, DE, KHi, MH, MdBE

Our Flag, Tyler, Tex., Feb. 17-Mar. 13, 1864

Pacificator, Augusta, Ga., 1864-?

Port Hudson Freemen, Port Hudson, La., July 14, 1864, ICN, MH

School and Family Visitor, Louisville, Ky., 1864, DE, MH, MoS

Smith and Barrow's Monthly, Richmond, Va., 1864, DLC, ScU, TxU

Southern Friend. A Religious, Literary and Agricultural Journal. Richmond, Va., Oct. 1, 1864-Mar. 15, 1866. Suspended Apr.-Sept. 1865, CtY, NcGuG, MH

Southern Observer, Selma, Ala., 1864-? NcD

Swamp Angel, Charleston, S.C., 1864

Weekly Register. Devoted to a register of important documents and events of the times; with essays on subjects connected with arts, science, and literature. Lynchburg, Va., Jan. 2, 1864-65, CtY, DLC, NN

Western Presbyterian. A Religious Monthly. Louisville, Ky., 1864. Superseded by *Western Presbyterian* OClWHi

Christian Herald, Moulton, Tuscumbia, Ala.; Nashville, Tenn., July 21, 1865?-72? KyLoS

Cosmopolitan Monthly -- See *Scott's Monthly Magazine*

Free Christian Commonwealth, Louisville, Ky., Mar. 1865-68. Supersedes *True Presbyterian*, CtY, NcMHi, KyLoS

Free South, Newport, Ky., Mar. 29, 1865-?

Jewell, Mobile, Ala., 1865-?

Keystone, Raleigh, N.C., Jan. 1865-?

Kentucky Farmer, Bowling Green, Ky., 1865-current

Literary Index, Florence, Ala., 1865-?

Louisianais. Journal Politique, Litteraire et Compagnard. Gentilly, La., 1865-? NN, NjP

National Horseman, Louisville, Ky.,
1865-current, CtY, DA, NN, TxU

Scott's Monthly Magazine, Atlanta,
Ga., 1865-69. Became
Cosmopolitan Monthly DLC

Sixth Corps, Danville, Va., 1865-?

Teacher and Pupil, Maysville, Ky.,
1865, DE, MH

Texas Baptist Herald, Houston,
Waco, Dallas, Tex., 1865-1908,
NN, PCA

Baltimore Episcopal Methodist --
See *Episcopal Methodist*

*Baptist Church and Sunday School
Messenger*, Yorkville, S.C., 1866?
KyLoS

Baptist Visitor, Baltimore, Md.,
Sept. 1866-July 1878, DLC,
MdBE, KyLoS

Crescent Monthly, New Orleans, La.,
1866-67, DLC, NN, LU

Episcopal Methodist, Baltimore, Md.,
1866-94. 1866-83 as *Baltimore
Episcopal Methodist*, DLC, NN,
NcD

*Farmer. Devoted to Agriculture,
Horticulture, the Mechanic Arts
and Household Economy*,
Richmond, Va., 1866-67, DA, DLC,
IaAS, Vi

*Gaillard's Medical Journal and the
American Medical Weekly* -- See
Gaillard's Southern Medicine

Gaillard's Southern Medicine,
Savannah, Ga., 1866-1911.
1866-68 as *Richmond Medical
Journal*, 1868-79 as *Richmond
and Louisville Medical Journal*,
1879-83 as *Gaillard's Medical
Journal*, 1883-85 as *Gaillard's
Medical Journal and the
American Medical Weekly*,
1885-1904 as *Gaillard's Medical
Journal*, 1904-05 as *Southern
Medicine and Gaillard's Medical
Journal*, DSG, DLC, NN

Galveston Medical Journal,
Galveston, Tex., 1866-71, n.s.
1880. v.3, no.1 as *Texas
Medical Journal*. v.3, no.2-4
as *Galveston and Texas Medical
Journal*, DSG, ICJ, NNN, TxU

Gospel Advocate, Nashville, Tenn.,
1866-? NN, KyL, KyLxT, NcD,
NjMD, TxU

*Home Monthly. Devoted to
Literature and Religion.*
Nashville, Tenn., July 1866-73?
LNHT, NcD, TxU

Ladies' Home Gazette, Atlanta, Ga.,
1866-Oct. 19, 1972? 1866-Apr.
20, 1867 as *Ladies' Gazette.*
NcD

*The Land We Love. A Monthly
Magazine*, Charlotte, N.C.,
1866-68. Merged with *New
Eclectic* in 1869, NN

Lutheran Visitor, Staunton, Va.,
1866-99? NcD, ViU

Miss Barber's Weekly, Newnan, Ga.,
1866?

Presbyterian Index, Mobile, Ala.,
1866-?

Protestant Missionary,
Jacksonville, Fla., 1866-69? IEG

*Richmond and Louisville Medical
Journal* -- See *Gaillard's
Southern Medicine*

Richmond Eclectic, Richmond, Va.; Baltimore, Md., 1866-75. Later as *Southern Magazine*. CtY, DLC, ICU, NcU, Vi, ViU

Richmond Medical Journal -- See *Gaillard's Southern Medicine*

Southern Magazine -- See *Richmond Eclectic*

Southern Medicine and Gaillard's Medical Journal -- See *Gaillard's Southern Medicine*

Southern Portfolio. Devoted to Polite Literature, Wit and Humor, Prose and Poetic Gems, Richmond, Va., May 12, 1866-?

Southern Ruralist, Tangipahoa, La., Jan. 3, 1866-Jan. 18, 1867? Suspended Feb. 28-Apr. 12 1866, MWA

Southwestern Christian Advocate, New Orleans, La., 1866-? DLC, NN

Southwestern Magazine, Devoted to Literature, Art, and the Prosperity of the Country. New Orleans, La., Oct.-Nov. 1866, LNHT, TxU, WHi

Texas Medical Journal -- See *Galveston Medical Journal*

Visitor, Selma, Ala., 1866-?

Western Presbyterian, Danville, Ky., 1866-69, DLC, ICU, PPPrHi

Alabama Pulpit, Selma, Ala., 1867-? Ala. Dept. of Archives and History

Burke's Weekly for Boys and Girls, Macon, Ga., July 6, 1867-Dec. 24, 1870. Superseded by *Burke's Magazine for Boys and Girls* GA, NcD, ViU

Christian Index, Jackson, Tenn., 1867-1937, NN, IEG, NcD, NjMD

Christian Observer, Catlettsburg, Louisville, Ky., 1867-1930, later as *Central Methodist*, NcD, NN, KyL

Farmer's Home Journal, Lexington, Louisville, Ky., 1867-1932, DA, DLC, ICJ, KyLF

Native Virginian, Orange, Va., Nov. 15, 1867-Dec. 17, 1869

New Orleans Advocate and Journal of Education, New Orleans, La., 1867-71, LNHT

Old Dominion. A Monthly Magazine of Literature, Science and Art, Richmond, Va., 1867-73? As *Seminary Magazine*, 1867-69, DLC, MiD-B, NcD, NcU, Vi, ViU, WHi

Our Monthly . . .A Monthly Magazine of Christian Thought and Work for the Lord, Clinton, S.C., 1867-? DLC, NN

Phillips' Southern Farmer, Memphis, Tenn., 1867-74? v.1-5 as *Southern Farmer*. DA, NcD, T, TU

School and Fireside, Louisville, Ky., 1867, MdBJ

Seminary Magazine -- See *Old Dominion. A Monthly Magazine of Literature, Science and Art*

Southern Boys' and Girls' Monthly, Richmond, Va., Jan. 1867-July 1868, LNHT, NcD, NcU, Vi, ViW

Southern Journal of Music, Louisville, Ky., Oct. 5, 1867-68? PPi

The Southern Opinion, Richmond, Va., 1867-69, NN, Vi

The Southern Review, Baltimore, Md.; Saint Louis, Mo., 1867-79, DLC, ICN, NN, ScU, Vi

Square and Compass, Raleigh, N.C., 1867-68

Twelve Times a Year, Louisville, Ky., 1867-71, DLC, OCl

Banner of the South and Planters' Journal, Augusta, Ga., 1868-Oct. 19, 1872, MWA, NcD, NjP

Boys' and Girls' Literary Journal, Montgomery, Ala., 1868-? Ala. Dept. of Archives and History

Christian Examiner, Richmond, Va., Jan. 1868-Dec. 1878, NcD

Church Register, Montgomery, Ala., 1868-?

Dixie Farmer, Knoxville, Nashville, Tenn.; Atlanta, Ga., 1868-82, MB, MWA

Farm and Family, Louisville, Ky., 1868-1918. Merged into *Inland Farmer*, DA, KyBgW, OO

Farm and Garden, Clinton, S.C., 1868, ScU

Insurance Times, New York, N.Y.; Richmond, Va., 1868-1937, DLC, NN

Literary Pastime, Richmond, Va., Aug. 8, 1868-?

Little Gleaner, Fredericksburg, Va., 1868-69? NcD

Masonic Record. A Monthly Magazine, Devoted to the Interests of the Fraternity and General Literature, Nashville, Tenn., 1868-Dec. 1870, NcD, T, TN

Missionary, Columbia, S.C., 1868, 1870, 1873-76, ScU

Missionary. An Illustrated Monthly Magazine, Nashville, Tenn., 1868-1911. United with *Home Mission Herald* to form *Missionary Survey*, CtY, DLC, ICU, NN, OO, TxU

Our Portfolio, New Orleans, La., 1868, LNHT

Rural Southerner, Atlanta, Ga., 1868-76? DA, DLC, NcU

Southern Banner, Augusta, Ga., 1868?

Southern Collegian, Lexington, Va., 1868-1918, DLC

Southern Journal of Education, Shelbyville, Ky., 1868

Southern Pulpit and Pew, Columbia, Tenn., Jan. 1868-?

Southern Son. A Literary, Agricultural and Temperance Monthly Magazine, Nashville, Tenn., 1868, NN

Southwestern Presbyterian, New Orleans, La., 1868-1908. United with other journals to form *Presbyterian of the South*, NN, NcD, TxU, VRT

Textile World, Atlanta, Ga., 1868-current

Academy Journal, Alexandria, Va., 1869-?

American Grocer, Jamaica, N.Y.; Bay Harbor Island, Fla., 1869-current

Apostolic Guide -- See *Christian Weekly*

Apostolic Times -- See *Christian Weekly*

Baptist Courier, Greenville, S.C., 1869 -? ScU, NN, NcD, KyLoS, OO, TxU

Catholic Advocate, Louisville, Ky.,
1869-70? DLC

Central Methodist -- See *Christian
Observer*

Christian Companion -- See
Christian Weekly

Christian Guide -- See *Christian
Weekly*

Christian Weekly, Lexington,
Louisville, Ky.; Cincinnati,
Ohio, 1869-1907. 1869-85 as
Apostolic Times, 1885-93 as
Apostolic Guide, 1894-1902 as
Christian Guide, 1903-05 as
Christian Companion. Merged
with *Christian Standard*?
KyLoS, KyLxCB, NN

East Tennessee Baptist, Knoxville,
Tenn., 1869-70? KyLoS

Educational Journal of Virginia,
Richmond, Va., 1869-91.
Superseded by *Virginia School
Journal*, CtY, DE, DLC, N, OO,
Vi

*Farmers' Gazette and Industrial
Index*, Richmond, Va., 1869-71?
DA, MB, NcD, NcU, Vi

Florida Dispatch, Jacksonville,
Fla., 1869-1910. 1869-89 as
Florida Dispatch, 1890-03 as
*Florida Dispatch, Farmer and
Fruit Grower*, 1894-1910 as
*Florida Farmer and Fruit
Grower*. Absorbed *Farmer's
Alliance* in 1889, DA, MB, OT,
DLC

*Florida Dispatch, Farmer and
Fruit Grower* -- See *Florida
Dispatch*

Florida Farmer and Fruit Grower
-- See *Florida Dispatch*

Methodist Advocate, Chattanooga,
Knoxville, Jackson, Tenn.,
1869-1931, NN, IEG, NcD, NjMD

Model Farmer -- See *Southern
Agriculturist*

Nineteenth Century, Charleston,
S.C., 1869-70, ScU, NN, CtY,
DLC, NcD, ViU

Reconstructed Farmer, Tarboro,
N.C., 1869-Oct. 1872? Nc, NcD,
NcRS, NcU

*Rural Carolinian, an Illustrated
Magazine of Agriculture,
Horticulture and the Arts.*
Charleston, S.C., 1869-76, CU,
DLC, NN, PPi, TxU, ScU

Rural Southland, New Orleans, La.,
1869-73. Consolidated in 1873
with *Our Home Journal*, also of
New Orleans, LNHT, DA

Southern Agriculturalist, Corinth,
Miss.; Nashville, Tenn., Apr. 1,
1869-Dec. 1949. Originally as
Model Farmer. Merged with
Farm and Ranch to form *Farm
and Ranch--Southern
Agriculturist*, DA, NN, TU, KyL,
ViU

Southern Farm and Home, Macon,
Ga.; Memphis, Tenn., 1869-73?
DA, LNHT, NcD, NcU, TxU, ViU

Southern Horticulturist, Canton,
Miss., 1869-70? Continued as
Swasey's Southern Gardener,
CU, DA, TxU, ViU

The Southern Monthly Magazine,
New Orleans, La., 1869? LNHT

Working Christian, Yorkville,
Charleston, Greenville, S.C.,
1869-77. Also as *Baptist
Courier*, NN, TxU, PCA

American Literary Realism,
Arlington, Tex., 1870-1910, 1967

American Practitioner, Louisville,
Ky., 1870-85. Continues *Western
Journal of Medicine*. United
with *Louisville Medical News* to
form *American Practitioner and
News*, 1886, CSt, Ct, DLC, DSG,
NN, NNN

Banner of the Church, Atlanta,
Ga.; Memphis, Tenn., 1870-71?
DLC, NBuG

Cosmopolitan Monthly, Atlanta, Ga.,
Jan. 1870. Supersedes *Scott's
Monthly Magazine*.

Gulf States, New Orleans, La.,
Jan.-Feb., 1870, LNHT, LU, NcD,
NjP

Insurance Advocate, Richmond, Va.,
Jan. 1870-July 1881. Merged
into *American Exchange and
Review*. NN, ViU, ViW

*L'Entr'Acte, journal des theatres,
litteraire et artistique*. New
Orleans, La., 1870? LNHT

The Heptasoph, New Orleans, La.,
1870? LNHT

Journal of Science, Louisville,
Ky., 1870, CtY, PPAN

One/Two, Nashville, Tenn., 1870-?

Plantation, Atlanta, Ga., 1870-73,
GU, NcD, TxU, ViU

The Present Age, New Orleans, La.,
1870-72? LNHT

Rutter's Political Quarterly,
Memphis, Tenn., 1870, DLC

Southern Druggist, Crystal
Springs, Miss., 1870

Sugar Bowl and Farm Journal, New
Iberia, New Orleans, La.,
1870-1910. Later as *Sugar
Planter*. Merged into *Modern
Sugar Planter*, DA, DLC, NN,
PPF

Sugar Planter -- See *Sugar Bowl
and Farm Journal*

Alabama Journal of Education,
Montgomery, Ala., 1871-?
Succeeded after a few months
by *Advance*, a political weekly,
DE, MH

Arkansas Journal of Education,
Little Rock, Ark., 1871-73.
Issued as a newspaper in 1870,
as a magazine 1871-73, DE, DLC,
OO, TxU

*Burke's Magazine for Boys and
Girls*, Macon, Ga., Jan.-Dec.
1871. Supersedes *Burke's
Weekly for Boys and Girls*, GA,
NcD, ViU

Clinical Record, Richmond, Va.,
1871?

*Earnest Worker in the Sabbath
School and the Family*,
Richmond, Va., 1871-? NNU

Georgia Medical Companion -- See
Southern Medical Record

Good Health and Mental Bliss, New
Orleans, La., 1871?-73? LNHT

Louisville School Messenger,
Louisville, Ky., 1871.
Superseded by *Home and School*,
DLC, MH

Masonic Jewel, Memphis, Tenn.,
1871-July 1878, DLC, NN, TMC

Masonic Monitor, Goldsboro, N.C.,
1871-72

Memphis Presbyterian, Memphis,
Tenn., 1871? KyLoS

*Mississippi Educational Journal.
Devoted to Popular Instruction
and Literature*. Jackson, Miss.,
Feb. 1871-Feb. 1872, DE, DLC,
MH, NSU

Monthly Record, Charleston, S.C.,
1871-80, ScU

Monthly Visitor, Norfolk, Va., 1871-72? KyLoS, GEU

New Monthly Magazine: a Literary Journal, Nashville, Tenn., 1871, CtY, ICN, NcD, NcU

Our Home Journal, New Orleans, La., 1871-75? DLC, IU, LN, LNHT, NjP, TxU

Rural Messenger, Petersburg, Va., 1871-82?

School Recorder, Russellville, Ark., 1871

Southern Medical Record, Atlanta, Ga., 1871-99. 1871-72 as *Georgia Medical Companion*. United with *Atlanta Medical and Surgical Journal* to form *Atlanta Journal-Record of Medicine*, DSG, CSt-Y, NNN, N

Southern Musical Journal. Monthly review of the news, literature and science of music. Savannah, Ga., 1871-82. Continued as *Southern Musical Journal and Educational Eclectic*, DLC, ICN, PP

Southern Rural Gentleman, Grenada, Miss., 1871-75?

Swasey's Southern Gardener, Tangipahoa, La., 1871. Continues *Southern Horticulturist*, DA

True Knight, Richmond, Va., 1871?

Virginia Clinical Record. A Monthly Journal of Medicine, Surgery, and the Collateral Sciences. Richmond, Va., 1871-74., CSt-L, NNN, DSG, ICN, NBM, ViU

Weekly Guide, Richmond, Va., 1871-?

Home and School. A Magazine of Popular Education, Literature and Sciences. Louisville, Ky., Jan. 1872-Oct. 1876. Superseded the *Louisville School Messenger*. Merged into *Educational Weekly* of Chicago, Jan. 1877, CtY, DE, DLC, KyU, MH

Masonic Tablet, Jackson, Miss., 1872-73

The Rising Generation, New Orleans, La., 1872, LNHT

Rural Sun. Devoted to the Family and Industrial Interests of the Country. Nashville, Tenn., Oct 3, 1872-Dec. 4, 1879, NcD, T, TN, ViU

Rural Alabamian, Mobile, Ala., 1872-73? DA, PPi, TxU

Southern Law Review, Nashville, Tenn.; Saint Louis, Mo., 1872-82. Merged into *American Law Review*, C, CU, InU, NN, TU, TxU

Southern Workman, Hampton, Va., 1872-? DLC, MH, NN, NIC

Texas Masonic Mirror, Houston, Tex., 1872-73

Alabama University Monthly, A Magazine Devoted to Education, Literature, Science and Art. Montgomery, Ala., Dec. 1873-June 1887? GEU, InU, NcD, Vi

Georgia Home Journal, _____, Ga., 1873?

Georgia Music Eclectic, Atlanta, Ga., 1873-74? NcD

Journal of Industry. Devoted to Agriculture, Horticulture, Immigration, Manufactures, Commerce, etc. Richmond, Va., Jan. 1873? Vi

Le Carillon, journal peu politique, encore moins litteraire, et pas de tout serieux. New Orleans, La., 1873, AU

Louisville, Ky., Public Library Paper, Louisville, Ky., May 17-Nov. 8, 1873

Moon's Bee World, Rome, Ga., 1873-77? DA, NIC-A, WU

Our Living and Our Dead. Newbern, Raleigh, N.C., July 2, 1873-March 1876, CtY, DLC, ICN, N, NN, NcU, TxU

Rural Southerner and Wilson's Herald of Health, Atlanta, Ga., 1873-74? May 1873-March 1974 as *Wilson's Herald of Health and Atlanta Business Review*, NNN, DSG, N, PPC

Southern Field and Factory, Jackson, Miss., 1873, DA, LNHT, NcD

Texas Farm and Home, Calvert, Tex., Nov. 1873-? DA, TxU

Wilson's Herald of Health and Atlanta Business Review -- See *Rural Southerner and Wilson's Herald of Health*

Alabama Baptist, Birmingham, Ala., 1874-? 1902-03 as *Southern and Alabama Baptist*, DLC, NN, KyLoS, NcD, TxU

American Medical Weekly, Louisville, Ky., 1874-83. v.6-13 as *American Medical Bi-Weekly*. Continued as *Gaillard's Medical Journal*, later *Gaillard's Southern Medicine*, CtY, DLC, DSG, ICJ, NN

American Sketch Book, LaCrosse, Wis.; Austin, Tex., 1874-82? DLC, MWA, N, TxU

Journal of Education, Selma, Ala., 1874

Louisiana State Agricultural and Mechanical College Journal, New Orleans, La., 1874? LNHT

Louisville Medical Reporter, Henderson, Ky., 1874, DSG, NNN, PPC

New Orleans Monthly Review, New Orleans, La., 1874-76? CtY, DLC, LN, LNHT, NN, NcD, NcU

North Carolina Journal of Education, Raleigh, N.C., 1874-75? NN, NcU, Nc, NcGW

Old Folks' Historical Record, Memphis, Tenn., 1874-75? DLC, PPHi, TxU

Pharmacal Gazette, Nashville, Tenn., 1874-75. Also as *Tennessee Pharmacal Gazette*, MBM, WU, CSt-L, PPC, T

Religious Messenger -- See *Texas Baptist*

Sacred Music, Irving, Tex.; Saint Paul, Minn., 1874-current

Southern Catholic, Memphis, Tenn., 1874-?

Southern Plantation, Montgomery, Ala., 1874-77? NcD

Tennessee Pharmacal Gazette -- See *Pharmacal Gazette*

Tennessee School Journal, Nashville, Tenn., 1874-75, DE, T

Texas Baptist, Paris, Dallas, Tex., 1874-July 8, 1886. v.1-2 as *Religious Messenger*, KyLoS

Texas Farmer and Orchardist, Palestine, Tex., 1874-80?

Tobacco Reporter, Raleigh, N.C., 1874-current

Virginia Medical Monthly,
Richmond, Va., 1874-current.
Apr. 1896-1918 as *Virginia
Medical Semi-Monthly*, CtY, DSG,
ICJ, N, NNN

Virginia Medical Semi-Monthly --
See *Virginia Medical Monthly*

American Baptist Flag -- See
Baptist Flag

American Spiritual Magazine -- See
The Spiritual Magazine

Arkansas Farmer, Little Rock,
Ark., 1875-95? DA, DLC

*Baptist Battle Flag and Church
Historian* -- See *Baptist Flag*

Baptist Flag, Saint Louis, Mo.;
Fulton, Ky., Jan. 1875?-Sept.
17, 1925, v.1-5, no.28 as *Baptist
Battle Flag and Church
Historian*. v.5, no.30-v.31,
no.14 as *American Baptist Flag*.
v.51, no.27-50 as *Diagram of
Truth and the American Baptist
Flag*, DLC, KyLoS, NN

*Diagram of Truth and the American
Baptist Flag* -- See *Baptist Flag*

Home and Farm, Louisville, Ky.,
1875-1918. Merged into *Inland
Farmer*, DA, DLC, OO, TxU, NN,
NcD, KyU

Kentucky Church Chronicle,
Louisville, Ky., 1875-89, DLC,
NNG

Kentucky Livestock Record -- See
Thoroughbred Record

Live Stock Record -- See
Thoroughbred Record

Louisiana Law Journal, New
Orleans, La., 1875-76, NNB, LNHT

North Alabama Farm and Home,
Florence, Ala., 1875?

The Spiritual Magazine, Memphis,
Tenn., Jan. 1875-Dec. 1877.
1876-77 as *American Spiritual
Magazine*, DLC, PU, TMC, ViU

*Sunny South, Devoted to
Literature, Romance, Fact and
Fiction*. Atlanta, Ga.,
1875-1903. Became a weekly
edition of the *Atlanta
Constitution* in 1903, was
discontinued 4 years later, DLC,
GA

Thoroughbred Record, Lexington,
Ky., 1875-current. 1875-85 as
Kentucky Live Stock Record.
1886-95 as *Live Stock Record*,
CSt, DA, DLC, IU

Weekly Budget, New Orleans, La.,
1875-76? LNHT, ICU

Associate Reformed Presbyterian,
Due West, S.C., 1876-1971, DLC,
NN, NcD, NcMHi, VRT

Carolina Teacher, Columbia, S.C.,
1876-77, ScU, DE

*Les Comptes-Rendus de L'Athenee
Louisianais*, New Orleans, La.,
1876-? LNHT

*Eclectic Teacher and Kentucky
School Journal* -- See *Eclectic
Teacher and Southwestern
Journal of Education*

*Eclectic Teacher and Southwestern
Journal of Education*, Carlisle,
Ky., 1876-83, v.1-7 as *Eclectic
Teacher and Kentucky School
Journal*, DE, N, MH, TxU

Holland's Magazine -- See
*Holland's, The Magazine of the
South*

*Holland's, The Magazine of the
South*, Dallas, Tex., 1876-19?
Also as *Holland's Magazine*,
DLC, KyU, NN, ScU, TxH, TxU

Louisville Medical News, Louisville, Ky., Jan. 1, 1876-Dec. 26, 1885. United with *American Practitioner* to form *American Practitioner and News*, later *American Practitioner*, CtY, DSG, KyU, NNN, ViU

Masonic Journal, Louisville, Ky., 1876-?

North Carolina Farmer, Raleigh, N.C., 1876-93. Later *Southern Farmer*, NcU, NcD

The North Carolina Mason, Raleigh, N.C., 1876-current

Southern Farmer -- See *North Carolina Farmer*

Southern Historical Monthly, Raleigh, N.C., 1876-77? NcU, PP, PPHi

Southern Historical Society. Richmond, Va., 1876-1959? APS

Star of Zion, Charlotte, N.C., 1876-current, DLC, NN

Arkansas Law Journal, Fort Smith, Ark., 1877, NNB, NBM

Baptist Banner, Cumming, Ga., 1877? KyLoS

Baptist Record, Clinton, Jackson, Miss., 1877-? v.1 as *Mississippi Baptist Record*, 1879-1905 as *Baptist*, KyLoS, NN, TxU

Farmer and Mechanic. A Southern Family Newspaper for Town and Country, Devoted to the Welfare of Carolina, Dixie, and the American Confederacy. Raleigh, N.C., 1877-1908. Merged into *State Chronicle*, NcU, NbU

Farmer's Magazine and Kentucky Live-Stock Monthly, Louisville, Ky., 1877-82? ICU, KyLF, OO

Horseman and Fair World; Devoted to the Trotting and Racing Horse, Indianapolis, Ind.; Lexington, Ky., 1877-current. As *Western Sportsman and Live Stock News*, 1877-Oct. 1891, as *Western Horseman*, 1891-June 1920, DA, DLC, IU, KyU, PP

Legal Reporter, Nashville, Tenn., 1877-79. v.1-2 as *Tennessee Legal Reporter*. Merged into *Southern Law Journal*, CtY-L, DLC, NcD-L, T, TU

Mississippi Baptist Record -- See *Baptist Record*

South Atlantic. A monthly magazine of literature, science, and art, Wilmington, N.C., 1877-82? DLC, MB, MH, NcU

Southern Farmers' Monthly, Savannah, Ga., 1877-82. Merged into *Southern Cultivator*, DA

Tennessee Legal Reporter -- See *Legal Reporter*

Texas Law Journal, Tyler, Tex., 1877-82, MH-L, N, NIC, NNB, TxU

Tobacco News and Prices Current, Louisville, Ky., Nov. 3, 1877-Jan. 24, 1880? DLC, MH-BA

Virginia Law Journal, Richmond, Va., 1877-93, C, Ct, DLC, ICU, M, N

Western Horseman -- See *Horseman and Fair World*

Western Sportsman and Live Stock News -- See *Horseman and Fair World*

Annals of the Army of Tennessee and Early Western History, Nashville, Tenn., Apr.-Dec. 1878, CtY, DLC, NN, NcU, T, TN, TU, TxU

Arkansas Medical Record, Little
Rock, Ark., 1878, CSt-L, DSG,
MBM, MiU, NNN

Baptist Informer, Raleigh, N.C.,
1878-current

Gulf Citizen, Mobile, Ala.,
June-Oct. 1878, LNHT, NjP, NjR,
RPB

Memphis Law Journal, Memphis,
Tenn., 1878-79, NIC, NNB, MH-L,
N, TMC, TxU, WaU

New Medicines, Atlanta, Ga.,
Apr.-Aug. 1878, DSG, NNN, PPC

*The New Orleans Quarterly
Review,* New Orleans, La., 1878,
DLC, CtY, IU, LN, NjP

North Carolina Medical Journal,
Charlotte, N.C., 1878-1908., DSG,
ICJ, MBM, NNN, NcU

Our Home, Louisville, Ky., 1878-79

Richmond Standard, Richmond, Va.,
1878-82, DLC, MiU, WHi

Southern Clinic, Richmond, Va.,
1878-1919? CSt-L, CtY, DSG, N,
NNN

Southern Law Journal, Tuscaloosa,
Ala.; Nashville, Tenn., 1878-81,
Ia, MH-L, NIC, NNB

Strong Words, New Orleans, La.,
1878, LNHT

*Tusculum Record. Education,
Industry, Church and State.*
Tusculum, Tenn., May 2,
1878-Apr. 28, 1881? DLC

Warrington's Musical Review, New
Orleans, La., 1878?-84? LNHT

Age, Louisville, Ky., 1879, DLC,
ICU, MB

Alabama Historical Reporter,
Tuscaloosa, Ala., 1879-85, CU,
DLC, MH, WHi

Church Messenger, Charlotte, N.C.,
1879-85? NNG, NcD, NcU

*Dental Luminary. A Quarterly
Journal Devoted to the Interests
of the Dental Profession,* Macon,
Ga., 1879-93, DSG, IEN-D, MBM,
NNN

Eclectic Medical Journal -- See
Georgia Eclectic Medical Journal

Every Saturday Journal, Richmond,
Va., 1879-1905.

*Florida Agriculturist. A Journal
Devoted to State Interests.*
Deland, Fla., 1879-1911, DA, NN,
FDS, FPY, FU, MWA, NcRS

Georgia Eclectic Medical Journal,
Atlanta, Ga., 1879-1904. 1879-80
as *Eclectic Medical Journal.*
1881-82 as *Georgia and
Tennessee Eclectic Medical
Journal,* CSt-L, DSG, MBM, MiU,
NNN

*Georgia and Tennessee Eclectic
Medical Journal* -- See *Georgia
Eclectic Medical Journal*

Iron Tradesman -- See *Hardware
and Implement Journal*

*Journal of Education for Home and
School,* New Orleans, La.,
1879-88. 1879-83 as *Louisiana
Journal of Education,* DE, LNHT,
NN

Louisiana Journal of Education,
New Orleans, La., 1879-88, LNHT,
LNTC

Louisville Monthly Magazine,
Louisville, Ky., 1879-80, MB, NN,
TxU, DLC, ICU, KyL, KyLF,
LNHT, MWA, V

New Southern Poultry Journal,
Louisville, Ky., 1879-? NIC

Opera Glass, Galveston, Tex.,
1879-1916

Parents' and Teachers' Monthly,
Lexington, Ky., 1879, OkEP

Presbyterian Survey, Atlanta, Ga.,
1879-current

The Phi Gamma Delta, Lexington,
Ky., 1879-current

*Southern Hardware and Implement
Journal*, Atlanta, Ga., 1879.
1879-1915 as *Tradesman*.
1915-1918 as *Iron Tradesman*,
DLC, ICJ, NN

Southern Practitioner, Nashville,
Tenn., 1879-1918. Merged into
Medical Review of Reviews, CtY,
DSG, ICJ, MBM, NN, NNN

Southern Quarterly Review,
Louisville, Ky.; New Orleans,
La., 1879-80? DLC, TxU, WHi

Spectrum, Columbia, S.C., 1879, ScU

Tradesman -- See *Southern
Hardware and Implement Journal*

*Virginia State Agricultural Society
Journal of Agriculture*, ___,
Va., 1879? DA, CSmH, NcD, ViU

Arkansas Medical Monthly, Little
Rock, Ark., 1880. Continued as
*Mississippi Valley Medical
Monthly*, later *Memphis Medical
Monthly*, CSt-L, DSG, MBM, MiU,
NNN

Arkansas School Journal, Little
Rock, Ark., 1880-83. 1882 as
Kellogg's Eclectic Monthly, TxU,
ArU, DE, MWA, N, NNC-T

Atlantic Missionary, Gordonsville,
Va., 1880?-86? DLC, NcD

*Cumberland Presbyterian
Quarterly Review*, Lebanon,
Tenn., 1880-84? KyLoS

Dental Headlight, Nashville, Tenn.,
1880-1910. Continued as *Oral
Hygiene*, DSG, NNN

Gavel, Danville, Ky., 1880?

Georgia Baptist, Augusta, Macon,
Ga., 1880-? PCA

Kellogg's Eclectic Monthly -- See
Arkansas School Journal

Kentucky Law Reporter, Frankfort,
Ky., 1880-1908, CtY, DLC, IU,
M, N

Masonic Age, Louisville, Ky.,
1880-81

*National Cooperator and Farm
Journal* -- See *Texas Farm
Cooperator*

Our Country and Village Schools,
Decatur, Ga., 1880-87, IU, N

Texas Farm Co-operator, San
Antonio, Tex., 1880-1913, v.1-21
as *Texas Stock and Farm
Journal*. Also as *Texas Farm
Journal* and as *National
Cooperator and Farm Journal*.
Merged into *National Field*, DA,
NN, TxU

Texas Farm Journal -- See *Texas
Farm Cooperator*

Texas Farmer, Belton, Tex.,
1880-91. Became the Texas
edition of *Progressive Farmer
and Farm Woman* in 1913.

Texas Journal of Education,
Austin, Tex., 1880-82.
Continued as *Texas School
Journal*, DE, TxU, N

Texas Stock and Farm, Fort Worth,
Tex., 1880-1911, v.1-29 as *Texas
Stockman-Journal*. Merged into
Texas Farm Cooperator, DA

Texas Stock and Farm Journal --
See *Texas Farm Co-Operator*

Texas Stockman-Journal -- See
Texas Stock and Farm

Thornwell Orphanage Messenger,
Clinton, S.C., 1880-89, 1890-93,
1895-1903, 1906-16, 1918,
1927-30, 1932-34, 1936-38,
1940-42, ScU, CtHC, DLC, LNHT,
NN, NcMHi, PPPrHi, ScClP, VRT

*Virginias, a Mining, Industrial
and Scientific Journal, Devoted
to the Development of Virginia
and West Virginia,* Staunton,
Va., 1880-85. Merged into
Industrial South, CtY, DGS,
DLC, ICJ, NN, NNE

Alabama Christian Advocate -- See
Methodist Christian Advocate

Alumni Journal, Hampton, Va.,
1881-94, 1904-?

Arkansas Baptist, Little Rock,
Ark., 1881-1905. Was *Arkansas
Evangel* 1881-86, *Arkansas
Baptist* 1887-1903, *Landmark
Baptist* 1904-05, DLC, NN, PCA

Arkansas Doctor, Harrisburg, Ark.,
June-Sept. 1881? MBM

Arkansas Evangel -- See *Arkansas
Baptist*

Arkansas Methodist, Little Rock,
Ark., 1881-? Also as *Western
Christian Advocate* and as
Western Methodist, DLC, NNUT,
OO, NN, NcD, TxU

Collector's Home Companion -- See
Naturalist's Companion

College Mirror, Greenville, S.C.,
1881-82, ScU

*Country Visitor's Summer
Magazine,* New Orleans, La.,
1881-83? LNHT

Educational Record, Nashville,
Tusculum, Tenn., 1881-83

Industrial South, Richmond, Va.,
1881-86, DLC, NNE, PPAP, MB,
MH, NN, Vi, VLxW

Intermediate Quarterly, Nashville,
Tenn., 1881-1912, GEU

Kentucky Law Journal, Louisville,
Ky., 1881-82? MH-L, NIC, NNB

Landmark Baptist -- See *Arkansas
Baptist*

Memphis Medical Monthly, Memphis,
Tenn., 1881-1922. Continues
Arkansas Medical Monthly, v.1-8
as *Mississippi Valley Medical
Monthly,* CtY-M, DSG, ICJ, N,
NNN, PPC

Methodist Christian Advocate,
Birmingham, Ala., May 25, 1881-?
v.1-75 as *Alabama Christian
Advocate,* ABS, NN, NcD

Mississippi Valley Medical Monthly
-- See *Memphis Medical Monthly*

Naturalist's Companion, Wytheville,
Va., 1881-82. Also as
Collector's Home Companion, DLC

*North Carolina Educational
Journal,* Chapel Hill, N.C.,
1881-85, N, NcU

L'Opera et ses Hotes, New Orleans,
La., 1881, LNHT

Quarterly Review, Galveston, Tex.,
Jan. 28-Aug. 28, 1881. MWA

Reformer, Atlanta, Ga., Sept.-Nov.
1881. Supersedes *Southern
Medical Reformer.* Superseded
by *Journal of American Medicine
and Surgery,* DSG

Southern Lumberman, Nashville,
Tenn., 1881-current, DLC, NN,
TU

Southern Medical Reformer,
Atlanta, Ga., Jan.-Aug. 1881.
Superseded by *Reformer,* DSG,
MBM, NNN

*Texas Medical and Surgical
Record*, Galveston, Tex.,
1881-83. Continued as *Texas
Courier-Record of Medicine*,
CSt-L, DSG, ICJ, MBM, NN, TxU

Texas Planter and Farmer, Dallas,
Tex., 1881-85?

*United Methodist Christian
Advocate*, Birmingham, Ala.,
1881-current

Western Christian Advocate -- See
Arkansas Methodist

Western Methodist -- See *Arkansas
Methodist*

Alabama Law Journal, Montgomery,
Ala., 1882-85, M, MH-L, NNB

Arkansaw Traveler, Little Rock,
Ark.; Chicago, Ill., 1882-1916?
DLC, IU, MWA

Blue Ridge Baptist, Hendersonville,
N.C., 1882-86? KyLoS

The Colored American Journal,
Palestine, Tex., 1882-?

*Cotton Plant. Devoted to the
Development of the Agricultural
Resources of the South.*
Columbia, S.C., 1882-1904.
United with *Progressive Farmer*
to form *Progressive Farmer and
Cotton Plant*, later *Progressive
Farmer and Farm Woman*, DA,
NcD

*Cotton Review. A Monthly Journal
Devoted to the Cotton Trade and
the Collection of Cotton
Statistics.* New Orleans, La.,
Oct. 1882, LNHT

Educational Journal, Jackson,
Miss., 1882

*Industrial Development and
Manufacturers Record*, Atlanta,
Ga., 1882-?

The Mascot, New Orleans, La.,
1882-95? LNHT, NN, NcD

Olivette, New Orleans, La., 1882,
LNHT

Prairie Flower -- See *Texas
Prairie Flower*

*Rural Record. A Journal for the
Farm, Plantation and Fireside*,
Chattanooga, Tenn., 1882-?
DLC, NcD

*Southern Bivouac: A Monthly
Literary and Historical
Magazine*, Louisville, Ky.,
1882-87. Merged into *Century*,
DLC, ICN, ICU, Ia, NN, NcU, TxU

Southern Dental Journal -- See
*Southern Dental Journal and
Luminary*

*Southern Dental Journal and
Luminary*, Atlanta, Ga.,
1882-1900. 1882-93 as *Southern
Dental Journal*, CU-M, DSG, MBM,
NNN, PPC

Southern Mercury, Dallas, Tex.,
1882-1901? DLC, WHi, KHi

*Southern World. A Journal of
Industry for the Farm, Home,
and Workshop.* Atlanta, Ga.,
1882-84? GA, GMM, MH

Southwestern Poultry Journal,
Galveston, Tex., 1882-?

Southern Pulpit, Richmond, Va.,
1882-84. Merged into
Treasury, ICU, NNG, NNU

Texas Law Reporter, Austin, Tex.,
1882-85, MH-L, NNB, TxU, WaU,
NIC

*Texas Prairie Flower. A Literary
Monthly Devoted to the Pure, the
True, the Beautiful.* Corsicana,
Tex., 1882-85? v.1-2 as *Prairie
Flower*, TxH, TxU, CSmH, NcD

Texas Siftings, Austin, Tex.; New
York, N.Y.; London, England,
1882-97, DLC, MiU, NN, TxU,
MWA, N, OCHP, TxDN

Texas Wool Grower, Fort Worth,
Tex., 1882-84. Merged into
Texas Live Stock Journal, KHi

Alabama School Journal,
Birmingham, Ala., 1883, NNC-T,
OO

American Medical Monthly, Austin,
Tex.; New Orleans, La.;
Baltimore, Md., 1883-1904.
1883-84 as *Texas Homoeopathic
Pellet*. 1885-97 as *Southern
Journal of Homoepathy*, DSG,
ICJ, MBM, NNN

Atlantic Journal of Medicine,
Richmond, Va., Aug. 1883-Feb.
1885, v.1, no.1 as *Atlantic
Journal of Medicine and
Surgery*, DSG, N

*Atlantic Journal of Medicine and
Surgery* -- See *Atlantic Journal
of Medicine*

Carolinian, Columbia, S.C.,
1883-1940, ScU

The Delta, Lexington, Va.,
1883-current

Eclectic Star, Atlanta, Ga.,
1883-86, DSG, AU

Electrical Age, New York, N.Y.;
Atlanta, Ga., 1883-1910. 1883-99
as *Electric Age*. United with
Southern Electrician to form
Electrical Engineering, DLC, NN

Electrical Engineering -- See
Electrical Age

*Elisha Mitchell Scientific Society
Journal*, Chapel Hill, N.C.,
1883/84-? CtY, DLC, NN, NcD,
NcU

Farm and Ranch, Dallas, Tex.,
1883-? 1883-89 as *Texas Farm
and Ranch*, DLC, WHi, TxU, NN

Figaro, New Orleans, La., 1883?-84?
LNHT

Florida Baptist Witness,
Jacksonville, Fla., 1883-current.
1904-05 as *Southern Baptist
Witness*. 1905-08 as *Southern
Witness*, NN, PCA, FU, NHC,
KyLoS, FDS

Home, Farm and Factory, Atlanta,
Ga., 1883-95?

Kentucky Stock Farm, Lexington,
Ky., 1883-1907. 1908-12 as *Stock
Farm. Pub. in the Blue Grass,
the National Trotting Horse
Journal*. Superseded by
Kentucky Trotting Record, DA,
DLC, ICU, CSt, KMK, KyU, MWA,
ViU

*La Revista Mercantil de Neuva
Orleans*, New Orleans, La., 1883?
LNHT

Masonic Home Journal, Louisville,
Ky., 1883-current

North Carolina Teacher, Raleigh,
N.C., 1883-95, DE, N, NcU, TxU

Rural and Workman -- See *Rural
Workman*

Rural Workman, Little Rock, Ark.,
1883-91, v.15 as *Rural and
Workman*, DA, DLC, TxU, PPHi

Southern Baptist Witness -- See
Florida Baptist Witness

Southern Journal of Education,
Nashville, Tenn., 1883-95.
1883-84 as *Tennessee Journal of
Education*. Merged into
Progressive Teacher, DE, DLC,
MH, N, OU, NcD

Southern Journal of Homoepathy
-- See *American Medical Monthly*

Southern Miller, Nashville, Tenn.,
1883-?

*Southern Musical Journal and
Educational Eclectic*, Macon, Ga.,
1883, DLC

*Stock Farm. Pub. in the Blue
Grass, the National Trotting
Horse Journal* -- See *Kentucky
Stock Farm*

Tennessee Journal of Education --
See *Southern Journal of
Education*

Texas Courier-Record of Medicine,
Fort Worth, Tex., 1883-1917?
Continues *Texas Medical and
Surgical Record*, DSG, MBM, N,
NN, NNN, TxU

Texas Dental Journal, Dallas,
Austin, Tex., 1883-current,
DSG, ICJ, MBM, NN, NNN, TxU

Texas Farm and Ranch -- See *Farm
and Ranch*

Texas Homoeopathic Pellet -- See
American Medical Monthly

Texas Law Review, Austin, Tex.,
1883-86, CU, DLC, MH-L, N, TxU

Texas School Journal, Dallas, Tex.,
1883-? Continues *Texas Journal
of Education*, DE, N, NN, OO,
TxH, TxU

A.M.E. Church Review,
Philadelphia, Pa.; Nashville,
Tenn.; Atlanta, Ga.,
1884-current. Philadelphia,
1884-1908; Nashville, 1908-09;
Atlanta, ?-current, DLC, NN, OO

*Agricultural and Commercial
Review. Devoted to Southern
agricultural, manufacturing
and commercial interests.* New
Orleans, La., 1884-85? LNHT

Arkansas Teacher, Little Rock,
Ark., 1884-86? DE, MH

Educational Courant, Louisville,
Ky., 1884-94. Merged into
Southern School, DE, DLC, N

Educational Herald, Louisville,
Ky., 1884?

Georgia Law Journal, Atlanta, Ga.,
1884, NNB

The Laborer, New Orleans, La.,
1884, LNHT

Lutheran Home, Salem, Va.,
1884-Jan. 1890? NcD

Medical Progress, Louisville, Ky.,
1884-? v.1-3 as *Progress.* CtY,
DSG, ICJ, NN, NNN, OO, PPC, TxU

Naturalist in Florida, Saint
Augustine, Fla., Sept. 1884-May
1885, NNM, PPAN

School Messenger, Ada, La.,
1884-88, TxU, MH, MWA, ViU

*Southern Letter. Devoted to the
education of the hand, head,
and heart*, Tuskegee, Ala.,
1884-? DLC, IEG, NN, CtY, NIC

Southern Naturalist, Nashville,
Tenn., 1884, T

Southern Pharmacist, New Orleans,
La., 1884-85? NNN, WU, DSG

Stylus, Newberry, S.C., 1884,
1898-1910, 1913, 1915, 1921, 1923,
1925-29, ScU

Werlein's Musical Journal, New
Orleans, La., 1884? LNHT

Alabama Teachers' Journal,
Huntsville, Ala., 1885-90? DE,
N, MH, NcD

American School, Henderson, Ky.,
1885

The Cadduceus, Charlottesville,
Va., 1885-current

Carolina Teacher, Columbia, S.C.,
1885-86, 1888, ScU, DE, MH

*Dixie. A Monthly Journal Devoted
to Southern Industrial
Interests*, Atlanta, Ga.,
1885-1908. Later *Dixie
Wood-Worker. Devoted to the
Technical Features of
Sawmilling and Woodworking*,
DLC, NN, NcD, OO, TxU

Dixie Wood-Worker -- See *Dixie.
A Monthly Devoted to Southern
Industrial Interests*

*Florida Medical and Surgical
Journal*, Jacksonville, Fla.,
1885-86, CSt-L, DSG, NNN

Georgia Farmer, Barnesville, Ga.,
1885-95?

Georgia Law Reporter, Atlanta,
Ga., 1885-86, C, M, NNB, AZ,
MH-L, N

The Holy Family, New Orleans, La.,
1885?-99, LNHT

Jewish Spectator, New Orleans, La.;
Memphis, Tenn., 1885-? NN,
NNJ, OCH, MB

Primitive Baptist, Fordyce, Ark.,
1885, PCA

Southern Geologist, Nashville,
Tenn., 1885-86? DLC, KHi, NIC

Southern Journal of Health,
Asheville, N.C., 1885, DSG, MBM,
NNN, NcD, PPC

Southern Law Times, Chattanooga,
Tenn., 1885-86, DLC, N, NIC, NNB

Spelman Messenger, Atlanta, Ga.,
1885-current, CSt, CtY, DE, DLC,
GU, KHi

Texas Court Reporter, Austin,
Tex., 1885-86, MH-L, NNB, TxU

*Afro-American Churchman. A
Monthly Magazine Devoted to the
Work of the Church Among
Afro-American People.* Norfolk,
Va., 1886-90, NPV

*Alabama Medical and Surgical
Journal*, Birmingham, Ala.,
1886-87, CSt-L, DSG, ICJ, NNN

American Economic Review,
Nashville, Tenn., 1886-current

Berea Reporter, Berea, Ky.,
1886-June 12, 1899, KyBB

Cumberland Collector, Nashville,
Tenn., 1886-87, DGS, NNC, PPi

Florida Christian Advocate,
Leesburg, Fla., 1886-? NN

Free-Will Baptist, Ayden, N.C.,
1886-? KyLoS, NcU

Georgia Cracker, Athens, Atlanta,
Ga., 1886?-88? NN, CtY

Georgia Teacher, Atlanta, Ga.,
1886-95, DE, GEU, GU, NcD

Gulf Messenger, San Antonio, Tex.,
1886-March 1898. Merged into
Texas Magazine, LNHT, TxH, TxU

The Lantern, New Orleans, La.,
1886-89? LNHT

*The Musical Messenger. Devoted
to Music, Literature, and Art*,
Montgomery, Ala., 1886-?;
Washington, D.C., 1888-89, DLC

The Nautilus, Melbourne, Fla.,
1886-current

Our Schools, Mayfield, Ky., 1886?

People's Educational Quarterly,
Dayton, Va., 1886-87? ICN

Practice -- See *Richmond Journal
of Practice*

Progressive Farmer, Raleigh, N.C.;
Birmingham, Ala., 1886-present,
DLC, Nc, ViU

Progressive Teacher, New Orleans,
La., 1886-89, DE

Protestant Episcopal Review,
Theological Seminary, Va.,
1886-1900? v.1-5 as *Virginia
Seminary Magazine*, DLC, NNG,
NcD, OO, Vi, ViU

Richmond Journal of Practice,
Richmond, Va., 1886-1911.
1886-94 as *Practice*. DSG, MBM,
NNN

Southern Farmer, Athens, Ga.,
1886-1907., DA, NN, ViU

*Southern Progress. A Monthly
Magazine Devoted to Health,
Happiness and the Advancement
of Florida.* Leesburg, Fla.,
1886, DSG, MWA

The South Illustrated, New Orleans,
La., 1886-89? LNHT

Sunny South Oologist, Gainesville,
Tex., 1886, ICJ, MH-Z, NNM

Texas and Southwestern Druggist,
Waco, Tex., 1886-88? v.1-2 as
Texas Druggist, DLC, DSG, NBM,
NNN, OCL, PPC, TxU, WU, MdU

Texas Druggist -- See *Texas and
Southwestern Druggist*

Texas Pharmacy, Austin, Tex.,
1886-current

Texas Public Schools, Fort Worth,
Tex., 1886

Virginia Seminary Magazine -- See
Protestant Episcopal Review

American Journal of Psychology,
Ithaca, N.Y.; Austin, Tex.,
1887-? CLU, DLC, NN, TxU

America's Textiles, Greenville,
S.C., 1887-current

Art and Letters, New Orleans, La.,
1887, CSt, DLC, LU, MWA, TxU,
AU

Charity and Children, Thomasville,
N.C., 1887-current

Charleston Philatelist, Charleston,
S.C., 1887-89, NNCo, MWA

Chautauguan, Bennettsville, S.C.,
1887-88, ScU

Le Diamant, New Orleans, La., 1887?
LNHT

Educational Advocate, Collinsville,
Ala., 1887, MH, N

Educational Advocate, Dublin, Ga.,
1887-91

Farmers' Alliance, Jacksonville,
Fla., 1887?-91? Merged into
*Florida Dispatch Farmer and
Fruit Grower* in 1889, later
*Florida Farmer and Fruit
Grower*, OT

Fisk Herald, Nashville, Tenn.,
1887-?

Florida School Journal, Lake City,
Fla., 1887-95, DE, FU

Fort Worth Drug Reporter, Fort
Worth, Tex., 1887-89? DSG

Gospel Expositor, Elberton, Ga.,
1887/88-88/89? United with
Gospel Standard to form
Standard Expositor, later
Review and Expositor, KyLoS

The Miscellany, New Orleans, La.,
1887-89? LNHT

Mississippi Teacher, Oxford, Miss.,
1887-90, DE

Nashville Medical News, Nashville,
Tenn., 1887, DSG, ICJ, MBM, NNN

School Teacher, Winston, Durham,
N.C., 1887-93. Became *Southern
Educator*, Durham, N.C. in 1890.,
DE, MH, NNC-T, Nc, NcD, RPB

Southern Educator -- See *School
Teacher*

Southern School Journal, Walnut
Grove, Miss., 1887-94

Southern Teacher, Chattanooga,
Tenn., 1887-94. Merged into
Southern School Journal, DE

Southern Tobacco Journal,
Winston-Salem, Greensboro, N.C.,
1887-current, NcU, KyU, DA, NN,
NcD

Southwestern Medical Gazette,
Nashville, Tenn., 1887-88, DSG,
ICJ, MBM, CSt-L, KyLF, KyLoU,
NBM, NNN, PPC

*Western North Carolina Journal of
Education*, Glenwood, N.C.,
1887-90

Alabama Medical and Surgical Age
-- See *Alabama Medical Journal*

Alabama Medical Journal, Anniston,
Birmingham, Ala., 1888-1911.
v.1-12 as *Alabama Medical and
Surgical Age*, CSt-L, DSG, MsSM,
NN

Alabama Philatelist, Mobile, Ala.,
Nov. 1888-Oct. 1889? MWA

Armor, Fort Leavenworth, Kan.;
Washington, D.C.; Richmond, Va.;
Fort Knox, Ky., 1888-current.
1888-1918 as *Journal of the U.S.
Cavalry Association*. 1920-46
as *Cavalry Journal*. 1946-50
as *Armored Cavalry Journal*.
CSt, CtY, DLC, NN

Armored Cavalry Journal -- See
Armor

Baptist News -- See *Baptist
Standard*

Baptist Standard, Dallas, Tex.,
Dec. 1888-? Also as *Baptist
News*, as *Western Baptist*, and
as *Texas Baptist Standard*.
DLC, NN, NcD, Tx, TxU

Georgia Educational Journal,
Atlanta, Ga., 1888-91.
Consolidated with *Piedmont
Educator* to form *Educational
Monthly*, DE

Home Field, Atlanta, Ga., 1888-1916.
1888-1909 as *Our Home Field*.
Also as *Mission Journal of the
Southern Baptist Convention*.
United with *Foreign Mission
Journal* to form *Home and
Foreign Fields*. PCA, CtY-D,
NN, NcD, KyLoS, TxU

Insurance Herald -- See *Southern
Underwriter*

*Journal of American Folklore
Quarterly*, Boston, Mass.; New
York, N.Y.; Lancaster, Pa.;
Austin, Tex., 1888-? CLU, DLC,
KyU, NN, NcD, NcU, TxU

*Journal of the U.S. Cavalry
Association*-- See *Armor*

Louisiana Educator, Baton Rouge,
La., 1888-92, LU, N

*Louisiana Planter and Sugar
Manufacturer* -- See *Planter
and Sugar Manufacturer*

Louisiana Review, New Orleans, La.,
Nov. 28, 1888-94? 1888-Oct. 1890
as *Weekly Louisiana Review*.
LU

*Mission Journal of the Southern
Baptist Convention* -- See *Home
Field*

Modern Farming, Richmond, Va.,
1888-May 1909. v.1-16, no.30 as
*Southern Tobacconist and
Manufacturers Record*. v.16,
no.31-v.20, no.9 as *Southern
Tobacconist and Modern Farmer*.
DA, DLC, NN, Vi, ViU

National Pilot, Petersburg, Va., 1888-1900

New Education, Daleville, Miss., 1888-89

Our Home Field -- See *Home Field*

Our Women and Children, Louisville, Ky., 1888-?

Piedmont Educator, Atlanta, Ga., 1888. United with *Georgia Educational Journal* to form *Educational Monthly*. DE

Planter and Sugar Manufacturer, New Orleans, La., July 1888-Nov. 9, 1929. v.1-73 as *Louisiana Planter and Sugar Manufacturer*. Merged into *Sugar*. CtY, DLC, NN, LNHT, LU

Progressive Educator, Raleigh, N.C., 1888?-?

Southern Insurance, New Orleans, La., 1888-current

Southern Tobacconist and Manufacturers Record -- See *Modern Farming*

Southern Tobacconist and Modern Farmer -- See *Modern Farming*

Southern Underwriter, Louisville, Ky.; Atlanta, Ga., 1888-1913. Also as *Insurance Herald*. NN, MH-BA, N

Tennessee Agricultural Experiment Station Bulletin, Knoxville, Tenn., 1888-current

Texas Baptist Standard -- See *Baptist Standard*

Texas Health Journal -- See *Texas Medical Practitioner*

Texas Medical Practitioner. A Monthly Magazine for the General Practitioner, Dallas, Tex., 1888-98. v.1-9 as *Texas Health Journal*, CSt-L, DSG, ICJ, MBM, NNN, TxU

Upholstering Today, High Point, N.C., 1888-current

Weekly Louisiana Review -- See *Louisiana Review*

Western Baptist -- See *Baptist Standard*

Advance, New Orleans, La., 1889-1903

Arkansas Educational Journal, Searcy, Ark., 1889-90. United with *Popular Educator* to form *Southern School Journal*

Associate Messenger, Columbia, S.C., 1889-90, ScU

Carolina School Journal, Orangeburg, S.C., 1889, ScU

Cotton Gin and Oil Mill Press; the Magazine of The Cotton Ginning and Oilseed Processing Industries, Dallas, Tex., 1889-?

Cumberland Presbyterian Quarterly, Nashville, Tenn., 1889-92. Also as *Cumberland Presbyterian Review*. Suspended 1893-1901., NcMHi, OWC, NjPT, TC

Cumberland Presbyterian Review -- See *Cumberland Presbyterian Quarterly*

Educational Exchange, Birmingham, Ala., 1889-? DE, N, NN, OO

Home and School, Louisville, Ky., 1889-93. Supersedes *Louisville School Messenger*. Merged into *Southern School*, DE

Jewish Sentiment, Atlanta, Ga.,
1889-1901. Merged with
Southwestern Jewish Sentiment,
NN

*Memphis Journal of the Medical
Sciences*, Memphis, Tenn.,
1889-93, DSG, ICJ, NNN

The Mercerian, Macon, Ga.,
1889-current

Methodist Herald, Russellville,
Harrison, Ark., 1889-93? NjMD

Missionary, Richmond, Va., 1889,
NN, OO

Mountain Educator, Marshall, Ark.,
1889-94? N

Pentecostal Herald, Louisville, Ky.,
1889-? IEG, NN, OO

Popular Educator, Little Rock,
Ark., 1889-90. United with
Arkansas Educational Journal
to form *Southern School Journal*

Round Table, Dallas, Tex., 1889-93,
DLC, LNHT, Tx, TxU

The SAR Magazine, Louisville, Ky.,
1889-current

Southern Architect -- See *Southern
Architect and Building News*

*Southern Architect and Building
News*, Atlanta, Ga., 1889. Also
as *Southern Architect* and as
*Southern Architect and
Contractor*, DLC, NN, OU, PU,
TxU

Southern Architect and Contractor
-- See *Southern Architect and
Building News*

Southern Philatelist, Charleston,
S.C., 1889, 1890, 1893-96, ScU,
CtY, NN, PPi

Southern School Journal,
Lexington, Cynthiana, Ky.,
1889-? DLC, NN, DE, KyL, NcD,
NcU

Stage, Columbia, S.C., 1889-90, ScU

Teacher at Work, Huntsville, Ala.,
1889-90? DE

Teachers' Guide, Haynesville, Ala.,
1889-90

Texas Baptist Worker, San Antonio,
Tex., 1889-95, NHC

Texas Journal of Education,
Galveston, Tex., 1889-91. ·
Merged into *Texas School
Journal*, DE, N, TxU

Virginia Medical Advance,
Warrenton, Va., 1889-90? DSG,
PPC

The A.M.E. Zion Church Quarterly,
Pittsburgh, Pa.; Wilmington,
Salisbury, Charlotte, N.C.,
1890-1909. Pittsburgh, 1890-91;
Wilmington, 1892-94;
Salisbury/Wilmington, 1895-96;
Charlotte, 1896-1909, CtY, DHU,
MH, MH-AH, OO

American Osprey, Ashland, Ky.,
1890, DSI, MH-Z, NNM

The Animal Herald, New Orleans,
La., 1890-91? LNHT, LU

Arkansas Medical Society Journal,
Little Rock, Ark., 1890-?
1890-92 as *State Medical Society
of Arkansas Journal*, DSG, ICJ,
NNN, PPC, CLSU, CU-M

The Arkansas Thomas Cat, Hot
Springs, Ark., 1890-1948

Asheville Medical Review,
Asheville, N.C., Aug.-Nov. 1890,
DSG, MBM, NNN

Baptist Trumpet, Killeen, Tex.,
1890-? NHC

Current Topics for Leisure Hours,
New Orleans, La., 1890-95, CtY,
LNHT, LU, NcU

Dixie Doctor, Atlanta, Ga., 1890-91,
DSG, ICJ, MBM, NNN

Florida Home-Seeker, Avon Park,
Fla., Jan. 1890-June 1891? DA,
FU

Home Missionary, Atlanta, Ga., July
1890-May 1894, NcMHi, VRT

The Jewish Chronicle, New Orleans,
La., 1890-? LNHT

*Kentucky State Journal of
Education*, Falmouth, Ky., 1890?

Naval Stores Review, Savannah,
Ga.; New Orleans, La.,
1890-current. v.1-20 as
Savannah Naval Stores Review,
CtY, DA, DLC, NN, NcD

Palmetto School Journal, Columbia,
S.C., 1890-91, ScU, DE

Palmetto Teacher, Greenwood, S.C.,
1890-94? MWA

Savannah Naval Stores Review --
See *Naval Stores Review*

Southeastern Underwriter, Atlanta,
Ga., 1890-1912? ICJ, NN

Southern School Journal, Little
Rock, Ark., 1890-96. Formed by
merger of *Popular Educator* and
the *Arkansas Educational
Journal*, DE, TxU

The Southland, Salisbury, N.C.,
1890; Winston, N.C., 1891, DLC,
MWA

St. Mark's Echo, Charleston, S.C.,
1890, ScU

*State Medical Society of Arkansas
Journal* -- See *Arkansas Medical
Society Journal*

University of the South Magazine,
Sewanee, Tenn., 1890

Virginia Manufacturer, Buchanan,
Va., 1890-91? NNE

Way of Faith, Columbia, S.C.,
1890-? NN, GDC, NcD, NjMD

The Woman's World, New Orleans,
La., 1890, LNHT

Brann's Iconoclast, Waco, Austin,
Tex., 1891-98. As *Iconoclast*,
1891-94, DLC, MoS, PP, WHi

The Church Advocate, Norfolk, Va.,
1891; Baltimore, Md., 1891-1934,
NNG

Educational Monthly, Atlanta, Ga.,
1891-93. Formed by union of
Georgia Educational Journal
and *Piedmont Educator*.
Continued as *Southern
Educational Journal*, DE

Faith at Work Magazine, Waco,
Tex., 1891-?

Hospodar, Omaha, Neb.; West, Tex.,
1891-current, DA, IU, NN, TxCM

Iconoclast -- See *Brann's
Iconoclast*

The Living Age, Denison, Tex.,
1891-?; Langston, Okla. Terr.,
?-1904

Living Water, Nashville, Tenn.,
1891-1909, NN, NjMD

*Medical Insurance and Health
Conservation*, Austin, Tex., Nov.
1891-Sept. 1922. v.1-4 as *Texas
Sanitarian*, v.5-25 as *Texas
Medical News*. United with
Practical Medicine and Surgery
to form *Medical Insurance*,
CtY-M, DSG, NN, TxU

Mississippi Baptist, Newton, Miss.,
1891-1915? KyLoS

Mississippi Medical Monthly,
Vicksburg, Miss., 1891-1914.
Merged into *Pan American
Surgical and Medical Journal,*
CSt-L, DSG, N, NNN

National Fancier -- See *Poultry
Life of America*

*North Carolina Journal of
Education,* Fairview, N.C., 1891?

*Our Times. A Biblical Interpreter
of the News* -- See *These Times.
A Biblical Interpreter of the
News*

Poultry Life of America, Belton,
Tex.; Indianapolis, Ind.,
1891-1917. v.1-13 as *National
Fancier,* DA

Shield and Diamond, Memphis,
Tenn., 1891-current

*Southern Critic. A Critical
Amateur Journal, Devoted to the
Cause, Especially in the South,*
Dalton, Ga., Mar. 1891, CtY

Southern Educational Journal,
Atlanta, Ga., 1891-1902, n.s.
1905-07, ICU, N, NN, GEU, MH,
NcD

*Southern Stenographer and
Typewriter,* Macon, Ga.,
Feb.-May 1891? NN

Southern Watchman -- See *These
Times. A Biblical Interpreter
of the News*

*Southron, the Leading Humorous
Illustrated Monthly of the
South,* New Orleans, La., Sept.
1891-Sept. 1893, CtY, AU, LNHT

Southwestern Druggist, Dallas,
Tex., 1891-1904, NNN

*Tennessee Journal of Meteorology
and Monthly Agricultural
Review,* Nashville, Tenn., Dec.
15, 1891-Oct. 1895? DLC, T

*Texas Historical and Biographical
Magazine,* Austin, Tex., 1891-92,
DLC, NHC, NN, TxU

Texas Medical News -- See *Medical
Insurance and Health
Conservation*

*Texas Monthly. Devoted to the
History and Development of the
State,* Seguin, Tex., Jan. 1891-?
NcD, TxKT

Texas Sanitarian -- See *Medical
Insurance and Health
Conservation*

*These Times. A Biblical
Interpreter of the News,*
Nashville, Tenn., 1891-?
1891-Apr. 4, 1905 as *Southern
Watchman.* May 1905-Dec. 1945
as *Watchman Magazine.* Jan.
1946-Apr. 1951 as *Our Times.
A Biblical Interpreter of the
News,* DLC, NN, TU

Trident of Delta Delta Delta,
Arlington, Tex., 1891-current

Unsere Lustigen Blatter, New
Orleans, La., 1891, LNHT

Virginia Historical Magazine,
Richmond, Va., 1891-92, CtY,
DLC, MHi

Watchman Magazine -- See *These
Times. A Biblical Interpreter
of the News*

Charlotte Medical Journal -- See
Southern Medicine and Surgery

Church in Georgia, Atlanta, Ga.,
1892-1903? NNG

Church Record of Alabama,
Tuscaloosa, Ala., 1892-1916?
DLC, NNG, NcD

The Dictator, New Orleans, La.,
1892-93? LNHT

Dixie Miller. A Monthly Journal Devoted to Milling, Flour and Grain. Atlanta, Ga., 1892-1924. United with *Miller's Review* to form *Miller's Review and Dixie Miller*, DA, DLC, NN

Educational Worker, Springville, Ala., 1892

Fetter's Southern Magazine, Louisville, Ky., 1892-95. Became *Southern Magazine*, 1893. Suspended Nov.-Dec. 1894, Apr. 1895. Re-named *Mid-Continent Magazine*, 1895. Merged with *Scribner's Magazine*, 1895, DLC, MdBE, WHi, NN, NcD, NcU

Florida Health Notes, Jacksonville, Fla., July 1892-99?, n.s. 1906-? CtY-M, DLC, DNLM, MiU, TxU

Florida Philatelist, Thonotosassa, Fla., July 1892-Jan. 1893? MWA, OClWHi

Florida Teacher, Dade City, Fla., 1892

Hot Springs Medical Journal, Hot Springs, Ark., 1892-1908, DSG, ICJ, MBM, N, NNN

Illustrated Kentuckian, a Journal of Art, Literature, Education, Lexington, Ky., 1892-94? MH, ICU, KyLoU

Kentucky Homestead, Lexington, Ky., Feb. 5, 1892-? KyU

The Ladies' Companion, New Orleans, La., 1892-93? LNHT

The Medical and Surgical Observer. Devoted to the Interests of Medicine, Dentistry, and Pharmacy. Jackson, Tenn., 1892-? CSt-L, DSG, PPC, ICJ, MBM, NNN

Mid-Continent Magazine -- See *Fetter's Southern Magazine*

New Charlotte Medical Journal -- See *Southern Medicine and Surgery*

Our Homes, Nashville, Tenn., 1892-1910? GEU, NcD, NjMD

Pine Forest Echo, Charleston, S.C., 1892, ScU

Puck, Jr. New Orleans, La., 1892? LNHT

The Sewanee Review, Sewanee, Tenn., 1892-current, DLC, NN, NcU, TU, TxU, NcD, ScU

Southern Education, Florence, Ala., 1892. Sold to *Educational Exchange*, DE, N, MH, MWA, NcD, T

Southern Magazine -- See *Fetter's Southern Magazine*

Southern Medicine and Surgery, Charlotte, N.C., 1892-1921. Also as *Charlotte Medical Journal* and as *New Charlotte Medical Journal*. Absorbed *Carolina Medical Journal*, DSG, NNN, NcU, CSt-L

Southland, Waco, Tex., 1892-? TxU

Tatler of Society in Florida, Saint Augustine, Fla., 1892-1908? DLC, NN, FPY, NBuG

Texas Live Stock Journal, Fort Worth, Tex., 1892-93. DLC, DA

Virginia School Journal, Richmond, Va., 1892-1905? Supersedes *Educational Journal of Virginia*, DE, N, NcD, Vi VR, VRU, ViU, ViW

William and Mary Quarterly, Williamsburg, Va., July 1892-Apr. 1919; Jan. 1921-Oct. 1943, Jan. 1944-? July 1894-Dec. 1943 as *William and Mary College Quarterly Historical Magazine*, CtY, DLC, NN, NcD, NcU

*William and Mary Quarterly
Historical Magazine* -- See
William and Mary Quarterly

American Textile Manufacturer --
See *Textile Manufacturer*

Arkansas Eclectic Medical Journal,
Heber, Ark., 1893-94? MiU, NNN

Chat, Nashville, Tenn., Dec. 2,
1893-Jan. 12, 1896, T

*Expositor Biblico; Para Maestros
de Intermedios, Jovenes,
Mayores, Adultos,* El Paso, Tex.,
1893-?

Florida Life, Jacksonville, Fla.,
1893-? DLC, FU

*Freedom. A Journal of Realistic
Idealism.* Sea Breeze, Fla.,
June 1893-Apr. 23, 1902? DLC,
NN, OO

*Journal of Surgery, Gynecology
and Obstetrics,* Atlanta, Ga.,
1893, CSt-L, DSG, ICJ, MBM, NNN

Kentucky Baptist, Louisville, Ky.,
1893-95? KyLoS

Lee's Magazine -- See *The Period*

Lee's Texas Magazine -- See *The
Period*

Methodist Advocate Journal,
Chattanooga, Athens, Tenn.,
1893-1924. Later published as
*Southeastern Christian
Advocate,* still later as S.C.
edition of *Christian Advocate,*
NN

Palmetto Leaves, Georgetown, S.C.,
1893, ScU

The Period, Dallas, Tex., 1893-1906.
Re-named *Lee's Texas Magazine,*
later *Lee's Magazine* after
moving to Boston in 1901, DLC,
MoS, TxU

Progressive Teacher, Morristown,
Tenn., 1893-?

School Farmer, Dallas, Tex.,
1893-95. United with *Texas
School Journal,* N, TxU

South Kentucky Evangelist, Elkton,
Henderson, Ky., 1893-1903,
KyLxCB

Southeastern Christian Advocate
-- See *Methodist Advocate
Journal*

*Southern and Western Textile
Excelsior* -- See *Textile
Manufacturer*

*Southern Industrial and Lumber
Review,* Houston, Tex.,
1893-1920? CtY, TxH, TxU

Southern Ruralist, Atlanta, Ga.,
1893-? DA, NN, KyU, NcD, LNHT,
TU

Southern Unitarian, Atlanta, Ga.,
1893-95? IEG, ICM, LNHT,
MH-AH, ScU

Textile Manufacturer, Charlotte,
N.C., 1893-1921. 1893-1907 as
*Southern and Western Textile
Excelsior.* 1907-09 as *American
Textile Manufacturer,* DA, DLC,
NN, RPB

*Virginia Magazine of History and
Biography,* Richmond, Va.,
1893-current, C, DLC, NN, OO

Virginia Odd Fellow, Richmond,
Va., 1893-Dec. 1917, n.s. Jan.
1918-? DLC, Vi, VBP, ViU

Wachovia Moravian, Winston-Salem,
N.C., 1893-?

Wofford College Journal,
Spartanburg, S.C., 1893-94,
1896-1901, 1903-09, 1911-13,
1916, 1921, 1923, 1926-27, 1935,
1937-41, 1952, ScU

Atlanta Clinic, Atlanta, Ga.,
1894-97. Merged into *Magazine
of Medicine*, DSG, MBM, NNN

Atlanta Dental Journal, Atlanta,
Ga., 1894-98? DSG, IEN-D, NNN,
CU-M, NBuG, PPiU-M

*Breeder and Horseman; A Weekly
Journal Devoted to the Beef and
Livestock Interests Generally*,
Nashville, Tenn., Sept.
1894-1901, TN

*Christian: A Journal for the
Individual* -- See *Scientific
Christian*

Collegian, Clinton, S.C., 1894-96,
1902-11, 1916, 1919, 1921,
1923-24, ScU

Concept, Spartanburg, S.C., 1894,
1896-1909, 1913, 1916, 1919, 1945,
1921, 1927, 1932, ScU

Desmos, Chapel Hill, N.C., 1894-?

Dixie Game Fowl, Columbia, Tenn.,
1894-1907? v.14+ as *Dixie
Poultry Breeder*, DA

Dixie Philatelist, Alexander City,
Ala., 1894-Aug. 1896. Merged
into *Lone Star State
Philatelist*, CtY, MWA, NNCo

Dixie Poultry Breeder -- See *Dixie
Game Fowl*

Dixie School Journal, Waldo, Miss.,
1894-96. United with
Mississippi Journal of Education
to form *Mississippi School
Journal*, DE

Epworth Era, Nashville, Tenn.,
1894-Dec. 1931. United with
Highroad to form *Epworth
Highroad*, DLC, NN, NcD, NcU,
TNG

Erskinian, Due West, S.C.,
1894-1910, 1912, 1916, ScU

The Family Mirror, New Orleans,
La., 1894-?

Florida Ruralist, Interlachen, Fla.,
1894-97, FPY, FU

Florida School Exponent,
Tallahassee, Jacksonville, Fla.,
1894-1914? DE, DLC

Florida School Journal, Cocoa,
Fla., 1894-1922? 1894-1919 as
Florida Schoolroom, IU, FTS, FU,
OO

Florida Schoolroom -- See *Florida
School Journal*

Iconoclast -- See *The Rolling Stone*

The Jewish Times, New Orleans, La.,
1894-? LNHT

Journal of Labor, Nashville,
Tenn., 1894-97, ICJ

Lone Star State Philatelist,
Abilene, Tex., Sept. 3,
1894-Sept. 1899, CtY, MWA, NNCo

Louisville Medical Monthly,
Louisville, Ky., 1894-99. United
with *Louisville Journal of
Surgery and Medicine* to form
*Louisville Monthly Journal of
Medicine and Surgery*, later
Medical Life, DSG, KyLoU-M, NNN

*Men and Matters. A Magazine of
Fact, Fancy and Fiction*, New
Orleans, La., 1894-1904, DLC,
LNHT, LU, NN

Methodist Protestant Herald,
Greensboro, N.C., Nov. 1894-Oct.
1939. Also as *Our Church
Record*, NcD, NcU

Mississippi Journal of Education,
Aberdeen, Miss., 1894-95.
United with *Dixie School
Journal* to form *Mississippi
School Journal*, DE

The National Baptist Magazine,
Washington, D.C.; Nashville,
Tenn., 1894-1901. Washington,
D.C., 1894-99; Nashville, 1899;
Washington, D.C., 1900-01, NHC,
PCA, DLC

*Naturalist. A Monthly Magazine
Devoted to Natural Science.*
Austin, Tex., 1894-95. Merged
into *Oregon Naturalist,* CtY,
DLC

The Negro Educational Journal,
Cartersville, Ga., 1894-95;
Athens, Ga., 1895, DHEW

Our Church Record -- See
Methodist Protestant Herald

Progressive Teacher, Augusta, Ga.,
1894-?

The Rolling Stone, Austin, Tex.,
Apr. 28, 1894-Apr. 27, 1895.
v.1, no.1-2 as *Iconoclast,* TxU

Scientific Christian, Little Rock,
Ark.; Denver, Colo., 1894-1921?
1914 as *Christian: A Journal
for the Individual,* DLC, OO

Seaside Thoughts, Charleston, S.C.,
1894, ScU

Southern Garden, New Orleans, La.,
1894? LNHT

Southern Medical Review, Houston,
Tex., 1894. Merged into *Texas
Sanitarian,* later *Medical
Insurance and Health
Conservation,* CSt-L, DSG, MBM,
NBM, PPC

Southern Pit Games, Blakely, Ga.,
1894-1909? DA, NN

Southern Poultry Journal, Dallas,
Tex., 1894-1914? DA

Southern Stenographer,
Charleston, S.C., Jan.-Dec. 1894,
CtY, NN

Southwest Texas Magazine,
Beeville, Tex., 1894, TxU

*Tennessee Journal of Medical
Diseases of Women and Children,
and Abstracts of the Medical
Sciences,* Nashville, Tenn.,
1894-95 DSG, MBM, NNN, PPC

Texan Philatelist, Abilene, Tex.,
Dec. 1894-Feb. 1899, MWA, NNCo

*University of Tennessee Scientific
Magazine,* Knoxville, Tenn.,
1894-97, ICJ, DLC, IU, MiU, PP,
T, TU

Woman, Richmond, Va., 1894-97

American Homes, Knoxville, Tenn.;
New York, N.Y., 1895-1904, DLC,
MB, NN

Berea Quarterly, Berea, Ky.,
1895-Oct. 1916, CtY, DLC, KyU,
MH, NN

Citadel Magazine, Charleston, S.C.,
1895, ScU

Coraddi, Greensboro, N.C., 1895-?

Horticultural Gleaner, Austin,
Tex., 1895-97? DA, NIC

Jubilate Deo, Charleston, S.C.,
1895, 1897, 1903-04, 1905,
1910-13, 1930-44, 1969, 1971-72,
ScU

LaSalle's Isonomy -- See *Reed's
Isonomy*

*L'Observateur Louisianais, revue
mensuelle religieuse, politique
et litteraire.* New Orleans, La.,
1895-97, LU, MiU, NcD, TxU

Louisiana School Review, New
Orleans, La., 1895?-1907? DE,
ICU, LU, LNHT, MH, N, NNC-T

*Magazine of Tennessee History and
Biography,* Nashville, Tenn.,
Jan.-Feb. 1895, CtY, N, TU

Mississippi State University Alumnus, State College, Miss., 1895-current

Oil Mill Gazeteer, Houston, Wharton, Tex., 1895-? DA, LNHT, NN, TxH

The Owl, New Orleans, La., 1895-99? LNHT

Pigeon News, Medford, Mass.; Brownwood, Tex., 1895-1979, DA, NN, ViU

Postmasters' Advocate, Alexandria, Va., 1895-current, DL, DLC, NN

Progressive Teacher and Southwestern School Journal, Morristown, Nashville, Tenn., 1895-? 1895-97 as *Tennessee School Journal*, 1898-1901 as *Southwestern School Journal*. CtY, DE, DLC, N, NcU, TU, TxU

Reed's Isonomy, A Journal of Justice. San Antonio, Tex., 1895-1905. 1895-1901 as *LaSalle's Isonomy*, DLC, NN

Sabbath School Companion, Charleston, S.C., 1895, DLC

St. Augustine's Record, Raleigh, N.C., 1895-98? NNG

The Southern Educator, Hawkinsville, Ga., 1895?-?

Southern Journal of Pharmacy and Materia Medica, Nashville, Tenn., 1895-96? NNN, WU, OCL, PPC

Southern Stenographic Magazine, Nashville, Tenn., June 1895, CtY, NN

Southland Queen, Beeville, Tex., Sept. 1895-July 1904. Merged into *Lone Star Apiarist*, later as *Western Bee Journal*, DA, MAA, WU

Southwestern Medical and Surgical Reporter, Fort Worth, Tex., 1895-97. Merged into *Texas Medical News*, later *Medical Insurance and Health Conservation*, DSG, ICJ, NNN, CSt-L, PPC, TxU

Southwestern School Journal -- See *Progressive Teacher and Southwestern School Journal*

Tennessee School Journal -- See *Progressive Teacher and Southwestern School Journal*

Texas Ranger, Austin, Tex., 1895-?

Virginia Law Register, Charlottesville, Va., 1895-1915, n.s. 1915-? C, CtY, DLC, M, N, TxU

American Historical Magazine and Tennessee Historical Society Quarterly, Nashville, Tenn., 1896-1904, CtY, DLC, NN, TU, TxU, NcU

Arkansas School Journal, Little Rock, Ark., 1896-1913, DE, TxU, ArU, MWA, N, NNC-T

Atlanta Illustrator, Atlanta, Ga., 1896

Carolina Teachers' Journal, Greenwood, S.C., Oct. 1896-Dec. 1901. Superseded by *Educational*, ScU

Church Messenger, Columbia, S.C., 1896, ScU

The Creole Monthly, New Orleans, La., 1896-98. Superseded by the *Creole Magazine* in 1899, LNHT, LU

The Cricket, New Orleans, La., 1896, LNHT

The Diocese of Louisiana, New Orleans, La., 1896-1925? LNHT

Dixie Manufacturer. A Semi-Monthly Journal Reflecting Southern Industrial Development. Birmingham, Ala., 1896-? AU

Docket, San Antonio, Tex., 1896, NIC, PU-L, TxU

Down in Dixie, New Orleans, La., 1896, LNHT

Journal of Physical Education, Recreation and Dance. Reston, Va., 1896-current

Magpie. One of the Ephemerals. Charlottesville, Va., June-Oct. 1896, CtY, DLC, ICN

Mississippi School Journal, Jackson, Miss., 1896-1911. Formed by union of *Dixie School Journal* and *Mississippi Journal of Education.* Merged into *Mississippi Educational Journal,* De, MsAM, MsU, TxU

Newberry Collegian, Newberry, S.C., 1896, ScU

North Carolina White Ribbon, Greensboro, N.C., July 1896-? Nc, NcU

Primitive Baptist Quarterly Review, Griffin, Ga., 1896, NcU, TxFS

South Carolina Tobacconist, Sumter, S.C., 1896, ScU

Southern Farmer, New Orleans, La., 1896-1900? DA

Southern Florist and Gardener, Louisville, Ky.; Chattanooga, Tenn., 1896-99? DA, MoSB

Southern Fruit Grower, Chattanooga, Tenn., 1896-1921, DA, NN, TU, WU, IU, LNHT, TC, WvU, IaAS

Southern Missioner, Lawrenceville, Va., 1896-1905, CtY, WHi, MnHi, MH, NNG, VBP, VR, NcD

Southwestern Medical Record, Houston, Tex., 1896-99, DSG, ICJ, MBM, TxU

Texas Magazine, Austin, Dallas, Tex., 1896-98. Feb.-Mar. 1898 not issued., DLC, NN, TxU

American Dental Weekly, Atlanta, Ga., 1897-98, DSG, ICJ, NNN, MH-M, MiU, NBM

American Ginner, Meridian, Miss., June-Oct. 1897, DA

Church Worker, Lexington, N.C., 1897-1904, PCA

Clemson College Chronicle, Greenville, S.C., 1897-1913, 1921, 1923, 1961-62, ScU

Colored Preacher, Spartanburg, S.C., 1897-1900. As *Lowery's Religious Monthly,* 1899-1900?

Cotton and Farm Journal, Memphis, Tenn., Nov. 1897-Mar. 1903? v.1-5 as *Cotton Planter's Journal,* DA, OO

Cotton Planter's Journal -- See *Cotton and Farm Journal*

Criterion, Columbia, S.C., 1897-1909, 1916, 1921, 1923, 1927, 1932, 1936-37, 1943, 1945, 1950, 1961, ScU

Educational Courier, Poplarville, Miss., 1897, LNHT

Epworth Leaguer, Columbia, S.C., 1897-98, ScU

Fancy Fowls -- See *Poultry Fancier*

Georgia Journal of Medicine and Surgery, Savannah, Ga., 1897-1903. Continued as *Southern Medicine,* DSG, ICJ, MBM, NNN

Gospel Tidings, Siloam Springs, Ark.; San Jose, Calif., 1897-1900? PCA

Ideal American Magazine, New Orleans, La., 1897?-1902? LNHT

Lowery's Religion Monthly -- See *Colored Preacher*

Medical Record of Mississippi -- See *Mississippi State Medical Association Journal*

Medical Register, Richmond, Va., 1897-1900, DSG, ICJ, MBM, NNN

Mississippi Medical Record -- See *Mississippi State Medical Association Journal*

Mississippi State Medical Association Journal, ____, Miss., 1897-1905. 1897-98 as *Medical Record of Mississippi*, v.4-8 as *Mississippi Medical Record*, DSG, LU, MB, NNN, MiD

Mississippi Teacher, Jackson, Miss., 1897-1905, MsU

Modern Philosopher: A Monthly Magazine for Progressive People. Knoxville, Tenn., May 1897-Apr. 1899, CtY, DLC, TU

The National Association Notes, Tuskegee, Ala., 1897-? NcD

National Stamp Collector, New Orleans, La., Dec. 1897-Feb. 1898, MWA, NNCo, OClWHi

North Carolina Home Journal, Trinity, N.C., Sept. 1897-Dec. 1898, Nc, NcD

Penn School Chronicle, Saint Helena Island, S.C., 1897, ScU

Poultry Fancier, Hopkinsville, Ky., 1897-Mar. 1915. v.1-11, no.8 as *Fancy Fowls*, DA, NIC

Quarterly of the Texas State Historical Association -- See *Southwestern Historical Quarterly*

Religious Outlook, Columbia, S.C., 1897-98, DLC, KyL, OO, TxU

Southern Tribute. A Monthly Magazine Devoted to the Daughters of the Confederacy. Austin, Tex., Nov. 1897-May 1898? DLC, NNHi, TxWB

Southland. A Journal of Patriotism. Devoted to History and the Cause of Confederate Veterans. Greenville, N.C., 1897-98? CtY, Nc, PPHi

Southwestern Historical Quarterly, Austin, Tex., July 1897-current. As *Quarterly of the Texas State Historical Association* until 1912, ArU, C, CtY, DLC, NN, NcD, NcU, TU, TxH, TxU

Texas State Historical Association Quarterly, Austin, Tex., 1897-current

Tobacco Worker, Louisville, Ky., Jan. 1897-Mar. 1924, n.s. Nov. 1940-? CtY, DLC, KyLoU, NN

Virginia Philatelist. A Monthly Magazine Devoted to the Interests of Philately in Virginia. Richmond, Va., Sept. 1897-Jan. 1905, IU, PPi, Vi, ViW

Weekly Livestock Reporter, Fort Worth, Tex., 1897-?

Youth's Magazine, New Orleans, La., 1897-1901? LNHT

Arkansas Farmer, Nashville, Tenn., 1898-?

Armstrong's Magazine, Knoxville, Tenn.; Atlanta, Ga., Apr. 1898-Mar. 1899? v.1 as *Southern Review*, DLC, NcU

Bryoloist, Brooklyn, N.Y.;
Pittsburgh, Pa.; Lafayette, La.;
College Station, Tex.; Durham,
N.C., 1898-current

Business Educator, Charleston,
S.C., 1898, ScU

Cherokee Gospel Tidings, Siloam
Springs, Ark., 1898-1902?   DLC,
NN

Colton's Magazine, New Orleans,
La., 1898?   LNHT

*Cotton, Serving the Textile
Industries* -- See *Textile
Industries*

Dental Clippings, Houston, Tex.,
1898-1902, IaU, NNN

Educator, Kittrell, N.C., 1898-?
MWA

Floral Magazine, Greenwood, S.C.,
1898, 1964, ScU

Florida Schools, Tallahassee, Fla.,
1898-?

*The Hospital Herald. A Monthly
Journal Devoted to Hospital
Work, Nurse Training, Domestic
and Public Hygiene.* Charleston,
S.C., 1898-?

Journal of Labor, Atlanta, Ga.,
Nov. 1898-?   GEU

Lynk's Magazine, Jackson, Tenn.,
1898-?

Memphis Lancet, Memphis, Tenn.,
1898-1900.   Merged into *Memphis
Medical Monthly*, CSt-L, DSG,
ICJ, MiU, NNN

Nature's Finer Forces Library,
New Orleans, La., 1898-99?   LNHT

The New Orleans Magazine, New
Orleans, La., 1898, LNHT

New Orleans Trade Journal -- See
*Southern Trade Journal.   A
Statistical Journal of Finance,
Commerce and Manufactures*

*North Carolina Journal of
Education*, Greensboro, N.C.,
1898-1901

Presbyterian Quarterly, _____,
_____, 1898, ScU

Religious Review of Reviews, Salem,
Va., 1898-99?   DLC, NN, OO, PCC

Rice Journal -- See *Rice Journal
and Southern Farmer*

*Rice Journal and Gulf Coast
Farmer* -- See *Rice Journal and
Southern Farmer*

*Rice Journal and Southern
Farmer*, Crowley, New Orleans,
La., 1898-current, v.1-8 as *Rice
Journal and Gulf Coast
Farmer*.   Also as *Rice, Sugar
and Coffee Journal* and as *Rice
and Sugar Journal.*   Currently
as *Rice Journal*, DA, DLC, NN,
TxH, ICJ, LNHT

Rice, Sugar and Coffee Journal
-- See *Rice Journal and
Southern Farmer*

Southern Journal of Osteopathy,
Franklin, Ky., 1898-99?   DSG,
NNN, PPC

Southern Lumber Journal,
Jacksonville, Fla., 1898-?   CtY,
DA, FU, MB, NN, NcD, ICJ

The Southern Magazine, New
Orleans, La., 1898?   LNHT

Southern Review -- See *Armstrong's
Magazine*

*Southern Trade Journal.   A
Statistical Journal of Finance,
Commerce and Manufactures.* New
Orleans, La., Aug. 1898-Dec.
1900?   v.1-2 as *New Orleans
Trade Journal*, NjR

Southwestern Progressive Medical Journal, Rogers, Ark., 1898-1901? NNN, CSt-L, DSG, OCL, PPC

Tennessee Philatelist -- See *Tennessee Philatelist and Home Worker*

Tennessee Philatelist and Home Worker, Knoxville, Tenn., Mar. 15-May 15, 1898. v.1-2 as *Tennessee Philatelist*, MWA

Texas Clinic, Dallas, Tex., 1898-1901? CSt-L, DSG, ICJ, MBM, NNN, TxU

Texas School Magazine, Dallas, Tex., 1898-1914? CtY, NNC-T, TxU, DE, N, Tx, TxDaM

Textile Industries, Atlanta, Ga.; Greenville, S.C.,   1898-current. 1898-1946 as *Cotton, Serving the Textile Industries*, DA, DLC, NN, NcRS, NcU

University of Texas Record, Austin, Tex., 1898-1913. v.1-3 as *University Record*, CU, CtY, DLC, NN, TxU

University Record -- See *University of Texas Record*

Arkansas Farmer and Homestead, Little Rock, Ark., 1899-? v.1-13 as *Arkansas Homestead*, DA, IU, NN, TU-M, UPB

Arkansas Homestead -- See *Arkansas Farmer and Homestead*

Atlanta Journal-Record of Medicine, Atlanta, Ga., 1899-1918. Formed by union of *Atlanta Medical and Surgical Journal* and *Southern Medical Record*, CtY, DSG, ICJ, MBM, NNN

Bible Student, Columbia, S.C., 1899, 1901-02, ScU

Building and Engineering Digest, Dallas, Tex., 1899-Dec. 15, 1925. v.1-25, no.19 as *Texas Trade Review and Industrial Record*, NN, TxU

Circuit Rider, Columbia, S.C., 1899-1900, ScU

Cotton. A Monthly Technical Journal Devoted to Cotton, Its Utilization and Products. Atlanta, Ga., 1899-1908? DLC, NN, ICU, LNHT, MiD, TxU

Cotton Ginners' Journal, Waco, Tex., Apr. 1899-1901, DA, N

Cotton Mill News, Charlotte, N.C., 1899-May 25, 1922. 1899-June 1921 as *Mill News*. Merged into *American Wool and Cotton Reporter*, NN

The Creole Magazine, New Orleans, La., 1899-1900? LNHT, LU

The Criterion, New Orleans, La., 1899, LNHT

Dental Hints, Augusta, Ga., 1899-1905, IaU, IEN-D, NNN

Dental World, Atlanta, Macon, Ga., 1899-1902? NBuG, NNN

"Echo," New Orleans, La., 1899?-1915? LNHT

Educator, Huntsville, Ala., 1899-?

Elite, New Orleans, La., 1899-1902? LNHT

Farmer and Stockman -- See *Florida Farmer*

Farmers' Union Sun, Columbia, S.C., 1899-1913, DA

Florida East Coast Homesteader -- See *Florida Farmer*

Florida Farmer, Jacksonville, Fla., 1899-Nov. 1932. v.1-16, no.5 as *Florida East Coast Homeseeker*; v.16, no.6-v.18, no.12 as *Florida Farmer and Homeseeker*; v.19-20, no.18 as *Florida Farmer and Stockman*, v.20, no.19-v.27, no.2 as *Farmer and Stockman*, DA, FJ, FU, NN

Florida Farmer and Homemaker -- See *Florida Farmer*

Florida Farmer and Stockman -- See *Florida Farmer*

Georgia Education, Atlanta, Ga., 1899-1900? DE, N, GEU, NcD

Georgia Poultry Herald -- See *Southern Poultryman*

Grit and Steel, Gaffney, S.C., 1899-? DA, NN, OU

Gulf Fauna and Flora Bulletin, Ruston, La., June-Dec. 1899? ICJ, NbU, TU, VHS

The Harlequin, New Orleans, La., 1899-1909, LNHT, DLC, NN, NjR

Home and School, Lexington, Ky., 1899. Formerly *Southern School*.

Insurance Field, Louisville, Ky., Nov. 9, 1899-1909, DLC, KyL, NN, TxU

Jewish Chronicle, Mobile, Ala., Nov. 1899-? OCH

The Jolly Joker, New Orleans, La., 1899-1900, LNHT

Journal of Tuberculosis, Asheville, N.C., 1899-1903, DLC, DSG, ICJ, MBM, NNN

Kentucky Historical and Genealogical Magazine, Lexington, Ky., May-June 1899, KyBgW, Nh, OCHP, OHi

Keystone. A Monthly Journal Devoted to Women's Work. Charleston, S.C., June 1899-June 1913, DLC

Lincoln Herald, Harrogate, Tenn., 1899-current. 1899-Oct. 1937 as *Mountain Herald*, CtY, DLC, KyL, KyLF, NN

Mill News -- See *Cotton Mill News*

Mountain Herald -- See *Lincoln Herald*

Our Young People, Newberry, S.C., 1899, ScU

Presbyterian, Rutherfordton, Shelby, N.C., Apr. 1899-Mar. 1905. v.1-2 as *Rutherfordton Presbyterian*, NcMHi

Southern Magazine, Manassas, Va., June-Dec. 1899. Merged into *Dixie. A Monthly Magazine*, DLC, NcD, ViU

Southern Medical Journal, La Grange, N.C., 1899-1902, DSG, ICJ, NNN

Southern Poultry Courier -- See *Southern Poultryman*

Southern Poultryman, Dallas, Tex., 1899-1906? 1899-1902 as *Georgia Poultry Herald*. 1902-1906 as *Southern Poultry Courier*. Merged into *Tri-State Poultry Journal*, DA

St. Andrew's Messenger, Charleston, S.C., 1899, ScU

Texas Trade Review and Industrial Record -- See *Building and Engineering Digest*

Truck Farmer -- See *Truck Farmer of Texas*

Truck Farmer of Texas, Dallas, San Antonio, Tex., 1899-1907? v.1-9 as *Truck Farmer*, DA, DLC, TxU

Virginia University School of Teutonic Languages Monographs, Charlottesville, Va., 1899-1904?   CtY, DLC, MnU

Baptist Herald, Milligan, Fla., 1900-03

Baptist Young People, Nashville, Tenn., 1900-?

Christian Home -- See *Home Quarterly*

Common Carrier -- See *Railroad Record and Common Carrier*

Cotton Seed Oil Magazine, Atlanta, Ga., 1900-Nov. 1930, DA, LN, LNHT, NN

The Defender, New Orleans, La., Oct. 1900-Nov. 1902, LNHT

Florida Magazine, Jacksonville, Fla., Jan. 1900-Sept. 1903. Began as *Sunny Lands*, St. Augustine, Fla., 1900. Only one number under this title, then moved to Jacksonville. Merged with *Alkahest*, Atlanta, in Oct. 1903, DLC, F, FJ, FU, NN

Florida School Herald, St. Augustine, Fla., 1900-05, DLC, FTS, FU

Florida's Financial and Industrial Record, Jacksonville, Fla., 1900-Nov. 1, 1912.   v.1-10, no.4 as *Weekly Industrial Record*; v.10, no.5-v.19, no.42 as *Industrial Record*, DA

Gulf Coast Record, Mobile, Ala., 1900-?   DLC, LNHT

The Herald, New Orleans, La., June-Oct. 1900, LNHT

Home Quarterly, Nashville, Tenn., 1900-Jan. 1938.   United with *Childhood Guidance in Christian Living* to form *Christian Home*, DLC, GEU

Industrial Record -- See *Florida's Financial and Industrial Record*

James Sprunt Studies in History and Political Science, Chapel Hill, N.C., 1900-?   DLC, NN, NcD, NcU

Legal Gazette, Huntington, Tenn., Jan.-Feb. 1900, ICU, MH-L, NIC

Light, A Quarterly Magazine Devoted to Religion, Science, Literature, Art, New Orleans, La., Oct. 1900-Apr. 1905, Ia, LNHT

North Carolina Historical and Genealogical Register, Edenton, N.C., Jan. 1900-July 1903, CtY, DLC, NN, NcD, NcU

North Carolina Law Journal, Tarboro, Raleigh, N.C., Mar. 1900-Mar. 1923, DLC, N, NcD-L, NcU

Poultry Gem Siloam Springs, Stuttgart, Ark., 1900-July 15, 1905.   Merged into *Poultry Life of America*, DA

Railroad Herald, Atlanta, Ga., 1900-Mar. 1933, CtY, NN, NcD

Railroad Record and Common Carrier, Atlanta, Ga., 1900-Apr. 1909.   1900-June 1903 as *Common Carrier*, DIC, DLC

Rice Industry, Houston, Tex., 1900-11, DA, DLC, TxH, TxU

Seaboard Medical and Surgical Journal, Norfolk, Va., Jan.-May 1900, DSG, NNN, PPC

South Carolina Historical and Genealogical Magazine, Charleston, S.C., Jan. 1900-current, CtY, DLC, ICN, NN, NcD, NcU, ScU

Southern Evangelist, Lexington, Ky., 1900-02?   NN, NcMHi

Sunny Lands -- See *Florida Magazine*

Teachers' Outlook, New Orleans, La., Jan. 1900-Mar. 1906, DE, LNHT, LU, MH, N

VUU Informer, Richmond, Va., 1900-current

Weekly Industrial Record -- See *Florida's Financial and Industrial Record*

Woman's World, Fort Worth, Tex., 1900-?

Cockrill's Magazine, Louisville, Ky., 1901-07

Cotton Trade Journal Savannah, Ga., Aug. 1901-Aug. 1907. United with Cotton Trade Journal to form *Cotton Trade Journal; An Illustrated Monthly*, later *Cotton Record*, DA, DLC, NN

Food Executive, Alexandria, Va., 1901-?

Furniture Merchandising, High Point, N.C., Feb. 1901-June 1932, DLC, NN

Furniture Retailer & Furniture Age, Nashville, Tenn., 1901-? AzU, DLC, KU, NN, NN

Gas, A Weekly Publication Devoted to General News and Literature, New Orleans, La., Nov. 1901-Jan. 1902, LNHT

Georgia Dental Association Journal, Macon, Ga., June 1901-June 1922, n.s. Mar. 1928-current, G, I, MiU, NNN

Gulf Ports Marine Journal, New Orleans, La., Nov. 9, 1901-July 12, 1902, MoS

Journal of Physical Education, New Orleans, La., 1901-? CLSU, DLC, MnU, NSU

Louisiana Grocer, Metairie, New Orleans, La., Jan. 1901-current, LNHT

Memphis Engineering Society Journal, Memphis, Tenn., 1901-June 1906, TNV, TU

North Carolina Booklet. Great Events in North Carolina History. Raleigh, N.C., May 10, 1901-Jan/Oct. 1926, CtY, DLC, NN, Nc, NcD, NcRS, NcU

Practical Dental Journal, San Antonio, Tex., 1901-Apr. 1926, MiU, NNN

Southern Druggist, Atlanta, Ga., 1901-08, NNN

Southern Furniture Journal; the Journal of the Southern Furniture Interests, High Point, N.C., 1901-? DLC, NcU

Southern Law Review, Atlanta, Ga., 1901-02, ICU, Ia, N, NIC

Southern Merchant, Atlanta, Ga., 1901-? NN

The Southland Magazine. A Magazine of the South, Norfolk, Va., 1901-Dec. 1910? NN, Vi, ViU

Southwestern Jewish Sentiment, Atlanta, Ga.; Dallas, Tex., 1901-19, NN

Sunday School Adults, Nashville, Tenn., 1901-current, DLC, NHC

Texas Banker, Dallas, Tex., 1901-10. Merged into *Texas Banker's Journal*, TxU

Texas Medical Gazette, Fort Worth, Tex., 1901-May 1905, DSG, NBM, NN

Texas Railway and Industrial Journal, Fort Worth, Tex., Jan. 1901-05? DLC, OO

Arkansas Baptist Little Rock,
Ark., 1902-current, KyLoS, NN,
PCA, TxU

Brethren Journal, Austin, Tex.,
1902-current.

Church and Society World, Atlanta,
Ga., 1902-? OCH, NN

*Club Life, A Journal Devoted to
the Interests of Southern
Clubdom*, New Orleans, La.,
1902-? LNHT, Louisiana State
Museum Library

Cross Roads, Tupelo, Miss., 1902-?

*Echo; A Magazine Devoted to
Society, Literature, and Stage
in the South*, Richmond, Va.,
Feb. 15, 1902, ViU

Farming, Knoxville, Tenn., 1902-26,
DA, MnU, NIC

Gulf State Historical Magazine,
Montgomery, Ala., July
1902-Mar./May 1904, AAP, ArU,
Ct, CtY, IU, DLC, GU, NcD, NcU,
NN

*Gulf States Journal of Medicine
and Surgery and Mobile Medical
and Surgical Journal*, Mobile,
Ala., 1902-Nov. 1910, CtY, DSG,
MBM, NNN, NcD

Harbinger, Raleigh, N.C., 1902-05,
NNC

Johnny on the Spot, New Orleans,
La., Feb. 1-March 1, 1902, LNHT,
Louisiana State Museum Library

Journal of Geography, Houston,
Tex., 1902-? ScU

Kentucky Oil Journal, Barbourville,
Ky., 1902, DLC

Lone Star Apiarist, Floresville,
Tex., Jan.-May 1902, DA, NIC-A,
WU

NARD Journal, Alexandria, Va.,
1902-current

*Oracle; An Illustrated Monthly
Magazine*, Richmond, Va., 1902,
DLC, MWA, Vi, ViU

Shippers' Guide -- See *Southern
Shippers' Guide*

South Atlantic Quarterly, Durham,
N.C., 1902-current, DLC, ICN,
N, NN, NcU, TxU

Southern Advance, Athens, Ga.,
Jan. 1902-Jan. 1905, DLC, GEU,
GMM, TxU

Southern Drug Journal, Atlanta,
Ga., 1902-06, NNN, WU, NcU

Southern Education Notes,
Knoxville, Tenn., 1902-03? DE

Southern School and Home,
Tallahassee, Fla., Apr. 1902-Nov.
1903? Merged into *Southern
Educational Review*, DE, DLC,
NNC-T

Southern Shippers' Guide,
Lamarque, Houston, Tex.,
1902-05? Also as *Texas Truck
Grower and Shippers' Guide*,
and as *Shippers' Guide*, DA

*Tennessee Medical Association
Journal*, Nashville, Tenn.,
1902-current. Also as *Tennessee
State Medical Association
Journal*, DSG, ICJ, N, NNN, TU

*Tennessee State Medical Association
Journal* -- See *Tennessee
Medical Association Journal*

*Tennessee Valley Historical Society
Circular*, _____, Tenn.,
1902-03? DLC, MHi

*Texas Field and National
Guardsman* San Antonio, Tex.,
Feb. 1902-June 1915. v.1-8,
no.6 as *Texas Field and
Sportsman*, DA, DLC, TxH, TxU

Texas Field and Sportsman -- See *Texas Field and National Guardsman*

Texas Truck Grower and Shippers' Guide-- See *Southern Shippers' Guide*

Alabama Christian, Birmingham, Ala., 1903-? KyLxCB

American Home Journal; A Monthly Magazine for the Home, Dallas, Tex., 1903-10? DLC, OO

American Society for Horticultural Science Journal, Alexandria, Va., 1903-? CLSU, NNC, IaU, CtY, LU, TU, ViU, WU

Baptist Builder, Martin, Tenn., 1903-20. v.14, no.41-v.16, no.26 as *Baptist Builder and Benton Baptist*, KyLoS

Baptist Builder and Benton Baptist -- See *Baptist Builder*

Bulletin of the Kentucky State Medical Association -- See *Kentucky Medical Journal*

Cotton Bale. Devoted to the Interests of the Southern Farmer, Shreveport, La., Mar. 1903-Feb. 1904? DA

International Commonwealth, Austin, Houston, Tex., 1903-22? v.1-7 as *State Topics: A Journal of the People*; v.8, no.1-2 as *Texas Weekly Review*, v.8, no.3-23 as *State Topics and the Texas Weekly Review*, v.8, no.24-v.10 as *State Topics and the Texas Monthly Review*, DLC, Tx, TxU

Journal of the Arkansas Medical Society Fort Smith, Ark., 1903-current, ArU

Journal of the Kentucky Medical Association, Louisville, Ky., 1903-current, KyU, KyL, DLC, NN

Kentucky Christian, Lexington, Ky., 1903-? Also as *Kentucky Evangel*, KyBgW, KyLxCB

Kentucky Evangel -- See *Kentucky Christian*

Kentucky Historical Society Register, Frankfort, Ky., 1903-? DLC, KyU, KyL, NN, ViU

Kentucky Medical Journal, Bowling Green, Ky., June 1903-? v.1 as *Bulletin of the Kentucky State Medical Association*, DLC, DSG, ICJ, KyL, KyU, MBM, N, NNN, NcD

North and South -- See *Southland*

Parks and Recreation; A Journal of Park and Recreation Management, Arlington, Va., 1903-?

The Register of the Kentucky Historical Society, Frankfort, Ky., 1903-current, CtY, DLC, KyLF, KyU, NN, ViBlbV

Southern Baptist, Jacksonville, Gainesville, Fla., 1903-04. Merged into *Florida Baptist Witness*, PCA, NN, KyLoS

Southern Bell Views, Atlanta, Ga., 1903-?

Southern Education, Knoxville, Tenn., 1903, DE, DLC, NN, TU

Southern Lutheran, New Orleans, La., Jan. 1903-Feb. 1922? LNHT, NcD

Southern Mills, a Monthly Devoted to the Industries of the South, Charlotte, N.C., 1903-08? MdBJ

Southland; Devoted to the Industrial and Agricultural Resources of the Territory Served by the Louisville and Nashville Railroad, Louisville, Ky., 1903-37? v.1-28, no.8 as *North and South*, DA, DLC, NN, NcD, FPY, TU

State Topics: A Journal of the People -- See *International Commonwealth*

State Topics and the Texas Monthly Review -- See *International Commonwealth*

State Topics and the Texas Weekly Review -- See *International Commonwealth*

Virginia Farm Journal, An Illustrated Magazine for Progressive Virginia Farmers, Alexandria, Va., Dec. 15, 1903-Mar. 1904?   DA

Young Men's Hebrew Association Magazine, New Orleans, La., June 1903?-Sept. 1907?

American Cotton Manufacturer; Cotton and Cotton Textiles, Charlotte, N.C., 1904-07. Merged into *Textile Manufacturer*, DA, DLC

American Fruit and Nut Journal, Petersburg, Va., 1904-13? 1904-06 as *American Nut Journal*, DA, DLC, NN

American Nut Journal -- See *American Fruit and Nut Journal*

Appalachian Journal, Knoxville, Tenn., 1904-Jan. 1937, DLC, T, TU

Army, Arlington, Va., 1904-current, DLC, OCU, NN, WM, WA, WyU, WvU

Dixieland; the Illustrated Home Magazine of the South, Dallas, Tex., Feb. 1904-? LNHT, TxU, ViU

Economic Geology, El Paso, Tex., 1904-current, ArU, AzU, AAP, IdU

Energy Engineering, Atlanta, Ga., 1904-current, DLC, IU, PPF, OC, NIC, NNE

Insurance News Graphic, Houston, Dallas, Tex., 1904-?   v.1-17, no.10 as *Texas Insurance*, DLC, Tx, TxH, TxU

Kentucky Farmer, Lexington, Louisville, Ky., Feb. 1904-12? v.1-5 as *Kentucky Farmer and Breeder*, v.7 as *Southern Farmer's Gazette*, DA, KyU, NN, ViU

Kentucky Farmer and Breeder -- See *Kentucky Farmer*

Medical Recorder. Medicine, Surgery and Allied Sciences, Shreveport, La., 1904-09. Continued as *Southern Medical Association Journal*, DSG, ICJ, N, NNN

Merchants' Journal and Commerce, Richmond, Va.; Raleigh, N.C., 1904-Dec. 1928, NN

Modern Eclecticism, A Journal of Specific Medication, Atlanta, Ga., Dec. 1904-July 1908. Supersedes *Georgia Eclectic Medical Journal*, MiU, NNN, OCL

National Rice and Cotton Journal -- See *Southwestern Farmer*

The New Citizen: A Magazine of Politics, Literature, and Current Events, Columbia, S.C., 1904-?   DLC, NN

News and Truths, Murray, Ky., 1904?-32, KyLoS, TxFS

North Carolina Journal of Law, Chapel Hill, N.C., Jan. 1904-Dec. 1905, Ct, DLC, N. NcU

Producers' Review, Dallas, Tex., 1904-06? v.1 as *Texas Producers Review*, DA

Review and Expositor, Louisville, Ky., 1904-current, KU, KyU

Southern Banker, Atlanta, Ga., 1904-current, DLC, GEU, GU, N, NN, NcU

Southern Educational Review, Chattanooga, Tenn., 1904-09, DE, DLC, NcU, NN, TU

Southern Engineer, A Practical Southern Journal Devoted to the Operation of Steam, Electrical, Gas and Refrigeration Machinery, Atlanta, Ga.; Raleigh, N.C., 1904-current. Also as *Southern Power Journal, Southern Power and Industry*, DLC, N, NcD, NcU, NN, TxU

Southern Farmer's Gazette -- See *Kentucky Farmer*

Southern Guardsman, New Orleans, La., Nov. 1904-Feb. 1908? LNHT

Southern Homes, Columbia, S.C., 1904-05? ScU

Southern Medicine, Savannah, Ga., 1904. Continues *Georgia Journal of Medicine and Surgery*. Merged into *Gaillard's Medical Journal*, later *Gaillard's Southern Medicine*, DSG, ICJ, NNN, MBM

Southern Medicine and Surgery, Chattanooga, Tenn., 1904-11, CSt-L, DSG, ICJ, MBM, NNN

Southern Power and Industry -- See *Southern Engineer*

Southern Power Journal -- See *Southern Engineer*

Southern Woman's Magazine, Atlanta, Ga., Feb. 1904-Aug. 1905, GA, NN

Southwest Magazine of Texas, Fort Worth, Tex., 1904-? TxU, TxWB, DLC, NN, MiU

Southwestern Farmer, Houston, Tex., 1904-12? v.1-3 as *National Rice and Cotton Journal*, DA, NN, TxH, TxU

Tennessee Christian, Nashville, Tenn., 1904-? KyLxCB

Texas Insurance -- See *Insurance News Graphic*

Texas Law Journal, Austin, Tex., 1904-05, TxU

Trusts & Estates, Atlanta, Ga., 1904-current, DLC, KyU, NNC, ICU, NIC

The Voice of the Negro, Atlanta, Ga.; Chicago, Ill., 1904-07, DLC, NN

ASHRAE Journal, Atlanta, Ga., 1905-current, CtY, DLC, MnU, NN, NcD, TU

American Bottler -- See *American Soft Drink Journal*

American Carbonator and Bottler -- See *American Soft Drink Journal*

American Soft Drink Journal, Jonesboro, Ga., 1905-? Also as *Southern Carbonator and Bottler*, as *Carbonator and Bottler*, as *National Carbonator and Bottler*, as *American Carbonator and Bottler*, and as *American Bottler*, CtY, DLC, NN

Architectural Art and Its Allies, New Orleans, La., July 1905-Jan. 1913. 1905-June 1906 as *Architecture and Allied Arts*, DLC, LN, AU

Architecture and Allied Arts -- See *Architectural Art and Its Allies*

Bob Taylor's Magazine -- See *Taylor-Trotwood Magazine*

Carbonator and Bottler -- See *American Soft Drink Journal*

Carolinas, Asheville, N.C., May
1905? LNHT, NNN, NcD

Charleston Museum, Charleston,
S.C., 1905-Oct. 1922. 1905 as
*College of Charleston Museum
Bulletin.* Superseded by its
Quarterly, Ct, DLC, ICJ, NN,
NcD, NcU

Classical Journal, Chicago, Ill.;
Gainesville, Fla., 1905-current,
AzU, CtY, DLC, NN, NcD

*College of Charleston Museum
Bulletin* -- See *Charleston
Museum*

*Farmer's Union News. A National
paper published in the interest
of the farmer*, Union City, Ga.,
1905-12? DA, DLC, NN

Florida Medical Journal,
Jacksonville, Fla., Jan.-Aug.
1905? NNN, PPC

Florida Signal, Emporia, Fla., Jan.
1905-July 1906? DLC

Georgia Baptist, Vidalia, Ga.,
1905-07? KyLoS

Georgia Practician, Savannah, Ga.,
1905-Dec. 1906, DSG, GEU, GU,
ICJ, MBM, NNN, NcD

Gulf Coast Line Magazine -- See
Gulf Coast Magazine

Gulf Coast Magazine, Corpus
Christi, Kingsville, Tex.,
1905-July 1912. v.1-2, no.3 as
Gulf Coast Line Magazine, DIC,
DLC, LNHT, TxH, TxU

La Hacienda, Buffalo, N.Y.; North
Miami Beach, Fla., 1905-current,
DA, DLC, N, NN, ViU

National Carbonator and Bottler
-- See *American Soft Drink
Journal*

National Shorthand Reporter,
Vienna, Va., 1905-current, CtY,
ICJ, NN

Practical Machinist -- See
Southern Machinery

R-MWC Alumnae Bulletin,
Lynchburg, Va., 1905-current

*South Carolina Medical Association
Journal*, Greenville, Columbia,
S.C., 1905-current, DSG, MBM,
N, NNN, NcD, ScU

Southern Carbonator and Bottler
-- See *American Soft Drink
Journal*

Southern Machinery, Atlanta, Ga.,
May 1905-Dec. 1910. 1905-07 as
Practical Machinist. Absorbed
Modern Machinery in 1911.
United with *Tradesman* to form
Iron Tradesman, later *Southern
Hardware and Implement
Journal*, DLC, NN, TNV

*The Southern Teacher's Advocate:
A Negro Journal of Education*,
Lexington, Ky., 1905-06, DE

Southwestern Electrician, Houston,
Tex., 1905-21? NN, NNE, TxH,
TxU

Taylor-Trotwood Magazine,
Nashville, Tenn., Apr. 1905-Dec.
1910. The Taylor Publishing
Co., 1905-06 as *Bob Taylor's
Magazine.* Absorbed *Trotwood's
Monthly* in Jan. 1907. Merged
into *Watson's Jeffersonian
Magazine*, later *Watson's
Magazine.* Absorbed by *Watson's
Jeffersonian Magazine* in Feb.
1911, DLC, MiU, NN, OO, TU

Texas Medicine, Austin, Tex.,
1905-current

Texas State Journal of Medicine,
Fort Worth, Austin, Tex., July
1905-current, DLC, ICJ, N, NN,
NNN, TxH, TxU

Town Talk, New Orleans, La., June, __-Feb. 1905

Trotwood's Monthly, Nashville, Tenn., Oct. 1905-Dec. 1906. Merged in Jan. 1907 with *Bob Taylor's Magazine* of Nashville to form *The Taylor-Trotwood Magazine*, DLC, LU, MnU, T, TN, TU

Yeanhelskyj Ranok, Dunwoody, Ga., 1905-current,

Alabama Citizen -- See *Citizen*

American Eagle, Estero, Fla., 1906-?

Arkansas Sketch Book, Little Rock, Ark., July 1906-Jan. 1910? 1906-Apr. 1908 as *Sketch Book*, DLC, LNHT, TxU

Bent of Tau Beta Pi, Knoxville, Tenn., 1906-current

Bohemian Scribbler, San Antonio, Tex., 1906-12. v.1-6 as *Passing Snow*. v.6, no.16-25 as *Mackay's Weekly*. v.6, no.26-v.7, no.39, as *Southern Sentinel*. Continued as *International Magazine*, DLC, TxU

Citizen, Birmingham, Ala., Aug. 1906-May 1941. 1906-July 1908 as *Alabama Citizen*, DLC

Cotton Journal, Atlanta, Ga., 1906-09? DA, NN, NcU

Cotton Seed, Atlanta, Ga., 1906-12, IU, ScCc, WU

The Dollar Mark, Newport News, Va., 1906-?

Farmers' Union Guide, Birmingham, Ala., 1906-11. Merged into *Progressive Farmer*, DA

Industrial Index, Columbus, Ga., 1906-? GEU, NN

Jewish Hope, San Antonio, Tex., 1906-07? NN

Kentucky Farming, Louisville, Ky., 1906-18? 1906-14? as *Our Country*. Merged into *Inland Farmer*

Krauss' Southerner, New Orleans, La., 1906-? LNHT

Mackay's Weekly -- See *Bohemian Scribbler*

Mississippi Valley Contractor, Memphis, Tenn.; Saint Louis, Mo., 1906-? v.1-22, no.22 as *Southern Contractor*

North Carolina Education; A Monthly Journal of Education, Rural Progress and Civic Betterment, Durham, N.C., 1906-24. 1906-Dec. 1908 as *North Carolina Journal of Education*. Superseded by *North Carolina Teacher*, DE, NcD, NcU, OO

North Carolina Journal of Education -- See *North Carolina Education*

On Dit, New Orleans, La., Mar.-May 1906, LNHT

Our Country -- See *Kentucky Farming*

Our Mission Fields -- See *Royal Service*

Palm Beach Life, Palm Beach, Fla., 1906-current

The Passing Snow -- See *Bohemian Scribbler*

Practical Advertising, Atlanta, Ga., 1906-Dec. 1909? NN

Ridgway's, A Militant Weekly for God and Country, New Orleans, La., Oct. 6, 1906-Feb. 9, 1907, DLC, IC, LNHT, Mi, NN, OO

Royal Service, Birmingham, Ala.;
Baltimore, Md., 1906-current.
As *Our Mission Fields*,
1906-Sept. 1914, CtY-D, DLC,
KyLoS

Sketch Book -- See *Arkansas
Sketch Book*

*South Carolina Live Stock
Association Report*, _____, S.C.,
1906-12, DA, NN, ScCc, ScU

Southern Contractor -- See
Mississippi Valley Contractor

Southern Magazine, Richmond, Va.,
Sept. 1906-June 1907, MiDU, Vi,
ViU, ViW

Southern Sentinel -- See *Bohemian
Scribbler*

Stained Glass, Chicago, Ill.; Mount
Vernon, N.Y.; Concord, N.H.;
Fairfax, Va.; Saint Louis, Mo.,
1906-current, DLC, IU, MH, OT,
PP

Studies in Philology, Chapel Hill,
N.C., 1906-current, CtY, DLC,
NN, NcU

Texas Churchman, Austin, Tex.,
1906-? TxH, TxU

Texas Libraries, Austin, Tex.,
1906-current, CU, DLC, IU, NN,
NcD, NcU, TxU, TxWB, Vi

Virginia Masonic Herald, Highland
Springs, Richmond, Va.,
1906-1932. v.1-26, no.6 as
Virginia Masonic Journal, v.26,
no.7 - v.27, no.6 as *Virginia
Masonic Herald and Virginia
Masonic Journal*, Vi

*Virginia Masonic Herald and
Virginia Masonic Journal* -- See
Virginia Masonic Herald

Virginia Masonic Journal -- See
Virginia Masonic Herald

Word and Work, Louisville, Ky.,
1906-? IEG, KyL

Cotton Record, Savannah, Ga., May
1, 1907-28. v.1, no.1-4 as
Cotton Trade Journal, v.1, no.5
as *Cotton Trade Journal; An
Illustrated Monthly*, DA, NN

Cotton Trade Journal -- See *Cotton
Record*

*Cotton Trade Journal; An
Illustrated Monthly* -- See
Cotton Record

Forest, Fish, and Game, Athens,
Ga., 1907-Apr. 1911. v.1-2 as
Southern Woodlands, DA, MH

Gospel Herald, Deland, Fla., Feb.
7, 1907-June 4, 1908, FU, NN

The Guide, Norcross, Ga., 1907-?

*The Horizon: A Journal of the
Color Line*, Alexandria, Va.;
Washington, D.C., 1907-10, CtY,
TNF

Jewish Herald-Voice, Houston, Tex.,
1907-? v.1-31, no.41 as *Texas
Jewish Herald*, NN, NNJ

The Kentucky Pharmacist,
Frankfort, Ky., 1907-? DA,
IU-M, KyL

Magazine of Wall Street, New York,
N.Y.; Ormond Beach, Fla.,
1907-current, DLC, FU, ICU, NN,
NcU

*Mechanical and Electrical
Engineering Record*, Lexington,
Ky., Oct. 1907-Mar. 1909, DLC,
KyU, TU

Musical Advance, Richmond, Va.,
1907-?

Refrigeration, Atlanta, Ga., June
1907-current, DA, NN, TxU

Schoolmates, New Orleans, La.,
Feb.-Apr. 1907, LNHT

Southern Highlander, Rome, Ga.,
1907-? DLC, NN, MH

Southern Orchards and Farms --
See *Southland Farmer*

Southern Woodlands -- See *Forest,
Fish, and Game*

Southland Farmer, Houston, Tex.,
May 1907-May 1926. v.1 as
*Texas Fruits, Nuts, Berries and
Flowers*, v.2-6, no.1 as
Southland Orchards and Homes,
v.6, no.2 - v.10 as *Southern
Orchards and Farms*. Absorbed
Texas Stockman and Farmer,
Jan. 1916, DA, DLC, ICJ, MBA,
TxU

Southland Orchards and Homes --
See *Southland Farmer*

Southwestern Banker -- See
*Southwestern Banking and
Industry*

Southwestern Banker's Journal --
See *Southwestern Banking and
Industry*

*Southwestern Banking and
Industry*, Fort Worth, Tex.,
Feb. 1907-Dec. 1943. v.1-16 as
Texas Banker's Journal,
v.17-27, no.6 as *Southwestern
Banker's Journal*, v.27,
no.7-June 1941 as *Southwestern
Banker*. Absorbed *Texas
Banker*, July 1910, DLC, LNHT,
NN, Tx, TxH

Southwestern Railway Journal, Fort
Worth, Tex., 1907-? v.1-16 as
Texas Railway Journal, DIC,
DLC, NN, TxH, TxU

Texas Banker's Journal -- See
*Southwestern Banking and
Industry*

*Texas, Fruits, Nuts, Berries and
Flowers* -- See *Southland
Farmer*

Texas Jewish Herald -- See *Jewish
Herald-Voice*

Texas Observer, Houston, Austin,
Tex., Sept. 26, 1907-current,
DLC, TxU

Texas Railway Journal -- See
Southwestern Railway Journal

Texas Realty Journal, Houston,
Tex., 1907-July 1914? DLC, Tx,
TxH

Uncle Remus's Home Magazine -- See
Uncle Remus's Magazine

Uncle Remus's Magazine, Atlanta,
Ga., 1907-13. Supersedes *Sunny
South*, 1907. Absorbed *Home
Magazine*, May 1908. May
1908-July 1909 as *Uncle Remus's,
the Home Magazine*, Aug.
1909-1913 as *Uncle Remus's Home
Magazine*, DLC, GA, GU, NN, NcD,
OO

Uncle Remus's, the Home Magazine
-- See *Uncle Remus's Magazine*

The Union Magazine, New Orleans,
La., 1907-?

Virginia Journal of Education,
Richmond, Va., Oct. 1907-? CtY,
DE, DLC, NN, NcD, NcU, Vi, ViU

Watson's Jeffersonian Magazine,
Atlanta, Ga., Jan. 1907-17.
Absorbed *The Taylor-Trotwood
Magazine*, Jan. 1911. As
Watson's Magazine after Feb.
1912, DLC, GA, GEU, LNHT, NN,
NcD, NcU

Watson's Magazine -- See *Watson's
Jeffersonian Magazine*

Adult Student, Nashville, Tenn.,
1908-? ViU

Carolina Union Farmer, Charlotte,
N.C., 1908-May 1, 1913? NcU

Evangeliumi Hirnok, Palm Bay,
Fla., 1908-current.

Florida Fruit and Produce News
  -- See *Florida Grower*

Florida Grower, Jacksonville,
  Tampa, Fla.; Raleigh, N.C.,
  1908-current. v.1-3 as *Florida
  Fruit and Produce News*. Also
  as *Florida Grower and
  Rancher*, CU, DA, ICJ, NN, OO,
  TU

Florida Grower and Rancher -- See
  Florida Grower

Florida Historical Quarterly,
  Jacksonville, Gainesville, Fla.,
  1908-current. Suspended
  1910-23, CtY, DLC, MH, N, NN,
  NcD, TxU

Georgia Agriculturist, Athens, Ga.,
  1908-? DA, GEU, GS, GU-A

Georgia Education Journal, Macon,
  Atlanta, Ga., May 1908-? v.1-15,
  no.11 as *School and Home*, v.15,
  no.12 - v.18, no.6 as *Home,
  School and Community*, DE, G,
  GS, GU, MH, NNC-T, TxU

Hertzberg's Weekly, New Orleans,
  La., March 28, 1908-Jan.15, 1910,
  LNHT

Home Mission Herald, Atlanta, Ga.,
  Jan. 1908-Oct. 1911. United
  with *Missionary*, to form
  Missionary Survey, later
  Presbyterian Survey, CtY-D,
  NcMHi, VRT

Home, School and Community -- See
  Georgia Education Journal

*Lookout, A Newspaper Devoted to
  Society, Art and Literature*,
  Chattanooga, Tenn., 1908-?
  DLC, MoS, NN

Mathematics Teacher, Herndon, Va.,
  1908-current, KU, MoS, FU, CLU,
  DLC, MB

*National Eclectic Medical
  Association Quarterly*, Pompano
  Beach, Fla., 1908-?

Pan Pipes of Sigma Alpha Iota,
  Sarasota, Fla., 1908-current

The Pioneer, New Orleans, La.,
  1908-? LNHT

Poultry Science, College Station,
  Tex., 1908-current, TU, DLC,
  MdU, PU, OU, OkS

Presbyterian of the South,
  Richmond, Va., 1908-current,
  DLC, ViU, NN, OO

Primary Teacher, Nashville, Tenn.,
  1908-17, GEU

School and Home -- See *Georgia
  Education Journal*

*Southeastern Drug/Southern
  Pharmaceutical Journal* -- See
  Southern Pharmacy Journal

Southern Advertising Journal,
  Richmond, Va., Dec. 1908-Nov.
  1909, DLC

Southern Medical Journal,
  Nashville, Tenn.; Birmingham,
  Ala., 1908-current, DLC, DSG,
  N, NNN, NcD, NcU, TU-M, VRM

Southern Pharmacy Journal,
  Dallas, Tex.; Atlanta, Ga.,
  1908-current. Formed by merger
  of *Southern Pharmaceutical
  Journal* and *Southeastern Drug
  Journal*. Also as *Southeastern
  Drug/Southern Pharmaceutical
  Journal*, DA, DSI, MnU, N, TxU,
  NNN

Southwestern Judaist, Dallas, Tex.,
  1908-? NN

Texas Carpenter, Dallas, Tex.,
  1908-? TxH

Virginia Magazine, Lynchburg, Va.,
  Dec. 1908-Mar. 1909? Vi

*Word and Work; a monthly magazine
  whose purpose is to declare the
  whole counsel of God*. New
  Orleans, La., 1908-15? LNHT

American Journal of Agricultural Economics, Lexington, Ky., 1909-current

American Motorist, Washington, D.C.; Richmond, Falls Church, Va., Apr. 1909-Sept. 1930, DA, DLC, IU, NN, MoS

Arkansas State Rice Journal and Farmer -- See *Rice*

The Athenaeum, A Magazine for Jewish Homes, New Orleans, La., 1909?-1915? LNHT, NNC, NN, DCU, NjP

Carolina Churchman, Raleigh, Greensboro, N.C., 1909-current, NcU

Church of God Evangel, Cleveland, Tenn., 1909-current, DLC, KyLxCB

Coca-Cola Bottler, Atlanta, Ga., 1909-current,

College of the Bible Quarterly -- See *Lexington Theological Quarterly*

Dixie Philatelist, Shreveport, La., Dec. 1909-Apr. 1911, NNCo

The Down Homer, Elizabeth City, N.C., 1909-Sept. 1912, NcD

El Paso County Medical Society Bulletin, El Paso, Tex., 1909-16. United with *Arizona Medical Journal* to form *Southwestern Medicine*, DSG, N, NNN

Florida Review, Jacksonville, Fla., 1909-11, DLC, FJ, FPY, FU

Gulf States Banker, New Orleans, La., May 1909-June 1913. Merged into *Southern Banker*, LNHT

Jewish Record. A Weekly Magazine for Jewish Interests, Richmond, Va., Sept. 1909-Oct. 14, 1910, DLC, NN, Vi

Journal of the National Medical Association: A Quarterly Publication Devoted to the Interests of the National Medical Association and Allied Professions of Medicine, Surgery, Dentistry and Pharmacy, Tuskegee, Ala., 1909-?

Kentucky's Young Men, Louisville, Ky., 1909-30? KyLoS

Lexington Theological Quarterly, Lexington, Ky., 1909-current. Also as *College of the Bible Quarterly*, KyLxCB, KyU, NcD

Louisiana Trucker and Farmer -- See *Trucker and Farmer*

McConico's Monthly Magazine, Birmingham, Ala., 1909-? CtY, DLC

Men and Women, Memphis, Tenn., Feb. 1909-Jan. 1910, DLC, NjR

North Carolina Review, Raleigh, N.C., Oct. 1909-April 1913, NN, NcU, DLC ICU, MiU

Presbyterian Outlook, Atlanta, Ga.; Richmond, Va., 1909-current. Supersedes *Central Presbyterian* 1909-Mar. 1944 as *Presbyterian of the South*. Absorbed *Presbyterian Tribune*, 1955, DLC, NN, NcD, VRT

Rice, Carlisle, Ark., 1909-? v.1-4 as *Arkansas State Rice Journal and Farmer*, DA, IU

South Carolina Odd Fellow, Columbia, S.C., 1909-25? ScU

Southern Industrial Educational Association Quarterly Magazine, ____, ____, 1909-26, DE, IU, NN, OO

Southern Medical Association Journal, Shreveport, La., Jan.-Feb. 1909. Supersedes *Medical Recorder*. Merged into *Gulf States Journal of Medicine and Surgery* and *Mobile Medical and Surgical Journal*, DSG, MBM, NBM, NNN, NcD

Southern Philatelist, Shreveport, La., Aug. 1909-Nov. 1912, MWA, NNCo

Southern School News, Columbia, S.C., 1909-17? CtY, DE, NNC-T, ScU, ViW

Southern Scribe, a magazine about people, New Orleans, La., July 3, 1909-June 20, 1911, DLC

Southwest Farmer and Investor, San Antonio, Tex., 1909-Sept. 1920? DA

Southwest Monthly, Pulaski, Va., May-Aug. 1909? DA

Sunday School Primary Pupil, Nashville, Tenn., 1909-current, DLC, MiU

The Texas Magazine, Houston, Tex., Oct. 1909-Aug. 1913, DLC, MB, NN, Tx, TxU

Texas Methodist Historical Quarterly, Georgetown, Tex., July 1909-Jan. 1911, CtY, NN, TxH, TxU

Theological Institute, Atlanta, Ga., 1909-?

Trucker and Farmer, New Iberia, New Orleans, La., 1909-14. v.1-2 as *Louisiana Trucker and Farmer*. United with *Modern Sugar Plants* to form *Modern Farming*, DA, OrCA

Virginia Farm Journal, Richmond, Va., Sept.-Oct. 1909? Vi

Alabama Presbyterian -- See *Gulf States Presbyterian*

Baptist Intermediate Union Quarterly, Nashville, Tenn., 1910-?

Citrus Fruit Grower and Gulf Coast Orchardman -- See *Gulf Coast Citrus Fruit Grower and Southern Nurseryman*

Commercial Fertilizer -- See *Commercial Fertilizer and Plant Food Industry*

Commercial Fertilizer and Plant Food Industry, Atlanta, Ga., 1910-? As *Commercial Fertilizer*, 1910-32, DA, NN, NcRS, OrCA

Dixie, Jacksonville, Fla., Dec. 3, 1910-Dec. 1917, FU, NN

Gulf Coast Citrus Fruit Grower and Southern Nurseryman, Houston, Tex., Dec. 1910-Feb. 1912. 1910-Feb. 1911 as *Citrus Fruit Grower and Gulf Coast Orchardman*, DA, DLC, TxH

Gulf States Farmer -- See *Woman's Home Review*

Gulf States Presbyterian, Birmingham, Ala., 1910-14? 1910-11 as *Alabama Presbyterian*, NcMHi, PPPrHi, TxU, VRT

Hunter's Magazine of Frontier History, Border Tragedy, Pioneer Achievement, Carlsbad, Tex., Nov. 1910-June 1912? DLC, TxU

Landscape Architecture, Boston, Mass.; Louisville, Ky.,1910-current

Missions in Georgia, Savannah, Ga., 1910-16, NNG

Modern Paint & Coatings, Atlanta, Ga., 1910-current

Modern Sugar Planter, New
Orleans, La., 1910-1913.
Absorbed *Sugar Planters'
Journal*, Dec. 1910. United with
Trucker and Farmer to form
Modern Farming, DA, DLC, LNHT

New South Baker, Atlanta, Ga.,
1910-? NN

North Carolina Churchman,
Raleigh, N.C., 1910-? NNG, Nc,
NcU

*North Carolina High School
Bulletin*, Chapel Hill, N.C.,
1910-17. Superseded by *High
School Journal*, DE, DLC, N,
NcU, TxU

Pan-American Review, New Orleans,
La., 1910-June 1916, LNHT

Plating and Surface Finishing,
Winter Park, Fla., 1910-current,
DLC, IU, MiU, NN

Rural Educator, Jonesboro, Ark.,
1910-16? DA, KMK, OO

Southern Architectural Review,
Houston, Tex., 1910-11? TxH

*Southern Good Roads. A monthly
magazine devoted to highway
and street improvement*,
Lexington, N.C., 1910-20.
Sept.-Dec. 1918 not published,
DLC, N,NN, NcU, TU, Vi

Texas Tradesman, Houston, Tex.,
1910-June 1913, DA, TxH

*Woman's Era, A Magazine of
Inspiration for the Modern
Woman*, New Orleans, La., Feb.
1910-Jan. 1911? LNHT, Louisiana
State Museum Library

Woman's Home Review, New Orleans,
La., 1910-July 1928. v.1-13,
no.5 as *Gulf States Farmer*,
v.13, no.6 - v.14, no.2 as
*Woman's Home Review and Gulf
States Farmer*. Merged into
Home Circle, DA, IU

*Woman's Home Review and Gulf
States Farmer* -- See *Woman's
Home Review*

Boy's Life, Dallas-Fort Worth,
Irving, Tex., 1911-current

Christian Education Magazine --
See *Church and Campus*

Christian Education Monthly   --
See *Church and Campus*

Church and Campus, Nashville,
Tenn., 1911-? Also as *Christian
Education Monthly*, and as
Christian Education Magazine,
CtY, DE, NN, NcD, TNG

Church Herald, Saint Augustine,
Pensacola, Fla., Nov.
1911-Feb./Mar. 1919, FPY

Farmer-Stockman, Oklahoma City,
Okla.; Dallas, Tex.,
1911-current, CU, DA, OkU, TxCM

The Foundation, Atlanta, Ga.,
1911-?

*Journal of the Medical Association
of Georgia*, Atlanta, Ga.,
1911-current, DLC, DSG, GEU,
GU, InU, NBM, NcD

Latin America, New Orleans, La.,
Mar. 1911-Apr. 1916, LNHT, MH,
NN, OrU

*Magazine of Antique Firearms. A
Monthly Periodical Devoted to
the History of Firearms*,
Athens, Tenn., Apr. 1911-Aug.
1912? LNHT, NN

*Mercurio, revista mensual Instrada
de' actualidades ciencias,
artes, critica, viajes, politica,
industrias, modes, etc.* New
Orleans, La., 1911-27, LN, LNHT

Missionary Survey -- See
Presbyterian Survey

Missionary Voice -- See *World
Outlook*

Mississippi Educational Advance,
Jackson, Miss., May 1911-?   DE,
ICU, MsSM, MsU

Mississippi Visitor, Jackson, Miss.,
Oct. 1911-Oct. 1940, NcMHi, VRT

Neustros Ninos, El Paso, Tex.,
1911-current.

New World Outlook -- See *World
Outlook*

Presbyterian Survey, Richmond,
Va., Nov. 1911-current.   Formed
by union of *Missionary,* and
Mission Herald, 1911-24 as
Missionary Survey, DLC, NcD,
VRT, ViU

South Carolina State Magazine,
Aiken, S.C., Jan.-May 1911, DLC,
ScU

Southern Hotel, Atlanta, Ga.,
1911-13?   DLC

Southern Missioner, Lawrenceville,
Va., 1911-21, CtY, OO, WHi

*The Southern Patriot, and The
Southern Scribe,* New Orleans,
La., 1911?   LNHT

Southern Textile Bulletin,
Charlotte, N.C., 1911-?   Ct,
DLC, NN, NcRS, NcU

Star and Lamp, Charlotte, N.C.,
1911-current, DLC, NN, NcU,
TxH, TxU

Textile Bulletin -- See *Southern
Textile Bulletin*

Westminister Magazine, Oglethorpe,
Ga., 1911-Spring 1939, MoK, TxU,
ViU

World Outlook, Nashville, Tenn.,
1911-?   1911-32 as *Missionary
Voice,* currently as *New World
Outlook,* of New York.   CtY-D,
DLC, NcD, TxDaM, TxU

Alumni Review, Chapel Hill, N.C.,
1912-current, NcU

Arkansas Engineer, Fayetteville,
Ark., 1912-13, n.s. 1921-current,
ArU

Arkansas Fruit and Farms, Fort
Smith, Ark., 1912-16?   v.1-2 as
Ozark Produce Journal, v.3-5
as *Ozark Fruit and Farms,* DA,
ICJ

Baptist Progress, Dallas, Tex.,
1912-current, KyLoS, PCA, TxFS

The Challenge, New Orleans, La.,
1912-Jan. 1913, LNHT

East Tennessee Farmer -- See
*Tennessee Farmer, and Southern
Stockman*

The Ensign, Raleigh, N.C., 1912-?

Farmers' Fireside Bulletin,
Arlington, Tex., 1912-?   DA,
PPAN

Good Words, Atlanta, Ga., 1912-Apr.
1938.   Superseded by *Atlantian,*
CtY, ScU

High School Quarterly -- See
*School and College; Dedicated
to the Interests of the Schools
and Colleges of Georgia*

Kentucky Druggist, Louisville, Ky.,
1912-26.   Superseded by *J.K.P.A.*

Kentucky Law Journal, Lexington,
Ky., 1912-current, CtY-L, DLC,
KyU, Mi, N, NcD-L, NcU, TxU

Kentucky Trotting Record,
Lexington, Ky., Oct. 1912-Nov.
1913.   Supersedes *Stock Farms*
Merged into *Horse Journal,* DLC

Modern Druggist, New Orleans, La.,
1912-?   NBM, NNN

The New Citizen, New Orleans, La.,
1912-14?   LNHT, Louisiana State
Museum Library

New South, Dallas, Tex., Jan.
1912–May 1913? CLSU

Ozark Fruit and Farms -- See
Arkansas Fruit and Farms

Ozark Produce Journal -- See
Arkansas Fruit and Farms

Poultry News, Dallas, Tex.,
1912–Apr. 1936, NN

*School and College; Dedicated to
the Interests of the Schools and
Colleges of Georgia*, Athens,
Ga., Oct. 1912–June 1937.
v.1–24 as *High School
Quarterly*, CtY, DE, G, GU, NcD,
NcU

Southern Medical Bulletin,
Birmingham, Ala., 1912–? Later
as *Southern Medicine*, DA, NN,
Vi, CtY, VR, ViU

Southern Medicine -- See *Southern
Medical Bulletin*

Southwestern Horticulturist, Fort
Worth, Tex., 1912–13, DA

*Tennessee Agriculture; A Magazine
Devoted to the Conservation and
Development of the Agricultural
Interests of Tennessee*,
Nashville, Tenn., May 1912–Dec.
1922, DA, DLC, NcRS, T, TU

*Tennessee Farmer, and Southern
Stockfarm*, Knoxville, Tenn.,
Sept. 21, 1912–Aug. 30, 1918?
v.1–6 as *East Tennessee
Farmer*. Merged into
*Progressive Farmer and
Southern Ruralist*, DA, NcD

Terrazzo Topics, Alexandria, Va.,
1912–current. Formerly as
Terrazzo Trends

Terrazzo Trends -- See *Terrazzo
Topics*

Texas Hotel News -- See *Texas
Hotel and Catering News*

Texas Hotel and Catering News,
Dallas, San Antonio, Tex., 1912–?
v.1–26 as *Texas Hotel News*, DLC

La Trompeta, Corpus Christi, Tex.,
1912–?

Vaughan's Family Visitor,
Lawrenceburg, Tenn., 1912–?

*Virginia Federation of Labor
Journal*, Richmond, Va., Jan.
1912–June 1913, DL, MdBJ

Alcalde, Austin, Tex.,
1913–current, MoU, Tx, TxU

Arkansas, Fayetteville, Ark., Feb.
1913–Apr. 1920.

Arkansas Teacher, Conway, Ark.,
1913–22. United with the
association's *Journal* to form
Journal of Arkansas Education,
ArU, DE, IU

Carolina and the Southern Cross,
Kinston, N.C., Mar. 1913–Aug.
1914, DLC, NN, Nc, NcD

Church Herald, Charleston, S.C.,
1913–? NNG

Dixie Druggist, Hickory, N.C.,
April 1913? NNN, NcU

Gulf Coast Lumberman Houston,
Tex., 1913–current. Also as
*Gulf Coast Lumberman &
Building Material Distributor*,
DA, ICJ, TxH, TxU

*Gulf Coast Lumberman & Building
Material Distributor* -- See *Gulf
Coast Lumberman*

Hotel and Travel, Atlanta, Ga.,
1913–?

Louisiana School Work -- See
Southern School Work

*North Carolina Live Stock
Association Report*, _____, N.C.,
1913–17? AzU, DA, WU

Scouting Magazine New York, N.Y.;
Dallas, Tex., 1913-current, CtY,
DLC, NN, PP, Tx

*Sky-Land; Stories of Picturesque
North Carolina*, Charlotte, N.C.,
1913-15? DLC, MoS, OCL

Social Service Quarterly, Raleigh,
N.C., Apr. 1913-17, Nc, NcU

South Carolina Christian,
Charleston, S.C., 1913-? KyLxCB

Southern Bench and Bar Review
Jackson, Miss., 1913. Merged
into *Lawyer and Banker*, NNC,
ICU, MiU-L, CLL

*Southern Christian Courier; A
Voice for Christian Unity*,
Jackson, Miss., 1913-? KyLxCB

Southern School Work, Alexandria,
Zachary, La., 1913-June 1922.
1913-Feb. 1918 as *Louisiana
School Work*, DE, LU, OrU

*Southern Texas Truck Grower's
Journal*, San Antonio, Tex.,
1913-Oct. 1915, DA

Southern Woman's Magazine
Nashville, Tenn., May 1913-Dec.
1918, TN, TU, TxU, ViU

*Sunday; the Magazine for the
Lord's Day*, Atlanta, Ga.,
1913-current.

Tennessee Banker, Knoxville,
Nashville, Tenn., 1913-current,
IU

Texaco Star, Houston, Tex.,
1913-current, CtY, DLC, TxH,
TxU

Texas and Pacific Magazine Dallas,
Tex.; New Orleans, La., Aug.
1913-Nov. 1915? DBRE, LNHT

Texas Commercial News Sugar Land,
Tex., 1913-Feb. 1933, NN, Tx,
TxU

Truck and Chick, Tallahassee, Fla.,
1913-Mar. 1915, DA

*University of Virginia Alumni
News*, Charlottesville, Va.,
1913-current, ViU

*Virginia Folk-Lore Society
Bulletin*, Richmond, Va., 1913-24,
CtY, MH, NN, ViU

Virginia Law Review,
Charlottesville, Va.,
1913-current, CtY-L, DLC, N,
NcD-L, NcU, Vi, VRU

*Virginia State Horticultural
Society. Virginia Fruit*,
Bedford, Va., 1913-? DA, OCL,
Vi, ViU

Alchemist, Gainesville, Ga., 1914-?

The Cattleman, Fort Worth, Tex.,
1914-current, DA, IU, IdU, NN,
TxU, ViU

Dallas Medical Journal, Dallas,
Tex., 1914-current, CSt-L, DSG,
NNN, PPC, TxU-M

*Federal Reserve Bank of Richmond
Economic Review*, Richmond, Va.,
1914-current. Formerly as
*Federal Reserve Bank of
Richmond Monthly Review*

*Federal Reserve Bank of Richmond
Monthly Review* -- See *Federal
Reserve Bank of Richmond
Economic Review*

*Florida Medical Association
Journal*, Jacksonville, Fla.,
1914-current, DSG, NNN

Home Mission Herald, Louisville,
Ky., Apr. 1914-17, NcMHi

Jewish Monitor, Fort Worth, Dallas,
Tex., 1914-29? OCH

Kappa Alpha Psi Journal,
Nashville, Tenn., 1914-?

Mississippi Banker, Jackson, Miss., 1914-current, CtY, MsU, NN

Modern Farming, New Orleans, La., Feb. 1914-Apr. 1, 1929. Formed by union of *Trucker and Farmer* and *Modern Sugar Planter*. Merged into *Southern Ruralist*, DA

Music Educator's Journal, Madison, Wis.; Ann Arbor, Mich.; Herndon, Va., Sept. 1914-current, DE, DLC, KU, NN, NcD, WU

Negro Farmer -- See *The Negro Farmer and Messenger*

The Negro Farmer and Messenger, Tuskegee, Ala., 1914-18. v.1-2 as *Negro Farmer*, DA, IU

New Southern Citizen, New Orleans, La., Oct. 1914-May 1917, DLC, LNHT

Orange and Black, Barbourville, Ky., 1914-?

Southern Bulletin, Atlanta, Ga., 1914-? DBRE

Southern Farm and Dairy, Bryan, Tex., 1914-15? DA, IU

Southern Farmer, Baton Rouge, La., 1914-15? DA

Southern News Bulletin, Atlanta, Ga., 1914-Oct. 1931, DHU, DIC, T

Southwestern Retailer, Dallas, Tex., 1914-Feb. 1935, TxU

The Teachers' Forum, New Orleans, La., 1914-17.

Texas Laundry and Dry Cleaning Journal, Austin, Tex., 1914-?

Texas Municipalities -- See *Texas Town & City*

Texas Nativist, Bryan, Tex., Jan. 1914-Dec. 1915, TxU

Texas Town & City, Fort Worth, Austin, Tex., March 1914-current. 1914-58 as *Texas Municipalities*, CtY, DLC, NN, NcD, NcU, Tx, TxU

Alabama Farm Facts, Montgomery, Ala., 1915-23.

American Fruit Grower, Charlottesville, Va., Sept. 1915-Sept. 1917. Absorbed *Fruit Grower* Sept. 1917. United with *Green's Fruit Grower*, Oct. 1917, to form *Green's American Fruit Grower*, later *American Fruit Grower* of Chicago, DA, NN, OO

Carolina Chemist, Chapel Hill, N.C., Jan. 1915-May 1922, DLC, NcD, NcU

Carolina Journal of Pharmacy, Chapel Hill, N.C., 1915-current, NNN, Nc, NcU

The Cumberland Flag, Loudon, Tenn.; Huntsville, Ala., 1915-current, NcMHi

Dallas World, Granite City, Ill.; Dallas, Tex., 1915-40? KyLoS

Dixie Highway, Chattanooga, Tenn., Sept. 1915-25? KyL, OC, OCHP

Drug and Allied Industries, Washington, D.C.; Atlanta, Ga., 1915-monthly. Also as *Proprietary Drugs*, and as *Standard Remedies*, DA, ICJ, N, LNL

Facts and Figures; An Authoritative Food Trade Magazine, Jacksonville, Fla., 1915-? NN

Forest and Farms, Knoxville, Tenn., Apr.-July 1915. Merged into *East Tennessee Farmer*, later *Tennessee Farmer and Southern Stockman*, DA

Journal of Speech Education -- See *Quarterly Journal of Speech*

Journal of the Association of Official Analytical Chemists, Arlington, Va., 1915-current

Kentucky High School Quarterly, Lexington, Ky., 1915-? CtY, DE, N, NcU

Labor Review, Devoted to the Interests of Organized Labor, Augusta, Ga., 1915-? DL, GEU, IU, LNHT, NcD

The Lodestar, New Orleans, La., Jan. 1915, LNHT

Louisiana Engineer, New Orleans, La., Feb. 1915-current. 1915-55 as the society's *Proceedings*, CtY, DA, ICJ, ICW, LN, LNHT, NN

Matrix, Austin, Tex., 1915-?

Musicale -- See *Southwestern Musicale*

National Baptist Voice, Nashville, Tenn., 1915-? DHU, PCA

OMI Mission Magazine -- See *Oblate World and Voice of Hope*

Oblate World and Voice of Hope, San Antonio, Tex., 1915-current. Formerly as *OMI Mission Magazine*

Proprietary Drugs -- See *Drug and Allied Industries*

Quarterly Journal of Public Speaking -- See *Quarterly Journal of Speech*

Quarterly Journal of Speech, Falls Church, Annandale, Va., Apr. 1915-current. Also as *Quarterly Journal of Public Speaking* and as *Journal of Speech Education*, CtY, DLC, Mi, MnU, NN, NcD, ViU

Rebellion, New Orleans, La., Mar. 1915-June 1916, LNHT

Rice University Studies; Writings in All Scholarly Disciplines, Houston, Tex., 1915-?

Richmond College Historical Papers, Richmond, Va., 1915-17, CtY, DLC, NN, TxU

SI-DE-KA Magazine, Arlington, Va., 1915-current.

Southern Florist -- See *Southern Florist and Nurseryman*

Southern Florist and Nurseryman, Fort Worth, Tex., 1915-current. v.1-14, no.6 as *Southern Florist*, DA, IU, NN, Tx, TxU

Southeast Live Stock, Columbus, Ga., 1915-Oct. 1923, DA

Southern Miscellany, a monthly devoted to literature in the South, Montgomery, Ala., Nov. 1915-Jan. 1916, MWA, LNHT, CSmH, GU

Southwest Review, Austin, Dallas, Tex., 1915-current. v.1-9 as *Texas Review*, absorbed *Reviewer*, April 1926, CU, DLC, NN, NcD, NcU, Tx, TxU

Southwestern Hospital Reporter, Houston, Tex., 1915-? DSG, MBM, TxU

Southwestern Musicale, Dallas, Arlington, Tex., 1915-May 1933. v.1-15, no.9 as *Musicale*. Superseded by *Southwestern Musician*, Dec. 1934, MA, NN, TxH, TxU

The Southwestern Musician and Texas Music Educator, Lubbock, Austin, Tex., 1915-current. Supersedes *Southwestern Musicale*, absorbed *Texas Music Educator*, 1954, DLC, NN, TxCM, TxH

Southwestern Oil Journal, Fort Worth, Tex., 1915-July 29, 1921. Merged into *Oil Gazette*, DGS, NNC, TxH

Standard Remedies -- See *Drug and Allied Industries*

Tennessee Historical Magazine, Nashville, Tenn., Mar.1915-26, n.s. Oct. 30-Jan. 1937, CtY, DLC, M, NN, NcD, NcU, T, TU, TxU

Texas Mathematics Teachers' Bulletin, Austin, Tex., 1915-? CtY, DLC, N, NN, TxH, TxU

Texas Review-- See *Southwest Review*

Vanderbilt Alumnus, Nashville, Tenn., 1915-current.

Virginia Education Association Quarterly, _____, Va., Jan. 1915-Jan. 1, 1918? DE, Vi, ViU

Virginia State Teachers Quarterly, Richmond, Va., 1915-18, Vi

Alabama Markets Journal, _____, Ala., 1916-? CtY, DA, DLC, ICJ, NN

Anvil, Fort Worth, Tex., Apr.-July 1916, TxU

Beekeepers' Item -- See *Modern Beekeeping*

The Blood-Horse, Lexington, Ky., Aug. 1916-current. v.1-4 as *Kentucky Thoroughbred Association Bulletin*, v.5-12 as *Thoroughbred Horse*, v.12, no.6-8 as *Thoroughbred*, DA, DLC, KyU, LU, NN

Divine Word Messenger, Bay Saint Louis, Miss., 1916-?

Federal Bank of Atlanta Economic Review, Atlanta, Ga., 1916-current. Formerly as *Federal Reserve Bank of Atlanta Monthly Review*, CtY, DLC, GEU, NN, NcD, NcU

Federal Reserve Bank of Atlanta Monthly Review -- See *Federal Bank of Atlanta Economic Review*

Genetics, Princeton, N.J.; Austin, Tex.; Chapel Hill, N.C., 1916-current, CtY, DA, IU, NN, NcD, NcU, TxDN

Georgia Builder, _____, Ga., Mar. 1916-42. Superseded by *Georgia on the March*, v. 1-19, no. 7 as *City Builder*, GEU, GU

Georgia Grocer, Atlanta, Ga., 1916-current.

Georgia On The March -- See *Georgia Builder*

Gulf Coast Grower -- See *Gulf States Grower*

Gulf Coast Oil News -- See *World Oil*

Gulf States Grower, Mobile, Ala., March 1916-Aug. 1917? v.1-2, no.4 as *Gulf Coast Grower*, DA

Kentucky Magazine, Lexington, Ky., Nov. 1916-Jan. 1918, ICU, KyL, KyU, WHi

Kentucky Thoroughbred Association Bulletin -- See *The Blood-Horse*

La Luz Apostolica, San Antonio, Tex., 1916-?

Marine Corps Gazette, Quantico, Va., Mar. 1916-current, CtY, DLC, MoU, NN

The Mississippi Valley Voice, New Orleans, La., 1916-? LNHT

Modern Beekeeping, New Braunfels, Tex., 1916-? 1916-July 1946 as *Bee-keepers' Item*, DA, NN, NcRS, TxU

Modern Truck Grower, Wilmington, N.C., Jan. 11-Apr. 1, 1916? DA

Oil Weekly -- See *World Oil*

Rural Kentuckian, Lexington, Ky., 1916-22, KyU

San Antonian; Voice of the Chamber of Commerce, San Antonio, Tex., 1916-?

Southern Hospital Record, Atlanta, Ga., 1916-19? CSt-L, DSG, NNN

Southern Law Quarterly, New Orleans, La., 1916-18, CSt, CU, Ct, DLC, LNHT, N

Southwestern Medicine, El Paso, Tex., 1916-? DSG, NNN, TxU-M

Southwestern Mineral Resources -- See *Texas Industrial Resources*

Southwestern Resources -- See *Texas Industrial Resources*

Texas Industrial Resources, Austin, Tex., Nov. 1916-Sept. 1932. v.1-2, no.4 as *Texas Mineral Resources*; v.2, no.5 - v.4, no.6 as *Southwestern Mineral Resources*; v.4, no.7 - v.7, no.12 as *Southwestern Resources*, NN, PPAN, TxH, TxU

Texas Mineral Resources -- See *Texas Industrial Resources*

Texas Outlook, Fort Worth, Austin, Tex., 1916-current, DE, NN, OCl, Tx, TxU

Thoroughbred -- See *The Blood-Horse*

Thoroughbred Horse -- See *The Blood-Horse*

Tulane Law Review, New Orleans, La., 1916-current, CtY-L, DLC, LNHT, LU-L, M, N, NcD-L, NcU

Virginia Pharmacist, Richmond, Va., Sept. 1916-current, DLC, MBM, NcU, Vi, ViU

World Oil, Houston, Tex., 1916-current. Formerly as *Oil Weekly*, and as *Gulf Coast Oil News*, CLU, DLC, LU, NN, MnU, TxH, TxU

Advocate -- See *Pentecostal Holiness Advocate*

Alabama Dental Association Journal, Birmingham, Mobile, Ala., Sept. 1917-current. 1917-Apr. 1958 as the Association's Bulletin, AU-M, DLC, DSG, NNN, NcU-H

American Baptist and Commoner -- See *Baptist and Commoner*

Arkansas Banker, Little Rock, Ark., Apr. 1917-current, CtY, IU, NN, TxU

Arkansas Educational Association Journal, Little Rock, Ark., 1917-22. United with *Arkansas Teacher*, to form *Journal of Arkansas Education*, DLC

Automotive Executive, McLean, Va., 1917-current. Absorbed *Cars and Trucks*, 1979. Formerly as *NADA Magazine*

Baptist and Commoner, Little Rock, Ark., May 1917-? Supersedes *Baptist*. v.68, no.1-3 as *American Baptist and Commoner*, DLC, TxU

Baptist Fundamentalist -- See *The Fundamentalist*

Baptist Student, Fort Worth, Tex., 1917-20? KyLoS, LNHT, TxFS

The Bells, Belton, Tex., 1917-current.

Cars & Trucks, McLean, Va.,
1917-79. Absorbed by
Automotive Executive in 1979.

Dallas Spirit, Dallas, Tex., Mar.
17-31, 1917?   TxU

Elastomerics, New York, N.Y.;
Atlanta, Ga., 1917-current.
Formerly as *Rubber Age and
Tire News* and as *Rubber Age*,
DLC, GAT, MnU, NN, OkU

Farmers' Union Messenger, Fort
Worth, Tex., 1917-?   DA, IU

Florida Buggist -- See *Florida
Entomologist*

*Florida Engineering Society
Journal*, Tallahassee,
Gainesville, Fla., 1917-current,
DLC, F, FMU, FU

Florida Entomologist, Gainesville,
Fla., 1917-current.   v.1-3 as
Florida Buggist, CtY, DA, DLC,
FTS, FU, NNM, NcD, NN

Florida Newspaper News -- See
*Florida Newspaper News and
Radio Digest*

*Florida Newspaper News and Radio
Digest*, Tampa, Fla., 1917-?   Also
as *Florida Newspaper News*,
FPY, FU

The Fundamentalist, Fort Worth,
Wichita Falls, Tex.; Orlando,
Fla., 1917-?   v.1-10 as
Searchlight.   Also as *Baptist
Fundamentalist*, KyLoS, MnHi,
TMG, TxU

Georgia Historical Quarterly,
Savannah, Ga., 1917-current,
CtY, DLC, ICU, NN, TxH, TxU,
ViBlbV

*Gulf Marine Register and
Shipbuilding Review*, New
Orleans, La., 1917-Oct. 1923,
MoS, NN, TxU, LNHT

*Journal of the Alabama Dental
Association*, Mobile, Ala.,
1917-current, AU-M, DLC, DSG,
NNN, NcU-H

Labor World, Chattanooga, Tenn.,
1917-current, DL, NIC, NcU

Leatherneck Magazine, Quantico,
Va., 1917-current, Vi, ViU

Linen Supply News, Miami Beach,
Hallendale, Fla., 1917-current,
later as *Textile Rental
Magazine*.

Louisiana Historical Quarterly,
New Orleans, La., 1917-?   CtY,
DLC, ICJ, LNHT, N, NN, NcD,
NcU, TxU

Mental Hygiene, Arlington, Va.,
1917-?

NASSP Bulletin, Herndon, Va.,
1917-current.

North Carolina Beekeeper, Raleigh,
N.C., 1917-24, DA, NIC-A, NcRS,
NcU

Pentecostal Holiness Advocate,
Franklin Springs, Ga., 1917-?
Also as *Advocate*, DLC, GU, NNUT

Pioneer Magazine of Texas -- See
Texas Pioneer

Rubber Age -- See *Elastomerics*

Rubber Age and Tire News -- See
Elastomerics

Searchlight -- See *The
Fundamentalist*

Southwestern Evangel, Seminary
Hill, Tex., 1917-July 1931.
v.1-8 as *Southwestern Journal
of Theology*, ICU, NjPT, OO,
PCA, TxU

Southwestern Journal of Theology
-- See *Southwestern Evangel*

Teachers' Music Sentinel, Hudson,
N.C., Sept. 1917-May 1919, DLC

Tennessee Alumnus, Knoxville,
Tenn., 1917-current.

Texas Oil News, San Marcos, Tex.,
1917-?

Texas Pioneer, San Antonio, Tex.,
1917-Apr./May 1931? v.1-5 as
Pioneer Magazine of Texas, v.6
as *Texasland* DLC, Tx, TxH, TxU

Texasland -- See *Texas Pioneer*

Textile Rental Magazine -- See
Linen Supply News

University of Alabama News.
University of Alabama, Ala.,
1917-current.

Alabama Defense Record, _____,
Ala., 1918, DLC, ICU, IU, WHi

Appalachian Appeal, Bristol, Va.,
Nov. 1918-Nov. 1930, NcMHi, VRT

Arkansas Writer, Little Rock,
Ark., Dec. 1918-Apr. 1922, ArU

Extension News, Blacksburg, Va.,
1918-? Later as *Extension
Service News*, ViBlbV

Extension Service News -- See
Extension News

Head, Heart, Hands and Health,
Blacksburg, Va., 1918-current,
ViBlbV, ViU

High School Journal, Chapel Hill,
N.C., 1918-current, DE, DLC, N,
NcD, NcU, TNG, ViU

*Hispania; A Journal Devoted to the
Interests of the Teaching of
Spanish and Portuguese*,
Stanford, Calif.; University,
Miss., 1918-current, CtY, DLC,
MiU, NN, NcD, NcU

*The Hispanic American Historical
Review*, Baltimore, Md.; Durham,
N.C., 1918-current, CtY, DLC,
NN, NcD, NcU

Intermediate Leader, Nashville,
Tenn., 1918-?

Joe's Bulletin, Luthersville, Ga.,
1918-current.

*Journal of the Patent Office
Society*, Washington, D.C.;
Arlington, Va., 1918-current.
CtY-L, DLC, IU, NN, NcD-L

*Southern Marine Journal; the
Marine and Shipping Journal
of the South*, Houston, Tex.,
1918-22? PP, TxH

*Southwest and Texas Water Works
Journal*, Temple, Tex.,
1918-current. Also as *Southwest
Water Works Journal*, MH, NN,
TxCM, TxH, TxU

Southwest Water Works Journal --
See *Southwest and Texas Water
Works Journal*

Square and Compass, Clearwater,
Fla., 1918-?

*Tennessee Extension Review;
Agriculture and Home
Economics*, Knoxville, Tenn., May
10, 1918-? C, DA, DLC, TU

Virginia PTA Bulletin, Richmond,
Va., 1918-current, Vi, ViW

American Cotton News, Atlanta, Ga.,
1919-21, DA

Alabama Farmer, Auburn, Ala.,
1919-? AAP, DA, NbU

Alabama Food Merchants Journal
Montgomery, Ala., 1919-current.

American Gas Association Monthly,
Easton, Pa.; Arlington, Va.,
1919-current, CtY, DLC, IU, NN,
NjP, TU

Arkansas Legionnaire, Little Rock, Ark., 1919-?

Blue Ridge Voice, Nashville, Tenn., 1919-27, LNHT, NcU, TU, ViU

Communique, Hollywood, Fla., 1919-?

Cotton Facts, Raleigh, N.C., Nov. 14, 1919-Apr. 3, 1920. Merged into *Cotton News*, DA

Cotton Ginner, Dallas, Tex., Aug. 1919-Jan. 1922? Superseded by *Cotton Ginners' Journal*, DA

Cotton News, Saint Matthews, S.C., 1919-Nov. 1926? DA, NN

Dixie Beekeeper, Waycross, Ga., Apr. 1919-Mar. 1930. United with *Beekeepers' Item*, to form *Beekeepers' Item and Dixie Beekeeper*, later *Beekeepers' Item*, DA, NcRS, OU

Ecological Society of America Bulletin, Tucson, Ariz.; Durham, N.C.; Lawrence, Kan., 1919-current, CtY, DA, NBuG, NIC

Fish and Oyster Reporter, New Orleans, La., 1919-July 1941. Merged into *Fishing Gazette*, DLC

Florida Audubon Society Bulletin, Winter Park, Fla., 1919-Mar. 1925. Superseded by *Florida Naturalist*, DA

Florida Planter, Fort Myers, Fla., 1919-? FU

Georgia Farmer and Stockman, Macon, Ga., Feb. 1919-June 1921, DA, IU

Georgia Legionnaire, Atlanta, Ga., 1919-?

Journal of Dental Research, New York, N.Y.; Houston, Tex., 1919-current, CtY, DLC, NNN, NcD, TU-M, TxU-M

Lone Star Oilman, San Antonio, Tex., Mar. 8, 1919-? TxU

Marley Musical Review -- See *Whittle Musical Review*

Merchants Journal, Montgomery, Ala., 1919-?

The Military Engineer, Washington, D.C.; Alexandria, Va., 1919-current, CtY, DLC, ICJ, IU, NN, NcRS, NjR

Mississippian; The Business Builder of the State; A Modern Industrial Magazine, Jackson, Greenville, Gulfport, Miss., Jan.-Oct. 1919? MsJS

National Drainage Journal, Marietta, Ga., June 1919-? v.1, no.1-6 as *Southern Drainage Journal*, IU

National Forum: Phi Kappa Phi Journal, Baton Rouge, La., 1919-current. AzTeS, ViBlbV

New Orleans Illustrated News, New Orleans, La., Dec. 1919-May, 1922? LNHT, Louisiana State Museum Library.

North Carolina Agricultural Educational Monthly, Raleigh, N.C., 1919-? NcU

Presbyterian Progress, Marion, S.C., Nov. 1919-Sept. 1920, NNUT, NcMHi, VRT

South Atlantic Ports, Jacksonville, Fla., June 1919-Dec. 1930, IU, LNHT, NN

South Carolina Education, Columbus, S.C., 1919-? N, NN, NcD, ScU

Southern Drainage Journal -- See *National Drainage Journal*

Southern Farm Equipment and Supply, Nashville, Tenn., 1919-197?

Southern Funeral Director,
Atlanta, Ga., 1919-1956, NN, MnU

Southern Marine Review,
Jacksonville, Fla., 1919-May
1946? Merged into *Work Boat.*
1919-Sept. 1941 as *United States
Ports,* DLC, FU

Southern Musical Review -- See
Whittle Musical Review

Southern Pine Salesman, New
Orleans, La., 1919-June 1920?
DLC

Southern Shoe Journal, Houston,
Tex., Nov. 1919-July 1920? NN

*Southland Journal; In the Interest
of Farms, Schools and Roads,*
Petersburg, Va., 1919-Jan. 21,
1921? DA

*Tennessee Dental Association
Journal* -- See *Tennessee State
Dental Association Journal*

*Tennessee State Dental Association
Journal,* Nashville, Tenn., Feb.
1919-present. Also as *Tennessee
Dental Association Journal,*
CU-M, NNN, PU, TU-M

*Tennessee State Horticultural
Society Bulletin, _____, Tenn.,*
1919-20? MAA, PPi

Tyler's Quarterly -- See *Tyler's
Quarterly Historical and
Genealogical Magazine*

*Tyler's Quarterly Historical and
Genealogical Magazine,*
Richmond, Va., July 1919-April
1952. Superseded by *Tyler's
Quarterly,* CtY, DLC, NN, NcU,
ViU, ViBlbV

United States Ports -- See
Southern Marine Review

Virginia Publisher and Printer,
Richmond, Va., Oct.
1919-current. Later as
Virginia's Press, DLC, NN, Vi,
ViBlbV, ViU

Virginia's Press -- See *Virginia
Publisher and Printer*

Whittle Musical Review, Dallas,
Tex., Oct. 1919-May 1928. v.1,
no.1-7 as *Marley Musical
Review.* v.1, no.8-11 as
Southern Musical Review, TxU

Alabama School Progress,
Montgomery, Ala., Mar. 1920-Oct.
1921. Merged into *Alabama
School Journal,* MH

Chase Magazine, Lexington, Ky.,
1920-current.

Citrus Industry Magazine, Tampa,
Bartow, Fla., 1920-current, DLC,
FU, NN

The Civitan Magazine, Birmingham,
Ala., 1920-current

Ecology, Brooklyn, N.Y.; Durham,
N.C., 1920-current. Supersedes
Plant World, CtY, DLC, NN, NcD,
NcU, NjP, TxU

Florida Fisherman -- See *Florida
Fisherman and Guide*

Florida Fisherman and Guide,
Saint Petersburg, Fla.,
1920-July 1924? 1920-23 as
Florida Fisherman, FJ, FU

*Florida Industrial Record; A
Monthly Journal Devoted to the
Upbuilding of Florida,* Tampa,
Fla., Nov. 1920, FU

Florida Zephyr, Crocked Lake,
Fla., Sept.-Dec. 1920? DLC

Game and Fish Conservationist --
See *Virginia Wildlife*

Georgia Alumni Record, Athens,
Ga., 1920-current

Georgia Cotton Pool News, Atlanta, Ga., 1920-32? DA, NIC-A, NN

Gulf Ports Magazine, Galveston, Tex.; New Orleans, La., 1920-23, CtY, DLC, LN, MoS, NN, PPi

Interstate Index -- See *Pioneer*

K.E.A. Bulletin -- See *Kentucky School Journal*

K.E.A. Journal -- See *Kentucky School Journal*

Kaleidograph; A National Magazine of Poetry, Dallas, Tex., May 1920-Apr./June 1959. 1929-Apr. 1932 as *Kaleidoscope*, DLC, MH, NN, Tx, TxU

Kaleidoscope -- See *Kaleidograph*

Kentucky Music Teachers' Journal, Louisville, Ky., Nov. 1920-21? IU, KyL

Kentucky School Journal, Louisville, Ky., Dec. 1920-? Also as *K.E.A. Bulletin, K.E.A. Journal*, KyBgW, KyU, N, NcU

Master Barber and Beautician Magazine, Charlotte, N.C., 1920-?

Methodist Superintendent and His Helpers, Nashville, Tenn., 1920-24. Merged into *Worker's Council*, GEU

Miami Pictorial -- See *The Miamian*

The Miamian, Miami, Fla., 1920-72. Continued by *Miami Pictorial*, and *Miami Magazine*. Currently as *Miami/South Florida Magazine*, DLC, FU, KU

Miami/South Florida Magazine -- See *The Miamian*

Mississippi Legionnaire, Jackson, Miss., 1920-current

North Carolina Christian, Wilson, N.C., 1920-? NcD, NcU

P.G.A. Magazine -- See *Professional Golfer*

Pioneer, San Antonio, Tex., 1920-27? Also as *Interstate Index*, PP

Poultry and Eggs Marketing, Kansas City, Mo.; Gainesville, Ga., Oct. 1920-current. Formerly as *Poultry and Eggs Weekly*, DA, ICU, NN

Poultry and Eggs Weekly -- See *Poultry and Eggs Marketing*

Presbyterian Outlook, Covington, Decatur, Ga., Dec. 1920-May 1929? NcMHi

Professional Golfer, Palm Beach, Lake Park, Fla., 1920-77. As *P.G.A. Magazine*, after 1977.

Public Health Laboratory, Burlington, Vt.; Olean, N.Y.; Boiling Springs, N.C., 1920-current, DNLM, InU, MiU, PPC

The Ranch Magazine, San Angelo, Tex., 1920-current

Review of the Graphic Arts, Kissimmee, Fla., 1920-current. Formerly as *Share Your Knowledge Review*, DLC, MWA, NN

Rural Messenger, Tuskegee, Ala., 1920-24, DA

Share Your Knowledge Review -- See *Review of the Graphic Arts*

Sheep and Goat Raiser -- See *Sheep and Goat Raisers' Magazine*

Sheep and Goat Raisers' Magazine,
San Angelo, Tex., Aug. 1920-May
1941. Merged into *Southwestern
Sheep and Goat Raiser,* later
Sheep and Goat Raiser, DA, IU,
TxLT

Social Science Quarterly -- See
*Southwestern Social Science
Quarterly*

Southern Dairyman, Montgomery,
Ala., 1920-23? Some 1922
numbers as *Town and Country
Magazine,* DA

Southern Golfer, Jacksonville,
Fla., Jan. 1, 1920-Mar. 15, 1928.
1920-22 as *Southern Golfer and
Tourist.* Merged into
Metropolitan Golfer, DLC, FJ,
NN

Southern Golfer and Tourist -- See
Southern Golfer

Southern Review, Asheville, N.C.,
Jan.-Oct. 1920, DLC, MdBJ, MiU,
NN, Nc, TxU, ViU, WHi

*Southwestern Political and Social
Science Quarterly* -- See
*Southwestern Social Science
Quarterly*

*Southwestern Political Science
Quarterly* -- See *Southwestern
Social Science Quarterly*

Southwestern Purchaser, Dallas,
Tex., 1920-? NN, TxH, TxU

*Southwestern Social Science
Quarterly,* Austin, Tex., June
1920-current. Also as
*Southwestern Political Science
Quarterly,* and *Southwestern
Political and Social Science
Quarterly.* Currently as *Social
Science Quarterly,* CtY, DLC,
IU, MH, NN, NcU, TU, TxH, TxU

*Studies in Economics and
Sociology,* Lexington, Ky., Mar.
1920-23, DLC, KU, KyU, NN, NcD,
NcU

Sunday School Builder, Nashville,
Tenn., Oct. 1920-? DLC, NHC,
NjMD

Texas Co-operative News, Temple,
Tex., 1920-? DA, TxU

This is West Texas, Abilene, Tex.,
1920-current. Formerly as *West
Texas Today*

Town and Country Magazine -- See
Southern Dairyman

Virginia Conservationist -- See
Virginia Wildlife

Virginia Teacher, Harrisonburg,
Va., 1920-May 1939, DE, DLC, N,
NN, Vi, ViU

Virginia Wildlife, Richmond, Va.,
1920-current. As *Virginia
Conservationist,* until May 1922.
As *Game and Fish
Conservationist,* from May 1922
until September 1931, CU, DLC,
NN, NcD, ViBlbV, ViU

West Texas Today -- See *This Is
West Texas*

Abernathy Weekly Review,
Abernathy, Tex., 1921-current

Alabama Childhood, Montgomery,
Ala., Apr. 1921-June 1922, CU,
CtY, DLC, ICJ, IU, NNN, NcD

Alabama School Journal,
Montgomery, Ala., 1921-current,
ABS, ATT, DE, N, NcD, TxU

*American Logistics Association
Review; Magazine for
Government/Military
Marketing/Distribution/Procurement
Systems,* Washington, D.C.; Falls
Church, Va., 1921-current.
Formerly as *Quartermaster
Review,* CtY, DLC, NN, PP

Battery Man, Terre Haute, Ind.;
Largo, Fla., 1921-current, MoS,
NN, OCL

Cotton Trade Journal, New Orleans, La., 1921-?   DA, DLC, LNHT, NN

Delta Irrigation News, McAllen, Tex., July 1921-Sept. 1929. Merged with *Valley Farmer*, CU, DLC, NN

Democratic Review, Dallas, Tex., Jan.-Aug. 1921, DLC

The Double-Dealer, New Orleans, La., Jan. 1921-May 1926, DLC, LNHT, NN, NcD, NcU, TxU, ViU

Electrical Consultant, Atlanta, Ga.; Cos Cob, Conn., 1921-current

Electrical South, Atlanta, Ga., 1921-?   DLC, NN, NcRS, TxU, ViU u5. *Georgia's Health*, Atlanta, Ga., 1921-?

Home Circle, Louisville, Ky., 1921-? DGU, IU

Infantry School Quarterly -- See *Infantry; the Professional Magazine for Infantryman*

Infantry; the Professional Magazine for Infantrymen, Fort Benning, Ga., 1921-current. As *Infantry School Quarterly*, July 1947-Jan. 1957, CtY, DAL, DLC, DNW, MnU

Kentucky Grocer, Louisville, Ky., 1921-?

Lighting, East Stroudsburg, Pa.; Atlanta, Ga., 1921-?   Also as *Lighting Fixtures and Lighting*, and as *Lighting and Lamps*. Absorbed *Lamps*, Nov. 1933, DA, DLC, NN

Lighting and Lamps -- See *Lighting*

Lighting Fixtures and Lighting -- See *Lighting*

Lyric, Norfolk, Roanoke, Blacksburg, Va., 1921-current, DA, NN, NcD, ViU, ViW

Mississippi Demonstrator, Agricultural College, Miss., Aug. 1921-July 1924, Ct, DA, ICJ, IU, MsSM

The National Elementary Principal, Arlington, Va., May 1921-current. As *Principal* since Sept. 1980, CtY, DE, N, NcD, NcU, TxCaW, TxU

North Carolina Rural Life, Raleigh, N.C., Nov. 1921-June 1923. Superseded by *North Carolina Agriculture and Industry*, DA, IU, NIC-A

Occupations -- See *Personnel and Guidance Journal*

Owenwood Magazine, Fort Worth, Tex., Dec. 1921-?   TxU

Peanut Journal -- See *Peanut Journal and Nut World*

Peanut Journal and Nut World, Suffolk, Va., Nov. 1921-current. As *Peanut Journal* until 1931, DA, NN, ViU

Personnel and Guidance Journal, Easton, Pa.; Falls Church, Va., Aug. 1921-current. Also as *Vocational Guidance Magazine*, as *Occupations*, and as *The Vocational Guidance Journal*, CSt, DE, DLC, NN, NcD, ViU

Pioneer Pecan Press, San Saba, Tex., 1921-Feb. 1928. Merged into *National Nut News*, CU, DA, NN, TxU

Principal -- See *The National Elementary School Principal*

Quartermaster Review -- See *American Logistics Association Review*

The Review, Falls Church, Va., 1921-?

The Reviewer, Richmond, Va.;
Chapel Hill, N.C., Feb. 1921-Oct.
1925. Merged into *Southwest
Review*. Moved to Chapel Hill
in Dec. 1924, CtY, DLC, NN, NcD,
NcU, Vi

Scraper, Frankfort, Ky.,
1921-current

Southern Automobile Journal,
Atlanta, Ga., 1921-April 1979.
1921-Aug. 1930 as *Southern
Automotive Dealer*, DLC, NN, GS

Southern Automotive Dealer -- See
Southern Automobile Journal

Southern Methodist, Memphis,
Tenn., 1921-24, GEU, IEG

Southwestern Episcopalian,
Staunton, Va., 1921-? TxU, Vi,
ViU

Tennessee Churchman, Tullahoma,
Tenn., Sept. 1921-Nov. 1932?
TMC

*Tennessee Highways and Public
Works*, Nashville, Tenn., Oct.
1921-Apr. 1927, MiU, T, TMC, TU

Tennessee Horticulture, Knoxville,
Tenn., 1921-? N, NN, T, TU

Texas Aggie, College Station, Tex.,
1921-current

Tri-State Tobacco Grower, Raleigh,
N.C., 1921-26, IU

Virginia Dental Journal, Richmond,
Va., 1921-current. Continues
*Virginia State Dental
Association Bulletin*, DSG, IEN-D,
NNN, Vi, VRM

Virginia Guardsman, Richmond,
Va., Apr. 1921-May 31, 1939?
Suspended July 1929-Mar. 1931,
DLC, NN, Vi, ViU

Virginia Review, Chester, Va.,
1921-current

*Virginia State Dental Association
Bulletin*, Richmond, Va., 1921-?
Continued by *Virginia Dental
Journal*, DSG, ICJ, NNN, PU, Vi

The Vocational Guidance Journal
-- See *Personnel and Guidance
Journal*

Vocational Guidance Magazine --
See *Personnel and Guidance
Journal*

Alabama Farm Bureau, Montgomery,
Ala., 1922-?

American Horticultural Magazine
-- See *American Horticulturist*

American Horticulturist, Mount
Vernon, Va., Aug. 1922-current.
Formerly as *American
Horticultural Magazine*, CtY,
DA, DLC, NN

Arkansas Rice News, Stuttgart,
Ark., Mar. 1922-Dec. 21, 1927?
DA, NIC-A

Automobile Bulletin, Louisville,
Ky., 1922-?

Baptist Junior Union Quarterly I,
Nashville, Tenn., 1922-?

Baptist Student, Nashville, Tenn.,
1922-current. Later as
Student, CtY-D, KyLoS, KyU, TNG

Breeze, Harrisonburg, Va.,
1922-current

Car Owner, Greensboro, N.C., Oct.
1922-? Also as *Carolina
Motorist*, as *Carolina Motor
News*, and as *Carolina
Crusader*, NN, Nc

Carolina Club Boy, Clemson, S.C.,
1922-? DA, ScCc

Carolina Cooperator, Raleigh, N.C.,
July 1922-current. 1922-34 as
North Carolina Cotton Grower,
later as *FCX Carolina
Cooperator*, DA, DL, NN, NcD,
NcRS

Carolina Crusader -- See *Car
Owner*

Carolina Motor News -- See *Car
Owner*

Carolina Motorist -- See *Car Owner*

Dallas, Dallas, Tex., 1922-current.
v.14, no.7 - v.20, no.2 as
Southwest Business, and as
Southwest Purchasing, DLC, NN,
TxU

Daughters of America, Youngstown,
Ohio; Mount Morris, Ill.;
Chesapeake, Va., Apr. 1922-?
DLC, N, OCl

Dixie Farm and Poultry Journal
-- See *Dixie Farmer*

Dixie Farmer, Nashville, Tenn.,
1922-? v.1-12, no.1 as *Dixie
Poultry Journal*, v.12, no.2 -
v.18, no.5 as *Dixie Farm and
Poultry Journal*, DLC, NN, TU

Dixie Poultry Journal -- See *Dixie
Farmer*

FCX Carolina Cooperator -- See
Carolina Cooperator

Florida Clubwoman, Apopka, Winter
Garden, Fla., 1922-? DLC, FTS,
FU

Florida Dental Journal -- See
*Florida State Dental Society
Journal*

*Florida State Dental Society
Journal*, Clermont, Fla., Apr.
1922-Oct. 19, 1929, n.s. 1929-?
n.s. 3-8 as *Florida Dental
Journal*, FPY, IEN-D, NNN

The Fugitive, Nashville, Tenn.,
April 1922-Dec. 1925, DLC, InU

Furniture South, High Point, N.C.,
1922-current. v.1-6, no.9 as
*Southern Furniture Market
News*, v.6, no.10 - v.7, no.1 as
Southern Furniture Record,
later as *Furniture World*, DLC,
GAT

Furniture World -- See *Furniture
South*

Georgia Parent Teacher, Atlanta,
Ga., May 1922-? GEU

Hospital Buyer -- See *Hospital
Topics*

Hospital Digest and Buyer -- See
Hospital Topics

Hospital Topics, Chicago, Ill.;
Sarasota, Fla., 1922-current.
1922-25 as *Hospital Buyer*, Jan.
1926 as *Hospital Digest and
Buyer*, Feb. 1926-1949 as
Hospital Topics and Buyer,
1950-Aug. 1951 as *Hospital
Topics and Buyer's Guide*, DLC,
ICJ, NN, NNN, PP

Hospital Topics and Buyers -- See
Hospital Topics

Hospital Topics and Buyer's Guide
-- See *Hospital Topics*

Hydrocarbon Processing, Houston,
Tex., 1922-current

Izaak Walton Magazine -- See
Outdoor America

Journal of Social Forces -- See
Social Forces

Kentucky Road Builder, Louisville,
Ky., 1922-? DA, DLC, N, NN

Lone Pilgrim, Selma, N.C., Oct. 6,
1922-? NcD, NcU

MFC Co-op News -- See *MFC News*

MFC News, Madison, Miss., 1922-current. Also as *MFC Co-op News*

Mississippi Doctor, Booneville, Miss., 1922-? DSG, MoU, NcD, TU-M, ViU

Mississippi Farm Bureau News, Jackson, Miss., 1922-current

Mississippi Law Review, University of Miss., 1922-23, CtY, MH-L, MiU-L, N, NcD-L, TxU

Mississippi Veteran, Brandon, Miss., 1922-?

National Waltonian -- See *Outdoor America*

North Carolina Cotton Grower -- See *Carolina Cooperator* DA, NN

North Carolina Law Review, Chapel Hill, N.C., 1922-current, CtY, DLC, NNC, NcD-L, NcU, TxU

Outdoor America, Arlington, Va., 1922-current. Izaak Walton League. Also as *National Waltonian*, formerly as *Izaak Walton Magazine*, DA, DLC, IU, NN, PP, ViU

PTA Communicator -- See *Texas Parent Teacher*

Snowy Egret, Battle Creek, Mich.; Williamsburg, Ky., 1922-current, ICF, MB, MiU, NNM

Social Forces, Chapel Hill, N.C., Nov. 1922-current. v.1-3, no.4 as *Journal of Social Forces*, CtY, DA, DLC, NcU, NcD

Southern Furniture Market News -- See *Furniture South*

Southern Furniture Record -- See *Furniture South*

Southern Plumber, New Orleans, La., 1922-current? LNHT, T

Southern Poultry Journal, Montgomery, Ala., 1922-24? DA

Southern Retail Merchant, Jackson, Miss., 1922-? v.1-2 as *Mississippi Merchant*, NN

Southwest Business -- See *Dallas*

Southwest Purchasing -- See *Dallas*

Student -- See *Baptist Student*

Tarheel Banker, Raleigh, N.C., 1922-current, CtY, DA, NN, NcD, NcU

Tech Oracle, Cookeville, Tenn., 1922-current

Tennessee Law Review, Knoxville, Tenn., Nov. 1922-current, CtY-L, DLC, ICU, IU, N, NcD-L, NcU, T, TU

Texas Federation News, Austin, Tex., Sept. 1922-? TxDN, TxU

Texas Ginner, Dallas, Tex., June 1922-Apr. 1930. Supersedes *Cotton Ginner*, superseded by *Cotton Ginners' Journal*, DA, LU,TxH

Texas Law Review, Austin, Tex., 1922-current, CtY, DLC, N, NcU, TxU

Texas PTA Communicator -- See *Texas Parent Teacher*

Texas Parent Teacher, Dallas, Tex., 1922-current. Also as *Texas PTA Communicator, Texas PTA*, later as *PTA Communicator*, Tx, TxDN, TxLT

Tobacco Planter, Louisville, Ky., 1922-June 1929? DA, KyU, NN, NcRS

Virginia Churchman, Highland Springs, Richmond, Va., 1922-current, NcD, VR, ViU

Welding Journal, Easton, Pa.; Miami, Fla., Jan. 1922-current, CU, DLC, MoS, NN, NjR

Baptist News, Owenton, Ky., 1923-26? KyLoS

Better Crops with Plant Food, New York, N.Y.; Atlanta, Ga., Sept. 1923-current, DA, DLC, IU, NN, WU

Bible Searchers: Teacher -- See *Junior Teacher*

Charleston Museum Quarterly, Charleston, S.C., 1923-? CT, CtY, DLC, NN, NNM

Civic Forum, Arlington, Va., 1923-current

Conservation News -- See *Louisiana Conservation Review*

Dental Graduate -- See *Dental Student/Dental Practice*

Dental Student -- See *Dental Student/Dental Practice*

Dental Student/Dental Practice, Chicago, Ill.; Waco, Tex., 1923-current. Also as *Dental Student, Dental Students' Magazine*, also as *Dental Graduate; The National Magazine of First Practice*, ICJ, IEN-D, MoS, NNN, TxU-M

Dental Students' Magazine -- See *Dental Student/Dental Practice*

Digest, Auburn, Ala., Oct. 1923-? AAP, DA, DLC

Florida Christian, Ocala, Fla., 1923-? KyLxCB

Florida Clinic, Jacksonville, Fla., Aug. 1923-Feb. 1, 1926, FU, MBM, NNN, OO

Florida Education Association Journal, Tallahassee, Fla., Sept. 1923-current. Also as *United Teacher & Florida Education*, since 1980 as *Forum*, DE, FPY, FTS, FU

Florida Highways, Winter Garden, Fla., Dec. 1923-Feb. 1953. Suspended Aug. 1932-June 1941. Superseded by *Florida Public Works*, later *Industrial Florida*, DLC, F, FJ, FPY, FU

Florida Poultry Journal, Lakeland, Fla., Jan./Feb. 1923-? 1923 as *Poultry in Florida*, FU

The Forum -- See *Florida Education Association Journal*

Frontier Times, Bandera, Austin, Tex., Oct. 1923-? CtY, DLC, MH, NN, ICN, Tx, TxH, TxU, ViU

Georgia Peanut Grower, Albany, Ga., Mar. 29, 1923-June 1926. CU, DA, NIC-A

Georgia Tech Alumnus, Atlanta, Ga., 1923

Go, Charlotte, N.C., 1923-current

Gulf Coast Grower, Foley, Ala., Mar. 1923-Apr. 1925, CU, DA

Jewish Weekly Review -- See *San Antonio Jewish Weekly*

Journal of Arkansas Education, Little Rock, Ark., 1923-current, ArU, DE, IU, NNN

Junior Leader, Nashville, Tenn., 1923-?

Junior Teacher, Nashville, Tenn., 1923-current. Currently as *Bible Searchers: Teacher*

LAE Journal, Baton Rouge, La., 1923-?

Louisiana Conservation News -- See *Louisiana Conservation Review*

Louisiana Conservation Review, New Orleans, La., Mar. 1923-41. 1923-Nov. 1924 as *Conservation News*, 1927-1928/1929 as *Louisiana Conservation News*, suspended 1925-Aug. 1927, CtY, NIC, NN, IU, LNHT, LU, TxU

Louisiana Schools, Baton Rouge, La., May 1923-? v.1-9 as *The Louisiana Teachers Association Journal*, DE, LNHT, LNL, LU, MH, N, TxU

Louisiana Teachers Association Journal -- See *Louisiana Schools*

Miss Rutherford's Historical Notes, Athens, Atlanta, Ga., Jan. 1923-Dec. 1926, n.s. Jan.-June 1927. v.1-4, no. 9 as *Miss Rutherford's Scrap Book*, DLC, G, GU, NN, NcD, NcU

Miss Rutherford's Scrap Book -- See *Miss Rutherford's Historical Notes*

Mississippi Builder. A Modern Industrial Magazine, Jackson, Miss., Sept. 1923-July 1930? MsJS, MsSM, NN, MsU

Mississippi Educational Journal, Jackson, Miss., 1923-? MsAM

Modern Knitting Management, Coral Springs, Fla., 1923-current

Norfolk and Western Magazine, Roanoke, Va., 1923-current. Currently as *Norfolk Southern World*, DLC, NN, ViU

Norfolk Southern World -- See *Norfolk and Western Magazine*

North Carolina Agriculture & Industry, Raleigh, N.C., Oct. 17, 1923-May 27, 1926. Supersedes *North Carolina Rural Life*, DA, DLC, NN, NcRS, NcU

North Carolina Commerce and Industry, Chapel Hill, N.C., Oct. 1923-May/June 1926, CtY, DLC, N, NcU

North Carolina Lutheran, Stanley, N.C., 1923-current

North Carolina Water and Sewage Works Association Journal, _____, N.C., 1923-? NcU

Outdoors-South -- See *Southern Golf Magazine*

Peabody Journal of Education, Nashville, Tenn., 1923-current, CtY, DLC, MH, NN, NjR, TU

Poultry in Florida -- See *Florida Poultry Journal*

The Punch, New Orleans, La., 1923-?

San Antonio Jewish Weekly, San Antonio, Tex., 1923-Oct. 21, 1927. v.1, no.1-5 as *Jewish Weekly Review*, merged into *Jewish Record*, of Chicago, NN, TxU

Sanatorium Outlook, State Sanatorium, Ark., 1923-?

Southern Golf -- See *Southern Golf Magazine*

Southern Golf Magazine, Atlanta, Ga., June 1923-Oct. 1927. 1923-March 1926 as *Outdoors-South*, Apr.-May 1926 as *Southern Golf*, DA, NN

The Southern Literary Magazine, Atlanta, Ga.; Nashville, Tenn., 1923-Feb. 1924. Mar.-July 1924 as *The Southern Magazine*, CtY, DLC, GU, NcD, NcU, TN, TxH, VRT, ViU

The Southern Magazine -- See *The Southern Literary Magazine*

Southwestern Colonization Journal, Fort Worth, Tex., 1923-? N, TxU

Staple Cotton Review -- See
Staplreview

Staplreview, Greenwood, Miss.,
1923-current. Also as *Staple
Cotton Review*, DA, DLC, LNHT,
MsSM, NN, TxU

*Sunshine; A Florida Magazine of
Business, Art, and Advertising*,
Saint Augustine, Fla., Sept.
1923-Dec. 1925, FU

Techgram, Blacksburg, Va.,
1923-present, ViBlbV

Tennessee Farm Bureau News,
Columbia, Tenn., 1923-current

Texas Contractor, Dallas, Tex.,
1923-current, TxH, TxU

Texas Insuror, Austin, Tex.,
1923-current

Texas Tax Journal, Austin, Tex.,
1923-? NN, Tx, TxU

The United Teacher -- See *Florida
Education Association Journal*

United Teacher & Florida Education
-- See *Florida Education
Association Journal*

Virginia Review -- See *Virginia
Municipal Review*

White Wing Messenger, Cleveland,
Tenn., 1923-current

Wood Preserving News, McLean, Va.,
Jan. 1923-? CU, DA, DLC, NN,
ViU

Alabama 4-H Club News, Auburn,
Ala., July 1924-Sept. 1931, n.s.
Sept. 1937-? AAP, DA, DLC

*Alabama Academy of Science
Journal*, Birmingham, Ala.,
1924-26. Title varies. AAP,
ABS, CoU, DLC, NcD, NNM, WvU

Alabama Sportsman, Birmingham,
Ala., 1924-27, DA

American Baptist Monthly -- See
Baptist Monthly Magazine

American Cotton Ginner -- See
*American Ginner and Cotton Oil
Miller*

*American Cotton Ginner and Cotton
Market Reporter*, Little Rock,
Ark., 1924-? DA

*American Ginner and Cotton Oil
Miller*, Little Rock, Ark.,
1924-Feb. 1938. v.1-2 as
Arkansas Ginner, v.3-5, no.2
as *American Cotton Ginner*,
merged into *Cotton and Cotton
Oil Press*, DA, NN

Arkansas Agriculturist,
Fayetteville, Ark., 1924-? ArU,
DA, DLC

Arkansas Educator, Little Rock,
Ark., 1924-current

Arkansas Ginner -- See *American
Ginner and Cotton Oil Miller*

Baptist Monthly Magazine,
Louisville, Ky., Apr. 1924-Aug.
1925. no.1 as *American Baptist
Monthly*. Merged into *American
Baptist*, NNUT, PCA, KyLoS

Campus Comments, Staunton, Va.,
1924-current

*Church Management: The Clergy
Journal*, Cleveland, Ohio;
Austin, Tex., 1924-current, DLC,
ICU, NRCR, NcD, TxDaM, ViU

Cooperation, Columbia, S.C.,
1924-30. Superseded by *Cotton
Co-op of South Carolina*, DA,
NN, ScCc

*County Progress; the Business
Magazine for County Officials*,
San Antonio, Brownwood, Tex.,
1924-current, DLC, NN, TxCaW,
TxU

Emory Magazine, Atlanta, Ga.,
1924-current

Family News, Winnsboro, Tex.,
1924-?

Florida Engineer and Construction
-- See *Industrial Florida*

*Florida Engineering and
Construction* -- See *Industrial
Florida*

Florida Fruits and Flowers,
Bartow, Fla., 1924-Dec. 1926, CU,
DA, FU, NN

Florida Outdoors, Sanford, Fla.,
Jan. 4, 1924-Jan. 1926. v.1-2,
no.7 as *Florida Trucker*, DA,
FU

Florida Public Works -- See
Industrial Florida

Florida Trucker -- See *Florida
Outdoors*

Georgia Law-Maker, Atlanta, Ga.,
July 7, 1924-?   GU

Georgia State School Items,
Atlanta, Ga., 1924-Aug. 1933,
CtY, GU, TNG, TxU, ViU

Georgia Voter, Atlanta, Ga., 1924-?
1924-May 1928 as *Pilgrim*,
suspended 1937-42?   DLC, GEU,
GHi, GS, GU, NcU

Graphics -- See *Southern Graphics*

Industrial Florida, Winter Park,
Fla., Feb. 1924-1954. v.1-6 as
*Florida Engineer and
Construction*; v.7-9 as *Florida
Engineering and Construction*;
v.9, no.8 - v.22 as *Florida
Public Works*, DLC, F, FU, NN

*Journal of the Alabama Academy
of Science*, Auburn, Ala.,
1924-current, AAP, ABS, DLC,
MiU, NcD, OU

Kentucky Horticulture, Frankfort,
Ky., Feb. 1, 1924-May 1934.
Suspended Sept. 1932-July 1933,
CU, DA, DLC, NN

Lone Star Constructor, Dallas,
Tex., Oct. 1924-Nov. 1932, NN,
TxHR

*Louisiana State University Alumni
News*, Baton Rouge, La.,
1924-current

Lower Rio Grande Valley Magazine
-- See *Texas Farming and
Citriculture*

MTA, Jackson, Miss., 1924-?

Mayont, University, Ala., 1924-?

Memphis Medical Journal -- See
*Memphis and Mid-South Medical
Journal*

*Memphis and Mid-South Medical
Journal*, Memphis, Tenn., 1924-?
Earlier as *Memphis Medical
Journal*, DSG, Ia, MiU, NNN, TU,
TU-M

Methodist Layman, Nashville, Tenn.,
Feb. 1924-?   GEU, TxDaM, TxU

New Orleans Topics, New Orleans,
La., 1924, LNHT

New Southern Philatelist, Richmond,
Va., Nov. 1924-Oct. 1933. v.1-5
as *Southern Philatelist*.
Superseded by *Stamp and Cover
Collecting*, CtY, DLC, NN, Vi

North Carolina Historical Review,
Raleigh, N.C., 1924-current,
CtY, DLC, NN, NcD, NcU, ViBlbV

North Carolina Teacher, Raleigh,
N.C., 1924-current. Supersedes
North Carolina Education.
Superseded by *North Carolina
Education*, DE, IaU, NcD, NcU,
ViU

Pilgrim -- See *Georgia Voter*

The Sojourner, Alexandria, Va.,
1924-current

South, Hollywood, Fla., Nov.
1924-Jan. 1927. v.1-2, no.1 as
Hollywood Magazine, v.2, no.2
as *Tropical America*, DLC, FU,
NN, PP

Southern Builder, New Orleans,
La., 1924-28?

Southern Graphics, Kissimmee, Fla.,
1924-current. Formed by merger
of *Southern Printer*, and
Lithographer & Graphics. Also
as *Graphics*

The Southern Jewish Weekly,
Jacksonville, Fla., 1924-current.
As *Southern Jewish Monthly*,
1924-46, DLC, FU

Southern Philatelist -- See *New
Southern Philatelist*

Southern Printer -- See *Southern
Printer and Lithographer*

*Southern Printer and
Lithographer*, New Orleans, La.;
Atlanta, Ga., 1924-30? Also as
Southern Printer, LNHT

*Studies in Language and
Literature*, Chapel Hill, N.C.,
1924, CtY, DLC, IU, NN, OO

Tennessee Highways, Nashville,
Tenn., Mar.-Oct. 1924, MiU, T,
TMC, TU

*Texas Christian University
Quarterly; A Journal Devoted
to Science and the Humanities*,
Fort Worth, Tex., Apr. 1924-Jan.
1925, DLC, IU, N, TU, TxU

Texas Citriculture -- See *Texas
Farming and Citriculture*

Texas Farming and Citriculture,
Harlingen, Tex., 1924-? v.1-6,
no.1 as *Lower Rio Grande Valley
Magazine*, v.6, no.2 - v.11,
no.10 as *Texas Citriculture*,
v.11, no.11 - v.13, no.2 as
*Texas Citriculture and
Farming*, DA, DLC, NN, TxU

Texas Library Journal, Beaumont,
Tex., Nov. 1924-? CtY-L, DLC,
IU, NN, TxU

Tidewater Trail, Norfolk, Va., Nov.
1924-? DLC, Vi

Virginia Municipal Review,
Richmond, Va., Jan. 1924-1981.
Continued by *Virginia Review*,
1981, MH-PA, ViBlbV, ViU

The Wesleyan Alumna -- See
Wesleyan College Now.

Wesleyan College Now, Macon, Ga.,
1924-current. Formerly as *The
Wesleyan Alumna*.

Alabama Law Journal, Tuscaloosa,
Ala., Oct. 1925-May 1930, Ct,
CtY-L, DGU, DLC InU, N, NcD-L,
NcU, TU

Alumnae Magazine, Sweet Briar,
Va., 1925-current

Alumni Review, Lexington, Va.,
1925-current. Later as *W&L, The
Alumni Magazine of Washington
and Lee University*, Vi

American Speech, Baltimore, Md.;
University, Ala., Oct.
1925-current, CtY, DLC, NN,
NcD

Army and Navy Courier, San
Antonio, Tex., 1925-? Also as
Army-Navy-Air Force Courier,
DLC, NN

Army-Navy-Air Force Courier --
See *Army and Navy Courier*

Catholic Virginian, Richmond, Va.,
1925-current, DLC, Vi, ViW

Church Herald, Mariana, Fla., Mar.
1925-July 1935. v.1, no.1-2 as
Florida Herald, DLC, FPY, FU

Classical Bulletin, Chicago, Ill.;
Wilmore, Ky., 1925-current, IU,
InU, OCX, MChB, MH, NcU

Commonwealth College Fortnightly,
Mena, Ark., 1925-Mar. 15, 1938.
Superseded by *Commoner*, ArU,
DLC, NN

Dixie Dairies, Little Rock, Ark.,
1925-Nov. 1929. v.1-4 as *Dixie
Magazine*, DLC, NN, NjP

Dixie Guide, Gulfport, Miss., 1925-?

Dixie Magazine -- See *Dixie Dairies*

The Editor's Forum, Atlanta, Ga.,
1925-current, CU, NN

Family Lines Magazine, Louisville,
Ky.; Jacksonville, Fla.,
1925-current. Currently as
Seaboard System News

Florida Banker, Jacksonville, Fla.,
1925-31? FPY, FU

Florida Herald -- See *Church
Herald*

Florida Magazine -- See *Florida
Realtor*

Florida News, Miami, Fla., Sept.
1925-Apr. 12, 1926? FU, MH-BA,
NN

Florida Realtor, Orlando,
Bradenton, Fla., June
1925-current. 1925-Feb. 1940,
1941-Aug. 1949 as *Florida Realty
Journal*, Mar.-Nov. 1940 as
Florida Magazine, FPY, FTS, FU,
NN

Florida Realty Journal -- See
Florida Realtor

*Gas Digest, The Magazine of Gas
Operations* -- See *Gas Magazine*

Gas Magazine, Houston, Tex.,
1925-current. Currently as *Gas
Digest, The Magazine of Gas
Operations*

Georgia, Atlanta, Ga., 1925-Sept.
1930? CSt, GS, IU, NN

Kentucky Warbler, Bowling Green,
Ky., 1925-? KyBgW, KyU, MiU

L & N, Louisville, Ky., 1925-?

Language, Baltimore, Md.; Menasha,
Wis.; Austin, Tex., Mar.
1925-current, CtY, DLC, NN,
NcD, NcU, ViU

*Louisiana Colored Teachers'
Journal*, Baton Rouge, La.,
1925-? LNX, LU

Louisiana Highways Magazine,
Baton Rouge, La., Feb.
1925-Aug. 1928, DLC, DPR, LNHT,
LU

*Louisville & Nashville Employee's
Magazine*, Louisville, Ky., Mar.
1925-197? Also as *Louisville &
Nashville Magazine*, DLC, KyL,
ViU

Louisville & Nashville Magazine --
See *Louisville & Nashville
Employee's Magazine*

Mountain Life and Work, Berea,
Ky.; Nashville, Tenn.;
Clintwood, Va., 1925-current.
Formerly as *Southern Mountain
Life and Work*. Absorbed
Southern Highlights, DLC, IU,
MnU, NN, NcU, TU, ViU

The New Orleans Home Journal, New
Orleans, La., Summer
1925-Christmas 1929? LNHT

New Orleans Life, New Orleans, La.,
1925-27, LNHT, Louisiana State
Museum Library

Seaboard System News -- See
Family Lines Magazine

Southern Advertising/Markets,
Atlanta, Ga., 1925-79.
Superseded in 1980 by
*Adweek/Southwest Advertising
News*

*Southern Advertising and
Publishing*, Greensboro, N.C.,
Nov. 1925-? DLC, FU, LNHT, NN,
NcU

Southern Construction Magazine,
Miami, Fla., June 6, 1925-? FU

Southern Jeweler, Atlanta, Ga.,
1925-current, NcU

Southern Mountain Life and Work
-- See *Mountain Life and Work*

Tennessee Parent Teacher,
Nashville, Tenn., 1925-70.
Superseded by *Tennessee
Parent-Teacher Bulletin*, T,
TMC, TNG, TU

Texas Nursing, Austin, Tex.,
1925-current

VA PHCC Image, Richmond, Va.,
1925-current. Later as *Virginia
PHCC Image*

Virginia PHCC Image -- See *VA
PHCC Image*

Virginia Legionnaire, Richmond,
Arlington, Va., 1925-current, Vi

Virginia Musician, Norfolk, Va.,
Oct. 1925-? Vi, ViU

*Virginia Quarterly Review; A
National Journal of Literature
and Discussion*, Charlottesville,
Va., Apr. 1925-current, CtY,
DLC, NN, NcD, NcU, Vi, ViU

Virginia Tech Engineer,
Blacksburg, Va., 1925-? DBS,
MdU, OU

VOC ED, Arlington, Va.,
1925-current

*W & L, The Alumni Magazine of
Washington and Lee University*
-- See *Alumni Review*

The Whole Truth, Memphis, Tenn.,
1925-?

Xavier Herald, New Orleans, La.,
1925-?

Accounting Review, Menesha, Wis.;
Sarasota, Fla., Mar.
1926-current, CtY, DLC, NN, NcD

Baptist Historical Record,
Westminster, S.C., 1926-27,
KyLoS

*Baptist Young People's Union
Magazine*, Nashville, Tenn.,
1926-32

Certified Milk, Brooklyn, N.Y.;
Alpharetta, Ga., Apr. 1926-?
CtY, ICU, MiU, NN

Christian Messenger, Atlanta,
Macon, Ga., 1926-current,
KyLxCB

Cumberland Flag, Union City,
Tenn., Oct. 15, 1926-? NcMHi

*Distaff; A Critical Literary
Quarterly*, Tallahassee, Fla.,
1926-? FPY, ViU

Dixie Contractor, Atlanta, Decatur,
Ga., 1926-current, ICJ, ScU

Dixie Pharmaceutical Journal,
Atlanta, Ga., Oct. 1926-Jan.
1928? v.1-2, no.2 as *Georgia
Pharmaceutical Journal*, MdU-B

East Texas Magazine, Longview,
Tex., 1926-?

Florida Investor, Miami, Fla.,
Aug.-Nov. 1926? NN

Florida Review, Tallahassee, Fla.,
June 7, 1926-Oct. 20, 1930, DA,
FJ, FPY, FU, ViU

Free Baptist Herald, Winchester,
Va., 1926-28, PCA

Georgia Pharmaceutical Journal --
See *Dixie Pharmaceutical
Journal*

IGA Groceryman, Chicago, Ill.;
Greensboro, N.C., 1926-current.
Also as *Independent
Groceryman*, DA, DLC, ICU

Independent Groceryman -- See *IGA
Groceryman*

*Journal of the National Association
of Referees in Bankruptcy*,
Dallas, Tex., Dec. 1926-Oct.
1965. Continued by *Journal of
the National Conference of
Referees in Bankruptcy*, DLC,
MH-L

*Journal of the Tennessee Academy
of Science*, Nashville, Tenn.,
1926-current, DA, DLC, MiU, NN,
NcU, T, TU

*Kentucky Folk-Lore and Poetry
Magazine*, Bowling Green, Ky.,
Apr. 1926-Jan./Mar. 1931, DLC,
KyL, KyU, NN

Kentucky Optometrist, Somerset,
Frankfort, Ky., 1926-? NN, OU

Morehouse Journal of Science,
Atlanta, Ga., Apr. 1926-Apr.
1931, DLC, GU, NN

*Plant Food; A Balanced Ration for
Crops*, Atlanta, Ga., Jan.
1926-Jan./Feb. 1927, DA, LNHT

Presbyterian Youth, Richmond, Va.,
1926-? v.1-18 as *Program
Builder*, NcMHi, VRT

Program Builder -- See
Presbyterian Youth

Southern Automotive Journal -- See
Southwestern Automotive Journal

Southern Opportunity, Knoxville,
Tenn., 1926? IU, TU

Southern Registered Nurse,
Jacksonville, Fla., 1926-Aug.
1929. Merged into *Trained
Nurse and Hospital Review*, NNN,
PPPrHi

Southwestern Automotive Journal,
Dallas, Tex., Oct. 1926-Aug.
1930. United with *Southern
Automotive Dealer*, to form
Southern Automotive Journal,
DLC, PP

Southwestern Dental Mirror, Dallas,
Tex., 1926-31, NBM, NNN

TPA Messenger -- See *Texas Press
Messenger*

Tennessee Engineer, Knoxville,
Tenn., Oct. 1926-Jan. 1933, Mar.
1942-? TU

Tennessee Utility News, Nashville,
Tenn., Mar. 1926-Oct. 1929. T,
TMC, TU

Texas Accountant, Austin, Tex.,
1926-? TxCM

Texas Carrier, Linden, Tex.,
1926-current

Texas Press Messenger, Richardson,
Austin, Tex., 1926-current. As
TPA Messenger after July 1979.
NN, TxU

Texas Wheat Grower, ____, Tex.,
May 27, 1926-Oct. 5, 1929, DA,
NIC-A

*Virginia, First in the Heart of the
Nation*, Richmond, Va., 1926-37,
CtY, DLC, NN, NcD, TU, VR, ViU

Alabama Forest News, Montgomery,
Ala., 1927-Apr. 1939, CU, CtY,
DLC, IU, NcD, PP

American Newspaper Boy -- See
American Newspaper Carrier

American Newspaper Carrier,
Winston-Salem, N.C.,
1927-current. Formerly as
American Newspaper Boy

Arkansas Churchman, Little Rock,
Ark., 1927-current

Arkansas Publisher, Little Rock, Ark., Sept. 1927-? ArU

Arkansas Traveler Magazine, Little Rock, Ark., Mar.-Oct. 1927, MiU

Armed Forces, Virginia Beach, Va., 1927-current.

Armed Services, Virginia Beach, Va., 1927-current.

Baptist Program, Nashville, Tenn., 1927-current.

Beach & Pool -- See *Swimming Pool Age & Spa Merchandiser*

Beach & Pool and Aquatics -- See *Swimming Pool Age & Spa Merchandiser*

Beach & Pool Magazine -- See *Swimming Pool Age & Spa Merchandiser*

Bozart, Atlanta, Ga., Sept. 10, 1927-Sept. 1935. 1930 as *Bozart and Contemporary Verse*. United with *Westminster Magazine*, to form *Bozart-Westminster*. Later as *Westminster Magazine* again. CtY, DLC, GEU, KyL, NN, NjP, TxU, ViU

Bozart and Contemporary Verse -- See *Bozart*

Bozart-Westminster -- See *Bozart*

Church Administration, Nashville, Tenn., 1927-31, KyLoS

Church Herald for the Blind, Louisville, Ky., 1927-? DLC, Tx

Co-op Cotton, Memphis, Tenn., Feb. 1927-? DA

The Filson Club Historical Quarterly, Louisville, Ky., 1927-current. v.1-3 as *History Quarterly*, also as *History Quarterly of the Filson Club*, CtY, DLC, KyU, NN, NcU, ViBlbV

Fisk News, Nashville, Tenn., 1927-current.

Florida Bar Journal, Tallahassee, Fla., Aug. 1927-current. 1927-May 1934 as *Florida State Bar Association Law Journal*, June 1934-June 1953 as *Florida Law Journal*, CtY-L, DLC, F, FDS, NNB, NcD-L

Florida Farm and Grove, Jacksonville, Fla., 1927-? NN

Florida Law Journal -- See *Florida Bar Journal*

Florida Naturalist, Daytona Beach, Maitland, Fla., 1927-current. Supersedes *Florida Audubon Society Bulletin*, DA, FU, NNM

Florida PTA Bulletin, Orlando, Fla., 1927-current

Florida State Bar Association Law Journal -- See *Florida Bar Journal*

Georgia Law Review, Athens, Ga., Mar. 1927-June 1928, CtY-L, DLC, G, GU, N, NcD-L, NcU

History Quarterly -- See *Filson Club Historical Quarterly*

History Quarterly of the Filson Club -- See *The Filson Club Historical Quarterly*

Home Furnishings, Dallas, Tex., 1927-current. Formerly as *Southwest Home Furnishings News*, and as *Southwest Furniture News*

Home Missions College Review,
Raleigh, N.C.; Philadelphia, Pa.,
May 1927-May 1930, DLC, ICU,
NcU

J.K.P.A. _____, Ky., 1927-Sept.
1938. Supersedes *Kentucky
Druggist,* superseded by
Kentucky Pharmacist, DA, KyL,
MBM

Jewish Floridian, Miami, Fla.,
1927-current, FU

Little Theatre of Dallas Magazine,
Dallas, Tex., Oct. 1927-Dec. 2,
1935? NN

Louisiana Dairyman, _____, La.,
Jan. 1927-May 1930? DA, NN

Market Bulletin, Nashville, Tenn.,
Nov. 1927-? As *Tennessee
Market Bulletin,* after July
1928. DA, DLC, T, TU

*Memphis Lumberman and Southern
Woodworker* -- See *National
Hardwood Magazine*

Music Poster, Atlanta, Ga., Oct.
1927, DLC

National Hardwood Magazine,
Memphis, Tenn., 1927-current.
1927-July 1943 as *Memphis
Lumberman and Southern
Woodworker,* NN, TMC, TMG

*New South, A Magazine of Southern
Thought and Opportunity,*
Chattanooga, Tenn., Mar.-Sept.
1927, DLC, NN, NcU, T, TxU

The Orleanian, New Orleans, La.,
Dec. 1927-Jan. 1928, LNHT,
Louisiana State Museum Library

Palm Beach County Labor News West
Palm Beach, Fla., 1927-?

Peabody Reflector, Nashville,
Tenn., 1927-current

Poultry Quarterly, Marietta, Ga.,
Jan. 1927-Jan. 1930, DA

*Southern Dairy Products Journal,
a Monthly Publication Devoted
to Milk and Milk Products,*
Atlanta, Stone Mountain, Ga.,
1927-current, DA, GU-A, NN, GAT

Southern Dairyman, Atlanta, Ga.;
Shreveport, La., Dec. 1927-Oct.
1930, FU

Southerner, Lynchburg, Va., Nov.
1927?-June 1931? Vi, ViU

Southwest Furniture News -- See
Home Furnishings

Southwest Homefurnishings News --
See *Home Furnishings*

Southwestern Architect, Dallas,
Tex., July-Sept. 1927? DLC,
OkS, TxHR

Southwestern Highways, Fort Worth,
Tex., Dec. 1, 1927-Jan. 1930.
v.1-2, no.16 as *Texas Highways,*
DA, DPR, NN, PP, TxH, TxU

*Swimming Pool Age & Spa
Merchandiser,* New York, N.Y.;
Fort Lauderdale, Fla.; Atlanta,
Ga., 1927-current. Also as
Beach & Pool Magazine, as *Beach
& Pool and Aquatics,* as *Beach
& Pool,* and as *Swimming Pool
Weekly and Swimming Pool Age,*
DLC, NN, NcU

*Swimming Pool Weekly and Swimming
Pool Age* -- See *Swimming Pool
Age & Spa Merchandiser*

Teachers and Schools, Columbus,
S.C., Feb. 15, 1927-Nov. 1929?
KyL, ScU, ViU

Tennessee Market Bulletin,
Nashville, Tenn., Nov. 1927-?
As *Market Bulletin* until July
1928. DA, DLC, T, TU

Texas Business Review, Austin,
Tex., Apr. 25, 1927-current,
DLC, NN, NcD, Tx, TxH, TxU

Texas Grower and Valley Farmer,
Mercedes, Tex., Oct. 1927-Aug.
1935. v.1-4, no.8 as Valley
Farmer, v.4, no.9 - v.7, no.1
as Valley Farmer and South
Texas Grower. Merged into
Texas Farming and
Citriculture, DA, NN, TxU

Texas Highways -- See
Southwestern Highways

Tides and Strides, Norfolk, Va.,
1927-Sept. 1929, NN

Tulanian, New Orleans, La.,
1927-current

Valley Farmer -- See Texas Grower
and Valley Farmer

Valley Farmer and South Texas
Grower -- See Texas Grower and
Valley Farmer

Vets Voice, Virginia Beach, Va.,
1927-current

Westminster Magazine -- See Bozart

Alabama Farm Production,
Montgomery, Ala., Feb.
1928-Sept. 1936, AAP, AU, DA,
DLC, NIC

Alabama Libraries, Montgomery,
Ala., 1928-? IN, LNHT, NcU

American Fur Animals, Charlotte,
N.C., July/Aug. 1928-Jan. 1933.
Also as Carolina Fur Animal,
as Southern Fur Animals and
Poultry Digest, and as American
Fur Animals and Poultry
Digest, merged into Successful
Rabbit Breeding, DA, NN, NcU

American Fur Animals and Poultry
Digest -- See American Fur
Animals

Aviator -- See Southern Aviator

The Broadcaster, Nashville, Tenn.,
1928-? DHEW, KyBB, NN

Bunker's Monthly -- See Texas
Monthly

CPA, Dallas, Tex., 1928-current

Carolina Fur Animal -- See
American Fur Animals

Carolina Play-Book, Chapel Hill,
N.C., Mar. 1928-? DLC, NN, NcD,
NcU

Cotton Digest, Houston, Tex., Oct.
20, 1928-current. Currently as
Cotton Digest International, DA,
DLC, TxH, TxU

Cotton Digest International -- See
Cotton Digest

The Expected, Lynchburg, Va.,
1928-?

Faro Dominical -- See Marchemos

Florida Clearing House News,
Winter Haven, Fla., Sept.
1928-July 15, 1933, DA, DLC,
FPY, FU

Florida Fruit World, Tampa, Fla.,
May 1928-Jan. 1929. Merged into
Florida Farmer, CU, DA, FPY,
NN

Florida Municipal Record,
Jacksonville, Tallahassee, Fla.,
Apr. 1928-current, DLC, FJ, FU,
NN, ViU

Fort Worth, Fort Worth, Tex.,
1928-current

Free Baptist Quarterly,
Winchester, Va., June 1928-Aug.
1930, PCA

Future Farmer -- See Texas Future
Farmer

The Houston Gargoyle, Houston,
Tex., Jan. 1928-Sept. 25, 1932.
v.1, no.1-2 as Houston's New
Weekly, DLC, NN, TxH, TxU, ViU

Houston's New Weekly -- See *The Houston Gargoyle*

Kentucky Progress Magazine, Louisville, Ky., Sept. 1928-Feb. 1936. Superseded by *In Kentucky*, DLC, KyL, KyU, NN, NcU, TxU

Lawman, Cayce, S.C., 1928-?

Louisiana Parent-Teacher, New Orleans, La., 1928-June 1932? LNHT, MH

Marchemos, El Paso, Tex., 1928-? Formerly as *Faro Dominical*

Mississippi Law Journal, University, Miss., July 1928-current, DLC, MH-L

Mississippi Legion-Aire, Brandon, Miss., 1928-current

Morehouse Alumnus, Atlanta, Ga., 1928-current

Motor Transport, Austin, Tex., Aug. 1928-Apr. 1936. 1928-32 as *Motor Transportation*, DLC, ICU, Tx, TxU

Motor Transportation -- See *Motor Transport*

N.C.S.U. Alumni News, Raleigh, N.C., 1928-?

New Orleans Young Man, New Orleans, La., 1928-? LNHT

Panhandle-Plains Historical Review, Canyon, Tex., 1928-? DLC

Pipeline, Houston, Tex., 1928-current. Formerly as *Pipe Line News*

Pipe Line News -- See *Pipeline*

Saco-Lowell Bulletin, Boston, Mass.; Greenville, S.C., 1928-? DA, DLC, MCM, NN

Southern Aviator, Temple, Tex., May 1928-Oct./Nov. 1930. v.1-2, no.5 as *Aviator*, DLC, WaS

Southern Business, Knoxville, Tenn., 1928-34, TU

Southern Business Builder, New Orleans, La., 1928-31, LNHT

Southern Fur Animals and Poultry Digest -- See *American Fur Animals*

The Stater, Raleigh, N.C., 1928-?

Tennessee Road Builder, Nashville, Tenn., Mar. 1928-? ICJ, T,TMG, TU

Texas C.P.A. Dallas, Tex., 1928-?

Texas Future Farmer, Austin, Tex., 1928-current. 1928-Aug. 1946 as *Lone Star Farmer*, Sept. 1946-Feb. 1954 as *Future Farmer*, DA, TxH, TxKT, TxU

Texas Legion News, Austin, Tex., 1928-current

Texas Monthly, Fort Worth, Dallas, Tex., Jan. 1928-July 1930. v.1-2, no.4 as *Bunker's Monthly*, merged into *Texas Weekly*, later *Texas Digest*, DLC, NN, Tx, TxH, TxU

U.S. Piper, Birmingham, Ala., 1928-current

Virginia Libraries, Richmond, Va., Apr. 1928-Jan. 1932, MiU, NNC, TxU, Vi, ViU

Agricultural Education Magazine, Des Moines, Iowa; Mechanicsville, Va., 1929-current, DA, DLC, IU, MnU, NcRS

Alabama Conservation, _____, Ala., July 1929-current. v.1-12, no.4 as *Alabama Game and Fish News*, AAP, ABS, AU,Ct, DLC, N, NN, NcD

Alabama Game and Fish -- See
   Alabama Conservation

American Literature, Durham, N.C.,
   1929-current, CtY, DLC, NN,
   NcD, NcU, NjP, TxU

Business Farming, Monroe, La.,
   1929-?

*Carolina Skyland, A Monthly
   Devoted to Western North
   Carolina*, Asheville, N.C., 1929-?
   NcD

Dallasite, Dallas, Tex., Sept. 28,
   1929-Apr. 5, 1930, NN

Dental Bulletin -- See *Houston
   District Dental Society Journal*

Dixie Business, Atlanta,
   Dawsonville, Ga., 1929-current,
   DLC, GDS

Dixie Dentist, New Orleans, La.,
   Jan. 1929-Nov. 1931, MH-M, MiU,
   NNN

EM Report, Dallas, Tex., 1929-?
   Formerly as *PM Report*

Echo, Huntsville, Tex.,
   1929-current

Florida Christian Endeavor News,
   Tampa, Fla., 1929-?   FU

Florida Commercial, Jacksonville,
   Fla., Apr. 1929-May 21, 1930?
   DLC, FJ, FTS, NN

*Florida Optometric Association
   Journal*, Miami Beach, Fla.,
   1929-?   v.9-15 as *Florida
   Optometrist*.   Suspended 1938-42
   or '43, DLC

Florida Optometrist -- See *Florida
   Optometric Association Journal*

Florida Parent Teacher, Tampa,
   Fla., 1929-?   FTS, FU

Florida Woods and Waters,
   Tallahassee, Fla., 1929/30-31,
   DA, DLC, F, FJ, FU, MiU

*Galveston Wharf Co. Employees
   Magazine*, Galveston, Tex., May
   1, 1929-?   DLC

Georgia Business, Athens, Ga.,
   1929-current.   1929-Mar. 1942?
   as *Georgia Business Review*.
   Suspended 1933-Sept. 1941; Apr.
   1942-May 1947.   Currently as
   *Georgia Business and Economic
   Conditions*, CtY, DA, DLC, G,GS,
   GU, ICJ, NN

*Georgia Business and Economic
   Conditions* -- See *Georgia
   Business*

Georgia Business Review -- See
   Georgia Business

Greater Lubbock, Lubbock, Tex.,
   1929-current

*Houston District Dental Society
   Journal*, Houston, Tex., Dec.
   1929-?   1929-Apr. 1934 as *Dental
   Bulletin*, MiU, NNC-M, NNN, TxH

Jewish Press, Dallas, Tex., Oct.
   1929-Sept. 1936, NN, NNJ, OCH

Kentucky Press, Lexington, Ky.,
   1929-current, IU, NN

Lighted Pathway, Cleveland, Tenn.,
   1929-current

Louisiana, Baton Rouge, La., Mar.
   1929-July 1930, C, LU, NN

Louisiana Future Farmer, Houma,
   La., 1929-?

PM Report -- See *EM Report*

Petroleum Engineer -- See
   *Petroleum Engineer
   International*

Petroleum Engineer International,
Tulsa, Okla.; Dallas, Tex.,
1929-current.   Earlier as
Petroleum Engineer, supersedes
Hydrocarbon News, and
Petro/Chem Engineer, DLC, NN,
TxU

*Sheepman; The Practical Sheep
Magazine for Farm Flock Owners
of America,* Lexington, Ky.,
July 1929-54. Absorbed by
Sheep Breeder and Sheepman,
Jan. 1955, DA, KyU

Southern Aviation, Atlanta, Dalton,
Ga., Sept. 1929-May 1933.
Merged into *Popular Aviation,*
DLC, FU, GEU, GU, NN, NcD, TxU

Southern City, Atlanta, Ga.,
1929-33, DLC, ICU, NN, ViU

Texas Civil Engineer, Houston,
College Station, Tex., Nov.
1929-?   Formerly as *Texas
Engineer,* ICJ, NN, TxH, TxU

Texas Engineer -- See *Texas Civil
Engineer*

Threefold Advocate, Siloam Springs,
Ark., 1929-?

Alabama Business, University of
Alabama, Ala., Nov. 1930-81.
Also as *University of Alabama
Business Review,* and as
*University of Alabama Business
News,* Ct, FU,MH-BA, NN, NcD

Alabama Economic Review, Auburn,
Ala., Dec. 1, 1930-June 1933, DA,
ICU, KyU, NN, ViU

Alabama Historical Quarterly,
Montgomery, Ala., 1930-current.
Suspended 1931-39. ABS, CtY,
DLC, GA, IU, NN, NcD, NcU, ViU

*American Alliance for Health,
Physical Education and
Recreation* -- See *Research
Quarterly for Exercise and
Sport*

Arkansas Dental Journal, Little
Rock, Ark., Mar. 1930-current.
Mar.-May 1930 as *Dentark,*
IEN-D, MoS, NNN, OCo, NNC-M

Arkansas Libraries, Little Rock,
Ark., 1930-30, n.s. June
1944-current, ArU, DLC, GEU,
ICU, IU, MnU, NN, NcU, Vi

Baptist Adults, Nashville, Tenn.,
1930-current

Baylor's Quarterly, Louisville,
Ky., Jan. 1930-? DLC, TxU

Co-operator -- See *Sheep and Goat
Raiser*

Dentark -- See *Arkansas Dental
Journal*

The Digest, Baton Rouge, La.,
1930-?

Dixie Underwriter -- See *Southern
Underwriter*

Florida Dental Journal, Tampa,
Fla., 1930-current. Later as
*Florida State Dental Society
Journal,* then again as *Florida
Dental Journal,* IEN-D, NNN

*Florida Oil Reporter and Florida
Investor,* Tampa, Fla., Oct.
1930-June 1936? FTS, FU

*Florida State Dental Society
Journal* -- See *Florida Dental
Journal*

Georgia Lawyer, Macon, Ga., June
1930-Jan. 1932, CtY-L, DLC, G,
GU, InU, N, NcD, TxU

Gulf Coast Sportsman, Houston,
Tex., Apr. 1930-June 1931, TxH

Home Missions, Atlanta, Ga.,
1930-current. Also as *Southern
Baptist Home Missions.*
Currently as *Missions USA,*
CtY-D, GMM, NRCR, PCA, KyLoS

Houston Bar Journal, Houston, Tex., Nov. 1930-Dec. 1931. Suspended by *First District Bar Journal of Texas*, CtY-L, DLC, NcD-L, TxH, TxU

Houston Magazine, Houston, Tex., 1930-current

Journal of Air Law -- See *The Journal of Air Law and Commerce*

The Journal of Air Law and Commerce, Chicago, Ill.; Dallas, Tex., 1930-current. v.1-9 as *Journal of Air Law*, CtY-L, DLC, NN, TxU

Kentucky City, Louisville, Lexington, Ky., Apr. 12, 1930-Aug. 1954. Superseded by *Kentucky City Bulletin*, KyL, KyU, MiU, NN, ViU

Lone Star Bulletin -- See *Sheep and Goat Review*

Louisville State Dental Society Impressions: A Journal of Friendly Relations, New Orleans, La., 1930/31-? LNHT, NNC-M, NNN

Methodist Herald, Jackson, Tenn., Jan. 22, 1930-Aug. 10, 1932. Formed by union of *Methodist Advocate* and other periodicals. GEU, NcD

Methodist Herald, Louisville, Ky., 1930-32, GEU, KyLoS

The Migrant, Nashville, Tenn., 1930-current, DA, DSI-M, MiU, NNM, T, TNV, TU

Missions USA -- See *Home Missions*

The New Orleanian, New Orleans, La., Sept. 6, 1930-? LNHT, Louisiana State Museum Library

North Carolina Farm Business, Raleigh, N.C., 1930-Nov. 1931, DA, NN, NcRS

North Carolina Guernsey News, Salisbury, N.C., 1930-Dec. 1932, DA, NcU

North Carolina Teachers Record, Raleigh, N.C., Jan. 1930-? NNC-T, NcU, NcRS

Raven, Lynchburg, Va., 1930-current, MiU, NNM, Vi, ViU

Research Quarterly for Exercise and Sport, Ann Arbor, Mich.; Reston, Va., Mar. 1930-current. As *American Alliance for Health, Physical Education and Recreation Research*, C, DE, DLC, N, NN, NcD, ViU

Sheep and Goat Raiser, San Angelo, Tex., Oct. 1930-? v.1, no.1-5 as *Lone Star Bulletin*, v.1, no.6 - v.4, no.18 as *Co-operator*, v.4, no.19 - v.11 as *Southwestern Sheep and Goat Raiser Magazine*. Absorbed *Sheep and Goat Raisers' Magazine*, Oct. 1941, DA, DLC, NN, TxU

South Carolina Dental Association Journal, Columbia, S.C., 1930-41. Superseded by *South Carolina Dental Journal*, GEU, NNN

Southern Baptist Home Missions -- See *Home Missions*

Southern Office Outfitter, Atlanta, Ga., 1930-current. Formerly as *Southern Stationer and Officer Outfitter*, DLC

Southern Stationer and Officer Outfitter, Atlanta, Ga., 1930-current. Currently as *Southern Office Outfitter*, DLC

Southern Underwriter, Jacksonville, Raleigh, N.C., Jan. 1930-Nov. 1937? v.1, no.1-2 as *Tar Heel Underwriter*, v.1, no.3-7 as *Dixie Underwriter*, DLC, FU, Nc, NcD, NcU, VR, ViU

Southern Worker, Chattanooga,
Tenn., Aug. 1930-Sept. 1937.
Suspended Feb. 13, 1932-May 13,
1933. DA, DHU, NN, TxU

Southwestern Poultry Journal, San
Antonio, Tex., 1930-May 1934,
NN

*Southwestern Sheep and Goat
Raiser Magazine* -- See *Sheep
and Goat Raiser*

*State Government; The Journal of
State Affairs*, Lexington, Ky.,
1930-current, DLC, KyU, NN, NcU

Tar Heel Underwriter -- See
Southern Underwriter

Tennessee Industry, Nashville,
Tenn., Sept. 1930-June 1932, T,
TU, ViU

Texas Highways, Dallas, Tex., Sept.
1930-Aug. 1933, NN, Tx, TxU

Texas Lawman, Austin, Tex.,
1930-current, NN, TxU, TxWB

Texasky Rolnik, Fort Worth, Tex.,
1930-?

Tobacco News, Florence, S.C., Dec.
1930-Oct. 1931? NIC-A

The Torch, Knoxville, Tenn., 1930-?

*University of Alabama Business
News* -- See *Alabama Business*

*University of Alabama Business
Review* -- See *Alabama Business*

*Virginia-Carolina Jewish
Messenger*, Richmond, Va.,
1930-Mar. 1938? Vi

Virginia P-H-C-C Image, Richmond,
Va., 1930-current

Alabama Medicine -- See *Journal
of the Medical Association of
the State of Alabama*

Allied Youth, New York, N.Y.;
Arlington, Va., 1931-? CtY,
DLC, NN, VRT

Atlantic Sportsman, Winston-Salem,
N.C., Sept. 1931-Dec. 1933, DA,
DLC, NN, NcU

B.E.A. Bulletin Birmingham, Ala.,
1931-?

The Baker, Houston, Tex., 1931-?

Beginning Teacher, Nashville,
Tenn., 1931-?

Berea Alumnus, Berea, Ky.,
1931-current

Carolina Mountain-Air, Asheville,
N.C., 1931-34/35? MBM, NNN,
PPC

*Duke University Research Studies
in Education*, Durham, N.C.,
1931-? CtY, DLC, N, NcD, NcU

*Ecological Monographs; A Journal
for All Phases of Biology*,
Durham, N.C., 1931-current, CtY,
DA, DLC, MH, NcD, NcU, NcRS

Epoca, San Antonio, Tex., June 7,
1931, IU

Forestry-Geological Review,
Atlanta, Ga., Jan. 1931-Mar.
1937. 1931-Jan. 1932 as *Georgia
Forest Lookout*, CtY, DA, DLC,
GU

Foundation Fellowship, Asheville,
N.C., 1931-33, NN

*Free Economy; The Way Out for
Democracy* -- See *Freedom and
Plenty*

Freedom and Plenty, San Antonio,
Tex., Nov. 1931-May/June 1950.
v.1-7, no.3 as *Way out*, Apr.
1937-July 1940 as *Free Economy;
The Way Out for Democracy*,
CtY, DLC, NN

Georgia Forest Lookout -- See
Forestry-Geological Review

Industrial Medicine and Surgery,
Chicago, Ill.; Miami, Fla., 1931-?
Also as *Industrial Medicine; the
Journal of Industrial Health,
Occupational Medicine, and the
Surgery of Trauma*, DLC, NN,
ViU

*Industrial Medicine; The Journal
of Industrial Health,
Occupational Medicine, and the
Surgery of Trauma* -- See
*Industrial Medicine and
Surgery*

Iron Worker, Lynchburg, Va.,
1931-? DLC, Vi, ViBlbV, ViW

ITE Journal -- See *Traffic
Engineering*

*Journal of the Medical Association
of the State of Alabama*,
Montgomery, Ala., 1931-current.
Currently as *Alabama Medicine*

Louisiana Legionnaire, Baton
Rouge, La., 1931-?

Louisiana State University Studies
Baton Rouge, La., 1931-? CtY,
DLC, LN, LNHT, LU, NN, NcD,
NcU

Mississippi Highways, Jackson,
Miss., 1931-? DLC, DPR, MsSM,
MsU

The New Orange Peel, Gainesville,
Fla., 1931-?

Polio Chronicle, _____, Fla., July
1931-Feb. 1934, IU, N, NNN, ViU

Popular Government, Chapel Hill,
N.C., 1931-current, CtY, DLC,
NN, NcD, NcU

The Restaurant Review, Jackson,
Miss., 1931-?

South Texan, San Antonio, Tex.,
1931-?

Southern Fine Arts, Memphis,
Tenn., Apr. 1931-current, MWA

Southwestern Baker, Houston, Tex.,
May 1931-? NN

Southwestern Bottler, San Antonio,
Tex., 1931-34? DLC,

Sunrise; The Florida Magazine,
Saint Augustine, Fla., Nov.
1931-June 1933? DLC, FJ, FU

Tennessee Libraries, Knoxville,
Tenn., June 1931-Sept. 1947.
Suspended Feb. 1933-Dec. 1937,
Feb. 1941-Mar. 1947. Superseded
by *Tennessee Librarian*, N, T,
TU

Traffic Digest -- See *Traffic
Engineering*

Traffic Engineering, New York,
N.Y.; Arlington, Va., May
1931-current. Also as *Traffic
Digest*, and as *Transportation
Engineering*. Currently as *ITE
Journal*, CtY, NN, OCL

Transportation Engineering -- See
Traffic Engineering

*Ventana; Missionary Magazine for
Women*, El Paso, Tex.,
1931-current

Virginia Agricultural Economics --
See *Virginia Farm Economics*

Virginia Farm Economics,
Blacksburg, Va., July
1931-current. Currently as
*Virginia Agricultural
Economics*, DA, FU, NN, Vi, VBP

Virginia Intermont Cauldron,
Bristol, Va., 1931-?

Way Out -- See *Freedom and Plenty*

American Surgeon, Atlanta, Ga.,
Apr. 1932-current. Suspended
Dec. 1942-July 1946, DLC, NNN,
NcU, ViU

Baptist Voice, Tampa, Fla., 1932-41?
KyLoS

Beach & Town Visitor, Miami Beach,
Fla., 1932-?

Blue and Gray, Harrogate, Tenn.,
1932-?

Campus Canopy, Valdosta, Ga.,
1932-?

*Carolinas Magazine, Devoted to the
Progress of the Carolinas*,
Charlotte, N.C., June 1932-?
DA, NcD, NcU

Character and Personality,
Durham, N.C., Sept.
1932-Mar./June 1945. Continued
by *Journal of Personality*, InU

*Cumberland Empire; A Magazine of
Lore and Legend*, Big Laurel,
Va., 1932-33, ICU, MH, MWA, NN,
Vi, ViU

Duke Bar Association Journal,
Durham, N.C., Mar. 1932-42,
CtY-L, DLC, NNU, NcD, NcU

Epworth Highroad, Nashville,
Tenn., 1932-Sept. 1941. Formed
by union of *Epworth Era*, and
High Road, CtY-D, DLC, NcD, ViU

*First District Bar Journal of
Texas*, Houston, Tex., June
1932-May 29, 1933. Supersedes
Houston Bar Journal, CtY-L,
DLC, NcD, TxU

Florida Fireman, Williston,
Chattahoochee, Fla.,
1932-current, F, FU

Florida Funeral Director,
Jacksonville, Tallahassee, Fla.,
1932-? FU

*Historical Magazine of the
Protestant Episcopal Church*,
Garrison, N.Y.; Richmond, Va.,
Mar. 1932-current, CtY, DLC, NN,
NcD, TxU, ViU

Industrial Medicine and Surgery
-- See *Occupational Health &
Safety*

*International Journal of
Occupational Health and Safety*
-- See *Occupational Health &
Safety*

*Interpreter; A Magazine of
Excellent Things*, Kirstenstad,
Tex., 1932-Feb. 1933, MWA, TxU

Journal of Personality, Durham,
N.C., 1932-current, CtY, DLC,
NN, NcD, ViU

Lepidopterists News, Miami, Fla.,
June 1932-Dec. 1933? NNM

The Masonic Monthly, Mobile, Ala.,
1932-present

*Modern Concepts of Cardiovascular
Disease*, New York, N.Y.; Dallas,
Tex., 1932-current, CtY-M, DLC,
MiU, NNN, ViU

*North Carolina Historical and
Genealogical Record; A
Quarterly Magazine of North
Carolina Genealogy, Biography,
and Local History*, Forest City,
N.C., Jan. 1932-Oct. 1933, DLC,
InU, NN, Nc, NcD, NcU

Occupational Health & Safety, Waco,
Tex., Oct. 1932-current. As
*International Journal of
Occupational Health and
Safety*, until 1976. Earlier as
*Industrial Medicine and
Surgery*, DLC, ICJ, MH-M, NN,
TU-M

Presbyterian Evangel, Shreveport,
La., Jan. 1932-33? LNHT, NcMHi

Religion in Life, New York, N.Y.;
Nashville, Tenn., 1932-80.
Superseded in 1980 by *United
Methodist Board of Higher
Education and Ministry
Quarterly*, CtY-D, DLC, MH-AH,
NN, NcD

Rice Industry, Beaumont, Tex.,
Nov.-Dec. 1932, DA, LU

Ruritan, Dublin, Va., 1932-current.
Formerly as *Ruritan National.*

Ruritan National -- See *Ruritan*

*Southern Baptist Brotherhood
Journal*, Knoxville, Tenn.,
1932-? 1932-43 as *Southern
Baptist Brotherhood Quarterly*,
KyLoS, TxFS, ABH

*Southern Baptist Brotherhood
Quarterly* -- See *Southern
Baptist Brotherhood Journal*

Southern Highway Journal,
Atlanta, Ga., 1932-Sept. 1938?
GAT

Southern Hospitals, Charlotte,
N.C.; Greenville, S.C.,
1932-current, NN, NcD, NcU,
TxU, VRM

Southern Salesman, Nashville,
Tenn., Nov. 1932-Sept. 1933?
Suspended June-July 1933.
DLC, NN

Southern Sportsman, Richmond, Va.,
May-June 1932, Vi, ViU

The Southern Surgeon, Atlanta,
Ga., 1932-? DLC

Sou'wester, Americus, Ga.,
1932-current

Tar Heel Universalist, Kinston,
N.C., 1932-? NcU

Tennessee Genealogical Records,
Nashville, Tenn., 1932-37? DLC,
NcU

*Texas Bluebonnet; The Family
Monthly for Every Texas Home*,
New Braunfels, Tex., Aug. 1932-?
TxU

Texas Chess Magazine -- See
Western Chess Magazine

Texas Cooperative Dairyman,
Houston, Tex., Aug. 1932-Jan.
1933, DA

Texas Grower and Shipper,
Harlingen, Tex., Jan. 1932-Apr.
1933. Merged into *Texas
Citriculture*, DA

Texas Opinion, Houston, Tex.,
1932-Feb. 1934, Tx, TxH, TxU

The Tie, Louisville, Ky.,
1932-current

Tobacco Grower, Farmville, Va.,
Oct. 21, 1932-Oct. 1941. Merged
into *Virginia Farmer*, DA, NIC-A

*Tobacco Tips for the Grower,
Warehouseman Dealer,
Manufacturer and Allied
Tobacco Interests*, Manning,
S.C., Feb. 4, 1932-Jan. 5, 1933,
DA, NN

Virginia Drama News,
Charlottesville, Va., 1932-?
DLC, NN, ViU, ViW

Visitor Slick Magazine, Miami
Beach, Fla., 1932-?

Western Chess Magazine, Dallas,
Tex., Aug. 1932-Apr. 1933. v.1
as *Texas Chess Magazine*, OCl

American Horseman, Lexington,
Ky., 1933-50. Also as *Kentucky
Horseman, New American
Horseman.* Absorbed
Sportologue, July 1942, DLC,
KyL, NN

The American Rose Magazine,
Harrisburg, Pa.; Shreveport,
La., Mar./Apr. 1933-current, DA,
FU, IU, MH, NN

Bahama's Magazine, Miami, Fla.,
1933-current

Columbus Balboa Review,
Birmingham, Ala., Oct. 1933-Oct.
1938? MWA

Construction, Arlington, Falls
Church, Va., 1933-current

*Cotton Economist; Agricultural,
Commercial, Financial,
Industrial*, New Orleans, La.,
Jan. 5-Feb. 23, 1933, DA

*East Texas Oil Journal and East
Texas Oil*, Longview, Tex.,
1933-?

*Engineering Progress at the
University of Florida*,
Gainesville, Fla., 1933-?   Ct,
DLC, F, FU, MoU

Florida Dispatch, Saint Augustine,
Fla., 1933-?   FU

Florida Radio News, Lakeland, Fla.,
Jan.-Aug. 1933, FU

Food Marketer, Atlanta, Ga., 1933-?

Georgia Future Farmer, Atlanta,
Ga., 1933-current

*Georgiaman; For Stamp Collectors
and Hobbyists*, Atlanta, Ga.,
1933.   Merged into *White
Elephant*, DLC, NNCo, PP

Golf Course Reporter, Saint
Charles, Ill.; Jacksonville
Beach, Fla.; Lawrence, Kan.,
July 1933-current.   Also as
*Greenkeepers' Reporter,
Greenkeeper's Bulletin.*
Currently as *Golf Course
Management*, DLC, MnHi, NN, NIC

The Hindsonian, Raymond, Miss.,
1933-current

Journal of Insurance -- See *The
Journal of Risk and Insurance*

*The Journal of Risk and
Insurance*, Fort Worth, Tex.;
Athens, Ga., 1933-current.
Formerly as *Journal of
Insurance*, DE, DLC, MiU, NN,
NcD, ViU

Kentucky Horseman -- See *American
Horseman*

Law and Contemporary Problems,
Durham, N.C., Dec. 1933-?   CtY,
DLC, MH-Ed, NN, NcD, NcU

*Little Theatre of the South
Magazine*, New Orleans, La.,
Aug. 1933-?   DLC, LU, TxH

Louisiana Leader, Baton Rouge,
La., Dec. 1933-June 1942, LNHT,
MoU, TxU

New American Horseman -- See
American Horseman

North Carolina Poetry Review,
Gastonia, N.C., July 1933-June
1936.   Merged into *Poetry
World*, DLC, IU, NN, Nc, NcD,
NcU

*The Observer; A Literary
Publication*, Memphis, Tenn.,
1933-34, MWA, NN, NjP, T

Ole Miss Alumni Review, Oxford,
Miss., 1933-?

Pelican News, New Orleans, La.,
1933-?   DNLM

*Quarterly Review of Higher
Education Among Negroes*,
Charlotte, N.C., 1933-?   CtY,
DE, NcD, NcU, PP

Railway Dispatch, Saint Augustine,
Fla., 1933-?   Merged into
Railway Mechanical Engineer,
DLC, KU, MiU, NN

Rice News, Lake Charles, La., Nov.
1933-?   DA, LNHT, NN

Richmonder, Richmond, Va., Feb.
1933-July 1934, Vi

Shell News, Houston, Tex., 1933-?

Southern Broadcast, Monroe, La.,
1933-June 26, 1937, NN

Southern Economic Journal, Chapel Hill, N.C., Oct. 1933-current, CtY, DLC, NN, NcD, NcU, Vi

Southern Freemason, Montgomery, Ala., Oct. 1933-Jan. 1934? NN

Southern Home and Garden, Fort Worth, Dallas, Tex., Nov. 1933-Sept. 1946. Absorbed by *Sun-up*, DA, TxCM, TxU, TxDN

Stamp and Cover Collecting, Richmond, Va., Nov. 1933-Oct. 1936. Supersedes *New Southern Philatelist*, superseded by *Stamp and Cover Collectors' Review*, CtY, NN, TxU, Vi, VR

Stamp Collector; An Independent Monthly Magazine Devoted to the Study and Dissemination of Philately in All Its Phases, New Orleans, La., Aug. 1933-Apr. 1934. Merged into *Stamp Collectors' Digest*, NN, TxU, WU

The State, Raleigh, N.C., 1933-current, Nc, NcD, NcRS, NcU

T.A.B. Quarterly, Houston, Tex., 1933-? As *Texas Industry*, until 1976, DLC, TxH, TxU

Tennessee Avifauna, Nashville, Tenn., 1933-? DSI-M, NH-Z, TNV, MiU

Texas Bond Reporter, Dallas, Tex., 1933-? DLC

Texas Industry -- See *T.A.B. Quarterly*

Tidewater Motorists, Norfolk, Va., 1933-current

Virginia Nurse, Richmond, Va., 1933-current. Formerly as *Virginia Nurse Quarterly*, Vi, ViRM

Virginia Nurse Quarterly -- See *Virginia Nurse*

Virginia Trucks, Richmond, Va., 1933-?

Alabama Future Farmer, Auburn, Ala., 1934-? AAP, DA, NIC-A

American Journal of Medical Technology, Detroit, Mich.; Dallaire, Tex., 1934-83. Merged with *American Medical Technologists Journal* in 1984 to form *Journal of Medical Technology* DLC, ICJ, NNN, OCL, TxU-M

American Motor Carrier, Atlanta, Marietta, Ga., 1934-current, DLC, NN

Arkansas Historical Review, Little Rock, Ark., Feb.-June 1934, ArU, CU, DLC, MnU, NN, TxU

Arkansas Municipal Bulletin -- See *City & Town*

Arkansas Municipalities -- See *City & Town*

Arkansas Nurse, Little Rock, Ark., 1934-75

Beta Club Journal -- See *National Beta Club Journal*

Breeder-Feeder, Houston, Tex., Sept. 1934-? TxCM

Brickbats & Bouquets, Dallas, Tex., 1934-current

Carolina Radio--News Weekly, Durham, N.C., 1934-? NcD

The Catholic Week, Mobile, Ala., 1934-current

City & Town, North Little Rock, Ark., Aug. 15, 1934-current. Formerly as *Arkansas Municipalities*, v.1 as *Arkansas Municipal Bulletin*, ArU, DLC, MH, NN, ViU

Claytonia, Lynchburg, Va., June 1934-Apr. 1939. Superseded by *Virginia Journal of Science*, DA, NcD, NcU, Vi, ViU

Commonwealth Magazine -- See *Commonwealth; The Magazine of Virginia*

Commonwealth; The Magazine of Virginia, Richmond, Norfolk, Va., 1934-85. Also as *Commonwealth Magazine*, DLC, NN, NcD, Vi, ViBlbV, ViU

Communication Monographs, Ann Arbor, Mich.; Annandale, Va., Sept. 1934-current. Formerly as *Speech Monographs*, CtY, DLC, NN, NcD, ViU

Construction News, Little Rock, Ark., 1934-current

Delta Kappa Gamma Bulletin, Austin, Tex., 1934-current

Exceptional Children, Herndon, Reston, Va., 1934-current. May 1935-May 1951 as *Journal of Exceptional Children*, DLC, IU, MH, NcD, ViU

Flight Magazine, Fort Worth, Fort Washington, Dallas, Tex., Apr. 1934-? 1934-Apr. 1936 as *Southwestern Aviation*, May 1936-Dec. 1950 as *Southern Flight*, DLC, NN, TxLT

Flight Operations Magazine, Atlanta, Ga., 1934-?

Florida Food & Grocery News, Indian Rocks Beach, Fla., 1934-current

Florida Poultry and Dairy Journal -- See *Florida Poultryman*

Florida Poultry and Farm Journal -- See *Florida Poultryman*

Florida Poultryman, Tampa, Fla., Feb. 1934-? May 1939-May 1948 as *Florida Poultryman and Stockman*, June 1948-Dec. 1951 as *Florida Poultry and Dairy Journal*, Jan. 1952-Jan. 1956 as *Florida Poultry and Farm Journal*, DA, FPY, FU, NN

Florida Poultryman and Stockman -- See *Florida Poultryman*

Floridian, Winter Park, Fla., July 1934-Mar. 1935? DLC, FU

Four Arts; Dedicated to Artistic Virginia, Richmond, Va., June 1934-June 1935, LNHT, NN, Vi, ViU

Humble Oilways; A Magazine for Industry, Houston, Tex., 1934-?

Insurance Record, Dallas, Tex., Nov. 1934-current. 1934-Aug. 31, 1944 as *Southwest Insurer*, Sept. 7-Dec. 28, 1944 as *Southwest Insurer and Insurance Record*, DLC, TxU

The International Fire Chief, New York, N.Y.; Alexandria, Va., 1934-current, DLC

Journal of Exceptional Children -- See *Exceptional Children*

LBA Banker -- See *Louisiana Banker*

Louisiana Banker, Baton Rouge, La., 1934-current. Formerly as *LBA Banker*, LU

Modern Business Education; A Magazine for Commerce Teachers, Lexington, Ky.; Baton Rouge, La., Nov. 1934-June 1951, DLC, KyU, LU

Museum News -- See *Tidewater Arts Review*

National Beta Club Journal,
Spartanburg, S.C., Sept.
1934-current. Formerly as *Beta
Club Journal*, DLC, FU, GU, ViU

National Educational Secretary,
Washington, D.C.; Chicago, Ill.;
Arlington, Va., 1934-current.
v.1-18 as *National Secretary*,
IU, N, NcDurC, OkU, UU

National Secretary -- See *National
Educational Secretary*

North Carolina Education, Raleigh,
N.C., Sept. 1934-current.
Supersedes *North Carolina
Teacher*, DE, NN, NcD, NcU, TxU

*North Carolina Labor and
Industry*, Raleigh, N.C., Aug.
1934-75, Ct, DL, IU, Nc, NcU,
TxU

North Carolina Legion News,
Raleigh, N.C., 1934-?

Notes, Chapel Hill, N.C., 1934-?

*The Orleans Parish Medical Society
Bulletin*, New Orleans, La.,
1934-current, LU-M, NNN

Photogrammetric Engineering, Falls
Church, Va., 1934-current.
Currently as *Photogrammetric
Engineering and Remote
Sensing*, DLC, NN, VBP

*Photogrammetric Engineering and
Remote Sensing* -- See
Photogrammetric Engineering

Sewanee News, Sewanee, Tenn.,
1934-current

Southern Flight -- See *Flight
Magazine*

Southern Magazine, Wytheville,
Va., Mar. 1934-May 1938, DLC,
GU, InU, NN, NcU, Tx, Vi, VR,
ViU

Southern Review, Jackson, Miss.,
1934, CtY, ViU

Southern States Sportsman,
Knoxville, Tenn., Nov. 1934-Feb.
1936. v.1 as *Tennessee
Sportsman*, DA, DLC, MoU, T, TU

Southwest Insurer -- See
Insurance Record

*Southwest Insurer and Insurance
Record* -- See *Insurance Record*

Southwest Texas Medicine, San
Antonio, Tex., 1934-May 1935,
MBM, NNN, PPC

Southwestern Aviation -- See *Flight
Magazine*

Southwestern Musicale -- See
*Southwestern Musician and
Texas Music Educator*

Southwestern Musician -- See
*Southwestern Musician and
Texas Music Educator*

*Southwestern Musician and Texas
Music Educator*, Lubbock, Tex.,
Dec. 1934-? Supersedes
Southwestern Musicale,
1934-Aug. 1954 as *Southwestern
Musician*. Absorbed *Texas Music
Educator*, Sept. 1954, AzU, DLC,
LU, NN, TxH

Speech Monographs -- See
Communication Monographs

*Story Art; A Magazine for
Storytellers*, Chevy Chase, Md.;
Harrisburg, Pa.; Dallas, Tex.,
1934-current, DLC, H, NN, OU

Sword of the Lord, Murfreesboro,
Tenn., 1934-current

*Tennessee Nurses Association
Bulletin*, Nashville, Tenn.,
1934-current

Tennessee Sportsman -- See
Southern States Sportsman

Tennessee Teacher, Nashville,
Tenn., Feb. 1934-current, DE,
N, T, TU

Texas Business and Professional Woman, Brownwood, Tex., July 1934-? TxH, TxLT

Texas Oil Journal, Longview, Tex., 1934-?

Tidewater Arts Review, Norfolk, Va., 1934-? v.1-2 as *Museum News*, DLC, ViU, ViW

Virginia Farmer, Hopewell, Richmond, Va., Mar. 1934-Nov. 1948. Mar.-Oct. 1934 as *Virginia Grange News*, absorbed *Tobacco Grower*, VBP

Virginia Grange News -- See *Virginia Farmer*

Virginia Trucker, Richmond, Va., 1934-?

Alabama Public Works and Highway Journal -- See *Progressive Alabama*

Alumni Gazette, Williamsburg, Va., 1935-current

American Digest, New Orleans, La., June 1935-Mar. 1936. no.1-5 as *Louisiana Author's Journal*, LNHT

Baptist Training Union Magazine, Nashville, Tenn., Jan. 1935-? NjMD, PCA

Coastal Cattleman -- See *Gulf Coast Cattleman*

Commonwealth; the Magazine of Democracy, Bradenton, Fla., 1935-85, CtY, DLC, NN, NcD

Dixie Ranger, Atlanta, Ga., Mar. 1, 1935-Apr. 1942, DA, DLC

Duke Mathematical Journal, Durham, N.C., Mar. 1935-current, CtY, DLC, NN, NcD, NcU

Expert Witness Journal, Miami, Fla., 1935-current. Formerly as *Law Lab Journal*

Farmer's Banner -- See *Texas Agriculture*

Florida Architecture, Miami, Fla., 1935-? 1935-48 as *Florida Architecture and Allied Arts*, 1943-46 not published, F, FM, FU, GAT, TxU

Florida Architecture and Allied Arts -- See *Florida Architecture*

Florida Beacon, Jacksonville, Fla., 1935-? FU

The Gamecock, Hartford, Ark., 1935-current, OU, WU

Gulf Coast Cattleman, Beaumont, Tex., 1935-current. Also as *Coastal Cattleman*, DA, NN, TxCM, TxU

Journal of Rehabilitation, Des Moines, Iowa; Chicago, Ill.; Alexandria, Va., Jan. 1935-current. 1935-Jan. 1945 as *National Rehabilitation News*, DE, DLC, N, ViU

Journal of Southern History, Baton Rouge, New Orleans, La.; Athens, Ga., Feb. 1935-current, CtY, DLC, F, GU, NN, NcD, ViBlbV

Kentucky Methodist, Paris, Ky., 1935-? GEU, KyLxCB

Law Lab Journal -- See *Expert Witness Journal*

Louisiana Authors' Journal -- See *American Digest*

The Message Magazine, Nashville, Tenn., 1935-Mar./Apr. 1978. Continued by *Message*, DLC

Mississippi Forests and Parks, Jackson, Miss., 1935-? DA, DLC, MsSM, MsU, NN

National Rehabilitation News -- See *Journal of Rehabilitation*

Presbyterian, Kinston, N.C., Aug. 1935-Dec. 1936, VRT

Presbyterian News, Greensboro, N.C., Sept. 1935-? NcMHi, NcU

Producer-Consumer, Amarillo, Tex., July 1935-July/Aug. 1952? DA, TxCaW, TxLT

Progressive Alabama; Highway and Industrial Review, Montgomery, Ala., June 1935-May 1936? v.1, no.1-8 as *Alabama Public Works and Highway Journal*, NN, TU

Richmond Gardens -- See *Virginia Gardens*

Richmond Milk Market Review, Richmond, Va., 1935-? DA, NIC-A

South Atlantic Bulletin, University, Ala., May 1935-Nov. 1978. Continued by *SAB, South Atlantic Bulletin*, DLC, LU, MiU, MoU, NjR

The Southern Review; A Literary and Critical Quarterly Magazine, Baton Rouge, La., July 1935-Apr. 1942, 1965-current, CtY, DLC, LN, LNHT, MiU, NcD, NcU, Vi, ViU

Southern Speech Communication Journal, Richmond, Va.; Winston-Salem, N.C., Oct. 1935-current. Formerly as *Southern Speech Journal*, DLC, FU, GU, LNHT, NcD, NcU, VBP

Southern Speech Journal -- See *Southern Speech Communication Journal*

Southern Voice; Devoted to the Interests of the Worker and Farmers of the South, Leesville, La., Feb. 22-Mar. 27, 1935? NN

Southwester; A Journal for Writers, Artists, and Members of Study Groups, Dallas, Tex., Summer 1935-May 1939, DLC, NN, TxH, TxU

Sunday School Young Adults -- See *Sunday School Young People*

Sunday School Young People, Nashville, Tenn., 1935-current. Currently as *Sunday School Young Adults*, KyLoS, NRAB

Tennessee Folklore Society Bulletin, Maryville, Murfreesboro, Tenn., 1935-current, CtY, DLC, MH, NN, NcU, T, TU

Texas Agriculture, Waco, Tex., Oct. 1935-? v.1-5 as *Farmer's Banner*, TxCM, IU

Texas Centennial Review, Dallas, Tex., Nov. 21, 1935-June 25, 1936, NN, TxDN, TxU

The Upper Room, Nashville, Tenn., 1935-current, DLC, IU, PP, ViRUT

Virginia Gardens, Richmond, Va., Dec. 1935-? v.1-3 as *Richmond Gardens*, Vi

Alabama Social Welfare, Montgomery, Ala., Jan. 1936-current, AU, CtY, DLC, IU, N, NN, TU, TxU

Alabama; The News Magazine of the Deep South -- See *South; The News Magazine of Dixie*

American Jewish Times -- See *American Jewish Times Outlook*

American Jewish Times Outlook, Greensboro, Charlotte, N.C., 1936-? Originally as *American Jewish Times*, absorbed *Southern Jewish Outlook*, NN, NcGuG, NcU, OCH

American Railroad Journal -- See *Railroad Journal*

Carolina Flyer, Charlotte, N.C., Feb. 1936-? DLC

Carolina Stage, Chapel Hill, N.C.,
Mar. 1936-? DLC, MH, NN, NcU

Castanea, Morgantown, W.Va.;
Charlotte, N.C., Jan.
1936-current, CLU, DA, DLC, IU,
N, NcD, NcU

Dallas Bar Speaks, Dallas, Tex.,
1936-? MnU-L

Doors and Hardware, McLean,
Arlington, Va., 1936-current

Duke Divinity School Review,
Durham, N.C., 1936-? NcD

DukEngineer, Durham, N.C.,
1936-current, NcD

Employment Service Envoy,
Frankfort, Ky., Mar. 1936-Dec.
1938. 1936-May 1937 as *National
Reemployment Service in
Kentucky*, DLC, KyL, KyU, NN

Farm Bureau Press, Little Rock,
Ark., 1936-?

*Florida Academy of Sciences
Quarterly Journal*, Gainesville,
Orlando, Fla., 1936-current. As
Florida Scientist since 1973.
CtY, DLC, FDS, FTS, FU, NN, NcU

Florida Cattleman -- See *Florida
Cattleman and Livestock Journal*

*Florida Cattleman and Dairy
Journal* -- See *Florida
Cattleman and Livestock Journal*

*Florida Cattleman and Livestock
Journal*, Kissimmee, Fla., Oct.
15, 1936-current. v.1, no.1-3
as *Florida Cattleman*, v.1, no.4
- v.7, no.6 as *Florida Cattleman
and Dairy Journal*, DA, FPY,
FU

Florida Foods Journal -- See
Florida Products Journal

Florida Fruit Digest, Jacksonville,
Fla., 1936-? FU

Florida Homes and Flowers, Saint
Petersburg, Fla., Oct. 1936-?
FU

Florida Products Journal, Orlando,
Fla., Aug. 1936-Dec. 1939? v.1-2
as *Florida Foods Journal*, DA,
DLC, FTS, FU, NN

Florida Scientist -- See *Florida
Academy of Sciences Quarterly
Journal*

Florida Teacher, Miami, Fla., May
1936-? v.1-3, no.13 as *Teacher
of Dade County, Florida*, v.3,
no.14 -v.4, no.5 as *Teacher of
Dade County and the Florida
Teacher*, FU

Gospel Tidings, Amarillo, Tex.,
1936-?

Gulf Coast Migrant, Houston, Tex.,
1936-? MiU, TxHR

Herpetologica, Shreveport, La.,
1936-current

*Journal of Religious Education of
the African Methodist Episcopal
Church*, Nashville, Tenn.,
1936-current

Kentucky Bar Journal, Frankfort,
Lexington, Ky., Dec. 1936-?
Also as *Kentucky Benches and
Bar*, CtY-L, DLC, Ia, KyBgW,
NIC, NcD-L

Kentucky Benches and Bar -- See
Kentucky Bar Journal

*Members' Bulletin of the Virginia
Museum of Fine Arts*, Richmond,
Va., 1936-current, DLC, Vi, ViU

Mississippi Libraries, Jackson,
Clinton, Miss., 1936-current.
Formerly as *Mississippi Library
News*, DLC, IU, Mi-U, MsSM, MsU,
NN, NcU

Mississippi Press, Jackson, Miss.,
1936-? MsSM, MsU

Motor Transportation Hi-Lights,
Columbia, S.C., 1936-current

*National Reemployment Service in
Kentucky* -- See *Employment
Service Envoy*

*New Orleans College of Pharmacy
Journal*, New Orleans, La.,
1936-?   DSG, LNL, NNN

*New South; A Journal of
Progressive Opinion*,
Birmingham, Ala., July 1936-?
TC, TNV

News Digest, Birmingham, Ala.,
1936-?   v.1-9, no.17 as *Alabama
News Digest*, DLC, NcU, WHi

North Carolina Farm Bureau News,
Raleigh, N.C., 1936-current

North Carolina Public Schools,
Raleigh, N.C., 1936-75

North Carolina Review -- See
Pseudopodia

Oriole, Atlanta, Ga.; North
Augusta, S.C., 1936-current, DA,
GEU, GU, LU, MiU

Pseudopodia, Atlanta, Ga., Spring
1936-Winter 1944/45.   Later as
The North Carolina Review, and
as *South Today*, CtY, DLC, GEU,
GS, GU, NcD, ViU

Public Welfare Journal, Dallas,
Tex., Feb. 1936-Oct. 1937, NN

*Quarterly Journal of the Florida
Academy of Sciences*, _____,
Fla., 1936-?   v.1-7 as its
Proceedings, DA, DLC, FU, NN,
NcU

Raiford Record, Quincy, Fla.,
1936-?

Railroad Journal, Richmond, Tex.,
Sept. 1936-?   Sept. 1936 as
Texas Booster, Feb.-June 1945
as *American Railroad Journal*,
DLC, ICJ, NcU

Rural Sociology, Ithaca, N.Y.;
Lexington, Ky., Mar.
1936-current, Ct, DLC, KyU,
NcD, NcU, TxU

Scripts n' Pranks, Davidson, N.C.,
1936-?   Davidson College Library

Social Services in North Carolina,
Raleigh, N.C., 1936-?

South, Birmingham, Ala., 1936-?

*South; the News Magazine of
Dixie*, Auburn, Ala., 1936-?
1936-Sept. 11, 1956 as *Alabama;
the News Magazine of the Deep
South*, ABH, NN

South Carolina Newsview, Columbia,
S.C., Apr. 18-Sept. 19, 1936, ScU

South Today -- See *Pseudopodia*

*Southern Architectural Review;
Architecture Engineering,
Decoration*, Atlanta, Ga.,
1936-May 1938, DLC, GEU, NN,
TxU, ViW

Southern Farm Leader, New
Orleans, La., 1936-37?   NcD

Southern Financial Review,
Nashville, Tenn., 1936-?   TNV

*Southern Historical Research
Magazine; History, Biography,
Genealogy*, Dallas, Tex., Feb.
1936-Apr. 1937, Ct, DLC, NN, T,
TxH, TxU, ViU

Southern Journal of Progress --
See *Southern Progress*

*Southern Progress; A Magazine
Devoted to Commerce,
Agriculture and Industry in the
South*, Atlanta, Ga., June-Oct.
1936?   June 1936 as *Southern
Journal of Progress*, DA, GEU

Southern Sportsman, Austin, Tex.,
Aug. 1936-?   DA, FU, TxU

Steering Wheel, Austin, Tex.,
1936-current

*Teacher of Dade County and the
Florida Teacher* -- See *Florida
Teacher*

Teacher of Dade County, Florida
-- See *Florida Teacher*

*Tennessee Technologist; A
Quarterly of Southern
Industry*, Knoxville, Tenn.,
June 1936-Apr. 1938, CtY, DLC,
T, TU

Tennessee Welfare Courier,
Nashville, Tenn., Apr. 1936-?
TNV

Texas Booster -- See *Railroad
Journal*

Texas Business and Texas Parade
-- See *Texas Parade*

Texas Music Educator, Borger,
Tex., 1936?-Aug. 1954?
Absorbed by *Southwestern
Musician*, later *Southwestern
Musician and Texas Music
Educator*, TxDN

Texas Parade, Austin, Tex., June
1936-78. Suspended May
1943-May 1948, merged with
Texas Business to form *Texas
Business and Texas Parade*.
Superseded by *Texas Business*,
CtY, DLC, NN, Tx, TxH, TxU

Texas Wild Life, Austin, Tex., Oct.
1936.   Superseded by
Southwestern Sports Magazine,
DA

Urchin, New Orleans, La., 1936-?

Virginia Engineering Magazine,
Charlottesville, Va., June
1936-Mar. 1937, ViU

Virginia Poultry News, Blacksburg,
Va., Apr. 1936-May 1938, DA

West Texas Catholic, Amarillo, Tex.,
1936-current.   Formerly as *West
Texas Register*

West Texas Register -- See *West
Texas Catholic*

Window Vues, Fort Worth, Tex.,
1936-?

Accion, El Paso, Tex.,
1937-current.   Formerly as
Revista Para Uniones de Adultos

Alabama, Today and Tomorrow,
Montgomery, Ala., 1937-?   AAP,
AU, ATT

Baptist Beacon -- See *Baptist
Beacon and the Berean Banner*

*Baptist Beacon and the Berean
Banner*, Dallas, Tex., 1937-42.
v.1-5 as *Baptist Beacon*, KyLoS

Bethel Beacon, McKenzie, Tenn.,
1937-?

Chat, Raleigh, N.C., Mar.
1937-current, NNM, NcRS, MiU

The Chronicle of the Horse,
Middleburg, Va., 1937-current

The Contract Bridge Bulletin,
Memphis, Tenn., 1937-current

*Delta Weekly; A Journal of Fact
and Opinion*, Greenville, Miss.,
Oct. 1937-Sept. 1938, NN

*Dixieana; the All-Southern
Magazine*, Louisville, Ky.,
Jan.-Sept. 1937, KyL, NN, Vi,
ViU

Flight Surgeon Topics, Randolph
Field, Tex., Jan. 1937-July
1939, DSG, NNN

Florida Architect, Miami, Fla.,
1937-Sept. 1946, n.s. 1947-?
1937-May 1954 as *Bulletin*, FM,
FMU, FU, MCM

Florida Pharmacist, Tallahassee, Fla., 1937-current. Also as *Florida State Pharmaceutical Association Journal*, and as *Florida Pharmacy Journal*, FPY, FU

Florida Pharmacy Journal -- See *Florida Pharmacist*

Florida State Pharmaceutical Association Journal -- See *Florida Pharmacist*

Florida West Coast Bird News, Saint Petersburg, Fla., July 1937-?   MiU

For Men, Louisville, Ky., Apr. 1937-Aug. 1939. Also as *For Men and Men Only*, and as *For Men Only*, DLC, TC

For Men and Men Only -- See *For Men*

For Men Only -- See *For Men*

Game and Fish -- See *Mississippi Game and Fish*

Glenmary Challenge, Vanceburg, Ky., 1937-current. Also as *Glenmary's Challenge*

Glenmary's Challenge -- See *Glenmary Challenge*

Growth; A Journal for Studies of Development and Increase -- See *Growth; Devoted to Problems of Normal and Abnormal Growth*

Growth; Devoted to Problems of Normal and Abnormal Growth, Menasha, Wis.; Ann Arbor, Mich.; Lakeland, Fla., 1937-current. Also as *Growth; A Journal for Studies of Development and Increase*, CU, DA, DLC, FU, NNN, NcD

Gulf Coast Baptist, Houston, Tex., 1937-?   KyLoS

Journal of Parapsychology, Durham, N.C., 1937-current, CtY, DLC, NN, NcD

Kentucky Farm Bureau News, Louisville, Ky., 1937-current

Kentucky Grower and Stockman, Lexington, Ky., June 1937-Nov. 1939, DA, KyU

Knitter, Charlotte, N.C., 1937-? NN, NcRS, ScCc

Lawyers Title News, Richmond, Va., Apr. 1937-current, CtY-L, MH-L, NcD-L

Literary South, Lincolnton, N.C., Jan. 1937-?   GEU, NcD, NcU

Louisiana Business Review, Baton Rouge, La., Jan. 1937-current, CtY, DL, DLC, IU, LN, LNHT, NcD

Louisiana Library Association Bulletin, New Orleans, Baton Rouge, La., 1937-current, DLC, LNHT, LNX, MH, NN

Louisiana Policy Jury Review, Shreveport, La., Apr. 1937-? DLC, LNHT

Mississippi Game and Fish, Jackson, Miss., Nov. 1937-current. 1937-Apr. 1938 as *Game and Fish*, CU, CtY, DA, FU, MsU, TxU

Modern Bulk Transporter, Houston, Tex., 1937-current

Motel/Motor Inn Journal, Temple, Tex., Oct. 1937-? Also as *Tourist Court Journal*, and as *Motor Inn Journal*, DLC, NN

Motor Inn Journal -- See *Motel/Motor Inn Journal*

Mountain Sentinel, Relief, Ky., Oct. 1937-?   ViU

New South, Chattanooga, Tenn.;
Birmingham, Ala., Nov. 1937-?
Supersedes *Southern Worker*,
DA, NN

*North Carolina Wildlife
Conservation* -- See *Wildlife in
North Carolina*

Open Windows, Nashville, Tenn.,
1937-current, DLC, KyLoS

Pioneer, Greenville, Tenn., 1937-?

The Professional Agent,
Alexandria, Va., 1937-current

Rayito, El Paso, Tex., 1937-current

Revista Para Uniones de Adultos
-- See *Accion*

Roosevelt Review, New Orleans, La.,
1937-?

South Carolina Magazine, Columbia,
S.C., 1937-? DLC, ScCc, ScU,
NN

Southern Association Quarterly,
Durham, N.C., 1937-? CtY, DE,
DLC, N, NcD, NcU, Vi, ViU

*Southern City; A Monthly Review
of Municipal Affairs of the
State*, Raleigh, N.C., Aug.
1937-Dec. 1948, n.s. Jan.
1949-current, IU, NN, NcD, NcU

Southern Folklore Quarterly,
Jacksonville, Gainesville, Fla.,
Mar. 1937-current, CtY, DLC,
FDS, FJ, FU, NSU, NcD, ScU

Southwestern Sports Magazine,
Waco, Tex., Aug. 1937-Feb. 1939.
Supersedes *Texas Wild Life*,
merged into *Southern
Sportsman*, DA

*Stamp and Cover Collectors'
Review*, Richmond, Va., Jan.
1937-Oct. 1939. Supersedes
Stamp and Cover Collecting, IU,
NN, Vi, VR

*Studies in Regionalism in
Kentucky*, Lexington, Ky.,
1937-? KyU, MdBE, NcD, TU

Tennessee Conservationist,
Nashville, Tenn., Feb.
1937-current. v.1-3 as
Tennessee Wild Life, v.4, no.2-7
as *Tennessee Wild Life and
Conservationist*, DA, IU, NN, T,
TMC

Tennessee Guardsman, Nashville,
Tenn., Oct. 1937-June 1938,
July-Nov. 1949, Feb.-Dec. 1952,
ICMILC, T, TMC

Tennessee Speech Journal,
Nashville, Tenn., 1937-Jan. 1944,
NhD, TNG, TNV, TU

Tennessee Valley Farmer,
Nashville, Tenn., June
1937-June 1939. United with
*Dixie Farm and Poultry
Journal*, to form *Dixie Farmer*,
DA, DLC, NN

Tennessee Wild Life -- See
Tennessee Conservationist

*Tennessee Wild Life and
Conservationist* -- See *Tennessee
Conservationist*

Texas Architect and Engineer, Fort
Worth, Tex., 1937-Nov. 1938,
DLC, TxCM, TxU

Texas Geographic Magazine, Dallas,
Tex., May 1937-Fall 1949, CU,
DLC, IU, TxH, TxU

Tourist Court Journal -- See
Motel/Motor Inn Journal

Wildlife in North Carolina,
Raleigh, N.C., Nov.
1937-current. 1937-Mar. 1938 as
*Wildlife Management in North
Carolina*. Apr. 1938-Aug. 1945
as *North Carolina Wildlife
Conservation*, DA, DLC, NN, NcRS

Wildlife Management in North Carolina -- See *Wildlife in North Carolina*

American Biology Teacher, Lancaster, Pa.; Herndon, Reston, Va., Oct. 1938-current, DLC, InU, MH, NNN, ViW

At-Fa Journal, Valdosta, Ga., 1938-?

Atlantian, Atlanta, Ga., July/Aug. 1938-? Supersedes *Good Words*, GS, GU, NN, NcU

Carolina Food Dealer, Charlotte, N.C., 1938-? NcRS, NcWsW

Carolina Tips, Burlington, N.C., 1938-current, ICF, NIC, ViU

Citrus and Vegetable Magazine, Tampa, Fla., June 16, 1938-current. 1938-Dec. 1941 as *Citrus*, Jan. 1942-June 1960 as *Citrus Magazine*, DA, KyU, NIC-A

Citrus Grower, Orlando, Fla., Nov. 15, 1938-May 15, 1942, DA, FU, NIC

Citrus Magazine -- See *Citrus and Vegetable Magazine*

Coach and Athlete, Atlanta, Decatur, Ga.; Baltimore, Md.; Montgomery, Ala., 1938-present. 1938-June 1952 as *Southern Coach and Athlete*, FU, GU, NN, ScU

Cotton Textile Institute -- See *Textile Hi-Lights*

Eastern Fruit Grower, Charlestown, W.Va.; Boyce, Va., Mar. 1938-? DA, MoU, NN, VBP

Florida Future Farmers, Tallahassee, Fla., 1938-?

Florida Justice, Miami, Fla., Nov. 1938-Apr. 1939, CtY-L, NIC, NcD-L, WU

Florida Liberator, West Palm Beach, Fla., Aug.-Nov. 1938. Superseded by *New Liberator*, DLC

Florida School Bulletin, Tallahassee, Fla., 1938-? Later as *Florida Schools*, DLC, FTS, FU, N, TU

Florida Schools -- See *Florida School Bulletin*

Georgia Bar Journal, Macon, Ga., Apr. 1938-63. Superseded in 1964 by *Georgia State Bar Journal*, Atlanta, C, CtY-L, DLC, G, GEU, GMM, N, NcD-L, NcU

Georgia Farm Bureau News, Macon, Ga., 1938-current

Kentucky Banker, Louisville, Ky., 1938-current, ICJ, ICU, KyL, NN

Kentucky Grocer's News, Louisville, Ky., 1938-?

Kentucky Pharmacist, Louisville, Ky., Oct. 1938-current. Supersedes *J.K.P.A.* DA, IU-M, KyL

Kentucky Sportsman, Somerset, Ky., Aug. 1938-? DA, KyL, KyU

"The Knickerbocker"-The International Netherlands Magazine, Fort Lauderdale, Fla., 1938-?

Leader's Magazine, Lexington, Ky., 1938-current

Louisiana Law Review, Baton Rouge, La., Nov. 1938-current, Ct, CtY-L, DLC, LNHT, LU-L, NcD-L, NcU

Louisiana Municipal Review, Shreveport, Baton Rouge, La., May/June 1938-current, LNHT, LU, NN

MAFES Research Highlights, Water Valley, Miss., 1938-current

Mission USA, Atlanta, Ga.,
1938-current. Formerly as *Home
Missions*

*New Orleans Medical, Dental and
Pharmaceutical Association
Journal*, New Orleans, La., Aug.
1938-? DSG

North Carolina Federationist,
Salisbury, N.C., July 1938-?
NN, NcD, NcU

PDCA Magazine -- See *PDCA Seventy*

PDCA Seventy, Falls Church, Va.,
1938-current. Formerly as
Spotlights, and as *PDCA
Magazine*. Currently as
*Painting and Wallcovering
Contractor*

*Painting and Wallcovering
Contractor* -- See *PDCA Seventy*

Petroleum Equipment and Services,
Dallas, Tex., 1938-?

*Professional Decorating & Coating
Action*, Falls Church, Va.,
1938-current

*Sanatorium Digest; Reassuring,
Reliable, Readable*, El Paso,
Tex., 1938, NNN

Searchlite, Saint Petersburg, Fla.,
1938-?

*South Carolina
Federationist...Published in the
Interest of South Carolina
Labor*, Columbia, S.C., Oct.
1938-Dec. 1949, NN

Southern Coach and Athlete -- See
Coach and Athlete

Southern Garden -- See *Southern
Life, Home and Garden Magazine*

Southern Home and Garden -- See
*Southern Life, Home and Garden
Magazine*

*Southern Life, Home and Garden
Magazine*, Raleigh, N.C.,
1938-41. v.1, no.1-2 as
Southern Home and Garden, v.1,
no.3-12 as *Southern Garden*,
DLC, NcGW, TC, ViU

Southern Methodist Layman,
Atlanta, Ga., 1938-50, GEU, NcD

Southern Pulp and Paper -- See
*Southern Pulp and Paper
Manufacturer*

Southern Pulp and Paper Journal
-- See *Southern Pulp and Paper
Manufacturer*

*Southern Pulp and Paper
Manufacturer*, Atlanta, Ga., Dec.
1938-current. Dec. 1938 as
*Southern Pulp and Paper
Journal*, currently as *Southern
Pulp and Paper*, DA, DLC, GAT,
GU, NcD

Spotlights -- See *PDCA Seventy*

Stamp Commentator, Dallas, Tex.,
Apr. 1938-July 1940? NNCo

Subpoena, San Antonio, Tex., Feb.
1938-Oct. 22, 1943, July 18,
1946-? CtY-L, NIC, ScCc, TxU

Sugar Journal, Crowley, New
Orleans, La., 1938-current, DA,
LN, LNHT, NN, PP, TxH

Tennessee Public Welfare Record,
Nashville, Tenn., Jan.
1938-current, CU, DLC, ICU, NcD,
T, TMG, TxU

*Texas and Southwest Hotel-Motel
Review*, San Antonio, Tex.,
1938-current. Formerly as
Texas Hotel Review, DLC, TxU

Texas Bar Journal, Houston,
Austin, Tex., Feb. 1938-current,
CtY-L, DLC, NcD-L, NcU, TxH,
TxU

Texas Genealogist, Dallas, Tex.,
Oct. 1938-Feb. 1939, DLC, TxH,
TxU

Texas Hotel Review -- See *Texas
and Southwest Hotel-Motel Review*

*Texas Journal of Plumbing,
Heating, Contracting*, Austin,
Tex., 1938-current

*Texas Veterinary Medicine
Journal*, Austin, Tex.,
1938-current, DA, MnU

Textile Hi-Lights, Charlotte, N.C.,
Apr. 11, 1938-?   1938-June 1957
as *Cotton Textile Institute*, DA,
DLC, NN, NcRS

Tobacco News, Greenville, N.C.,
Aug. 20-Nov. 16, 1938, DA

*Virginia Business and Professional
Woman*, Charlottesville, Va.,
Aug. 1938-?   DLC, Vi, ViU

Virginia Verse, Charlottesville,
Va., Feb.-June 1938, DLC

*Virginia Wildlife Federation
Record*, Norfolk, Va., 1938-?

Airports and Air Carriers,
Charlotte, N.C.; New York, N.Y.,
Jan. 1939-Apr. 1949.   Jan.
1939-Dec. 1942 as *Dixie Air
News*, Jan.-June 1943 as *America
Pilot and Air-Craftsman*, July
1943-Aug. 1944 as *American
Pilot*, Sept. 1944-Mar. 1948 as
*Airports; Construction,
Operations, Maintenance*,
absorbed *Aviation Equipment*,
Sept. 1947; absorbed by
American Aviation, later
Airlife, CtY, DLC, NN, NcRS

*Airports; Construction, Operations,
Maintenance* -- See *Airports and
Air Carriers*

Alabama Bar Bulletin, Birmingham,
Ala., Apr.-Oct. 1939.   Merged
into *Alabama Lawyer*, CtY-L,
MiU-L, MnU-L, NNB, NcD-L

American Checkerist, Abilene, Tex.,
Jan. 1939-?   PP

American Pilot and Air-Craftsman
-- See *Airports and Air
Carriers*

Armored News, Covington, Ga.,
1939?-?   Also as *Armored Force
News*, InU, NN

Baylor Dental Journal, Dallas,
Tex., Nov. 1939-?   CU-M, DNLM,
FU

Breeder-Stockman, Warrenton, Va.,
June 1939-57.   Also as *Virginia
Breeder*, and as *Eastern
Breeder*, absorbed *Stockman*,
July 1950.   United with
Southern Livestock Journal, to
form *Livestock Breeder*, DA,
DLC, NN, ViU

CEA Critic, College Station, Tex.,
Sept. 1939-current, CtY, DLC,
Mi, NcD, NjR, PU, ViU

Czechoslovak Specialist, Columbus,
Ohio; Chicago, Ill.; Fairfax, Va.,
1939-current, NNCo

Dixie Air News -- See *Airports and
Air Carriers*

Dr. Shelton's Hygienic Review, San
Antonio, Tex., Sept. 1939-Aug.
1980, DNLM

Drilling -- See *Drilling
International*

Drilling-DCW -- See *Drilling
International*

Drilling International, Dallas,
Tex., 1939-current.   Also as
*Drilling-DCW, Drilling-The
Wellsite Magazine*, currently as
Drilling, KU, IU, TxU

Drilling-The Wellsite Magazine --
See *Drilling International*

Eastern Breeder -- See
Breeder-Stockman

*Exponent; the Georgia Tech
Magazine*, Atlanta, Ga., 1939-?

Foodsman, Richmond, Va.,
1939-current

Georgia Petroleum Retailer,
Decatur, Ga., 1939-? GU

Georgia Tech Engineer, Atlanta,
Ga., 1939-?

Gospel Proclaimer, Austin, Tex.,
Jan. 1939-? TxU, TxDN

*Journal of Industrial Arts
Education* -- See
Man/Society/Technology

*The Journal of Mississippi
History*, Jackson, Miss., Jan.
1939-current, DLC, IU, LN, MsSM,
NN, NcD, NcU, ViBlbV

Journal of Politics, Gainesville,
Fla., Feb. 1939-current, CtY,
DLC, FDS, FTS, FU, MH, NN, NcD,
NcU

Kentucky Engineer, Lexington, Ky.,
June 1939-? KyU, KU, PSt

Louisiana Rural Economist,
University, La., Jan. 1939-? IU,
D, DLC, LU, NIC, NN

Man/Society/Technology, Reston,
Va., 1939-current. Also as
*Journal of Industrial Arts
Education*. Currently as
Technology Teacher

*Mississippi Academy of Science
Journal*, _____, Miss., 1939-?
DLC, LU, OU, MiU, MsU

Mississippi Business Review, State
College, Miss., June
1939-current, CU, DLC, GU, IU,
KyU, MsU, TxU

Mississippi News and Views,
Jackson, Miss., 1939-?

Mississippi RN, Jackson, Miss.,
1939-current

NCEE Registration Bulletin -- See
*National Council of Engineering
Examiners Registration Bulletin*

*National Council of Engineering
Examiners Registration
Bulletin*, Clemson, S.C.,
1939-current. Currently as
NCEE Registration Bulletin

Public Welfare in Mississippi,
Jackson, Miss., July/Sept.
1939-June 1952. Superseded by
Welfare Brief, DLC, LU, MsU

South Carolina Speech Bulletin,
Rock Hill, S.C., May 1939-? DE,
DLC, MnU, ViU

*Supervision; The Magazine of
Industrial Relations and
Operating Management*, New
York, N.Y.; East Stroudsburg,
Pa.; Sarasota, Fla.; Burlington,
Iowa, 1939-current. Supersedes
Foreman, CLSU, MCM, NN, NcU,
OCl

Tar Heel Nurse, Raleigh, N.C.,
1939-current, DNLM, NcU

Technology Teacher -- See
Man/Society/Technology

Texas Presbyterian Tidings,
Arlington, Tex., Feb. 1939-?
CSaT, NcMHi

Virginia Breeder -- See
Breeder-Stockman

Virginia Conference Messenger,
Franklin Springs, Ga., 1939-?
KyLxCB

Washington & Lee Law Review,
Lexington, Va., Fall
1939-current, CtY-L, DLC, IU,
N, NcD-L, NcU, Vi, ViLxW

Alabama Lawyer, Montgomery, Ala.,
Jan. 1940-current, CtY-L, DLC,
IU, InU, N, NcD-L, NcU, TU

American Church News, Nashville, Tenn., 1940–current As *New Oxford Review*, Oakland, Berkeley, Calif., since Mar. 1977, MiU, NjP

American Cover -- See *NSS Bulletin*

Arkansas Christian, Little Rock, Ark., 1940–? ArU, KyLxCB, TxFTC

Campus Echo, Durham, N.C., 1940–?

Central Christian Advocate, Nashville, Tenn., 1940–?

The Chuck Wagon, The Voice of the Texas Restaurant Industry, Austin, Tex., Aug. 1940–current, Tx, TxU

Cooperative Digest, Raleigh, Greensboro, N.C., July 1940–? DA, OU, TxLT

Dixie Mirror, Savannah, Ga., May 1940–Jan. 1941, DLC

Florida Future Farmer, Kissimmee, Fla., 1940–?

Florida Magazine of Verse, Winter Park, Fla., Nov. 1940–? CtY, FTS, FU, NN

For the Poor, Thornton, Ark., 1940–?

Georgia Music News, Statesboro, Ga., 1940–current

Georgia Observer, Atlanta, Ga., 1940–42? CSt-H

Intermediate Teacher, Nashville, Tenn., 1940–?

Interpreter, Durham, N.C., 1940–?

Kentucky Business, Lexington, Ky., Oct. 1940–Jan. 1942, DLC, KyU, IU, ViU

Kingdom Digest, Dallas, Tex., 1940–current

Louisiana Weather Journal and Agriculturist, New Orleans, La., 1940–? NNCoCi

Louisiana Welfare, Baton Rouge, La., Oct. 1940–? DLC, IU, LNX, LU, TxU

Louisville Insurance Pictorial, Louisville, Ky., Mar. 1940–? KyL

Mississippi Future Farmer, Long Beach, Miss., Jan./Feb. 1940–? DA, MsAM, MsSM

Motive, Waco, Tex., Apr./June-Aug./Oct. 1940, CtY

NSS Bulletin, Huntsville, Ala., 1940–current. Also as *American Cover*, DGS, DLC, NcD, OT, ViU

North Carolina Medical Journal, Winston-Salem, N.C., Jan. 1940–current, DLC, NNN, NcU, VRM

Of All Things, Comanche, Tex., Mar. 1940–? DLC, TxU

Oil, New Orleans, La., 1940–?

Our National Family, Dover, Del.; Atlanta, Ga., 1940–? DLC, NN, NcDurC

Phylon; the Atlanta University Review of Race and Culture, Atlanta, Ga., 1940–current, DLC, GU, NcU, TxU, ViBlbV

Quote Magazine, Atlanta, Ga., 1940–current, DLC

Rural Louisianian, _____, La., Mar. 1940–? DA, LU

Seafood Merchandising, New Orleans, La., 1940-? 1940-June 1957 as *Southern Fisherman*, July-Oct. 1957 as *Southern Fisherman and Seafood Merchandising*, absorbed *Fish & Oil Industry*, Nov. 1952, and *Seafood Business*, March 1953, DF, DLC, LNHT, NN

Sheep and Wool, Lexington, Ky., June-Oct. 1940, DA, TU

South-Central Bulletin, New Orleans, La.; Houston, Tex., Dec. 1940-current, LNHT, LNL, NcD, TxU

Southern Accent; A Magazine of Poetry from the Heart of the South, Jackson, Miss., July/Aug. 1940-Sept./Oct. 1941, CSmH, NN

Southern Canner & Packer -- See *Southern Food Processor*

Southern Fisherman -- See *Seafood Merchandising*

Southern Fisherman and Seafood Merchandising -- See *Seafood Merchandising*

Southern Food Processor, Atlanta, Ga., 1940-? 1940-Aug. 1951 as *Southern Canner & Packer*, DA, GAT

Southern Frontier, Atlanta, Ga., Jan. 1940-Dec. 1945. Superseded by *New South*, DLC, MsAM, NcD, CtY, TNV

Southern Genealogical Review, Mount Vernon, Ga., July-Dec. 1940, DLC, NN, Vi, WHi

Studies in the Romance Languages and Literatures, Chapel Hill, N.C., 1940-? CU, MiU, N, NcU

Tennessee Planner, Nashville, Tenn., Jan./Feb. 1940-? Supersedes *Tennessee Plan Topics*. Suspended Sept./Oct. 1941-Sept./Oct. 1942, IU, DL, MiU, NN, NcD, TC, TN, TU

Tennessee Valley Engineer, Knoxville, Tenn., Apr. 1940-? DLC, TU

Texas Archaeological News, Austin, Tex., Mar.-Dec. 1940, DLC, NN, TxU

Texas Art Teacher, Georgetown, Tex., Nov. 1940-? TxDN, TxU

Texas Historical and Biographical Record, Austin, Tex., July 1940-? TxDN

Virginia Engineering Review, Charlottesville, Va., Sept. 15, 1940-? NNC, NjR, ViU

Virginia Journal of Science, Blacksburg, Charlottesville, Richmond, Va., 1940-May 1943, n.s., Jan. 1950-current. Supersedes *Claytonia*, CtY, DLC, NN, NcD, NcU, Vi, ViW

Weevil Outlet, Monticello, Ark., 1940-?

Williamsburg Restoration Historical Studies, Williamsburg, Va., 1940-? DLC, NN, ViU

Abingdon Quarterly, Nashville, Tenn., Oct.-Dec. 1941-July-Sept. 1945. Supersedes *Illustrated Quarterly*, superseded by *Bible Lessons for Youth*, DLC, GEU

Annals of Kentucky Natural History, Louisville, Ky., Sept. 27, 1941-? DA, DLC, KyL, KyU

Arkansas Gardener, Batesville, Ark., Oct./Nov. 1941-? ArU, DA

BIB-Liner, Dallas, Tex., 1941-current

Bulletin of Florida Farm Bureau Federation -- See *Florida Agriculture*

Chipper/Snacker, Arlington, Va., 1941-current

Christian School, Nashville, Tenn., 1941-?

D. H. Hill Library Studies, Raleigh, N.C., Aug. 1941-? CLU, DLC, NN, NcD, NcU

Educational & Psychological Measurement, Chicago, Ill.; Durham, N.C., Jan. 1941-current, CtY-M, DA, DLC, NN, NcD, NcU

Florida Agriculture, Kissimmee, Orlando, Gainesville, Fla., 1941-current. v.1-8 as *Bulletin of Florida Farm Bureau Federation*, F, FM, FMU, FU

Florida Civilian Defense News, Tallahassee, Fla., 1941-Feb. 28, 1945, Ct, FCU, FTS, NN, NjP

Florida Contractor, Tallahassee, Fla., 1941-current. Formerly as *Florida Planning & Heating Contractor*

Florida Planning & Heating Contractor -- See *Florida Contractor*

Game Fowl News, Asheville, N.C., 1941-? OU

Gulf States Industry, Pensacola, Fla., Mar. 1941-Nov. 1947. Mar. 1941-June 1944 as *Wentworth's Magazine*, Apr.-June 1947 as *Industrial South*, merged with *Tung World*, Dec. 1947. F, FU

History News, Washington, D.C.; Montpelier, Vt.; Nashville, Tenn., July 1941-current. 1941-49 as *State and Local History News*, CtY, DLC, NN, TKL, Vi, ViU

Home Quarterly, Nashville, Tenn., Oct./Dec. 1941-July/Sept. 1954. Superseded by *Mature Years*, DLC, GEU, NcD

Human Organization, Boston, Mass.; Gainesville, Fla.; Washington, D.C., 1941-current, CtY, DLC, NN, NcD

Individual Grocer, Covington, Ky., 1941-?

Industrial South -- See *Gulf States Industry*

Journal of Economic History, Raleigh, N.C.; Atlanta, Ga., 1941-current, DLC, TxU

Journal of Public Health Dentistry, Raleigh, N.C., 1941-current

Junior Historian -- See *Texas Historian*

Key Houston, Houston, Tex., 1941-?

Louisiana Methodist, Little Rock, Ark., 1941-?

Methodist Messenger, Denton, Tex., Dec. 3, 1941-? TxDN

Mississippi Literary Review, University, Miss., 1941, DLC, MsU

Motive; A Magazine of the Methodist Student Movement, Nashville, Tenn., Feb. 1941-? DE, DLC, NcD, OCl, TxU

Mountaineer, Knoxville, Tenn., Feb. 1941-? DLC

National Dental Association Quarterly, Charlottesville, Va.; Tuskegee, Ala., 1941-current, AU-M, DLC, MiU, PP

Quarterly Review . . . A Survey of Southern Baptist Progress, Nashville, Tenn., Jan.-Mar. 1941-current, DLC, KyLoS, PCA, TxLT

Slipstick, Clemson, S.C., 1941-?

Southeastern Cattleman and Dairy Journal -- See *Southern Livestock Journal*

Southern Chemist, Memphis, Tenn., 1941-? 1941-47 as *Memph-ion*, DLC, TU, LNL

Southern Garment -- See *Southern Garment Manufacturer*

Southern Garment Manufacturer, Charlotte, N.C.; Atlanta, Ga., Aug. 1941-? Also as *Southern Garment*, NcU, NN

Southern Livestock Journal, Kissimmee, Fla., June 1941-Dec. 1957. 1941-Oct. 1943 as *Southeastern Edition of Florida Cattleman and Dairy Journal*, Nov. 1943-May 1946 as *Southeastern Cattleman and Dairy Journal*, DA

Southern Stockman -- See *Stockman*

Southwestern News, Fort Worth, Tex., 1941-current

Star; Radiating the Light of Truth on Hansen's Disease, Carville, La., 1941-current

State and Local History News -- See *History News*

Stockman, Memphis, Tenn., Mar. 1941-June 1950. 1941-Jan. 1946 as *Southern Stockman*, merged with *Eastern Breeder*, to form *Breeder-Stockman*, DA, DLC, IU, NN, TU

Surveying and Mapping, Washington, D.C.; Falls Church, Va., Oct. 1941-current, DGS, DLC, NN

Tennessee Anthropology Papers, Knoxville, Tenn., Nov. 1941-? DLC, ICU, MiU, NjP

Tequesta: The Journal of the Historical Association of Southern Florida, Coral Gables, Fla., Mar. 1941-? CU, DLC, F, FTS, FU, NN, NcD

Texas A & M Agriculturist, College Station, Tex., 1941-?

Texas Historian, Austin, Tex., Jan. 1941-current. Formerly as *Junior Historian*, DLC, TxDN, TxLT, TxU

Texas Journal of Public Health, Austin, Tex., Nov. 1941-Mar./Apr. 1946? NNN, Tx, TxH, TxU

Texas Resources, Austin, Tex., Jan. 1941-? Ct, DLC, N, TxU

Textiles Panamericanos; Revista Para la Industria Textile, New York, N.Y.; Atlanta, Ga., May 1941-current

Upward, Nashville, Tenn., 1941-69. Superseded by *Event*, in 1970.

Virginia Bar Weekly, Richmond, Va., Jan. 22, 1941-Jan. 4, 1944, CtY-L, MiU-L, MnU-L, NcD-L

Virginia Farm Bureau News, Richmond, Va., 1941-current

Wentworth's Magazine -- See *Gulf States Industry*

Wesley Quarterly, Nashville, Tenn., 1941-?

Ahora, El Paso, Tex., 1942-current. Formerly as *Revista Para Uniones de Intermedios*

Archeological Society of Virginia Quarterly Bulletin, Charlottesville, Va., 1942-current, DLC, NN, Vi, ViBlbV

Arkansas Historical Quarterly, Fayetteville, Ark., Mar. 1942-current, ArU, CU, DLC, NN, NcD, NcU, TxU

Bankers Digest, Dallas, Tex., 1942-current, TxU

Bicycle Journal, Fort Worth, Tex., 1942-?

Business Bulletin -- See *Mississippi's Business*

Education in Louisiana, Baton Rouge, La., Apr. 1942-May 1948. Apr. 1942-May 1945 as *Louisiana Education in Wartime*, CtY, LN, LNHT, LU, ViU

Explicator, Fredericksburg, Richmond, Va., Oct. 1942-current, CLU, DLC, MH, NN, NcD, ViU, ViW

Florida Jaycee News, New Port Richey, Fla., 1942-?

The Florida United Methodist, Lakeland, Fla., 1942-current

Forest Farmer, Valdosta, Atlanta, Ga., 1942-current, DA, GU

Georgia Entomologist, Atlanta, Ga., Jan. 1942-? DA, NIC-A

Guide Magazine, Saint Petersburg, Fla., 1942-current

Louisiana Education in Wartime -- See *Education in Louisiana*

Louisiana Game, Fur and Fish -- See *Louisiana Conservationist*

Kentucky Genealogical and Historical Recorder, Washington, Ky., 1942-? KyBB, MoK, OCl

Kentucky Sesquicentennial County History Series, Cynthiana, Ky., 1942-? CtY, DLC, KyU, MnU, NN

The Louisiana Bar, New Orleans, La., Jan. 1942-Apr. 1953, Ct, LNHT, M, NIC, NNC, NcD-L

Louisiana Conservationist, Baton Rouge, La., Dec. 1942-July 1948, n.s. Sept. 1948-current. July 1946-July 1948 as *Louisiana Game*, and as *Fur and Fish*, CU, DA, DLC, IU, LN, LNHT, LNX, NN

Mississippi Music Educator, Hattiesburg, Miss., 1942-current

Mississippi's Business, University, Miss., Oct. 1942-current. v.1-8 as *Business Bulletin*, CtY, DLC, MsU, NN, NcU

New Orleans Port Record, New Orleans, La., Sept. 1942-current, DLC, ICJ, LNHT, NN

North Carolina Libraries, Boone, N.C., Feb. 1942-current, Nc, NcD, NcU

North Carolina Plumbing & Heating Cooling Forum, Raleigh, N.C., 1942-current

Palomino Horses, Mineral Wells, Tex., 1942-current

Presbyterian Journal, Weaverville, Asheville, N.C., May 1942-current. 1942-Sept. 1959 as *Southern Presbyterian Journal*, DLC, NcMHi, VRT, ViU

Record Changer, Fairfax, Va., 1942-? DHU, DLC, NN

Research and Farming, Raleigh, N.C., Dec. 1942-Summer 1981. Continued by *Research Perspectives*, Fall 1981, CU-A, NcRS, TxLT

Revista Para Uniones de Intermedios -- See *Ahora*

Revista Para Uniones De Primarios, El Paso, Tex., 1942-current

South Carolina Dental Journal,
Greenville, S.C., 1942-Jan. 1982.
Supersedes *Journal of the South
Carolina Dental Association*,
absorbed *Palmetto State Dental
Journal* in 1944, NNN, NNN-D,
TU-M

*South Carolina Medical University
Bulletin*, Charleston, S.C.,
1942-?

Southern Patriot, Nashville, Tenn.;
Dallas, Tex., 1942-current. As
Southern Struggle, since 1977,
CtY, DLC, GEU, MnU, NN, NcD,
ViU

Southern Presbyterian Journal --
See *Presbyterian Journal*

Southern Struggle -- See *Southern
Patriot*

*Tar Heel Elementary School
Principal*, Greensboro, N.C.,
Nov. 1942-? NcGW, NcU

Tennessee Government, Knoxville,
Tenn., Sept./Oct. 1942-? CU,
CtY, NN, NcD, TU, ViU

Tennessee Historical Quarterly,
Nashville, Tenn., Mar.
1942-current, CLU, ICN, IU, InU,
NN, NcD, NcU, TC, TU

Texas Chiropractor, Austin, Tex.,
1942-current

Texas Fashions, Dallas, Tex.,
1942-?

Texas Game and Fish, _____, Tex.,
Dec. 1942-? CU, CtY, DA, DLC,
NN, TxCM, TxU

Texas Livestock Journal, Austin,
Tex., Jan. 1942-? Merged with
Weekly Livestock Reporter, DA,
NN, TxDN, TxU

Texas Personnel Review, Austin,
Tex., 1942-? TxDaM

Texas Professional Engineer,
Austin, Tex., Oct. 1942-current,
IU, Tx, TxDaM, TxLT, ViU

Texas Progress, Dallas, Tex., July
1942-July 1945, DA

Textile Forum, Raleigh, N.C., Jan.
1942-73, DA, DLC, NN, NcRS

Virginia Religious Work Journal,
Richmond, Va., July 1942-Apr.
1954. Superseded by
Sowing-Sharing, Vi

Alabama Local Government Journal
-- See *Alabama Municipal
Journal*

Alabama Municipal Journal,
Montgomery, Ala., 1943-current.
1943-May 1953 as *Alabama Local
Government Journal*, AAP, AU,
MiU, NIC, PV-L

American Patriot -- See *Free
Enterprise*

Atlanta News Digest -- See *Georgia
Labor News Digest*

Church Music, Richmond, Va., Sept.
1943-74. Merged in 1974 with
Life and Worship and continued
as *Music and Liturgy* DLC,
NcMHi, VRT

Educational Leadership,
Washington, D.C.; Alexandria,
Va., Oct. 1943-current, CtY, DE,
DLC, N, NcD, ViU

Florida DCT Journal, West Palm
Beach, Fla., Jan. 1, 1943-?

Free Enterprise, San Antonio,
Tex., Dec. 1943-current. As
American Patriot, Phoenix,
Ariz., since 1976, DLC, NN

*Georgia Academy of Science
Bulletin* -- See *Georgia Journal
of Science*

Georgia Engineer, Atlanta, Decatur, Ga., Feb. 1943-current, GAT, AzTeS

Georgia Journal of Science, Atlanta, Ga., July 1943-1976. As *Georgia Academy of Science Bulletin*, until 1976, CtY, DLC, GEU, GU, NcD, NcU

Georgia Labor News Digest, Atlanta, Ga., 1943-? v.1-4, no.14 as *Atlanta News Digest*, also as *Georgia News Digest*, DLC, GU, MH

Georgia News Digest -- See *Georgia Labor News Digest*

Guardsman, Houston, Tex., June 1943-? June-Dec. 1943 as *Texas Guardsman*, Tx, TxH, TxU

Horse World, Des Moines, Iowa; Lexington, Ky., Apr. 1943-current. Also as *Iowa Horseman*, and as *Mid-western Horseman*, DA, IaAS

Houston Engineer, Houston, Tex., 1943-? Formerly as *Slide Rule*, NN, TxCM, TxLT, TxU

Iowa Horseman -- See *Horse World*

Kentucky Monographs, Lexington, Ky., 1943-? DLC, IN, KyU, NN

Louisiana Peace Officer, Baton Rouge, La., 1943-? Supersedes *Louisiana Policeman*, LU, NNCoCi

Louisiana Pharmacist, New Orleans, La., Nov. 1943-current, DLC, DSG, IU-M

Mid-western Horseman -- See *Horse World*

Mississippi Dental Association Journal, McComb, Miss., July 1943-Apr. 1951, DSG, InU-D, NNN, NNU-D

Mississippi Notes, Bay Saint Louis, Miss., Mar. 1943-May 1951? DLC

Music and Liturgy -- See *Church Music*

NSS News, Alexandria, Va.; Huntsville, Ala., 1943-current, DLC, ICF, NN

North Carolina English Teacher, Chapel Hill, N.C., Apr. 1943-current, Nc, NcD, NcU

Quarterly Review of Literature, Chapel Hill, N.C., Autumn 1943-44, DLC, GU, MH, NN, NcRS, NcU, ViU

Raven, San Antonio, Tex., Spring 1943-Winter 1944. United with *Now* to form *Different*, NN, Tx, ViU

Rayburn's Ozark Guide; the Magazine of the Ozark, Lonedale, Ark., July/Aug. 1943-? ArU, CLU, DLC, MH

Rural Living, Richmond, Va., 1943-current

Slide Rule -- See *Houston Engineer*

Southern Building -- See *Southern Building Standards*

Southern Building Standards, Birmingham, Ala., 1943-current. Currently as *Southern Building*, DLC, NN

Southern Weekly, Dallas, Tex., Oct. 16, 1943-? Absorbed *Southwestern Banking and Industry*, CtY, NN, NjP, TxDN, TxU

Southernaire, Atlanta, Ga., Mar. 1943-? GAT

Tarheel Wheels, Raleigh, N.C., 1943-current

Taxicab Management, Asheville, N.C., 1943-current

Tennessee School News, Knoxville, Tenn., Apr. 1943-? IU

Texas Commons, Blanco, Tex., July
1943-? NN

Texas Food Merchant, Austin, Tex.,
1943-current

Texas Guardsman -- See *Guardsman*

*Texas Reports on Biology and
Medicine*, Galveston, Tex.,
Spring 1943-? CtY, DLC, NN-M,
TxU-M, ViU

Texas Trends, Fort Worth, Tex.,
Sept. 1943-? Also as *Texas
Trends in Mental Health*, DSG,
LNHT, TxH, TxU-M

Texas Trends in Mental Health --
See *Texas Trends*

Volunteer Gardener, Nashville,
Tenn., Oct. 1943-? DA, T, TU

We the People of North Carolina,
Raleigh, N.C., May 1943-current,
DLC, KyU, NcD, NcU

World-wide Missionary Crusader,
Lubbock, Tex., 1943-current

Accion Inter-Americana, Austin,
Tex., Nov. 1944-? DLC, TxU

Carolina Israelite, Charlotte, N.C.,
Feb. 1944-? DLC, MH, NN

Co-op Power, Austin, Tex.,
1944-current

Corrosion, Houston, Tex.,
1944-current, DLC, NN, TxH,
TxU, ViU

Delta Farm Press, Clarksdale,
Miss., 1944-current

Drilling Contractor, Houston, Tex.,
1944-current, DLC, OkT, OkU,
TxCM

Georgia Progress, Athens, Ga.,
Sept. 15, 1944-Feb. 1949, CtY,
DA, DLC, GEU, GU, NN

*Georgia Vocational Rehabilitation
News*, Atlanta, Ga., Sept. 1944-?
CtY, DLC, GAT, GMW, GU, NN

Georgia's Human Resources,
Atlanta, Ga., 1944-? CtY, DLC,
GEU, GMW, GU

Internal Auditor, Altamonte
Springs, Fla., Sept. 1944-? DLC

*Journal of the Texas Optometric
Association*, Austin, Tex.,
1944-current

*Louisiana Dental Association
Journal*, Shreveport, La.,
1944-current

Louisiana Highway News, Baton
Rouge, La., Aug. 1944-Oct. 1953.
Superseded by *LMTA News*, LU

Meharri-Dent, Nashville, Tenn.,
1944-current, InU-D, NNC-M, PU

Mississippi Transports, Jackson,
Miss., 1944-?

North Carolina Engineer, Raleigh,
N.C., Sept. 1944-? NN, NcD,
NcRS

Odd Fellows News of Texas, Dallas,
Tex., 1944-?

Rural Life, Jackson, Miss., June
1944-Jan. 1945, DA, NN, ViU

The SCEA Emphasis, Columbia, S.C.,
1944-current

Scenic South, Louisville, Ky.,
1944-71, AAP, AU, DLC, KyU,
ViBlbV

South Carolina Education Journal,
Columbia, S.C., 1944-?

South Carolina Farmer, Columbia,
S.C., 1944-current

Southern Business, Atlanta, Ga.,
1944-45, GU

Tennessee Archeologist, Knoxville, Tenn., Dec. 1944-? DLC, NN, TC, TU

Tennessee Industrial Hygiene News, Nashville, Tenn., 1944-? DLC, T, TU

Tennessee News, Nashville, Tenn., Jan. 28, 1944-? T, TMC

Tennessee Republican Age, Chattanooga, Tenn., Jan. 1944-? DLC

Texas A & M Engineer, College Station, Tex., 1944-?

Texas Co-op Power, Austin, Tex., July 1944-current. 1944-Jan. 1945 as *Texas Cooperative Electric Power*, DA, Tx, TxU

Texas Osteopathic Physicians' Journal, Fort Worth, Tex., 1944-? CLOst, DNLM, TxU

Textile Technology Digest, Charlottesville, Va., June 1944-current, DBS, InLP, OU

The Work Boat, New Orleans, Covington, La., 1944-current. Absorbed *Southern Marine Review* in 1946. DLC, FU, ICJ, NN, OCl

Alabama Bible Society Quarterly, _____, Ala., Jan. 1945-? DLC, ViU

Alabama Poultry Cooperative News, Montgomery, Ala., May 1945-? DA

Alabama Purchaser, Birmingham, Ala., Feb. 1945-current, AAP, AU, GEU, LNTC

Auburn Veterinarian, Auburn, Ala., Winter 1945-current, AAP, DA, FU, NIC

Better World for Our Crippled Children-- See *New Horizons*

Biometrics, Washington, D.C.; Raleigh, N.C.; Washington, D.C., 1945-? DSG, CtY, MCM, MiU

Business Girl, Dallas, Tex., Mar. 1945-Sept. 1947, DLC, TxDa

Cats Magazine, Port Orange, Fla., 1945-current, NN, OCl, PP

Christian Chronicle, Austin, Tex., 1945-?

Citizen, San Antonio, Tex., 1945-? DLC

Classified Exchange, Memphis, Tenn., 1945-?

The Cooperative Accountant, Durham, N.C.; Springfield, Va., Winter 1945-current, AU, LU, NcD

Cooperative Farmer -- See *Southern States Cooperative Farmer*

Cross Country News, Oklahoma City, Okla.; Cleburne, Tex., 1945-current, DLC, MoKL, TxU

El Hospital, North Miami Beach, Fla., 1945-current

Fairchild Tropical Garden Bulletin, Miami, Fla., May 1945-current, DA, FCU, MH

Florida Building -- See *Florida Contractor and Builder*

Florida Construction Industry -- See *Florida Contractor and Builder*

Florida Contractor and Builder, Miami, Orlando, Fla., 1945-current. 1946-June 1960 as *Florida Building*. Currently as *Florida Construction Industry*, F, FM, FMU

Flower & Feathers, Lookout
Mountain, Tenn., Aug.
1945-current, DLC, NN, TC, TCU,
ViU

General Aviation -- See *General
Aviation News: The Green Sheet*

*General Aviation News: The Green
Sheet*, Snyder, Tex.,
1945-current. Formerly as
General Aviation

Georgia Nursing, Atlanta, Ga.,
1945-current, DNLM

Houston Town and Country,
Houston, Tex., 1945-?

Journalism Educator, Columbia,
S.C.; Laramie, Wyo.; Reno, Nev.,
1945-current, ArU, IU, IaU, MoU,
NcU

Kentucky Happy Ground, Frankfort,
Ky., 1945-current. Originally
as *Kentucky Happy Hunting
Ground*, CU, DA, DLC, IU, KyL,
KyU

Kentucky Happy Hunting Ground
-- See *Kentucky Happy Ground*

Louisiana Genealogical Register,
New Orleans, La., July 1945-Oct.
1947, DLC, LN, LNHT, LU, MWA,
Mi, NN

*Louisiana State University
Engineering Experiment Station
News*, Baton Rouge, La., Jan.
1945-May 1947, LU, WaU

Louisiana Tech Engineer, Ruston,
La., 1945-current

Mid-South Stockman Farmer -- See
Stockman Farmer

Mississippi Valley Stockman Farmer
-- See *Stockman Farmer*

New Horizons, Chapel Hill, N.C.,
Sept. 1945-Apr. 1949. v.1,
no.1-4 as *Better World for Our
Crippled Children*, DNLM, NNC-M

Open Door, Richmond, Va., 1945-?
ViU

Piano Guild Notes, Austin, Tex.,
1945-current

*Pipeline and Underground Utilities
Construction*, Houston, Tex.,
1945-current

The Retired Officer, Washington,
D.C.; Alexandria, Va.,
1945-current, AMAU, DLC, MiD,
NN

Rural Georgia, Atlanta, Ga.,
1945-current

South; the Magazine of Travel, New
Orleans, La., Mar. 1945-Oct.
1948, DLC, GU, LN, NN

*South Carolina Education News
Emphasis*, Columbia, S.C., 1945-?

South Carolina Labor News,
Columbia, S.C., 1945-current

Southern Machinery and Metals,
Atlanta, Ga., Oct. 1945-Jan.
1950, GAT, ICJ, MoKL, NN, ViU

Southern Motor Cargo, Memphis,
Nashville, Tenn., 1945-current,
DLC, MiU, OkT

Southern Packet Asheville, N.C.,
Jan. 1945-1954, AAP, ABS, GEU,
GU, DLC, NN, Nc, NcD, NcU

Southern Plastics -- See *Southern
Plastics and Chemicals*

Southern Plastics and Chemicals,
Atlanta, Ga., Aug. 1945-Dec.
1946.   1945-Sept. 1946 as
Southern Plastics, DLC, GAT,
PPi

*Southern Plumbing, Heating and
Air Conditioning*, Atlanta, Ga.;
Greensboro, N.C., Dec.
1945-current. Also as *Southern
Plumbing, Heating, Cooling*, GAT

*Southern Plumbing, Heating,
Cooling* -- See *Southern
Plumbing, Heating and Air
Conditioning*

*Southern States Cooperative
Farmer*, Richmond, Va., Feb.
1945-current. Supersedes
Southern States Patron.
Feb.-Sept. 1945 as *Cooperative
Farmer*, 1945-? as *Southern
States Cooperative Farmer*,
?-current as *Cooperative
Farmer*, DA, DLC, NIC-A, ViU

Southern Textile News, Charlotte,
N.C., 1945-current, DA, GAT,
GEU

Southland, Atlanta, Ga., Dec.
1945-? DLC, FCU, GEU, GU

Stockman Farmer, Jackson,
Raymond, Miss., 1945-current.
Formerly as *Mid-South Stockman
Farmer*, and as *Mississippi
Valley Stockman-Farmer*

The Sun Colony, Fort Lauderdale,
Fla., 1945-?

*Tennessee Industrial Development
News*, Nashville, Tenn., Apr.
1945-? 1945-June 1953 as
*Tennessee Industrial Planning
Newsletter*, DLC, NN, NcU, T, TU

Tennessee Walking Horse,
Lewisburg, Tenn., Jan.
1945-June 1951, DA, DLC, MoU,
TU

Texas Butane News -- See *Texas
LP-Gas News*

Texas Chemurgic News, Dallas,
Tex., July 1945-Dec. 1950, DA,
TxU

Texas Hospitals, Austin, Tex.,
June 1945-current, DSG, ICJ,
NNN, TxH, TxU-M

Texas LP Gas News, Austin, Tex.,
1945-current. Formerly as
Texas Butane News, NN, OCl,
OkT, TxH, TxU

Texas Labor Market Review,
Austin, Tex., 1945-current.
Formerly as *Texas Manpower
Trends*

Texas Manpower Trends -- See
Texas Labor Market Review

*Texas Optometric Association
Journal* -- See *Texas Optometry*

Texas Optometry, Austin, Tex.,
1945-current. Formerly as
*Texas Optometric Association
Journal*

*Texas Spectator; A Weekly News
Magazine*, Austin, Tex., Oct. 12,
1945-May 24, 1948, CtY, NN, Tx,
TxU

Virginia Road Bulletin, Richmond,
Va., May 1945-? CU, DPR, NNC,
Vi, ViU

*Ad Week/Southwest Advertising
News*, Dallas, Tex., 1946-?

*Alabama's Industrial
Opportunities*, Montgomery, Ala.,
1946-48, ABS, AU-M, DA, KyU,
NN, OU, PP

American Building Supplies -- See
Southern Building Supplies

American Independent Jeweler --
See *Independent Jeweler*

Arkansas Law Review -- See
*Arkansas Law Review and Bar
Association Journal*

*Arkansas Law Review and Bar
Association Journal*, University,
Fayetteville, Ark., Winter
1946/47-current. v.1, no.1-2 as
Arkansas Law Review, ArU, CU,
DGW, DLC, MoU, N, KyU, NcU,
TxU

Arkansas Outdoors, Little Rock, Ark., 1946-current

Arkansas REA News, Little Rock, Ark., 1946-? DA, DLC

Arkansas Sportsman, Little Rock, Ark., July 1946-? DLC

Army Digest, Alexandria, Va., 1946-current. Currently as *Soldiers*

Asbury Seminarian, Wilmore, Ky., Spring 1946-current, CtY-D, DLC, IEG, KyU, MH-AH

Better Health for North Carolina, Raleigh, N.C., Dec. 1946-Apr. 1949, CU, DLC, Nc, NcD, NcU

The Camellia Journal, Fort Valley, Ga., 1946-current

Carolina Country, Raleigh, N.C., June 1946-current. Formerly as *Carolina Farmer*, CtY, DA, NcU

Carolina Road Builder, Raleigh, N.C., Sept. 1946-Dec. 1950. Superseded by *Road Builder*, CtY, Nc, NcRS, NcU

Dixie Sportsman, Knoxville, Tenn., 1946-? DLC, TU

Earth Science, Chicago, Ill.; Falls Church, Va., Aug. 1946-current, DLC, MiU, NN, OU, ViU

Eat, Memphis, Tenn., Apr. 1946-Aug. 1950? Apr.-Dec. 1946 as *Southern Refrigeration Journal*, Jan. 1947-Feb. 1949 as *Freezer's Journal*, Mar. 1949-Feb./Mar. 1950 as *Eat-Frozen Foods*, DA, DLC, NN

Estrella, El Paso, Tex., 1946-current

Eat-Frozen Foods -- See *Eat*

FCX Patron, Raleigh, N.C., 1946-?

Florida Builder, Tampa, Fla., July 1946-current, F, FM, FU

Florida Peace Officer, Orlando, Fla., 1946-? DLC, F, FCU

Florida Pharmaceutical Digest, Miami, Fla., July 1946-? FU

Florida Trees and Trails, Tallahassee, Fla., Aug. 1946-May/June 1951? F, FCU, FTS, FU

Freezer's Journal -- See *Eat*

Georgia Forestry Notes, Atlanta, Ga., 1946-48. Superseded by *Georgia Forestry*, GU

Georgia Osteopathic Medical Association Journal, Dublin, Tucker, Ga., 1946-? Also as *Georgia Osteopathic News*, CLOst, DNLM

Georgia Osteopathic News -- See *Georgia Osteopathic Medical Association Journal*

Georgia Presbyterian News, Decatur, Ga., Apr. 1946-Feb./Mar. 1951, NcMHi

Georgia Psychologist, _____, Ga., 1946-? 1946-54 as the association's *Bulletin*, GEU, GU

Independent Jeweler, Dallas, Tex., 1946-? Formerly as *American Independent Jeweler*, and as *Southwestern Watchmaker and Jeweler*,

Kentucky Naturalist, Louisville, Ky., Summer 1946-? DA, DLC, KyL, KyU, NNM

Kentuckiana Purchasor, Louisville, Ky., 1946-current

Key, Dallas, Tex., 1946-? Formerly as *Key Dallas*

Key Dallas -- See *Key*

L.M.T.A. News, Baton Rouge, La., 1946-current

Louisiana Labor Market, Baton Rouge, La., Jan. 1946-current, DL, DLC, IU, LN, LNHT, LU

Louisiana Rehabilitation News, Baton Rouge, La., Nov. 1946-? CSt, DLC, IU, LNHT, LNL, LNX, PP

Mississippi Sportsman, Memphis, Tenn., Feb. 1946-Mar. 1947. Merged into *Mississippi Valley Sportsman*, MsSM, NN

Mobile Home and R.V. News -- See *Mobile Home News*

Mobile Home and Trailer News -- See *Mobile Home News*

Mobile Home News, Miami, Altamonte Springs, Fla., 1946-current. Also as *Mobile Home and R.V. News* and as *Mobile Home and Trailer News*

NAWCAS Guild News, Atlanta, Ga., 1946-current

Nashville Cooperative Dairyman, Nashville, Tenn., June 1946-? DA

National Press Photographer -- See *News Photographer*

New South, Atlanta, Ga., Jan. 1946-? CtY, DLC, GU, NN, NcD, NcRS

News Photographer, Durham, N.C., 1946-current. As *National Press Photographer* until 1974. MoKL, NN, NRE

Orlando-Land, Orlando, Fla., 1946-?

Orlando Magazine, Orlando, Fla., 1946-81

Orthopedic and Prosthetic Appliance Journal -- See *Orthotics & Prosthetics Journal*

Orthotics & Prosthetics Journal, Alexandria, Va., Dec. 1946-current. Formerly as *Orthopedic and Prosthetic Appliance Journal*, DSG, NNC-M, PPiM

Quarterly Bulletin, Richmond, Charlottesville, Va., 1946-current, DLC, MiU, NN, Vi, ViU

Reading Guide, Charlottesville, Va., 1946-? CtY, DGW, NcD-L, Vi, ViU

Research Engineer, Atlanta, Ga., May 1946-? DLC, GU, NN

Revista Para Parvulos Y Principiantes, El Paso, Tex., 1946-current

Rural Arkansas Magazine, Little Rock, Ark., 1946-current

Rural Virginia, Richmond, Va., 1946-?

San Antonio District Dental Society Journal, San Antonio, Tex., 1946-70

Savannah Jewish News, Savannah, Ga., 1946-current

Shreveport Magazine, Shreveport, La., 1946-current

Signal, Burke, Falls Church, Va., 1946-current, DAL, DLC, NN

Soldiers -- See *Army Digest*

Southern Building Supplies, Atlanta, Ga., 1946-? Also as *American Building Supplies*, DLC, GAT

Southern Food Processing, New Orleans, La., Apr. 1946-Jan. 1948, MoKL

Southern Sportsman, Little Rock, Ark., 1946-? DLC

Southern States-man, Richmond, Va., July 1946-? DA

Southwest Advertising & Marketing, Dallas, Tex., 1946-? 1946-58 as *Southwestern Advertising & Marketing,* ArU, OkU, TxU

Southwestern Advertising & Marketing -- See *Southwest Advertising & Marketing*

Southwestern Watchmaker and Jeweler -- See *Independent Jeweler*

Sun-up, San Antonio, Tex., Feb. 1946-Jan. 1950. Absorbed *Southern Home and Garden,* DA, DLC, FU, NN

Tennessee Air Progress, Nashville, Tenn., Spring 1946-Winter 1948, Ct, DLC, TC, TU, ViU

Tennessee Business, Knoxville, Tenn., Jan. 1946-? CtY, DL, KyU, M, NN, TU

Tennessee Union Farmer -- See *Union Farmer*

Tennessee Valley Industrialist, Chattanooga, Tenn., Jan.-Apr. 1946. Superseded by *Southern States Industry and Business,* DLC, TC, TNJ

Texas; A Monthly Magazine Devoted to the Welfare of the People of Texas, Austin, Tex., Apr.-Aug. 1946, Tx, TxU-M

Texas Herald, Austin, Tex., Jan. 24, 1946-? Suspended May 1946-Mar. 1951, TxFTC, TxU

Texas News Digest; Current Statehouse Record Reviews, Austin, Tex., Jan. 18, 1946-? TxU

Texas Pageantry, Austin, Tex., Apr. 1946-? DLC, WHi

Texas Public Employee, Austin, Tex., Apr. 1946-? TxCM, TxU

Texas Week; Texas' Own Weekly Newsmagazine, Austin, Tex., Aug. 10, 1946-Feb. 22, 1947, NN, Tx, TxDN, TxU

Textile Review, Gastonia, N.C., 1946-? NcU, PPF

Union Farmer, Nashville, Tenn., Aug. 1946-May 1949. 1946-Jan. 1948 as *Tennessee Union Farmer,* DA, TNJ, ViU

Vegetable Growers News, Norfolk, Va., July 1, 1946-? 1946 as *Virginia Truck Experiment Station Vegetable Growers News,* DA, IU, WU

Virginia and the Virginia County -- See *Virginia Record*

Virginia and the Virginia Record -- See *Virginia Record*

Virginia Challenge, Altavista, Va., Sept. 1946-? Vi

Virginia Country -- See *Virginia Record*

Virginia Forests, Richmond, Va., Sept./Oct. 1946-current, DA, Vi, VBP, VR

Virginia Record, Richmond, Va., Oct. 1946-53, 1954-current. Formerly a newspaper. Also as *Virginia Country,* and as *Virginia and the Virginia Country,* and as *Virginia and the Virginia Record,* DLC, NN, Vi, ViU

Virginia Truck Experiment Station Vegetable Growers News -- See *Vegetable Growers News*

DECA Distributor, Falls Church, Va., 1947-current. Superseded by *New Dimensions*

AAA World -- See *Florida AAA Motorist*

Adult Teacher, Chicago, Ill.; Nashville, Tenn., Oct. 1947-current, DLC, IEG, NcD

African Violet Magazine, Knoxville, Tenn., 1947-current, DA, MiD, TKL

Air University Quarterly -- See *Air University Review*

Air University Review, Montgomery, Ala., 1947-current. Formerly as *Air University Quarterly Review*, AU, CtY, DLC, NN, NcD, TxU, ViU

Airman, Little Rock, Ark., June 1947-Sept. 1948, ArU, DLC

Alabama Cancer Bulletin, Montgomery, Ala., 1947?-? AU-M, DSG, UU

Alabama Nurse, Montgomery, Ala., May 1947-? AAP, AU-M, DNLM

All Outdoors Magazine, Denison, Tex., 1947-?

Alumni News, Hattiesburg, Miss., 1947-current

American Corrective Therapy Journal, New York, N.Y.; Houston, Tex., 1947-current. Until 1967 as *Association for Physical and Mental Rehabilitation Journal*, DSG, IU, KyU, PPC

Apalachee: The Publication of the Tallahassee Historical Society, Tallahassee, Fla., 1947-1970, CtY, ICN, ViBlbV

Association for Physical and Mental Rehabilitation Journal -- See *American Corrective Therapy Journal*

Bicycle Business Journal, Fort Worth, Tex., 1947-current

The Boardman, Baton Rouge, La., Apr. 1947-current, CU, DLC, FU, GU, LNHT, LU, NcD

Business Education Forum, Washington, D.C.; Reston, Va., Mar. 1947-current. Formerly as *UBEA Forum*, DLC, MnU, NN, TxDa

Coleopterists' Bulletin, Dryden, N.Y.; Gainesville, Fla., Apr. 1947-current, CU, DA, KU, LNHT, LU, MH, NcRS

Dade County Teacher, Miami, Fla., 1947-current. Currently as *U.T.D. Today*

Dallas Home Builder, Dallas, Tex., 1947-? DLC

Daylily Journal -- See *Hemerocallis Journal; Daylily Gardener's Magazine*

Dixie Handbook -- See *Dixie; The Magazine of Southern Progress*

Dixie; The Magazine of Southern Progress, Charleston, S.C., Jan./Mar. 1947-Fall 1948. v.1, no.1-3 as *Dixie Handbook*, DLC, NN, ScU

Florida AAA Motorist, Miami, Fla., 1947-current. As *AAA World* since 1981.

Florida Flying, Jacksonville, Fla., May 15, 1947-Mar. 1948, DLC

Florida Music Director, Tampa, Fla., Sept. 1947-current. Formerly as *Music Director* and earlier as *School Director*, FCU, FTS, FU

Florida Truck News, Jacksonville, Fla., 1947-current, F, FM, FMU, FTaSU, FU

Florida Wildlife, Tallahassee, Fla., 1947-current. Supersedes *Florida Game and Fish*, AAP, CU, DA, F, FCU, FTS, FU, NN

The Food Herald, Dallas, Tex., 1947-current

Georgia Pharmacist, Athens, Ga., 1947-? GU, LNL, PPiU-H

The Georgia Review, Athens, Ga., 1947-current, DLC, GA, GS, GU, NN, NcD

Gulfcoast Retail Grocer, Houston, Tex., 1947-current. Formerly as *Houston Retail Grocer*

Hemerocallis Journal; Daylily Gardener's Magazine, Minneapolis, Minn.; Signal Mountain, Tenn.; Walterboro, S.C., 1947-current. Currently as *Daylily Journal*, DA, DLC, NIC

The Herald, Houston, Tex., 1947-?

Home Life, Nashville, Tenn., Jan. 1947-current, ABH, DLC, KyLoS, TxFS

Houston Retail Grocer -- See *Gulfcoast Retail Grower*

Interpretation; A Journal of Bible and Theology, Richmond, Va., Jan. 1947-current. Supersedes *Union Seminary Review*, DLC, NcD, Vi, ViU

The Jag Journal, Alexandria, Va., Aug. 1947-current, DLC

The Journal of Comparative and Physiological Psychology, Arlington, Va., Feb. 1947-Dec. 1982. Continues *Journal of Comparative Psychology*, InU, KyU-M, TxU, ViU

Louisiana Highways, Baton Rouge, La., Apr. 1947-July 1950, Ct, DLC, LN, LNL, LU

Mecanica Popular, Miami, Fla., 1947-current

Miami Law Quarterly -- See *University of Miami Law Review*

Mississippi Methodist Advocate -- See *Mississippi United Methodist Advocate*

Mississippi United Methodist Advocate, Jackson, Miss., 1947-current. Formerly as *Mississippi Methodist Advocate*

Mississippi Valley Sportsman, Memphis, Tenn., Apr. 1947-? Supersedes *Bird Dog Gazette*, as *Mississippi Sportsman* and as *Florida Sportsman*, MsSM

Morticians of the Southwest, Dallas, Garland, Tex., 1947-current

Music Director -- See *Florida Music Director*

North Carolina Tree Topics, Raleigh, N.C., Aug. 1947-? DA, FTS

Nuclear Science Abstracts, Oak Ridge, Tenn., 1947-75, ABH, DF, DLC, MH, MN, TU

Orchid Lore, Houston, Tex., 1947-? DA, DLC, TxH

Panadero Latino Americano, Houston, Tex., 1947-?

Perkins School of Theology Journal, Dallas, Tex., Fall 1947-? CtY-D, OkTU, TxDaM, TxFS, TxHR

Presbyterian College Magazine, Clinton, S.C., 1947-?

Resort Management, Milwaukee, Wis.; Memphis, Tenn., June 1947-current, DLC, NN, OCl

Restaurant South, Greensboro,
N.C., 1947-current, FMU, FU, NcU

The Review, College Station, Tex.,
1947-?

School Director -- See *Florida
Music Director*

Security Searchlight, Nashville,
Tenn., Aug. 1947-?   T, TU

Skeet Shooting Review, Dallas,
Tex., 1947-current, NN

Southern Dairy Goat News, Union,
S.C., Jan. 1947-Sept. 1948, DA

Southern Hardwood Digest,
Memphis, Tenn., June
1947-June/July 1949, CU, DA

Southern Optometrist, Charlotte,
N.C., 1947-current, OU

Southern Wings, High Point, N.C.;
Orlando, Fla., 1947-current?
DLC, MoKL

Southwest Electrical, Dallas, Tex.,
1947-?

Southwestern Crop and Stock,
Lubbock, Tex., Jan. 1947-?
MoKL, TxCM, TxLT, TxWB

*Southwestern Horologist and
Jeweler*, Houston, Tex., 1947-?
MoKL, VBP, ViU

Southwestern Law Journal, Dallas,
Tex., 1947-current. v.1, no.1-2
as *Texas Law and Legislation*,
ArU, CtY-L, DLC, FU, GU, TxU

Tennessee Apiculture, Nashville,
Tenn., 1947-?   NIC, T, TMC

*Tennessee Vocational Rehabilitation
News*, Nashville, Tenn., Mar.
1947-Oct. 1949, DLC, TC, TMG,
TU

Tennessee Volunteer, Nashville,
Tenn., Apr. 1947-Feb. 1949, July
15, 1949-May 1953, T

Texas Law and Legislation -- See
Southwestern Law Journal

Time & Tide, Lorton, Va., 1947-?

Transportation Digest, Atlanta,
Ga., Oct. 1947-?   DLC

UBEA Forum -- See *Business
Education Forum*

U.T.D. Today -- See *Dade County
Teacher*

University of Miami Law Review,
Coral Gables, Fla., Mar.
1947-current. As *Miami Law
Quarterly*, 1947-Spring 1951,
CtY-L, DLC, F, FCU, FTS, FU,
N, NcD-L

Vanderbilt Law Review, Nashville,
Tenn., Dec. 1947-current, CtY-L,
DLC, N, NcU, TNJ, TU

Virginia Accountant, Richmond,
Va., June 1947-current, DLC,
NN, Vi, ViU

Virginia Economic Review,
Richmond, Va., Dec. 1947-?   DA,
DLC, IU, NN, Vi, ViU

Virginia Federalist, Richmond, Va.,
1947?-?   ViU

Virginia Foodsman, Richmond, Va.,
1947-?   DA, Vi, ViU

Virginia Poultryman, Richmond,
Harrisonburg, Va., Apr.
1947-current, DA, ViU, VBP

Virginia Trooper, Richmond, Va.,
Aug. 1947-?   DLC, Vi, ViU

West Texas Publishers, Hamlin,
Tex., 1947-?

AREA Magazine, Montgomery, Ala.,
1948-current. Formerly as
Alabama Rural Electric News,
DA

Aaron Burr Association Chronicle, Linden, Va., May 1948-? DLC, NjP, OCHP

Alabama Aviation News, Montgomery, Ala., July 1, 1948-? CSt, CU, DLC, NcD

Alabama Law Review, University, Ala., Fall 1948-present, AU, CtY-L, DAL, DLC, KyU, NcD-L, NcU, TU, TxU

Alabama Music Educator, Jacksonville, Ala., 1948-? DLC

Alabama Retail Trade, University, Ala., 1948-? 1948-Aug. 1949 as *Alabama Retail Trade Report*, Nov. 1949-Aug. 1955 as *Retail Trade Report*, AAP, AU, DLC, OkU

The Alabama Review, University, Ala., Jan. 1948-current, AAP, AU, CLU, LU, CtY, DLC, NN, NcU

Alabama Retail Trade Report -- See *Alabama Retail Trade*

Alabama Rural Electric News -- See *AREA Magazine*

American Musicological Society Journal Princeton, N.J.; Richmond, Va., Spring 1948-current, DLC, MH, NN, NcU, TxU

Apalachee Diary, Chattahoochee, Fla., 1948-current

Arkansas Delta Sig, Little Rock, Ark., 1948-current

Army Recruiting Journal, Hampton, Va., 1948-? Formerly as *U.S. Army Recruiting and Career Counseling Journal*

Art Education, Kutztown, Pa.; Herndon, Va., Jan./Feb. 1948-current, DLC, IU, NN, PP

Automatic Launderer and Cleaner -- See *Coin Launderer and Cleaner*

Baylor Law Review, Waco, Tex., Summer 1948-current, DLC, MH-L

Baylor Progress, Dallas, Tex., 1948-current

Carolina Quarterly, Chapel Hill, N.C., Fall 1948-current, CtY, DLC, NN, NcD, NcU

Coin Launderer and Cleaner, Atlanta, Ga., Nov. 15, 1948-current. Formerly as *Automatic Launderer and Cleaner*, DLC, OCl

Dallas Presbyter, Dallas, Tex., Apr. 1948-? NcMHi

El Paso Today, El Paso, Tex., 1948-current

Engineering Research -- See *Engineering Research News*

Engineering Research News, Raleigh, N.C., Jan. 1948-current. v.1, no.1 as *Engineering Research*, DLC, FU, KyU, NcRS, ViU

Flacs, Lakeland, Fla., 1948-current

Florida Anthropologist, Gainesville, Tallahassee, Fla., 1948-current, CtY, DLC, F, FCU, FU, NN, NjP

Florida Citrus Fruit: Acreage, Production, Utilization, Prices and Tree Numbers, Orlando, Fla., Dec. 1948-? DA, F, FTS

Florida's Children, Tallahassee, Fla., Mar. 1948-? 1948-Sept. 30, 1950 the *News Bulletin of the Florida Children's Commission*, CU, DLC, F, FU, IU

4-H Life Magazine, Atlanta, Ga., 1948-?

Georgia Forestry, Atlanta, Dry Branch, Ga., 1948-current. Supersedes *Georgia Forestry Notes*, DA, DLC, GS, KyU, N

Georgia Professional Engineer, Atlanta, Ga., 1948-current. As *Professional Engineer*, 1948-Mar. 1950, GAT, NN

Georgia Veterinarian, Atlanta, Ga., Sept. 1948-? DA, NIC, NNN

Golf World, Pinehurst, Southern Pines, N.C., 1948-current, DLC, KyU, NcD, ViU

Industrial Engineering, Norcross, Ga., 1948-? Supersedes *Journal of Industrial Engineering*

Jewish Monitor, Birmingham, Ala., 1948-?

Journal of Legal Education, Durham, N.C.; Lexington, Ky., 1948-current, CtY-L, DLC, KyU, N, NcD, NcU, ViU

Kentucky Electric Co-op News -- See *Rural Kentuckian*

Kentucky Weaver, Louisville, Ky., 1948-? DLC, OrP

Library Service Review, Durham, N.C., June 1948-? I, IU, MnU, NN

Library Service Review, Durham, N.C., June 1948-? I, IU, MnU, NN

Louisiana Stockman Farmer, Baton Rouge, La., Oct. 1948-Feb. 1950, DA, IU, LN, LNHT, LU

Manuscripts, New York, N.Y.; Tallahassee, Fla., Oct. 1948-Spring 1953, CU, CtY, DLC, KyU, NN, NcD

Miami Economic Research, Coral Gables, Fla., 1948-? v.1-4 as *Miami Residential Research*, DLC, FMU, FU, NN, NcU

Miami Lawyer, Miami, Fla., Nov. 1948-? 1948-June 1949 as *University of Miami Lawyer*, FCU, K, NcD-L

Miami Residential Research -- See *Miami Economic Research*

Missionhurst, Arlington, Va., 1948-current

Mississippi EPA News, Jackson, Miss., 1948-current

Mississippi Magic, Jackson, Miss., 1948-?

Mississippi Quarterly; The Journal of Southern Culture, Mississippi State, Miss., Dec. 1948-current. As *Social Science Bulletin*, 1948-July 1953. AU, DLC, GU, LU, MsU, NN, NcRS, ViU

Mississippi Rural Electric News, Jackson, Miss., 1948-?

National Stamp News, Sullivan's Island, S.C., 1948-?

North Carolina Artificial Breedings News Raleigh, N.C., Nov. 1948-? DA, NcRS

North Carolina Federalist, Greensboro, N.C., 1948-? NcD

North Carolina Folklore -- See *North Carolina Folklore Journal*

North Carolina Folklore Journal, Chapel Hill, Boone, N.C., June 1948-current. As *North Carolina Folklore* until 1972. Suspended July 1948-Aug. 1954, Oct. 1954-June 1955. DLC, NN, NcD, NcU

Personnel Psychology, Washington, D.C.; Durham, N.C., Spring 1948-current, CtY, DLC, NN, NcD, NcU, TxU, ViU

Polish Heritage -- See *The Quarterly Review of Polish Heritage*

Professional Engineer -- See
Georgia Professional Engineer

Quarter Horse -- See *Quarter
Horse Journal*

Quarter Horse Journal, Amarillo,
Tex., Sept. 1948-current.
Absorbed *Quarter Horse*, Nov.
1949.   As *Quarter Horse*, and
then *Quarter Horse Journal*,
DLC, TxCM, TxLT

Retail Trade Report -- See *Alabama
Retail Trade*

Rural Kentuckian, Louisville, Ky.,
Apr. 1948-current.   v.1-5, no.5
as *Kentucky Electric Co-op
News*, DA

Seafood Business Magazine, Port
Lavaca, Tex., Aug. 1948-Jan.
1953.   Absorbed by *Southern
Fisherman*, Mar. 1953, later
Seafood Merchandising, DF,
DLC, TxU

Seafood Merchandising -- See
Seafood Business Magazine

The Second Line, New Orleans, La.,
1948-current

Social Science Bulletin -- See
Mississippi Quarterly

South Carolina Law Quarterly,
Columbia, S.C., 1948-current.
Currently as *South Carolina
Law Review*, DLC, NcD-L, ScU,
TxU

South Carolina Law Review -- See
South Carolina Law Quarterly

South Carolina Presbyterian,
Columbia, S.C., May 1948-?
NcMHi

Southern Beverage Journal, Miami,
Fla., 1948-current

Southern Builder, Fort Worth,
Tex., 1948-?

Southern Fisherman -- See *Seafood
Business Magazine*

Southwest Retort, Dallas, Tex., Oct.
1948-?   TxU

Southwest Service Station Journal,
Brownwood, Tex., 1948-?

Southwestern Veterinarian, College
Station, Tex., 1948-current

Symphony Magazine, New York,
N.Y.; Vienna, Va., 1948-current.
As *Symphony News*, until May
1980.   DLC, IU, MiD, PP

Symphony News -- See *Symphony
Magazine*

TL, Tennessee Librarian -- See
Tennessee Librarian

The Technician, Marietta, Ga.,
1948-?

Tennessee Librarian, Nashville,
Tenn., Summer 1948-current.
Supersedes *Tennessee Libraries*,
currently as *TL, Tennessee
Librarian*, CLU, DLC, NN, NcU,
T, TU

Tennessee Libraries -- See
Tennessee Librarian

Tennessee Musician, Nashville,
Tenn.; Tampa, Fla., Sept.
1948-current, T, TJoS, TU

Tennessee Safety News, Nashville,
Tenn., May/June 1948-Dec. 1958,
T, TJoS

*Texas Journal of Secondary
Education*, Austin, Tex., Winter
1948-current.   Currently as
*Texas Study of Secondary
Education Research Bulletin*, IU,
TxDaM

Texas Literary Quarterly, Austin,
Tex., Summer 1948-?   CLU, NN,
TxU

*Texas Study of Secondary
Education Research Bulletin* --
See *Texas Journal of Secondary
Education*

The Texas Techsan, Lubbock, Tex.,
1948-?

Tipro Reporter, Austin, Tex.,
1948-current

University of Florida Law Review,
Gainesville, Fla., Spring
1948-current, CtY-L, DLC, F,
FCU-L, FU, NcD-L, NcU

University of Miami Lawyer -- See
Miami Lawyer

*U.S. Army Recruiting and Career
Counseling Journal* -- See *Army
Recruiting Journal*

Virginia Law Weekly,
Charlottesville, Va., May 27,
1948-current, DLC, NcD-L

AGRA News, Orlando, Fla.,
1949-current

*Abilene Geological Society
Geological Contributions*,
Abilene, Tex., 1949-? DLC, NNC,
TxLT, ViU

The Alabama Librarian,
Birmingham, Ala., Dec.
1949-current, AU, DLC, GAT,
NcU, Vi

Alabama Mental Health, Birmingham,
Ala., 1949-? AAP, ABH, AU, KyU,
NcU

Alabama Lumberman, Montgomery,
Ala., Jan. 1949-? AAP, AU, DA

American Breeds, San Antonio,
Tex., 1949-? As *Zebu Journal*
1949-Mar. 1952. DA, TxKT, TxLT

Aramco World Magazine, Houston,
Tex., 1949-current

Arkansas Ranger, Little Rock,
Ark., July 1949-? DA

Arkansas Recorder, Little Rock,
Ark., 1949-? ArU, DLC, NN

Baylor Business Studies, Waco,
Tex., Dec. 1949-current, CtY,
DLC, NN, NcD, NcU, TxDa

Cancer Bulletin, Houston, Tex.,
Mar./Apr. 1949-current, CLU,
DLC, ICJ, NNN, NcU, Tx, TxH,
TxU-M

Carolina Highways, Columbia, S.C.,
1949-current

*Chronicle of U.S. Classic Postal
Issues*, Falls Church, Va.,
1949-current

Commentary -- See *Georgia
Commentary*

Energy Management Report, Dallas,
Tex., 1949-current

Epos, A Quarterly of Poetry,
Branson, Mo.; Winter Park, Fla.,
Fall 1949-197? FCU, FU, MH, NN

Florida Italian Bulletin,
Hollywood, Fla., 1949-?

Florida Libraries, Gainesville,
Tallahassee, Fla., July
1949-current. Suspended Oct.
1949-June 1951, DLC, F, FMU,
NN, NcU, Vi

Florida Professional Engineer,
Jacksonville, Fla., Jan.
1949-Dec. 1954, FM, FMU, FTaSU,
FU

Georgia Commentary, Atlanta, Ga.,
Sept. 1949-May 1955. v.1 as
Commentary, Ct, GU, IU, LU, NNC

Georgia Democrat, Valdosta, Ga.,
1949, DLC, GMlW

Gospel Guardian, Lufkin, Tex.,
1949-? KyLxCB

Gulf Coast News Digest, Mobile,
Ala., 1949-?

Journal of Correctional Education,
New York, N.Y.; Huntsville,
Tex., Jan. 1949-current, C, MiU,
NN, TNJ

Journal of Petroleum Technology,
Dallas, Tex., Jan. 1949-current,
DLC, NN, NcRS

Kentucky Beverage Journal,
Frankfort, Ky., 1949-current

*Kentucky Dental Association
Journal,* Louisville, Ky., Jan.
1949-current, DSG, IaU, KyL,
KyLoU, NNU-D, TU-M

Kentucky Statistical Journal,
Frankfort, Ky., July 1949-?
KyL, KyU, NN

Livestock Weekly -- See *West Texas
Livestock Weekly*

Living in South Carolina, Cayce,
S.C., 1949-current

Louisiana News Digest, Baton
Rouge, La., Jan. 1949-June 1952?
Supersedes *Louisiana,* CU, DLC,
IU, LN, LNHT, LU, NN

Mercer Law Review, Macon, Ga.,
Fall 1949-? DLC, MH-L

National Public Accountant, Dallas,
Tex.; Alexandria, Va., Oct.
1949-current, AU, DLC, MoU, TxU

New Orleans Blue Book, New
Orleans, La., 1949-?

*North Carolina
Plumbing-Heating-Cooling
Forum,* Raleigh, N.C.,
1949-current

*Northern District Dental Society
Dental Mirror,* Atlanta, Ga.,
1949-?

The Overflow, Kissimmee, Fla.,
1949-current

Professional Gardener, New York,
N.Y.; McLean, Va., 1949-? DA,
DLC, NN

Professional Geographer, Hamilton,
N.Y.; Tallahassee, Fla.,
1949-current, CtY, DLC, NN,
NcD, PU

*Promotor de Educacion Cristiana;
Revista Para Lideres de
Iglesias,* El Paso, Tex.,
1949-current

Regional Action, Atlanta, Ga., Apr.
1949-? Also as *News of Regional
Action in Southern Higher
Education,* ArU, DLC, GAT, KyU,
LU, ViU

*Regional Action in Southern Higher
Education* -- See *Regional Action*

Rural Louisiana, Baton Rouge, La.,
1949-current

Schlumberger Sonde Off. Houston,
Tex., 1949-?

Shenandoah, Lexington, Va.,
1949-current, Vi, ViBlbV, ViU,
ViW

South Carolina Bibliographies,
Columbia, S.C., 1949-? DLC,
KyU, NN, NcD, NcU, Vi

South Carolina Schools, Columbia,
S.C., Fall 1949-? DLC, NcD,
ScCc

Southeastern Veterinarian,
Atlanta, Ga., 1949-? DA, GU

Southern Fireside, Birmingham,
Ala., Sept.-Nov. 1949, NN

*Southern Gardening; A Quarterly
Magazine Devoted to the Garden
and Home,* Forsyth, Ga., July
1949-Dec. 1950, GS, GU

Southern Indian Studies, Chapel
Hill, N.C., 1949-76, ICN, NjP,
OkTU, WHi

Studies in Germanic Languages and Literatures, Chapel Hill, N.C., 1949-?   CU, DLC, NN, NcU

Tappi Journal, New York, N.Y.; Atlanta, Ga., 1949-current, CtY, DA, DLC, NN

Tax Executive, Washington, D.C.; Arlington, Va., 1949-?

Technology Today, San Antonio, Tex., June 1949-current. As *Tomorrow*, then as *Tomorrow Through Research*, until 1978. DA, NN, TxDa, TxU-M

Tempo, Coral Gables, Fla., 1949-?

Tennessee Food Field, Chattanooga, Tenn., 1949-?

Texas Journal of Science, San Marcos, Huntsville, San Angelo, Tex., Mar. 1949-current, CtY, DLC, NN, Tx, TxH, TxU

Texas Petroleum Retailer, Austin, Tex., 1949-?

Texas Public Health Association Journal, Austin, Tex., June 1, 1949-?   Supersedes *Texas Journal of Public Health*, DSG, TxCM

Tomorrow -- See *Technology Today*

Tomorrow Through Research -- See *Technology Today*

Trux, Atlanta, Ga., 1949-current

VMEA Notes, Richmond, Va., 1949-?   DLC, ViU

West Texas Livestock Weekly, San Angelo, Tex., 1949-current. Currently as *Livestock Weekly*

William and Mary Review of Virginia Law, Williamsburg, Va., May 1949-July 1956. Superseded by *William and Mary Law Review*, DLC, Vi, ViU

Zebu Journal -- See *American Breeds*

Alabama Realtor, Birmingham, Ala., May 1950-?   AAP, AU

Arkansas Folklore, Fayetteville, Ark., July 1950-?   Also as *Ozark Folklore*, ArU, FU, MH, NN

Arkansas LP News, Little Rock, Ark., 1950-current

Arkansas Professional Engineer, Little Rock, Ark., 1950-?   ArU

Atlanta Economic Review, Atlanta, Ga., 1950-current, AU, DLC, GASU, GEU, NcD, NcU, ViU

Bulletin on Rheumatic Diseases, New York, N.Y.; Atlanta, Ga., Sept. 1950-current, ICJ, IU-M, NcU, ViRM

Business, Atlanta, Ga., 1950-current, GASU

The Church Musician, Nashville, Tenn., 1950-current, ABH, DLC, KyLoS, TxDaM

Circulation, New York, N.Y.; Dallas, Tex., Jan. 1950-current, CU, CtY-M, DLC, N, NcD, NcU, TxHMC, ViU

Dixie Lumberman, Jackson, Miss., Apr. 1950-?   Also as *Dixie Lumberman and Forester*, FU

Dixie Lumberman and Forester -- See *Dixie Lumberman*

F.P.   Jacksonville, Lakeland, Fla., Jan. 1950-current. Formerly as *Florida Psychologist*, FMU, FU

Fertility & Sterility, New York, N.Y.; Birmingham, Ala., 1950-current, AU, CtY-KS, DLC, IU, TxU, ViU

Florida Engineer, Gainesville,
Fla., Nov. 1950-? DLC, FMU, FU,
ICJ, ViU

Florida Mason, Miami, Fla., 1950-54,
FU

Florida Outdoors, Sun City, Fla.,
1950-June 1959. Absorbed
Florida Boating, Waterbug, and
Deep Sea Digest, DLC, FM, FMU

Florida Planning and Development,
Auburndale, Boca Raton, Fla.,
1950-current. Superseded by
*Florida Environmental and
Urban Issues*, FMU, FTaSU, NN

Florida Psychologist -- See *F.P.*

Floriland. For Garden and Home,
Tampa, Fla., Oct. 1950-May 1954,
FU

Georgia Game and Fish, Atlanta,
Ga., 1950-62, DLC

*Irrigation Engineering and
Maintenance*, New Orleans, La.;
Tampa, Fla., 1950-current. Also
as *World Irrigation*, currently
as *Irrigation Journal*, DLC, LU,
TxLT, ULA, ViBlbV

Irrigation Journal -- See
*Irrigation Engineering and
Maintenance*

Kentucky Revenue, Frankfort, Ky.,
July 1950-June 1958, DLC, KyU,
MH-L, TU

Law and Government, Chapel Hill,
N.C., 1950-? DLC, GU, MH-L,
NcU-L, ViU

Louisville, Louisville, Ky.,
1950-current, DLC, KyLoS,
KyLoU, NN

Metal Treating, New Rochelle, N.Y.;
Rocky Mount, N.C., Sept. 1950-?
DLC, ICJ, NN, WM

Negro Educational Review,
Orangeburg, S.C.; Jacksonville,
Fla., 1950-current, CtY, FMU,
FTaSU, GU, NN, NcD

Ozark Folklore -- See *Arkansas
Folklore*

Panama Canal Review, Miami, Fla.,
May 1950-? CtY, DLC, IU, MiU,
NN

Personnel Study -- See *Texas
University Studies in Personnel
and Management*

Photolith Magazine, Houston,
Lubbock, Tex., 1950-? FU, IaU,
IU, MoU

Primary Leader, Nashville, Tenn.,
1950-?

Safety Journal, Anderson, S.C.,
1950-current, AAP

The Second Line, New Orleans, La.,
1950-current, DLC, InU, MiD

Seedmen's Digest, San Antonio,
Tex., 1950-current, FU, GU, IU

The Sentinel, Jasper, Fla., 1950-?

*South Carolina Young Farmer and
Future Farmer Magazine*,
Columbia, Winnsboro, S.C.,
1950-current, DLC

Southern Exposure, Talladega,
Ala., 1950-current

Southern Innkeeper, Miami Beach,
Fla., 1950-? Also as *Southern
Innkeeper and the Florida
Chef*, FTaSU

*Southern Innkeeper and the
Florida Chef* -- See *Southern
Innkeeper*

The Specialty Worker, Pressmen's
Home, Tenn., 1950-68, DLC, FU,
IU, NN

The Spur: Life in Virginia--Past and Present, Fredericksburg, Va., 1950-July 1964, DLC, Vi, ViBlbV

Studies in Comparative Literature, Chapel Hill, N.C., 1950-? DLC, GU, MnU, NcD, NcU, NN, ViU

Tennessee Town & City, Nashville, Tenn., 1950-current, DLC, NN, NcU, T, TU, ViU

Texas Architect, Austin, Tex., 1950-current, DLC, TxDa, TxH

Texas Cooperative News, Austin, Tex., 1950-?

Texas Oil Jobber, Austin, Tex., Jan. 1950-current. Currently as *Texas Oil Marketer*, MoS, NN

Texas Oil Marketer -- See *Texas Oil Jobber*

Texas Petroleum Marketer, Austin, Tex., Oct. 1950-? DLC

Texas University Hispanic Studies, Austin, Tex., 1950-54, CtY, DLC, IU, MH, NcD, NN, TxDaM, TxU

Texas University Studies in Personnel and Management, Austin, Tex., 1950-? Also as *Personnel Study*, CtY, DLC, GU, MH-BA, NcD, NN, TxHR, TxU

Triangle, Lakeland, Fla., 1950-current

Tropical Living Homemaker and Gardener, Miami, Fla., 1950-64, DLC, FM, FMU, FTaSU

Vanguard, Birmingham, Ala., Oct. 1950-? DLC

Virginia GP -- See *Virginia General Practice News*

Virginia General Practice News, Richmond, Va., Oct. 1950-? Also as *Virginia GP*, DNLM, ViRM, ViU

World Irrigation -- See *Irrigation Engineering and Maintenance*

AAA Texas Motorist, Houston, Tex., 1951-current. Formerly as *Texas Motorist* and as *Texas Motor News*. As *AAA World* since 1982.

AAA World -- See *AAA Texas Motorist*

Alabama General Practitioner, Montgomery, Ala., 1951-? AAP, AU-M, DNLM

Alabama Pen Point, Birmingham, Ala., 1951-? Supersedes *Draper Inmate*, AU

American Patriot -- See *Free Enterpriser*

American String Teacher, Urbana, Ill.; Greenville, S.C., 1951-current, DLC, InU, NcD, NcU, TxU

Beautiful Atlanta Homes and Gardens, Atlanta, Ga., 1951-52, GU

Belmont Vision, Nashville, Tenn., 1951-?

BioScience, Washington, D.C.; Arlington, Va., Jan. 1951-current, CtY-M, DLC, N, NcD, NcU, ViBlbV, ViU

Bronze Thrills, Fort Worth, Tex., 1951-?

Bulletin of Marine Science, Miami, Fla., Mar. 1951-current. Formerly as *Bulletin of Marine Science of the Gulf and Caribbean*, CU, DLC, FMU, FU, TxU

Bulletin of Marine Science of the Gulf and Caribbean -- See *Bulletin of Marine Science*

The Contractors' Magazine, Baton Rouge, La., 1951-current. Currently as *Louisiana Contractor*

Current Podiatry, Brooklyn, N.Y.; Orlando, Fla., Aug. 1951-current, DLC, DNLM, MiDW

Duke Bar Journal -- See *Duke Law Journal*

Duke Law Journal, Durham, N.C., Mar. 1951-current. As *Duke Bar Journal*, 1951-57. C, DLC, MH-L, N, NcD, NcU, ScU

Episcopal Church Day, Miami, Fla., 1951-73. MCE

Escudo, El Paso, Tex., 1951-current

Flashback, Fayetteville, Ark., 1951-current, ArU, DLC, NN, TxU

Florida Academy of General Practice Journal -- See *Florida Family Physician*

Florida Dairy News, Jacksonville, Fla., 1951-? FMU, FU

Florida Family Physician, Jacksonville, Fla., 1951-Jan. 1968. Also as *Florida Academy of General Practice Journal*, DNLM, FU

Florida Gardener, Jacksonville, Fort Lauderdale, Fla., 1951-? DLC, FM, FU

Florida Home, Miami, Fla., 1951-? FM, GU

Florida Illustrated, Miami, Fla., 1951-? v.1-4 as *Florida Opportunity Bulletin*, v.5 as *Florida Opportunity Journal*, FM, FMU, FTaSU

Florida Motel Journal, Orlando, Fla., 1951-?

Florida Opportunity Bulletin -- See *Florida Illustrated*

Florida Opportunity Journal -- See *Florida Illustrated*

Florida Pioneer, Tampa, Fla., 1951-? NN

Forests & People, Alexandria, La., Mar. 1951-current, GU, LNHT, LNL, LU, MH, ViBlbV

Furman Magazine, Greenville, S.C., 1951-?

Georgia Alert, Atlanta, Ga., Nov. 1951-current, DLC, GU

Georgia Local Government Journal -- See *Georgia Municipal Journal*

Georgia Municipal Journal, Atlanta, Ga., 1951-current. Also as *Georgia Local Government Journal*. Currently as *Urban Georgia*. DLC, FU, GEU, GU, NcU, NN, ViU

Georgia Peace Officer, Atlanta, Ga., 1951-?

Group Practice, Charlottesville, Alexandria, Va.; New York, N.Y., 1951-current. Currently as *Group Practice Journal*, CtY-M, DNLM, IU-M, NcU-H, ViU

Group Practice Journal -- See *Group Practice*

Gulf Coast Sportsman, _____, _____, June 1951-? FTaSU

Heart of Texas, Houston, Tex., Summer 1951-? TxHMC

Inch, Houston, Tex., 1951-74, DLC, NN, OCl

Industrial Expansion in Texas -- See *Texas Industrial Expansion*

Industrios Lacteas, Houston, Tex., 1951-?

Jive, Fort Worth, Tex., 1951-?

Louisiana Contractor -- See *The Contractors' Magazine*

Medico-Legal Bulletin, Richmond, Va., 1951-current

Music Now, Knoxville, Tenn.; Radford, Va., 1951-current, DLC, FTaSU

NCAWE News, Arlington, Va., 1951-current, CLS, CLSU, IU, NbU

Norfolk Neck Historical Magazine, Norfolk, Va., Dec. 1951-Dec. 1978, ViBlbV

Outlook, Wake Forest, N.C., 1951-current, MBU-T

P.A.R. Analysis, Baton Rouge, La., Aug. 1951-current, DLC, LU, N

The Presbyterian -- See *Texas Presbyterian*

Review, Dotham, Ala., 1951-?   DLC, TxLT

Rotor Breeze, Fort Worth, Tex., 1951-?   DLC

Southeastern Librarian, Tucker, Ga., Spring 1951-current, DLC, FU, GA, GASC, GEU, GU, NcD, NcU, ViU

Southern Road Builder, Raleigh, N.C., 1951-?   ViU

Tampa Port, Tampa, Fla., 1951-?

Texas Industrial Expansion, Austin, Tex., 1951-current. v.1-5 as *Industrial Expansion in Texas*, DLC, IU, NN, TxCM, TxSaT

Texas Motor News -- See *AAA Texas Motorist*

Texas Motorist -- See *AAA Texas Motorist*

Texas Presbyterian, Austin, Denton, Tex., 1951-current. Currently as *Presbyterian*

Texas Social Worker, Austin, Tex., 1951-?   TxU

Urban Georgia -- See *Georgia Municipal Journal*

Virginia Cavalcade, Richmond, Va., Summer 1951-current, CtY, DLC, MH, N, NcD, NcU, ViBlbV, ViU

Virginia Engineer, Richmond, Cumberland, Va., 1951-current, Vi, ViBlbV, ViU

Virginia English Bulletin, Richmond, Va., 1951-current, ArU, DLC, Vi, ViBlbV, ViU

The Water Skier, Winter Haven, Fla., 1951-current

ACF Bulletin, Baton Rouge, La., 1952-current

Alabama Poultry Industry News, Montgomery, Ala., Fall 1952-? AAP

Alabama Trucker, Montgomery, Ala., Mar. 1952-current, AAP, ABH

Arc -- See *Mental Retardation News*

American College Health Association Journal, Coral Gables, Fla.; Washington, D.C., Oct. 1952-current. Also as *Student Medicine*. Currently as *Journal of American College Health*, CLS, DLC, FTaSU, FU, GU, MiU, ViU

American Horseman Sportologue, Lexington, Ky., July 1952-Aug. 1957, InU, KyU, NN, TU

Arkansas Farm Research, Fayetteville, Ark., Spring 1952-current, AAP, ArU, DLC, GU, NcRS, NN, ViBlbV

Aviation Mechanics Bulletin, New York, N.Y.; Arlington, Va., 1952-current, AMAU, NN

Baptist Intermediate Union Quarterly II, Nashville, Tenn., Jan. 1952-? DLC, KyLoS, NRAB

Buyers Purchasing Digest, Fort Lauderdale, Fla., 1952-? DLC

Cavalier, Greenwich, Conn.; Coral Gables, Fla., 1952-? DLC

Children Limited -- See *Mental Retardation News*

Communication Education, Falls Church, Va., Jan. 1952-current. As *Speech Teacher* until 1976. DLC, MnU, NcD, NcU, TxDaM, ViU

Confidential Forecaster, Austin, Tex., 1952-current

Deep Sea Digest, Miami, Fla., 1952-Sept. 1956. Absorbed by *Florida Outdoors*, FMU

Discussion, Millen, Ga., 1952-?

Dixie Logger & Lumberman, Wadley, Ga., 1952-current. Formerly as *Dixie Machinery and Lumberman*. Currently as *Logger and Lumberman*

Dixie Machinery and Lumberman -- See *Dixie Logger & Lumberman*

Emory Law Journal, Atlanta, Ga., 1952-current. As *Journal of Public Law* until 1974. DLC, FU, GASU, GEU, IU, NcU

Federal Accountant, Arlington, Va., Jan. 1952-current. As *Government Accountant's Journal* since 1976. DLC, NcU, NjR, TxU

Florida Civil Defense Digest, Jacksonville, Fla., Apr. 1952-? DLC, FMU, FU

Florida Explorer, Tampa, Fla., 1952-current, FU

Florida Newspaper News & Radio Digest, Tampa, Fla., 1952-?

Florida Sub-Tropical Gardener, Palm Beach, Fla., Sept. 1952-? FM, FMU, FU

Furniture Production, Nashville, Tenn., July 1952-current, CU, MiEM

Government Accountants Journal -- See *Federal Accountant*

Gulf Coast Plumbing, Heating-Cooling News, Brookshire, Tex., 1952-current

The Hose & Nozzle, Shreveport, La., 1952-current, LU

The Independent Garagemen, Austin, Tex., 1952-?

Jacksonville Seafarer, Jacksonville, Fla., Jan. 1952-current, DLC, FTaSU, FU, NN

Jewelers Digest, Atlanta, Ga., 1952-?

Journal of American College Health -- See *American College Health Association Journal*

Journal of Public Law -- See *Emory Law Journal*

Logger and Lumberman -- See *Dixie Logger & Lumberman*

Louisiana Baptist Builder, Denham Springs, Baton Rouge, La., 1952-current

Louisiana Cancer Reporter, New Orleans, La., 1952-current, DNLM

The Megaphone, Dallas, Tex., 1952-current, DLC

Mental Retardation News, New York, N.Y.; Arlington, Tex., 1952-current. Formerly as *Children Limited*. Currently as *Arc*, FM, LU, MoSW

Mobile Living, Chicago, Ill.; Sarasota, Fla., 1952-? DLC

National Future Farmer, Mount Morris, Ill.; Alexandria, Va., Fall 1952-current, DLC, IU, NN

The New Physician, Saint Louis, Mo.; Reston, Va., Jan. 1952-current, DLC, ICJ, NcU, TU-M, TxHMC, ViU

North Carolina Audio-Visualist, Red Springs, N.C., Nov. 1952-Mar. 1955, DLC, NcGU, NcRS

North Carolina Music Educator, Raleigh, High Point, N.C., 1952-? DLC

The Rice Engineer, Houston, Tex., Dec. 1952-? GAT, TxCM, TxHR, TxU

Scalpel and Tongs, Vienna, Va., 1952-current

Seafarer, Jacksonville, Fla., 1952-current

Sepia, Fort Worth, Dallas, Tex., Dec. 1952-? CtY, DLC, IU, NcRS, NN, TNF

South Carolina Trade and Industrial Education Magazine, Clinton, S.C., 1952-? DLC

Southern Industrial Supplier, Greensboro, N.C., 1952-current

Southern Philosopher, Chapel Hill, N.C., Jan. 1952-Jan. 1957, FU, KyU, MH, NcU, ViU

Southwest Trucker, Fort Worth, Tex., 1952-?

Spectroscopia Molecular, Chicago, Ill.; Lexington, Ky., 1952-? DLC, GAT, ICJ, NN

Speech Teacher -- See *Communication Education*

Student Medicine -- See *American College Health Association Journal*

Tar Heel Amvet, Durham, N.C., 1952-?

Tar Heel Economist, Raleigh, N.C., 1952-current. Formerly as *Tarheel Farm Economist*, CU, DLC

Tar Heel Farm Economist -- See *Tar Heel Economist*

Tennessee Farm and Home Science, Knoxville, Tenn., 1952-current, DLC, LU, T

Tennessee Lawyer, Nashville, Tenn., Sept. 1952-? DLC, IU, N, NcD-L, T

Tennessee Pilgrimage, Nashville, Tenn., 1952-? WHi

Tennessee Public Health, Nashville, Tenn., July 1952-? DLC, DNLM, T, TU-M

Texas Hi-Plains Irrigation Journal, Lubbock, Tex., 1952-?

Tidewater Motorist, Norfolk, Va., May 1952-? Supersedes *Tidewater Review*, ViU

Tyler's Quarterly: A Journal of American History, Biography, and Genealogy, Nashville, Tenn., July-Oct. 1952-? Supersedes *Tyler's Quarterly Historical and Genealogical Magazine*, CtY, DLC, NN, T, TNJ, ViBlbV, ViU

Union College Alumnus, Barbourville, Ky., 1952-current

Voice of Freedom, Dallas, Tex.,
1952-current

ABC Management, Houston, Tex.,
May 1953-current. Also as
Management Monthly and as
Management, DLC

Agricultural Ammonia News,
Memphis, Tenn., 1953-? Later
as *Agricultural Nitrogen News*,
IdU, MoKL

Agricultural Nitrogen News -- See
Agricultural Ammonia News

Alabama Bird-Life, Auburn, Ala.,
1953-? AAP, AU, GU

Alabama Dental Review, Birmingham,
Ala., 1953-Fall 1963, AAP, AU,
LNL, NNU-D

American Eagle, Louisville, Ky.,
Feb. 1953-?

Arkansas Grocer, Pine Bluff, Ark.,
1953-current

Arkansas Highways, Little Rock,
Ark., Nov. 1953-current, ArU,
DLC, In

Bell Helicopter News, Fort Worth,
Tex., 1953-? DLC

Blue Vulture, Miami, Fla., Jan.
1953-? NN

Bluegrass Tourist, Georgetown,
Ky., 1953-? KyU

Brangus Journal, Kansas City, Mo.;
San Antonio, Tex., 1953-current,
LU, NIC, OrCS

Cattle Business, Jackson, Macon,
Miss., 1953-current

Chain Saw Industry -- See *Chain
Saw Industry and Power
Equipment Dealer*

*Chain Saw Industry and Power
Equipment Dealer*, Shreveport,
La., 1953-current. Also as
Chain Saw Industry, DP

Circulation Research, New York,
N.Y.; Dallas, Tex., Jan. 1953-78.
Superseded by *Hypertension* in
1979. CLU, DLC, N, NcU, NjR,
TxU, ViU

Circus Review, Portland, Tenn.,
1953-? NjP, NN

Current Medicine for Attorneys,
South Miami, Fla., Sept.
1953-current, C, DLC, FU, LU-L,
MH-L, N, NcD-L, NcU

*Drill Bit-Southwestern Petroleum
News*, Odessa, Tex., 1953-? DLC,
TxCM, TxU

Elevator World, Mobile, Ala.,
1953-current

Florida Food Dealer, Ocala, Fla.,
1953-current

Florida Grocers' Bulletin, Miami,
Fla., 1953-?

Florida Nurse, Orlando, Fla.,
1953-current, DNLM, FMU, FU

Florida Police Journal,
Gainesville, Fort Lauderdale,
Orlando, Fla., 1953-? FM

Footprints, Plainview, Tex.,
1953-current

Glad Tidings of Good Things,
Abilene, Tex., 1953-current

*Gulf Coast
Plumbing-Heating-Cooling News*,
Houston, Tex., 1953-current

*Houston Studies in Business and
Economics* -- See *Studies in
Business and Economics*

Human Voice Quarterly -- See *Weid:
The Sensibility Revue*

Journal of Research in Music Education, Chicago, Ill.; Reston, Va., 1953-current, CLU, DLC, NN, ScU, ViU

Louisiana Bar Journal, New Orleans, La., July 1953-? Supersedes *The Louisiana Bar*, DLC, MH-L

Louisiana Motor Transport Association News, Baton Rouge, La., Oct. 1953-current, LU

Louisiana School News, _____, La., Sept. 1953-? DLC, NjP

Louisiana Traveler, Baton Rouge, La., Mar. 1953-? CU, DLC, NIC

Management -- See *ABC Management*

Management Monthly -- See *ABC Management*

Military Railway Service Journal, Laurens, Iowa; Vicksburg, Miss., 1953-? DLC

Mississippi Farmer, Jackson, Miss.; Nashville, Tenn., 1953-? MsU

Mississippi Language Crusader, University, Miss., 1953-current

Naples Guide, Naples, Fla., 1953-current

North Carolina Facts, Raleigh, N.C., Jan. 1953-? NcD, NcRS, NcU

Palmetto. A Magazine of Beautiful Poetry, Miami, Fla., Summer 1953-? FM, NN

Palmetto Piper, Columbia, S.C., 1953-current

Petal Paper, Hattiesburg, Miss.; Fairhope, Ala., 1953-? MH, MiEM, NcD, TxDaM

Potpourri, Lynchburg, Va., 1953-?

Pulpwood Production & Saw Mill Logging, Montgomery, Ala., 1953-current. Also as *Pulpwood Production and Timber Harvesting.* Currently as *Timber Harvesting*, AAP, DLC, GU, LU

Pulpwood Production and Timber Harvesting -- See *Pulpwood Production & Saw Mill Logging*

Roundup, Tucson, Ariz.; Bradenton, Fla., Apr. 1953-current, AzU, DLC, IU, NN, ViU

South Carolina Turkey News, York, S.C., Feb. 1953-? ScCleU

Southern Observer, Nashville, Tenn., Jan. 1953-June 1966, KyU, NcU, NN, ScU, TNJ, TU, Vi

Southern Outdoors, Montgomery, Ala.; Baton Rouge, La., 1953-current. Also as *Southern Outdoors/Gulf Coast Fisherman*, DLC, GAT, GU

Southern Outdoors/Gulf Coast Fisherman -- See *Southern Outdoors*

Southern Toy Journal -- See *Toy and Hobby Retailer*

Southwestern Toy Journal -- See *Toy and Hobby Retailer*

Studies in Business and Economics, Houston, Tex., 1953-? Also as *Houston Studies in Business and Economics*, DLC, FU, GU, MH, NcD, NN, TNJ

TSSA Reporter, Knoxville, Tenn., 1953-?

Tape Recording, Saverna Park, Md.; Alexandria, Va., 1953-? CLU, DLC, LU, MH-BA, NN

The Tennessee Journal of Purchasing, Knoxville, Tenn., 1953-?

Texas Defense Digest, Austin, Tex.,
1953-?   DLC

Texas Highways, Austin, Tex.,
1953-current, DLC, NN, TxHR,
TxSaT

Texas Police Journal, Dallas, Tex.,
1953-?   NN, TxDa, TxDaM, TxU

Texas Real Estate Magazine,
Austin, Tex., Jan. 1953-?   DLC

*Texas University Studies in
Marketing*, Austin, Tex., 1953-?
DLC, KyU, MH-BA, NcD, NN,
TxHR, TxU, ViBlbV

Timber Harvesting -- See *Pulpwood
Production & Saw Mill Logging*

Toy and Hobby Retailer, Atlanta,
Ga., 1953-Nov. 1962. Also as
Southern Toy Journal, and as
Southwestern Toy Journal, and
as *Toy Journal*, and as *Toy
Retailer*. Superseded by *Toy &
Hobby World*, NN

Toy Journal -- See *Toy and Hobby
Retailer*

True West, Austin, Tex., Summer
1953-current, DLC, NcD, NN,
TxLT

Virginia Bar News, Richmond, Va.,
Jan. 1953-current, DLC, IU,
NcD-L, ViU

Virginia Librarian,
Fredericksburg, Richmond, Va.,
1953-current. Currently as
Virginia Librarian Newsletter,
DLC, IU, KyU, NN, Vi, ViBlbV,
ViU

Virginia Veterinarian, Ashland,
Va., 1953-?   Vi, ViBlbV

Weid: *The Sensibility Revue*,
Homestead, Fla., 1953-?
Formerly as *Human Voice
Quarterly*, CLU, DLC, FMU, NcRS,
OrU

World Tennis, New York, N.Y.;
Houston, Tex., 1953-current,
CtY, DLC, MH, NcD, NcU, NN,
TxDaM, ViBlbV

A.S.B. Bulletin, Chapel Hill,
Burlington, N.C., Mar.
1954-current, DLC, NcD, NcU,
TxU, ViBlbV, ViU

Alabama Correctional Journal,
University, Ala., Apr. 1954-62.
Also as *Alabama Correctional
Research*, AU, FTaSU, IU

Alabama Correctional Research --
See *Alabama Correctional
Journal*

Alert, Annandale, Va., 1954-?

"Ansearchin'" News, Memphis,
Tenn., 1954-current, DLC, LNHT,
NN, OC, T

Arithmetic Teacher, Washington,
D.C.; Herndon, Va., Feb.
1954-current, C, DLC, MH, MiU,
NcU, ViBlbV, Vi

Astronautics -- See *Journal of
Astronautical Sciences*

Baton Rouge Digest, Baton Rouge,
La., Aug. 1954-58, LU

The Black Mountain Review, Black
Mountain, N.C., Spring
1954-Autumn 1957, CLU, CtY, LU,
NcU, NN, ViU

Boating Year Round/Outboard,
Tallahassee, Fla., Mar. 1954-July
1962. As *Outboard* until Aug.
1961, CLU, FU

Builders Association News, Fort
Worth, Tex., 1954-current

Business and Economic Review,
Columbia, S.C., Jan.
1954-current, DLC, FU, GU,
NcRS, NN

Christian Pathway, Opelika, Ala.,
Sept. 1954-?   NRAB

Church Recreation -- See *Church Recreation Magazine*

Church Recreation Magazine, Nashville, Tenn., 1954-current. Formerly as *Church Recreation*, IU, KyLoS, NcGU, TxDaM

Coast, Myrtle Beach, S.C., 1954-current

Courier, Charlottesville, Va., 1954-? ViU

Dixie Purchasor, Jonesboro, Ga., 1954-?

Doors to Latin America, Gainesville, North Miami Beach, Fla., Jan. 1954-? DLC, FMU, FU, NN, NcD, NcU

Flame, Alpine, Corpus Christi, Tex., Spring 1954-63, CtY, NN, TxU

Florida Tru-Sport, Miami, Fla., May-July 1954, DLC

The Florida Waterbug -- See *Waterbug. Underwater Sports*

Furniture Manufacturing Management, Germantown, Memphis, Tenn., 1954-current. Formerly as *Furniture Methods & Materials*, GU, NN

Furniture Methods & Materials -- See *Furniture Manufacturing Management*

Georgia Poultry Times, Gainesville, Ga., Feb. 1954-61. Absorbed by *Poultry Times*, GU

Green Thumb, Lexington, Ky., July 1954-? KyU

In Tech, Research Triangle Park, N.C., 1954-current

Interamerican, Denton, Tex., 1954-? CU, MH-P, PU-Mu

Journal of Astronautical Sciences, New York, N.Y.; Alexandria, Va., Fall 1954-current. Also as *Astronautics*, and as *Journal of Astronautics*, CtY, DLC, MiU, NcD, NjR, ViBlbV, ViU

Journal of Astronautics -- See *Journal of Astronautical Sciences*

The Kentucky City Bulletin, Lexington, Ky., Dec. 1954-May 1968. Continues *Kentucky City*. Continued by *Kentucky City*, DLC, KyLoU, NN

Kentucky Foreign Language Quarterly -- See *Kentucky Romance Quarterly*

Kentucky Romance Quarterly, Lexington, Ky., 1954-current. v.1-13 as *Kentucky Foreign Language Quarterly*, CtY, DLC, KyU, NN, NcD, TxU, ViU

Kentucky Writing, Morehead, Ky., 1954-? KyU, NIC, NN

Literature East and West, College Park, Md.; Austin, Tex., 1954-current, CtY, DLC, MH, NcU, NN, TxDaM, ViBlbV

Little Sphinx, Norfolk, Va., Feb. 1954-?

Louisiana's Family Doctor, New Orleans, La., 1954-? DNLM, LNL

Mathematics Student, Washington, D.C.; Reston, Va., Feb. 1954-current. Formerly as *Mathematics Student Journal*, CLU, DLC, IaU, MoS, NNU

Mathematics Student Journal -- See *Mathematics Student*

Mature Years, Nashville, Tenn., 1954-current. Supersedes *Home Quarterly*, DLC, GEU, NN

*Metropolitan Nashville Board of
Education News and Views*,
Nashville, Tenn., 1954-current

Mississippi Language Crusader,
University, Miss., 1954-current,
MsU

Mississippi Lawyer, Jackson, Miss.,
1954-?   IU, MH, NNC-L

Municipal South, Charlotte,
Lincolnton, N.C.; Greenville,
S.C., Jan. 1954-?   DLC, GU, N,
NcD, NcRS, ViBlbV, ViU

NACDL Journal -- See *NADL
Journal; The Voice of the Dental
Laboratory Industry*

*NADL Journal; The Voice of the
Dental Laboratory Industry*,
Alexandria, Va., 1954-current.
Formerly as *NACDL Journal*,
DLC, DNLM, ICADA

North Carolina Architect, Raleigh,
N.C., 1954-current. Formerly
as *Southern Architect*, DLC, NcD

North Carolina Bar -- See *North
Carolina State Bar Quarterly*

*North Carolina State Bar
Quarterly*, Raleigh, N.C., Feb.
1954-current. As *North
Carolina Bar* until 1978.   DLC,
NcD-L, NcU

North Carolina Veterinarian,
Raleigh, Smithfield, N.C., 1954-?
NcRS

Offshore, Conroe, Houston, Tex.;
Tulsa, Okla., 1954-current. Also
as *Offshore Operations*, and as
*Offshore; The Marine Oil
Operations Journal*, DLC, ICJ,
NN

Offshore Operations -- See
Offshore

*Offshore; The Marine Oil
Operations Journal* -- See
Offshore

Outboard -- See *Boating Year
Round/Outboard*

P.S. Public Schools in Action, Fort
Smith, Ark., 1954-current

Panhandle Geonews, Amarillo, Tex.,
Jan. 1954-?   OkU, TxCM, TxU

Pipe Line Industry, Houston, Tex.,
July 1954-current, DLC, ICJ,
NN, TxCM, TxU, ViU

Practical Nurses Digest, Norfolk,
Va., Apr. 1954-Jan. 1964. Also
as *Practical Nursing Digest*,
DLC, DNLM, MiD

Practical Nursing Digest -- See
Practical Nurses Digest

Progress, Belton, Tex., 1954-?

School Counselor, Falls Church,
Va., 1954-current. Formerly as
Elementary Counselor, DLC, MH,
NjR, ViBlbV, ViU

Sea Frontiers, Miami, Fla., Nov.
1954-current, DLC, FMU, FU,
IdU, LU, NN, ScU, ViU

Skylights, Murfreesboro, Tenn.,
1954-?   CLU, MiDW, TxSaT

South Carolina Wildlife, Columbia,
S.C., 1954-current, DLC, GU, LU,
NcD, NN, ScCleU

South Texas Law Journal, Houston,
Tex., 1954-current, DLC, FU,
MH-L, NcD-L, NcU-L, TxHR

*Southeast Furniture & Appliance
News*, Jackson, Miss., 1954-?

Southern Architect -- See *North
Carolina Architect*

*Southern Industry & Plant
Purchases*, Germantown, Tenn.,
1954-?

Southern Methodist University Studies in Jurisprudence, Dallas, Tex., 1954-? DLC, FU, LU, NcD, NN, TxHR, TxU

Southern Sawdust, Arlington, Va.; Sarasota, Fla., 1954-? NjP, NN

Southern School News, Nashville, Tenn., Sept. 1954-June 1965. Superseded by *Southern Education Report,* CtY, DLC, MiU, NN, NcD, NcU, T, TU, ViU

Southwestern Composers Journal, Austin, Tex., 1954-? TxHR

Tarheel Wheels Magazine, Raleigh, N.C., 1954-current

Task Force, Washington, D.C.; Annandale, Va., May 1954-? DLC, MH, NN

Tennessee Farmer, Nashville, Tenn., 1954-current,

Tennessee Farmer and Homemaker, Louisville, Ky., Sept. 1954-? KyU-ASC, T

Tennessee GP, Nashville, Tenn., Jan. 1954-? CtY-M, TNJ-M, TU-M

Tennessee Plumbing, Heating, Mechanical Contractor, Harrison, Tenn., 1954-?

Texas Lone Star -- See *Texas School Board Journal*

Texas School Board Journal, Austin, Tex., 1954-current. Currently as *Texas Lone Star,* TxCM, TxSaT, TxU

Texas School Business, Austin, Tex., Oct. 1954-? DLC, TxCM, TxU

Texas Thoroughbred, Dallas, Manor, Tex., Nov. 1954-current, TxDa

United States Conservation News, Miami, Fla., 1954-?

Virginia Antiquary, Richmond, Va., 1954-? DLC, MH, NcD, NN, ViU

Virginia Minerals, Charlottesville, Va., Oct. 1954-current, DLC, ICF, NcD, NcU, Vi, ViU

Waterbug. Underwater Sports, Clearwater, Fla., July 1954-Mar. 1956. Also as *The Florida Waterbug.* Absorbed by *Florida Outdoors,* IU

AREO Quarterly -- See *American Review of Eastern Orthodopy*

American Review of Eastern Orthodopy, New York, N.Y.; Indian Shores, Fla., 1955-? Formerly as *AREO Quarterly,* CtY-D, DHU, OO, TxDaM

American Salesman, New York, N.Y.; Sarasota, Fla.; Burlington, Iowa, Sept. 1955-current, DLC, FU, KU, NN

Approach; Naval Aviation Safety Review, Norfolk, Va., July 1955-current, DLC, FU, MnU, NN, ViU

Arkansas Faith, Crosett, Ark., Nov. 1955-June 1956, ArU

Arts in Louisville, Louisville, Ky., 1955-57, DLC, KyLoU, KyU, NN

Auburn Pharmacist, Auburn, Ala., 1955-current

Baptist Junior Union Quarterly II, Nashville, Tenn., 1955-? DLC, KyLoS

Bowling Proprietor, Park Ridge, Ill.; Arlington, Tex., 1955-current, DLC, NN

Carolina Rosarian, ____, ____, July 1955-? ScCleU

Citizen; A Journal of Fact and Opinion, Jackson, Miss., Oct. 1955-? DLC, MH, LU, MiU, NcD

Clinical Chemistry, Baltimore, Md.;
Winston-Salem, N.C., Feb.
1955-current, AAP, CLU, DLC,
MdU, NcU, ViU

Contracting in the Carolinas,
Richmond, Va.; Darlington, S.C.,
1955-current

*Echoes From the East Tennessee
Historical Society*, Knoxville,
Tenn., Apr. 1955-current, DLC,
KyU, NN, T, ViU

Escribano/Scribe, Saint Augustine,
Fla., 1955-? DLC, FM, FTaSU

Essays In Economics, Columbia,
S.C., Aug. 1955-? DLC, MH, NN,
NcD, ScU

Far East Reporter, Houston, Tex.,
1955-current

Fine Arts Philatelist -- See *Fine
Arts Philatelist Journal*

Fine Arts Philatelist Journal,
Muskogee, Okla.; Fort
Lauderdale, Fla., 1955-current.
Formerly as *Fine Arts
Philatelist*, IU, MBU

Florida Grocer, Miami, Fla.,
1955-current

*Florida Osteopathic Medical
Association Journal*, Ormond
Beach, Fla., 1955-? DNLM, FM,
FTaSU, FU-HC

Florida Purchaser, Jacksonville,
Fla., 1955-current

Florida's Business, Indian Rocks
Beach, Fla., Mar. 1955-? FTaSU

Flying Physician, Little Falls,
N.Y.; Lexington, Ky.,
1955-current, DNLM

Georgia Industrialist, Atlanta,
Ga., June 1955-? GU

Golf USA, Jackson, Miss., 1955-?

Ice Cap News, New York, N.Y.;
Irving, Tex., 1955-current,
CaQMAI, DLC, NhD

The Jewish Digest, Houston, Tex.,
1955-current, DLC, MH, NN, TxHR

Journal of Alabama Archaeology,
Moundville, Ala., 1955-current,
AAP, DLC, FU, MH-P, NN

*Journal of North Carolina
Genealogy* -- See *North Carolina
Genealogy*

Kentucky Farm and Home Science,
Lexington, Ky., July
1955-Summer 1962, DLC, IU, KyU,
MH, NN

Kentucky Folklore Record, Bowling
Green, Ky., 1955-current, DLC,
FU, KyBgW, KyU, MH, NcD, ViU

Kentucky State Health Journal,
Louisville, Ky., Sept. 1955-?
KyU-M

Key News, Nashville, Tenn., 1955-?
KyLoS

Louisville Lawyer, Louisville, Ky.,
Nov. 1955-? MH-L, N, NcD-L,
ViU-L

Lyric Louisiana, Baton Rouge, La.,
1955-? LU

The Mississippi Golfer -- See
Southern Golfer

Mississippi Grocers' Guide,
Jackson, Miss., 1955-current

Mississippi Municipalities, Jackson,
Miss., 1955-current, MsU, NN

*National Fluoridation News; A
General Information Medium for
Antifluoridation Forces,
National and International*,
Detroit, Mich.; Granette, Ark.,
1955-current, DLC, NN

North Carolina Genealogy, Raleigh, N.C., Mar. 1955-? Also as *North Carolinian*, 1955-61, and as *Journal of North Carolina Genealogy* 1962-66, DLC, ICN, KyU, NcD, NcRS, NN, ViBlbV

North Carolinian -- See *North Carolina Genealogy*

Northern Virginia Home-Garden News, Woodbridge, Va., 1955-current

Nursery Business, Tampa, Fla., 1955-current. Also as *Southeastern Nurseryman*, DLC, NcRS, ScCleU

Odd Fellow-Rebekah Star, Fort Worth, Tex., 1955-?

Orion, Lakemont, Ga., 1955-?

Our Country, Cardinal, Va., 1955-? ViU

Pan-American Trader, Miami, Fla., 1955-?

Photo News, West Palm Beach, Fla., 1955-current

Plant Science Bulletin, Tampa, Fla.; Ames, Iowa, 1955-current, DLC, NcRS, NcU, TxDaM, ViU

Power for Today, Nashville, Tenn., 1955-current

Prizewinner, Saint Petersburg, Fla., 1955-current

Public Affairs Comment, Austin, Tex., Jan. 1955-current, DLC, IU, MH, NcD, N, TxCM, TxU

Rental Service Forecasters, Boynton Beach, Fla., 1955-?

Southeastern Nurseryman -- See *Nursery Business*

Southern Golfer, Jackson, Miss., 1955-? Formerly as *The Mississippi Golfer*

Southwest Naturalist, Dallas, Tex., 1955-? ScCleU

Studies in Economics and Business Administration, Chapel Hill, N.C., 1955-? CtY, DLC, KyU, NcD, NcU, ViU

Texas Agricultural Progress, College Station, Tex., 1955-80, GU, TxKT, TxU

Texas Bellringer, Austin, Tex., Apr. 1955-? CLU, DNLM, LNHT

Texas Builder Magazine, Austin, Tex., 1955-?

Texas Caver, Waco, Tex., 1955-?

Texas Dental Assistants Association Bulletin, Houston, Tex., 1955-current

U.S. Golfer, Jackson, Miss., 1955-?

Virginia Builder, Richmond, Va., Nov. 1955-? Also as *Builder*, Vi

Virginian, Newport News, Va., July 1955-? NN, Vi, ViU

A.M.R.D. & C. Quarterly Bulletin, Athens, Ga., 1956-current

Alabama Bell, _____, Ala., Winter 1956-? AAP

Alabama Contractor, Birmingham, Ala., 1956-current

Alabama Wheel Cheer Magazine, Birmingham, Ala., Nov. 1956-? AAP

Alfred Hitchcock's Mystery Magazine, New York, N.Y.; North Palm Beach, Fla., 1956-? DLC

American Keepsake, Kingsport, Tenn., 1956-? DLC, KyU, NjR, NN

Armed Forces Comptroller,
Arlington, Va., July
1956-current, DLC, MiU, NIC, NN

Athletic Training, Greenville, N.C.,
1956-current

Atlanta Lawyer, Atlanta, Ga., Mar.
1956-? MnU-L, ViU-L

Aviation News Illustrated, Dallas,
Tex., 1956-?

Baptist Married Young People,
Nashville, Tenn., 1956-? KyLoS

Baptist Young Adults, Nashville,
Tenn., 1956-current, KyLoS

Behavioral Science, Ann Arbor,
Mich.; Louisville, Ky.; Santa
Barbara, Calif., 1956-current,
CtY, DLC, KyLoU, KyU, NN

The Blessings of Liberty,
Washington, D.C.; Pinehurst,
N.C., 1956-current, DLC

Catholic Counselor -- See
Counseling and Values

College Media Review -- See *College
Press Review*

College Press Review, University,
Miss.; Memphis, Tenn.,
1956-current. Currently as
College Media Review

Consultant, Miami, Fla.; Wake, Va.,
Feb. 1956-current, FU, NcD, NN

Counseling and Values, Falls
Church, Va., 1956-current.
Formerly as *National Catholic
Guidance Conference Journal*,
and *Catholic Counselor*, DCU,
DLC, KU

The Craftsman -- See *Make It With
Leather*

*Critique: Studies in Modern
Fiction*, Minneapolis, Minn.;
Atlanta, Ga., Winter 1956-?
CtY, GEU, GU, MH, NN, TxU

Descant, Fort Worth, Tex., Fall
1956-current, CoU, ICU, LNHT,
MH, NN, TxU, ViU

Every Day with Beginners,
Nashville, Tenn., 1956-? KyLoS

Every Day with Primaries,
Nashville, Tenn., 1956-? KyLoS

Fish Boat, Covington, La.,
1956-current. Currently as *Fish
Boat/Seafood Merchandising*,
DLC, FMU, NN

Fish Boat/Seafood Merchandising
-- See *Fish Boat*

*Florida Industrial Arts Quarterly
Bulletin*, Tampa, Fla., 1956-?
FMU

Florida Thoroughbred, Coral
Gables, Fla., Sept. 1956-? FM,
KyU

Forum, Houston, Tex.,
1956-current. Also as *Forum of
Texas*, DLC, MH, NcU, NN, TxHR

Forum of Texas -- See *Forum*

Georgia Farmer, Atlanta, Ga.;
Nashville, Tenn., 1956-? GU

Geotimes, Falls Church, Va.,
1956-current, CtY, DLC, NN,
NcU, ViBlbV, ViU

The Horseman, Houston, Tex.,
1956-current. Formerly as
*Texas and Southwestern
Horseman*, and as *Horseman:
The Magazine of Performance
Horsemanship*, CoFS, IaAS

*Horseman: The Magazine of
Performance Horsemanship* --
See *The Horseman*

The Hoskins Genealogist,
Alexandria, Va., Jan. 1956-Mar.
1960, DLC, WHi

Inhalation Therapy -- See
Respiratory Care

International Brahman Review,
Kissimmee, Fla., 1956-?

*Journal of the National Athletic
Trainers Association*,
Greenville, N.C., 1956-?

KAFP Journal, Louisville, Ky.,
1956-current

Latin American Report, New
Orleans, La., Mar. 1956-?   DLC,
FU, LU, NcU, NN

Leather Craftsman -- See *Make It
With Leather*

Louisiana Architect Builder, Baton
Rouge, La., July 1956-?   LU

Louisiana Republican, New Orleans,
La., Dec. 1956-?   DLC

Make it With Leather, Fort Worth,
Tex., 1956-current.   Formerly
as *Craftsman* and as *Leather
Craftsman*, OCl

*Moravian Music Foundation
Bulletin*, Winston-Salem, N.C.,
1956-current, DLC, ViU

*National Catholic Guidance
Conference Journal* -- See
Counseling and Values

Old Florida Cracker, Tallahassee,
Fla., Oct. 1956-?   Also as *Old
Florida Cracker and Sunshine
Salesman*, FTaSU, NN

*Old Florida Cracker and Sunshine
Salesman* -- See *Old Florida
Cracker*

Password, El Paso, Tex.,
1956-current, CtY, DLC, NcD,
NN, TxHR, TxU

Police, Springfield, Ill.; Fort
Lauderdale, Fla., 1956-?   CLSU,
DLC, FTaSU, NcU, NN

Preservation Progress, Charleston,
S.C., 1956-current, CU, DLC

Principes, Miami, Fla., Oct. 1956-?
DLC, FM, FTaSU, MiU, TxU

RC Respiratory Care -- See
Respiratory Care

Respiratory Care, Dallas, Tex.,
1956-current.   Also as
Inhalation Therapy and as *RC
Respiratory Care*, DLC, DNLM,
MiU

Retreader's Journal, Manchester,
N.H.; Louisville, Ky.,
1956-current, DLC

The South Carolina Librarian,
Columbia, S.C., 1956-current.
Supersedes *South Carolina
Library Bulletin*, DLC

Southern Landscape & Turf, Tampa,
Fla., 1956-current

Southern Theater, Salisbury, N.C.,
Fall 1956-?   As *Southern
Theater News*, 1956-62, FMU, LU,
MH, NcGU, NN

Southern Theater News -- See
Southern Theater

Southwest Properties Magazine,
Fort Worth, Tex., Apr. 1956-?
DLC

Southwestern Naturalist, Dallas,
College Station, Tex., Jan.
1956-current, CCC, DLC, LU,
NcD, NcU, TxCM, TxDaM

Studies in American English,
Austin, Tex., 1956-?   CtY, DLC,
MH, NcD, ScU, TxCM, TxU, ViBlbV

*Studies in Business and
Economics*, Atlanta, Ga., May
1956-?   AU, FU, GAT, ICU, NN,
ViU

*Sunday School Married Young
People*, Nashville, Tenn.,
Oct./Dec. 1956-?   KyLoS, NRAB

*Sunshine State Agricultural
Research Report*, Gainesville,
Fla., 1956-82. Superseded by
Florida Agricultural Report in
1982. DLC, FU, IU, LU, ScCleU

Tennessee Studies in Literature,
Knoxville, Tenn., 1956-? CtY,
DLC, GU, MH, NcD, NN, TNJ

Texas and Southwestern Horseman
-- See *The Horseman*

Texas Institutes, Austin, Tex.,
1956-? DLC, LU-L, NcD-L, TxU

Texas Poultry & Egg News,
Garrison, Tex., 1956-?

This is Auburn, Auburn, Ala., July
1956-? AAP, AU

*Together; the Magazine for the
United Methodist Church*,
Chicago, Ill.; Nashville, Tenn.,
Nov. 1956-73, CtY-D, DLC, NcD,
ScU, TNJ-R

*University of Tennessee Studies in
the Humanities*, Knoxville,
Tenn., 1956-? ArU, CtY, DLC,
LU, NcD, NN, TNJ, TU

Young People's Teacher, Nashville,
Tenn., Oct. 1956-? KyLoS

Academy of Management Journal,
Champaign, Ill.; Mississippi
State, Miss., Aug. 1957-current,
CtY, DLC, MCM, MiU, NcU, NN,
ViU

Airman, Washington, D.C.; San
Antonio, Tex., Aug. 1957-current
DLC, NbU, ScCleU

The Alabama Builder, Montgomery,
Ala., Mar. 1957-current, AAP,
AU

*Alabama Plaintiffs' Lawyer
Association Journal*,
Montgomery, Ala., June 1957-?
AAP, DLC, NcD-L

Alabama Roadbuilder, Montgomery,
Ala., Jan. 1957-? AAP, DLC

Albricias, Saint Petersburg, Fla.,
1957-current

*American Council of Polish
Cultural Clubs Quarterly Review*
-- See *Quarterly Review of
Polish Heritage*

*American Journal of Political
Science*, Detroit, Mich.; Austin,
Tex., May 1957-current.
Formerly as *Midwest Journal of
Political Science*, CtY, DLC, MH,
MiU, NcD, NN

Arlington Historical Magazine,
Arlington, Va., Oct. 1957-?
DLC, MH, NcD, NN, Vi, ViU

Avian Diseases, Ithaca, N.Y.;
College Station, Tex., May
1957-current, DLC, ICJ, MiU,
NcRS, TxCM

Beginner Leader, Nashville, Tenn.,
1957-? KyLoS

Builder/South -- See *Southern
Builder*

CLA Journal, Atlanta, Ga.,
1957-current

Church Nursery Guide, Nashville,
Tenn., 1957-? KyLoS

Coal Operator -- See *The
Independent Coal Operator*

College and Career, Nashville,
Tenn., 1957-?

Coloramic Magazine, Saint
Petersburg, Fla., July 1957-?

Cotton Farming, Memphis, Tenn.,
1957-current, ArU

Dopester, Avon Park, Fla.,
1957-197?

Educational Quest: A Journal of Educational Research and Service, Memphis, Tenn., Jan. 1957-Dec. 1981, DLC, IU, T, TU

El Paso Electronics, El Paso, Tex., Apr. 1957-?

Facts and Trends, Nashville, Tenn., 1957-?

Farm Reporter, Meridian, Miss., Apr. 1957-?

Florida Bowling Illustrated, Miami Beach, Fla., 1957-?   FM

Florida Review, Gainesville, Fla., Fall 1957-Spring 1958. Supersedes an earlier *Florida Review*, DLC, FU, KyU, NN

Florida Speleologist, Gainesville, Fla., Nov. 1957-?

Geologic Notes, Columbia, S.C., 1957-current. Currently as *South Carolina Geology*

Georgia Builder -- See *Southern Builder*

Guidepost, Falls Church, Va., 1957-current

Hep, Fort Worth, Tex., 1957-?

Hispanofila, Chapel Hill, N.C., 1957-current

Hogar Christiano, El Paso, Tex., Jan. 1957-current, KyLoS

Houston Business, Houston, Tex., 1957-?   IU, NIC

The Independent Coal Operator, Middlesboro, Ky., 1957-? Currently as *Coal Operator*

Individual Psychology -- See *Journal of Individual Psychology*

Journal of Individual Psychology, Austin, Tex., May 1957-Nov. 1981. Merged with *Individual Psychologist* to form *Individual Psychology*. Continues as *American Journal of Individual Psychology*, DLC, NN, TxU, VtU

Kentucky Farm Economics, Lexington, Ky., Jan. 1957-? KyU, NIC

Kentucky Soil and Water Conservationist, Louisville, Ky., Sept. 1957-?   KyU

Living with Children, Nashville, Tenn., 1957-current, KyLoS

Louisiana Agriculture, Baton Rouge, La., Fall 1957-current, DLC, IU, LNL, LU, NN

Louisiana Heart, New Orleans, La., 1957-60, LNL

Louisiana Journal of Plumbing-Heating-Cooling Contractors, Baton Rouge, La., 1957-?

Louisiana Spotlight, Baton Rouge, La., Jan. 1957-Apr. 1960, DLC, LNHT, LU, NN

Louisvillian, Louisville, Ky., Oct. 1957-June 1958. Supersedes *Arts In Louisville*. Superseded by *The Gazette of the Arts in Louisville*, DLC, KyU, NN, ViU

Manufactured Housing Reporter, Dallas, Tex., 1957-current

Midwest Journal of Political Science -- See *American Journal of Political Science*

Miscellany, Collegeboro, Ga., 1957-? GU

Mississippi Poetry Journal, Clinton, Miss., Summer 1957-? DLC, KyU, MsU, NN

Mobile Home Reporter, Dallas, Tex.,
1957-current. Also as *Mobile
Home Reporter & Recreation
Vehicle News*

*Mobile Home Reporter & Recreation
Vehicle News* -- See *Mobile Home
Reporter*

*National Association of Colleges
and Teachers of Agriculture
Journal*, New Orleans, La., Nov.
1957-current, NbU, NcRS, NIC

North Texas Dairyman, Arlington,
Tex., Oct. 1957-?

PHL Bulletin, Arlington, Va.,
1957-current, DLC

Pendulum of Time and the Arts,
Glendale, N.Y.; Winchester, Va.,
1957-?   OU

Polish Heritage -- See *Quarterly
Review of Polish Heritage*

Prizewinners, Saint Petersburg,
Fla., 1957-current

*Quarterly Review of Polish
Heritage*, Buffalo, N.Y.; Falls
Church, Va., 1957-current. As
*American Council of Polish
Cultural Clubs Quarterly Review*
until 1976. Since 1981 *Polish
Heritage*

SELA -- See *South Eastern Latin
Americanist*

South Carolina Geology -- See
Geologic Notes

South Eastern Latin Americanist,
Clemson, S.C., 1957-current.
Currently as *S E L A*, DLC, FMU,
FU, MH, NN, ScCleU

The Southern Bowler, Atlanta, Ga.,
1957-?

Southern Builder, College Park,
Ga., 1957-67. Also as
Builder/South and as *Georgia
Builder*, GAT, GU, NcRS, NN

*The Southern Genealogist's
Exchange*, Jacksonville, Fla.,
Spring 1957-?   DLC, FM, NN

Southwestern Brass Journal,
Huntsville, Tex., Spring 1957-?
DLC, KyLoS

Southwestern Louisiana Journal,
Lafayette, La., Jan. 1957-?
AAP, ArU, DLC, FU, GU, LNL,
LU, MH, NN

Space Journal, Huntsville, Ala.;
Nashville, Tenn., 1957-current,
AAP, CLU, DLC, GAT, NcRS, NN,
TNJ

Sunday School Lessons Simplified,
Nashville, Tenn., 1957-current

Tennessee Business, Knoxville,
Tenn., Sept. 1957-June 1965,
DLC, GAT, IU, NjR, TU

*Tennessee Law Enforcement
Journal*, Chattanooga, Tenn.,
Jan./Feb. 1957-current

Tennessee Magazine, Nashville,
Tenn., 1957-current, LU, MsU,
T, TNJ-P, TxU

Tennessee Taxpayer, Nashville,
Tenn., May 1957-?   MH-L, TNJ

Texas Archeology, Austin, Tex.,
Apr. 1957-?   DLC, FU, NN, TxDaM

Texas Baptists Today, Dallas, Tex.,
Oct. 1957-?   KyLoS

Texas Coach, Austin, Tex., Sept.
1957-current, TxU

Texas Supreme Court Journal,
Austin, Tex., 1957-?   DLC

Texas Tennis, Waco, Tex., 1957-?
TxSaT

*University of South Carolina
Education Report*, Columbia,
S.C., Dec. 1957-current, DLC, IU

Virginia Avifauna, Sweet Briar,
Va., Dec. 1957-? MH-Z, NIC, Vi,
ViU

William & Mary Law Review,
Williamsburg, Va., 1957-current.
Supersedes *William & Mary
Review of Virginia Law*, DLC,
MH-L, NcD-L, NcU-L, ViU

The Woman's World, Coral Gables,
Fla., 1957-?

Adhesives Age, Bristol, Conn.;
Atlanta, Ga., Oct. 1958-current,
DLC, GAT, GU, NcRS, ViBlbV

The Alabama Cattleman,
Montgomery, Ala., 1958-current,
AAP

Alabama Engineer, _____, Ala.,
June 1958-? AAP

Alabama Forest Products -- See
Alabama Forests

Alabama Forests, Montgomery, Ala.,
1958-current. Formerly as
Alabama Forest Products, CU

American Atheist, Austin, Tex.,
1958-current. Continues *The
Freethinker*, IU, MiU, NN

American Horticultural Magazine
-- See *American Horticultural
Society News and Views*

*American Horticultural Society
News and Views*, Washington,
D.C.; Mount Vernon, Va.,
1958-current. Also as
Gardeners Forum and as
*American Horticultural
Magazine*, currently as *American
Horticulturist*, NbU, NcU, ViU

American Horticulturist -- See
*American Horticultural Society
News and Views*

American International Travel,
Atlanta, Ga., 1958-?

*American Journal of Clinical
Hypnosis*, Baltimore, Md.;
Frankfort, Ky.; Atlanta, Ga.,
1958-current, CtY-M, DLC, GEU,
KyU, MdU-H, NcU-H, ViU

*American Journal of Orthopedic
Surgery*, Houston, Tex., Nov.
1958-? CtY-M, DLC, N, NcU,
TxHMC, ViU

Anglican Digest, Eureka Springs,
Ark., 1958-current

Antique Car Times, Corinth, Miss.,
1958-current

Architecture-South Carolina,
Columbia, S.C., Fall 1958-?
ScCleU

Arkansas Economist, Little Rock,
Ark., Fall 1958-64, ArU, AU,
DLC, GU, NcU, NN

Army Finance Journal, Alexandria,
Va., 1958-? DLC, NN

Arthritis and Rheumatism, New
York, N.Y.; Atlanta, Ga.,
1958-current, CtY-M, DLC, GEU,
GU, N, NcU-H, ViU

Atlantan Magazine, Atlanta, Ga.,
Apr. 26, 1958-? AAP, DLC, GAT,
GU, NN

Beauty, Dallas, Tex., 1958-?

Beefweek -- See *Breeder Journal*

Boating Progress, Jacksonville,
Fla.; New York, N.Y., 1958-Jan.
1963. Also as *Outboard
Progress*, DLC

Cancer Cytology, New York, N.Y.;
Boca Raton, Fla., 1958-80, DNLM,
ICJ, NcRS, TU, ViU

Carolina Christian, Greenville,
S.C., 1958-current

Contractor's Quarterly, Baton
Rouge, La., Jan. 1958-? DLC

Dixie Foods, Memphis, Tenn., 1958-?

E.D.P. Weekly, Annandale, Va., 1958-current, DNLM, GU, PSt

Education U.S.A. Arlington, Va., 1958-current, CLU, MiU, NdU, TxU

Fence Industry, Atlanta, Ga., 1958-current

Florida Forestry Reporter, Tallahassee, Fla., Feb. 1958-? FMU, FTaSU

Florida Horse, Ocala, Fla., 1958-? FTaSU, ViBlbV

Florida Orchidist, Miami Beach, Fla., 1958-? DLC, FMU, FTaSU

Florida States Righter, Miami, Fla., 1958-? FMU, NN

Florida Trend; Magazine of Florida Business and Finance, Saint Petersburg, Tampa, Fla., Apr. 1958-current, DLC, FM, FMU, FU

French Historical Studies, Raleigh, N.C.; Statesboro, Ga., 1958-current, CtY, DLC, NcD, NcU, NN

Frontier Times; the True West, Austin, Tex., 1958-?

Gardeners Forum -- See *American Horticultural Society News and Views*

Georgia Highways, Atlanta, Ga., Jan. 1958-Jan. 1959, DLC, GU

Go Boating, Houston, Tex., 1958-?

Greek, Roman and Byzantine Studies, Durham, N.C., 1958-current, NcD

Heart of Texas Records, Waco, Tex., 1958-current

Horizon, New York, N.Y.; Tuscaloosa, Ala., 1958-current, ABH, CLU, CtY, DLC, NN, NcD, Vi

Houston Geological Society Bulletin, Houston, Tex., 1958-current, LU, OCU, OkU, TxHR

Industria Turistica, South Miami, Fla., 1958-current, DLC

Jewelers & Watchmakers Journal, Memphis, Tenn., 1958-?

Journal of Air Traffic Control, Arlington, Va., July 1958-current, DLC, MiU, NN

Journal of the Evangelical Theological Society, Wheaton, Ill.; Jackson, Miss., 1958-current, CtY-D, DLC, ICU, MiU, MoSCS

Kentucky Civil War Round Table, Lexington, Ky., Mar. 1958-current, DLC, KyU, NN, ViU

Kentucky Negro Journal, Louisville, Ky., 1958-? DLC, KyU

Library Studies, Chapel Hill, N.C., 1958-? CtY, DLC, GU, MH, NcD, NcU, ViU

Livestock Breeder Journal, Macon, Ga., 1958-current. Currently as *Beefweek*, GU, IU, MoU, NcRS, ViU

Louisiana Folklore Miscellany, Lafayette, New Orleans, La., 1958-? ArU, LNL, LU, MH, NN

Military Law Review, Charlottesville, Va., 1958-current, DLC

Mississippi Valley Jeweler, Memphis, Tenn., 1958-?

Mississippi's Health, Jackson,
Miss., Jan. 1958-? DLC, DNLM,
MsU

Navy: The Magazine of Sea Power
-- See *Sea Power*

Non-Foods Merchandising -- See
Rack Merchandising

Now Hear This -- See *Sea Power*

Outboard Progress -- See *Boating
Progress*

Periodontology Today, San Antonio,
Austin, Tex., 1958-? GEU, LNL

Pimienta, Miami, Fla., 1958-current

Rack Merchandising, Atlanta, Ga.,
Jan. 1958-current. Currently
as *Non-Foods Merchandising*,
DLC, GU

Refuse Removal Journal -- See
*Solid Wastes Management, Refuse
Removal Journal & Liquid Wastes
Management*

Rehabilitation Counseling Bulletin,
Minneapolis, Minn.; Falls
Church, Va., Mar. 1958-current,
DLC, DNLM, MnU, NcRS

Sea Power, Arlington, Va.,
1958-current. Formerly as
*Navy: The Magazine of Sea
Power*, and as *Now Hear This*,
DLC, NN, ViU

*Solid Wastes Management/Refuse
Removal Journal* -- See *Solid
Wastes Management, Refuse
Removal Journal & Liquid Wastes
Management*

*Solid Wastes Management; Refuse
Removal Journal & Liquid Wastes
Management*, Atlanta, Ga.,
1958-current. Formerly as *Solid
Wastes Management/Refuse
Removal Journal*, and as *Refuse
Removal Journal*, DLC, NcRS, NN

South Carolinian, Columbia, S.C.,
1958-? ScCleU

Southern Baptist Deaf Worker,
Atlanta, Ga., Jan. 1958-? KyLoS

Southern Cemetery, Atlanta, Ga.,
1958-current

*Southern Jewish Historical Society
Journal*, _____, _____, Nov.
1958-? DLC, KyU, MH, NcD, NN,
Vi

Southern Poetry Review, Raleigh,
N.C., 1958-current, DLC, KyU,
MH, MsU, NcGU, ViU

Southwestern Journal of Theology,
Fort Worth, Tex., Oct.
1958-current, DLC, MH-AH,
TNJ-R, TxDaM

*Speech and Hearing Association of
Virginia Journal*,
Charlottesville, Va.,
1958-current, DLC

*Speech and Hearing Association of
Virginia Journal*,
Charlottesville, Va.,
1958-current, DLC

St. Luke's Journal of Theology,
Sewanee, Tenn., 1958-current,
DLC, MH-AH, NcD

State Government News, Chicago,
Ill.; Lexington, Ky.,
1958-current, CtY, DLC, MiU,
NcU, NN

The Steam Automobile, Chicago, Ill.;
Pleasant Garden, N.C.,
1958-current, DLC, DSI, NN

Texans For America News, Fort
Worth, Tex., Jan. 1958-Oct./Nov.
1959, NN

Texas Beverage News, Fort Worth,
Tex., 1958-current

Texas Farm and Ranch News, San
Antonio, Tex., 1958-current

Texas Quarterly, Austin, Tex.,
Feb. 1958-Winter 1978, CtY, DLC,
MH, NcD, NN, TxU

Texas Rail-ways, Austin, Tex.,
July 1958-? TxU

*Texas University Studies in
Banking and Finance*, Austin,
Tex., 1958-? CtY, DLC, GU, MA,
NcD, NN, TxHR, TxU

Torchlighter, New Orleans, La.,
1958-?

*Training Union Quarterly
Simplified*, Nashville, Tenn.,
1958-?

*University of Richmond Law
Review*, Richmond, Va., Spring
1958-current, DLC, MH-L, N,
NcD-L, NcU-L, ViU-L

Virginia Business Review,
Charlottesville, Va., Apr.
1958-Apr. 1960, DLC, KU, NjP,
Vi, ViU

Action in Kentucky, Louisville,
Ky., 1959-?

Adelante, El Paso, Tex.,
1959-current. Formerly as
Revista Para Jovenes

Alabama Genealogical Register,
Tuscaloosa, Ala.; Columbus, Pass
Christian, Miss., 1959-? AAP,
DLC, LNHT, NcD, NN

Alabama Star, Montgomery, Ala.,
Mar. 1959-? AAP

*Alabama State Teachers Association
Journal*, Montgomery, Ala., Feb.
1959-? AAP, GU, ICU

American Shipper -- See *Florida
Journal of Commerce*

Arkansas Agricultural Economist,
Little Rock, Ark., Feb. 1959-?
ArU, NIC

*Arkansas Journal of Business and
Industry*, Little Rock, Ark.,
Aug. 1959-? ArU, DLC

Arkansas Presbyterian, Little
Rock, Ark., 1959-? ArU

The Bell Tower, Memphis, Tenn.,
1959-current

Better Beef Business, Tulsa, Okla.;
Louisville, Ky., 1959-current.
Formerly as *Magic Circle
Stockman*, DLC, NIC

Bobbin, Columbia, S.C.,
1959-current, GAT, NcRS

The Choral Journal, Tampa, Fla.,
1959-current, DLC, FMU, NN

Church Administration, Nashville,
Tenn., Oct. 1959-current, ABH,
DLC, KyLoS

Coast Area Mississippi Monitor, Bay
Saint Louis, Miss., 1959/60-?
AAP, DLC, MsU, ViU

Councilor, Shreveport, La.,
1959-current, CSt, WHi

Crusader, Monroe, N.C., June
1959-? CtY, MiU, NcD

Dixie Wrestling News, Birmingham,
Ala., Spring 1959-?

El Barco Pesquero, New Orleans,
La., 1959-?

Faulkner Facts and Fiddlings --
See *Faulkner Facts and
Findings*

Faulkner Facts and Findings,
Conway, Ark., Sept.
1959-current. Also as *Faulkner
Facts and Fiddlings*, ArU, DLC,
KyU, NcD, NN

Flaming Torch, New Orleans, La.,
Mar. 1959-?

Florida Business and Opportunity
-- See *Florida Business Leader*

Florida Business Leader, Miami,
Fla., June 1959-?   Also as
*Florida Business and
Opportunity*, FM, FTaSU, FU, NN

Florida Construction Review,
Gainesville, Fla., Jan. 1959-Jan.
1965.   Superseded by *Business
and Economic Dimensions*, DLC,
FU, MH-BA, NN

Florida Journal of Commerce,
Jacksonville, Fla., Nov.
1959-current.   Also as *Florida
Journal of Commerce/Seafarer*,
and as *Florida Journal of
Commerce/American Shipper*,
currently as *American Shipper*,
DLC, FM, FMU, FU, NN

*Florida Journal of
Commerce/American Shipper* --
See *Florida Journal of Commerce*

*Florida Journal of
Commerce/Seafarer* -- See
Florida Journal of Commerce

*Florida Journal of Educational
Research*, Tallahassee, Fla.,
1959-?   DLC, FMU, FTaSU, FU

Florida Water News, Tallahassee,
Fla., July 1959-Aug. 1965.
Superseded by *Florida
Conservation News*, DLC, FMU,
FU, MH-PA

Food Promotions, Indian Rocks
Beach, Fla., 1959-current

Fountainhead, Alexandria, Va.,
1959-?   DLC

Friend O' Wildlife, Rocky Mount,
Raleigh, N.C., 1959-current,
NcRS

Furniture News, Charlotte, N.C.,
1959-76.   Superseded by
Furniture/Today

*G.S.E. General Support Equipment
Magazine*, Arlington, Va., 1959-?
DLC, GAT, ICJ, IU, NcRS, NN

Georgia Agricultural Research,
Athens, Ga., 1959-?   GAT, ICJ,
NcRS, NN

The Georgia CPA, Atlanta, Ga.,
Aug. 1959-77, GEU, TxCM, ViBlbV

Governmental Review, Columbia,
S.C., Feb. 1959-?   DLC, FU, NcU,
NN, ViU

Graduate Journal, Austin, Tex.,
1959-75, CtY, DLC, MH, NN, NcD,
TxU

Holiday Inn Magazine, Memphis,
Tenn., 1959-?

Inter-American Law Review, New
Orleans, La., 1959-66, DLC

International Geology Review, Falls
Church, Va., Jan. 1959-current,
CtY, DLC, MH, NcU, ViBlbV, ViU

Journal of Church and State, Waco,
Tex., 1959-current, CtY, DLC,
NcD, NN, TxHR, TxU

*Journal of College Student
Personnel*, Grand Forks, N.D.;
Falls Church, Va., 1959-current,
CLU, DLC, MH, NcU, ViBlbV, ViU

Kentucky School Boards Journal,
Lexington, Ky., 1959-?   KyU

Lawn Equipment Journal, Fort
Worth, Tex., 1959-?

Linage, Lubbock, Tex., 1959-?

Linguistic Reporter, Arlington,
Va., Apr. 1959-?   CLU, CtY, DLC,
MB, NcU, TxU, ViU

Louisiana Tech Forester, Ruston,
La., 1959-?   CU

Lynchburg College Magazine,
Lynchburg, Va., 1959-?

Magic Circle Stockman -- See
Better Beef Business

*Mississippi Future Business
Leader*, University, Miss., Apr.
1959-?   MsU

Mustang, Austin, Tex., Mar.
1959-Feb. 1965, ICF, NN, TxU

N.I.R.C. Voice, Bethesda, Md.;
Arlington, Va., 1959-?

*National Ornamental Metal
Fabricator*, Atlanta, Ga.,
1959-current. Currently as
*Ornamental/Miscellaneous Metal
Fabricator*

National Real Estate Investor, New
York, N.Y.; Atlanta, Ga.,
1959-current, DLC, GASU, InU,
NNC, TxDaM

Nuclear Safety, Washington, D.C.;
Oak Ridge, Tenn., Sept.
1959-current, DLC, KyU, TU-M

*Ornamental/Miscellaneous Metal
Fabricator* -- See *National
Ornamental Metal Fabricator*

Our Heritage, San Antonio, Tex.,
1959-current, DLC, ScU, TxSaT,
TxU

Outdoor Power Equipment, Fort
Worth, Tex., 1959-current

Paragraphs, Arlington, Va.,
1959-current

Port of Houston Magazine, Houston,
Tex., Jan. 1959-current, DLC,
IU, MiU, NN, TxHR

The Reflector, Amarillo, Tex.,
1959-? Continues *Bulletin,
Amarillo Genealogical Society*,
DLC

Romance Notes, Chapel Hill, N.C.,
Nov. 1959-current, CtY, DCU,
DLC, NcD, NcU, NN

Santa Gertrudes Journal, Fort
Worth, Tex., Sept. 1959-current,
TxCM, TxKT

South Carolina City, Columbia,
S.C., 1959-? DLC, NN, ScU

Southeastern Geology, Durham,
N.C., 1959-current, CtY, CU, FU,
NcD, NcU, NN

Southern Furniture News, High
Point, N.C., 1959-?

Southern Journal of Optometry,
Atlanta, Ga., 1959-current,
DNLM, InU

Southwest Magazine, Lafayette, La.,
Apr. 1959-?

Sports Car Digest, Odessa, Tex.,
1959-?

*Studies in Latin American
Business*, Austin, Tex., 1959-?
CtY, DLC, NcD, NjP, ScU, TxHR,
TxU, ViU

Stylus, Ashland, Va., 1959-? PPiU,
ViU

*Sunday School Extension Dept.
Quarterly*, Nashville, Tenn.,
Jan. 1959-? NRAB

Tennessee Cooperator, LaVergne,
Tenn., 1959-?

Tennessee Counties Today,
Nashville, Tenn., Oct. 1959-?
T

Texas Bridge, Houston, Tex.,
Summer 1959-? DLC

Texas Choirmaster, Galena Park,
Tex., Nov. 1959-? DLC, IU, TxU

Texas Heritage, Austin, Tex.,
Jan.-Mar. 1959-? DLC, NN, TxCM

*Texas Studies in Literature and
Language*, Austin, Tex.,
1959-current, CtY, DLC, MH,
NcU, NN, TxHR, TxKT

Theatre Organ, Middleburg, Va.,
1959-current

The Thunderbolt, Savannah,
Marietta, Ga., 1959-current.
Also as *Thunderbolt; The White
Man's Viewpoint*, DLC, MH

*Thunderbolt; The White Man's
Viewpoint* -- See *The
Thunderbolt*

Trailer/Body Builders, Houston,
Tex., 1959-current

Ultreya, Dallas, Tex., 1959-current,
CStclU

VEA News, Richmond, Va.,
1959-current

Virginia Numismatist, Hampton, Va.,
Sept. 1959-? ViU

Adjusters Reference Guide,
Louisville, Ky., 1960-current

*Alabama Market News; The Digest
of New Developments for
Executives*, Birmingham, Ala.,
1960-? AAP

*Alabama News of the Church of
God*, Birmingham, Ala., 1960-?
AAP

Alabama Sentinel, Montgomery,
Ala., 1960-? DLC

Alabama Sword of Hope,
Birmingham, Ala., 1960-? AAP

Arkansas Archeologist,
Fayetteville, Ark., Jan. 1960-?
ArU, DLC, LU, NN

*Around the Town and Horse Farm
Guide*, Lexington, Ky., Apr.
1960-current, KyU

Arts in Virginia, Richmond, Va.,
Fall 1960-current, CtY, DLC, MH,
NN, Vi, ViBlbV

Austin, Austin, Tex., 1960-current

*Austin Genealogical Society
Quarterly*, Austin, Tex., Nov.
1960-? NN, WHi

COPH Bulletin, Arlington, Va.,
1960-current, DLC

Campus Conservative, Jackson,
Miss., 1960-? ViU

Carolina Golfer, Charlotte, N.C.,
1960-current

Carolina Sportsman, Charlotte,
N.C., 1960-current

Church Library Magazine,
Nashville, Tenn., 1960-70.
Superseded by *Media: Library
Services Journal*,

Clubs & Recreation, Alexandria,
Va., 1960-current

*College Store News & Student
Supplies Wholesaler*, Atlanta,
Ga., 1960-?

ERB-Dom, Baton Rouge, Saint
Francisville, La., 1960-? NN,
WU

Florida Forum, Winter Park, Fla.,
1960-current

Georgia Anchorage, Savannah, Ga.,
1960-current, DLC

Georgia Taxpayer, Gainesville,
Ga., Aug. 1960-? GU

Go Boating, Miami Beach, Fla.,
1960-? Formerly as *"Go." Guide
on the Waterways*

"Go." Guide on the Waterways --
See *Go Boating*

*The Journal of Intergroup
Relations*, New York, N.Y.;
Louisville, Ky., 1960-? GEU,
IU-M, NN

*Journal of the Mississippi State
Medical Association*, Jackson,
Miss., Jan. 1960-current.
Supersedes *Mississippi Doctor*,
CtY-M, DNLM, MiU, MsSM, MsU

Kentucky Beekeepers' Quarterly, Frankfort, Ky., July 1960-?

LPA News, Fredericksburg, Va., 1960-current

Log Analyst, Tulsa, Okla.; Houston, Tex., 1960-current, DLC, TxDaM, TxU

Louisiana English Journal, Baton Rouge, La., Spring 1960-current, DLC, LNHT, LU

Louisiana History, Baton Rouge, La., Winter 1960-current, AU, CtY, DLC, LNHT, NcU, NN, TxU, ViBlbV

Louisiana Spotlight on Industry, Baton Rouge, La., Sept. 1960-Aug. 1964, DLC, LU, NN

MAIN, Fort Lauderdale, Fla., 1960-current

Medical World News, New York, N.Y.; Houston, Tex., Apr. 22, 1960-current, DLC, MiEM, TxHMC, ViBlbV

Miscellany; a Davidson Review, Davidson, N.C., 1960-current

Mississippi Law Enforcement Journal, Jackson, Miss., 1960-?

Mississippi University Studies in English, University, Miss., 1960-? CtY, DLC, LNHT, MH, MiDW, MiU, TU

New American Electronics Literature & Technical Data, Holly Hill, Fla., Feb. 1960-current

North Carolina Music Teacher, Charlotte, Chapel Hill, N.C., Apr. 1960-? NcGU

Point, Fort Lauderdale, Fla., 1960-?

Population Studies, Gainesville, Fla., 1960-current

Port of Hampton Roads Monthly Log, Norfolk, Va., 1960-current. As *Virginia Ports* until Oct. 1981

Production & Inventory Management Journal, Falls Church, Va., Jan. 1960-current, DLC, GAT, MCM, NcRS, NN, TxU

Sea Technology, Arlington, Va., 1960-current. Formerly as *Undersea Technology*, CU, DLC, GAT, NN, TxU, ViU

Southeastern Pest Control Journal -- See *Southern Pest Control Journal*

Southern Economic Development, Birmingham, Ala., Nov. 1960-Mar. 1961, AAP, DLC, MH

Southern Forest Research, New Orleans, La., Nov. 1960-? NN

Southern Gardens, Columbia, S.C.; Charlotte, N.C., 1960-current

Southern PBX Magazine, Atlanta, Ga., 1960-? GU

Southern Pest Control Journal, Atlanta, Ga., Jan. 1960-? Also as *Southeastern Pest Control Journal*, GU, KyU-ASC

Spur, Fredericksburg, Delaplane, Va., 1960-current. As *Spur of Virginia* until 1974, Vi, ViU, ViW

Spur of Virginia -- See *Spur*

The Student Store, Atlanta, Ga., 1960-?

Taylor Talk, Dallas, Tex., 1960-current, DLC

Tennessee Rifleman, Knoxville, Tenn., Jan. 1960-? DLC, NN

*Tennessee State University Faculty
Journal; Journal of Research,
Creative Writing, & Literary
Criticism*, Nashville, Tenn.,
1960-79

Texas Argus, San Antonio, Tex.,
1960-? DLC

Texas Football, Waco, Tex.,
1960-current

Texas Journal of Pharmacy,
Austin, Tex., Winter 1960-?
DNLM, LNL, TxHP, TxU

Textile Maintenance Reporter,
Austin, Tex., 1960-current, DLC

*Tips and Topics in Home
Economics*, Lubbock, Tex.,
1960-current, MiEM, OrCS

Trout, Vienna, Va., 1960-current

Undersea Technology -- See *Sea
Technology*

University Report, Chapel Hill,
N.C., 1960-current, NcU

*Virginia Journal of International
Law*, Charlottesville, Va.,
1960-current. Continues
*Journal of the John Bassett
Moore Society of International
Law*, DLC, MH-L

Virginia Ports -- See *Port of
Hampton Roads Monthly Log*

Voice of Liberty, Decatur, Ga.,
1960-current

Aid, Lubbock, Tex., Apr. 1961-?
MH

Alabama Farmer, Auburn, Eclectic,
Ala.; Nashville, Tenn., Jan.
1961-? AAP

*American Association of Teacher
Educators in Agriculture
Journal*, Blacksburg, Va., Apr.
1961-current, AzU, MnU-A,
ViBlbV

Arkansas Poultry Times, Little
Rock, Ark., 1961-current

Arkansas Speleologist,
Fayetteville, Ark., Spring
1961-? ArU

Arkansas Today, North Little
Rock, Ark., 1961-? ArU

Atlanta Magazine, Atlanta, Ga., May
1961-current. Supersedes *City
Builder*, DLC, GAT, GU, NcD, NN

Baptist Challenge, Little Rock,
Ark., 1961-current

Baylor Geological Studies Bulletin,
Waco, Tex., 1961-current, CtY,
DLC, NcD, NN, TxDaM, TxHR, TxU

Beachcomber, New Orleans, La.,
1961-? LU

Birmingham, Birmingham, Ala.,
1961-current, AU, MsSM

Boat/America, Pompano Beach, Fort
Lauderdale, Fla., 1961-?
Formerly as *Gondolier, Florida's
Boating Magazine*

The Christian Contender, Crockett,
Ky., 1961-current

Clef, Marietta, Ga., 1961-? DLC

Contract Management -- See *NCMA
Magazine*

*Dallas Forum: A Liberal Voice in
Dallas*, Dallas, Tex., May 1-June
16, 1961, TxDaM

Dixie Dairyman, Shreveport, La.,
1961-? GU, NcRS

Electronics of America, Holly Hill,
Fla., 1961-current

*Florida Certified Public
Accountant*, Gainesville, Fla.,
May 1961-74, FTaSU, FU, ViBlbV

Florida Field Report, Orlando, Fla., 1961-79. Incorporated into *Florida Grower and Rancher* in 1979

Florida Restaurant, Hotel and Motel Journal, Pensacola, Fla., 1961-?

Georgia Assessor, Atlanta, Ga., 1961-? GU

Georgia Genealogical Magazine, Homerville, Ga.; Easley, S.C., 1961-current, DLC, GU, NcD, NN

Georgian, Tucker, Ga., 1961-? GU

Gondolier, Florida's Boating Magazine -- See *Boat/America*

Grain and Fire, Cottonport, La., 1961-?

Howard Collector, Pasadena, Tex., Summer 1961-1973, CtY, DLC, ViU

Journal of Family Law, Louisville, Ky., 1961-current, CLL, DLC, KU, NcD-L, NcU, NN

Kentucky Heritage, Frankfort, Ky., Winter 1961-? KyU, MnHi, NN

Leaguer, Charlottesville, Va., 1961-current

Literary Sketches; A Magazine of Interviews, Reviews and Memorabilia, Williamsburg, Va., 1961-current, IU, ViU

Louisiana Architect, Baton Rouge, La., 1961-? LNHT, LU

Lounge Law, Waco, Tex., 1961-? WaU-L

Marina Merchandising, Clearwater, Fla., 1961-?

Market Place, Dallas, Tex., 1961-current

Military History of Texas and the Southwest, Austin, Tex., May 1961-current. Formerly as *Texas Military History*, DLC, NN, TxCM, TxHR, TxU

Millwork and Building Products, Memphis, Tenn., 1961-?

NCMA Magazine, Arlington, Va., 1961-current. Currently as *Contract Management*

The New Exponent, Athens, Tenn., 1961-?

New Guard, Washington, D.C.; Sterling, Va., Mar. 1961-current, DLC, MH, NcD, NN

North Carolina Agribusiness, Winston-Salem, N.C., 1961-current

North Texas State University Business Studies, Denton, Tex., 1961-? FU, GU, KyU, LU, TxHR, TxSaT

Ole Miss Engineer, University, Miss., 1961-current, GAT

The Outsider, New Orleans, La.; Tucson, Ariz., 1961-69, AzU, CtY, DLC, LU, MoU, NcD, NN

Poultry Times, Gainesville, Ga., 1961-current. Formed by merger of *Texas Poultry and Egg News* and *Southeastern Poultry Times*

The Quarter Racing Record, Fort Worth, Tex., 1961-current

Society of Petroleum Engineers Journal, Dallas, Tex., Mar. 1961-current, DLC, ICJ, NcRS, NN, TxHR, TxU

Southeastern Geographer, Athens, Ga.; Columbia, S.C., 1961-current, DLC, FU, GASU, GU, MH, NcD, NN, TxDaM

Southeastern Peanut Farmer, Tifton, Ga., 1961-current

Southern Hog Reporter, Macon, Ga.,
Mar. 1961-Oct. 1963, GU

Southern News and Views,
Hattiesburg, Miss., 1961-current

Southern Today, Morgan City, La.,
July 1961-?

Southwesterner, Columbus, N.M.; El
Paso, Tex., July 1961-? AzU,
CU, NN, OkU

Stirpes, Fort Worth, Tex., Mar.
1961-? DLC, NN, T, TxHR

*Studies in English Literature,
1500-1900*, Houston, Tex.,
1961-current, CtY, DCU, DLC,
NcD, NcU, NN, TxHR, TxU

Tennessee's Children, Nashville,
Tenn., 1961-? DLC

Texas Military History -- See
*Military History of Texas and
the Southwest*

Vanidades Continental, Miami, Fla.,
1961-? DLC

Virginia Chamber Review,
Richmond, Va., Jan. 1961-? ViU

Well Servicing, Dallas, Tex.,
1961-current, DLC, NN, TxCM

*Xavier University Studies; Journal
of Critical and Creative
Scholarship*, New Orleans, La.,
Apr. 1961-71, 1976-? CtY, DLC,
FU, LNHT, LNL, LU, NN

ACOS News, Coral Gables, Fla.,
1962-current

Action, Clearwater, Fla.,
1962-current. Formerly as *New
Pinellas Teacher*, and as
Pinellas Teacher

Adventure, Nashville, Tenn.
1962-current

American Notes & Queries, New
Haven, Conn.; Lexington, Ky.,
Sept. 1962-current, CtY, DLC,
KyU, NcD, NcU, NN

Area Digest, Atlanta, Ga., Spring
1962-Fall 1965, CLU, DLC, GAT,
NN

Arion, Austin, Tex., Spring 1962-?
CtY, DLC, MH, NcD, NN, TxCM,
TxHR, TxU

The Arkansas Amateur,
Fayetteville, Ark., 1962-current,
ArU, CU, NN

Arkansas Archeology, Fayetteville,
Ark., 1962. Absorbed by
Arkansas Archeologist, DLC, FU,
ICU, NN

Arkansas Family Historian,
Fayetteville, Ark., Mar.
1962-current, AAP, DLC, LNHT,
NN

*Atlanta Traffic and Safety
Counselor*, Atlanta, Ga., 1962-?
GU

Austin Dental News, Austin, Tex.,
1962-current. Currently as
Tenth Times

The Basketball News, Coral Gables,
Fla., 1962-?

Business Studies, Denton, Tex.,
1962-73

*Cardiovascular Research Center
Bulletin*, Houston, Tex.,
1962-current, DLC, ICJ, N,
TxHMC, ViU

*Clemson University Review of
Industrial Management and
Textile Sciences*, Clemson, S.C.,
1962-? AAP, DLC, GAT

Clin-Alert, Louisville, Ky.,
1962-current, CtY-M, DNLM, GU,
KyLoU-M, NcU-H

Coastal Research, Tallahassee,
Fla., 1962-current.   Formerly as
Coastal Research Notes, CtY,
DLC, FMU, FTaSU, FU, NjP

Coastal Research Notes -- See
Coastal Research

Conservation Contractor, Port
Lavaca, Tex., 1962-?

Corrosion Abstracts, Houston,
Tex., Jan. 1962-current, DLC,
NcRS, NN, TxHR, ViU

Custom Home Builders, Little Rock,
Ark., 1962-?

Enforcement Journal, Venice, Fla.;
Louisville, Ky., 1962-current,
NN, NcCU

Exxon USA, Houston, Tex.,
1962-current, NN, TxArU, TxCM

*Florida Audiovisual Association
AVA News*, Orlando, Fla.,
1962-75.   Superseded in part by
Florida Media Quarterly

*Florida FL Reporter; Journal of
Language and Culture in
Education*, Miami Beach, Fla.,
1962-74, DLC, FMU, FU, InNd

Florida Food Field, Miami Springs,
Fla., 1962-?

Forestry Economics -- See *Social
Sciences in Forestry*

Ft. Lauderdale Magazine, Fort
Lauderdale, Fla., June
1962-current

Georgia Bar News, Macon, Ga., Aug.
1962-June 1964.   Superseded by
Georgia Bar Reporter, DLC, GE,
NjR, ViU-L

Georgia Outdoors, Atlanta, Ga.,
Apr. 1962-?   GU, WaU

Georgia Realtor, Atlanta, Ga., Apr.
1962-?   GU

Humanist Educator -- See *Journal
of Humanistic Education and
Development*

JCI World, Coral Gables, Fla.,
1962-current, DLC

*Journal of Humanistic Education
and Development*, Alexandria,
Va., 1962-current.   As *Student
Personnel Association for
Teacher Education Journal* until
1975, as *Humanistic Educator*
until 1982.   DLC, FU, IU, MU,
ViU

Kentucky Architects, Louisville,
Ky., Jan. 1962-?   KyU

Key News, Dallas, Tex., 1962-?

Lifetimes -- See *Tennessee Life
Insurance/News*

*Lockheed Georgia Company
Quarterly* -- See *Lockheed
Georgia Quarterly*

Lockheed Georgia Quarterly,
Marietta, Ga., 1962-?   Also as
*Lockheed Georgia Company
Quarterly*, DLC, GAT, GU, OCl

Louisiana Studies, Natchitoches,
La., 1962-current.   Also as
*Louisiana Studies and
Interdisciplinary Journal of
the South*, currently as
*Southern Studies: An
Interdisciplinary Journal of
the South*, DLC, LNHT, LNL, LU,
NcD, NN

*Louisiana Studies and
Interdisciplinary Journal of
the South* -- See *Louisiana
Studies*

Market Showcase, Atlanta, Ga.,
1962-?

Materials Performance, Houston, Tex., Jan. 1962-current. Also as *Materials Protection*, and as *Materials Protection and Performance*, CtY, DLC, NN, TxHR, TxU, ViU

Materials Protection -- See *Materials Performance*

Materials Protection and Performance -- See *Materials Performance*

Methodist History, Lake Junaluska, Waynesville, N.C., Oct. 1962-current. Supersedes *World Parish*, CtY-D, DLC, NcD, NN, Vi

NCOA Journal Newspaper, San Antonio, Tex., 1962-current

NSPI Journal, San Antonio, Tex., 1962-current. Currently as *Performance & Instruction*, CtY-L, DLC, GU, N, NcRS, PU, TxSaT

New Norfolk, Norfolk, Va., Feb. 1962-77. Superseded by *Tidewater Virginian*, NN, Vi, ViU

New Pinellas Teacher -- See *Action*

New River News, Fort Lauderdale, Fla., July 1962-current, FU

North Carolina Law Enforcement Journal, Raleigh, N.C.; Columbia, S.C., 1962-82, DLC

Paper Money, Camden, S.C., 1962-current, DLC

Parts Line, Memphis, Tenn., 1962-current

Performance & Instruction -- See *NSPI Journal*

Pinellas Teacher -- See *Action*

Quartet; A Magazine of the Arts, College Station, Tex., 1962-79. Incorporated into *Descant* in 1979

Sida; Contributions to Botany, Dallas, Tex., Nov. 1962-current, DLC, GU, NcD, TxHR, TxU

Social Sciences in Forestry, Blacksburg, Va., 1962-current. Formerly as *Forestry Economics*, ViBlbV

Southeastern Peanut Farmer, Tifton, Ga., 1962-current

Southern Conservative, Lexington, Va., May 1962-? CLU, ViU

Southern Horseman, Meridian, Miss., 1962-?

Southern Motorsports Journal, Tuscaloosa, Ala., 1962-current

The Southern Quarterly; A Journal of Arts in the South, Hattiesburg, Miss., Oct. 1962-current, ArU, AU, CLU, CtY, DLC, MCM, MsU, NcD, NN, TxU

Southern Studies: An Interdisciplinary Journal of the South -- See *Louisiana Studies*

Student Activities -- See *Student Advocate*

Student Advocate, Reston, Va., 1962-current. Formerly as *Student Life Highlights* and as *Student Activities*, DeU, MsU, OkU

Student Life Highlights -- See *Student Advocate*

Student Personnel Association for Teacher Education Journal -- See *Journal of Humanistic Education and Development*

TNA News, Weslaco, Tex., 1962-?

Tarheel Principal, Greensboro,
N.C., 1962-?

Tennessee Highways, Nashville,
Tenn., Feb. 1962-?   DLC

Tennessee Life Insurance/News,
Nashville, Tenn., 1962-current.
Currently as *Lifetimes*

Texas Communicologist, Austin,
Tex., 1962-?   TxDaM, TxLT

Tri-ology Technical Report,
Gainesville, Fla., 1962-current,
HHS

*University of South Florida
Language Quarterly*, Tampa,
Fla., 1962-current, KyU, MiU,
OkU, TxHR

Vanguard Magazine, San Antonio,
Tex., 1962-?

*Voice of the Tennessee Walking
Horse*, Shelbyville, Lewisburg,
Tenn., 1962-current, ViBlbV

William and Mary Review,
Williamsburg, Va., 1962-current,
CaAEU, MH

AIDS International Voice,
Arlington, Va., 1963-current.
Formerly as *National Institute
of Rug Cleaning Voice*.
Currently as *Voice*

*Aid Journal of the Ambulance
Association of America*,
Charleston, S.C., 1963-?

Alabama Republican, Birmingham,
Ala., Sept. 1963-?   DLC

Alabama Veterinarian, Birmingham,
Ala., 1963-?   NIC

American Business Law Journal,
Bloomington, Ind.; Austin, Tex.,
1963-current, CLU, DLC, InU, N,
NcD-L, NcU, TNJ

Artifact, El Paso, Tex.,
1963-current, CU, MH-P

*Arkansas Department of Education
News Magazine*, Little Rock,
Ark., Mar. 1963-current, ArU,
DLC, LU

Business Direction -- See *New
Directions*

*Business Opportunities Digest;
Clearing House of Business
Opportunities Information*,
Farmington, N.M.; Atlanta, Ga.,
1963-?   CLSU, KMK

*Chesopeean: A Journal of North
American Archaeology*, Norfolk,
Va., 1963-current, DLC, MH-P,
NN, Vi, ViBlbV

Collegiate Journalist, Muncie, Ind.;
Gainesville, N.C., Fall 1963-?
CNoS, GASU, MoU

Dallas Review, Irving, Tex., Feb.
1963-?   DLC

*Deep South Genealogical
Quarterly*, Mobile, Ala., Aug.
1963-current, AAP, AU, DLC, NN

The Delta Review, Greenville, Miss.;
Memphis, Tenn., 1963-?   LNHT,
LU, MsU

*Ex-Umbra; A Magazine of the
Arts*, Durham, N.C., 1963-current

Faculty Research Journal, Raleigh,
N.C., 1963-?

Fashion Showcase-Retailer, Dallas,
Tex., 1963-current

*Florida Journal of Health,
Physical Education and
Recreation*, Tallahassee, Fla.,
Aug. 1963-?   FU

Forward -- See *Virginia Forward*

Georgia Epoch, Athens, Ga., Fall
1963-?   GU

Georgia Operator, Atlanta, Ga.,
Summer 1963-?   GAT, GU, NN

Green World; A Journal of Verse,
Baton Rouge, La., 1963-66, CU,
LNHT, LU, MH, NN

Houston Law Review, Houston, Tex.,
Spring 1963-current, DLC, N,
NcD-L, TxHR, ViU-L

Houston Lawyer, Houston, Tex.,
Nov. 1963-? Supersedes *Houston
Bar Bulletin*, CtY-L, DLC, NjR

Images; Fine Arts Magazine,
Asheville, N.C., 1963-?

Indian Sociological Bulletin -- See
*International Journal of
Contemporary Sociology*

*International Journal of
Contemporary Sociology*,
Raleigh, N.C., 1963-current.
Formerly as *Indian Sociological
Bulletin*, CtY, DLC, NcD, NN, ViU

*International Journal of
Gynaecology and Obstetrics*, New
York, N.Y.; Research Triangle
Park, N.C., Jan. 1963-current.
Also as *Journal of the
International Federation of
Gynaecology and Obstetrics*,
CLU, DLC, IU-M, NNACS

The Iscani, Waco, Tex., 1963-?

*Jackson County Historical Society
Quarterly* -- See *Stream of
History*

Jacksonville Magazine,
Jacksonville, Fla., Jan.
1963-current, FU

Journal of Economic Literature,
Cambridge, Mass.; Nashville,
Tenn., 1963-current, CtY, DLC,
MH, NcD, NN, TNF, ViBlbV

*Journal of the International
Federation of Gynecology and
Obstetrics* -- See *International
Journal of Gynecology and
Obstetrics*

Junior Musician -- See *Young
Musicians*

Louisiana Higher Education, Baton
Rouge, La., 1963-? DLC, LU,
MH, NcD, NN

Nashville Magazine, Nashville,
Tenn., Jan. 1963-? DLC, TNJ

*National Institute of Rug Cleaning
Voice* -- See *AIDS International
Voice*

New Directions, Roanoke, Va.,
1963-current. Formerly as
Business Direction

Peanut Research, Tifton, Ga., May
1963-? ICJ, ScCleU, TU, ViBlbV

Pipeline Digest, Houston, Tex.,
1963-current, DLC, ULA

Popular Rotorcraft Flying,
Raleigh, N.C., 1963-current

*Saint Augustine's College Faculty
Research Journal*, Raleigh, N.C.,
May 1963-? DLC, MH, NcD, NN

*South Carolina Genealogical
Magazine*, Liberty, S.C.; Pass
Christian, Miss., Feb. 1963-?
MoS, NN

*South Carolina Genealogical
Register*, Handsboro, Miss., Mar.
1963-? DLC, NcD, NN

*The Southern Journal of
Philosophy*, Memphis, Tenn.,
1963-current, CtY, DLC, NcD,
NN, TNJ, ViU

*Southwest Business and Economic
Review*, El Paso, Tex.,
1963-current. Continues *El
Paso Business Review*, InU, NN,
TxCM, TxDaM, TxLT, UU

Southwestern Genealogist, El Paso,
Tex., 1963-? CoU, In

Southwestern Studies, El Paso, Tex., Spring 1963-current, CtY, DLC, MH, NcU, NN, TxHR, TxU

Stream of History, Newport, Ark., Jan. 1963-current. Also as *Jackson County Historical Society Quarterly*, ArU, TxU

Studies in Scottish Literature, Lubbock, Tex.; Columbia, S.C., July 1963-? CtY, DLC, NcD, NN, TxDaM, TxHR

Studies in Short Fiction, Newberry, S.C., 1963-current, CtY, DLC, NcU, NN, ScCleU, ScU, ViBlbV

The Sunbelt Dairyman, Nashville, Tenn., Jan. 1963-current, GU, ScCleU

Texana, Waco, Tex., Winter 1963-? CtY, DLC, NcD, NN, TxHR, TxU

Texas Freemason, Austin, Houston, Tex., July 1963-? TxU

Texas Professor, Austin, Tex., Mar. 1963-? TxCM, TxHR

Theta: Exploring Human Potential in Life and Death -- See *Theta: The Journal of the Psychical Research Foundation*

Theta: The Journal of the Psychical Research Foundation, Durham, Chapel Hill, N.C., Apr. 1963-current. Currently as *Theta; Exploring Human Potential in Life and Death*, DLC, MH, NN

Toy and Hobby World, Atlanta, Ga., 1963-? NN

Virginia Forward, Richmond, Va., July 1963-? Also as *Forward*, DLC, Vi, ViBlbV, ViU

Virginia Genealogical Society Quarterly Bulletin, Richmond, Va., 1963-? DLC, NN, Vi, ViU

Voice, Arlington, Va., 1963-current. Formerly as *AIDS International Voice* and as *National Institute of Rug Cleaning Voice*

Young Musicians, Nashville, Tenn., 1963-current. Formerly as *Junior Musician*, DLC

Amica -- See *AMICA Bulletin*

AMICA Bulletin, Dallas, Tex., 1964-current. Formerly as *Amica*

Alabama Association of Secondary School Principals Bulletin, Huntsville, Andalusia, Ala., 1964-current, AAP

Alabama Journal of Medical Sciences, Birmingham, Ala., 1964-current, AAP, AU, DNLM, MoU, NcU-H

The America, Lexington, Ky., 1964-current

The American Eagle, Alexandria, La., 1964-?

American Killifish Association Journal, Dallas, Tex.; Atlanta, Ga., 1964-? DLC, NNM

The American Voice, Pigeon Forge, Tenn., 1964-?

Approaches; A Periodical of Poems by Kentuckians -- See *Kentucky Poetry Review*

Arkansas Football, Waco, Tex., 1964-current

Arkansas Outlook, Little Rock, Ark., 1964-78. Superseded by *Arkansas Economic Outlook*, ArU

Association of Engineering Geologists Bulletin, Sacramento, Calif.; Dallas, Tex., 1964-current. As *Engineering Geology*, 1964-67, CtY, DLC, NcD, NjP, TxDaM, ViU

Beehive, Nashville, Tenn., 1964-82

*Big Country 10-5 News
International* -- See *C. B.
Voice; The Big Picture of the
C. B. Radio*

**Birmingham Bar Association
Bulletin**, Birmingham, Ala., Feb.
1964-current, C, WaU-L

Blue Horse, Augusta, Ga.,
1964-current

*C. B. Voice; The Big Picture of the
C. B. Radio*, Statesville, N.C.,
1964-? Formerly as *Big Country
10-5 News International*

Christian Pathway, Crockett, Ky.,
1964-current

Citrus & Vegetable World, Winter
Haven, Barton, Fla., 1964-?
Also as *The Citrus World*

The Citrus World -- See *Citrus &
Vegetable World*

Consultant, Midland, Tex., 1964-78

Cotton Grower, Memphis, Tenn.,
1964-current

Courier, Nashville, Tenn., 1964-?
DLC

Daffodil Journal, Lorton, Va.;
Tyner, N.C.; Franklin, Tenn.,
Sept. 1964-current, DLC, ScCleU

Dog Lover's Digest, Greensboro,
N.C., 1964-current

El Paso Business Review, El Paso,
Tex., 1964-current. Formerly
as *El Paso Economic Review*,
currently as *Southwest Business
& Economic Review*

El Paso Economic Review -- See *El
Paso Business Review*

Engineering Construction, Dallas,
Tex., 1964-?

Engineering Facts from Gatorland
-- See *Facts From Gatorland*

Engineering Geology -- See
*Association of Engineering
Geologists Bulletin*

Engineering Technician, Everman,
Tex., 1964-?

FREN -- See *Florida Electric
Cooperative News*

Facts From Gatorland, Gainesville,
Fla., 1964-? Formerly as
*Engineering Facts from
Gatorland*, FU

Finite String, Arlington, Va., Jan.
1964-74. Superseded by
*American Journal of
Computational Linguistics*, AU,
KU, KyU, MH, NN, ViU

Florida Electric Cooperative News,
Tallahassee, Fla., 1964-current.
Formerly as *FREN*. Currently
as *Florida Rural Electric News*

Florida Farm & Ranch, Nashville,
Tenn., Jan.-Mar. 1964.

Florida Landscape Architecture,
Hollywood, Fla., 1964-? FU, GU

Florida Reading Quarterly,
Tallahassee, Fla., Dec.
1964-current, FMU, FTaSU

Florida Rural Electric News -- See
*Florida Electric Cooperative
News*

Flue Cured Tobacco Farmer,
Raleigh, N.C., 1964-current,
NcRS

GSN Gesneriad Saintpaulia News,
Knoxville, Tenn., 1964-current,
AAP, DLC, NIC

Georgia Bar Reporter, Atlanta,
Ga., Aug. 1964-? Supersedes
Georgia Bar News, DLC, FU,
GEU, NcD-L

*Georgia Genealogical Society
Quarterly*, Atlanta, Ga., Sept.
1964-? DLC, GU, NN

Georgia Librarian, Tucker, Ga.,
Mar. 1964-current, DLC, GAT,
GU, NN

*Georgia Pioneers Genealogical
Magazine*, Albany, Ga., Feb.
1964-?   GU, NcD, NN, TxU

Georgia State Bar Journal,
Atlanta, Ga., Aug. 1964-current.
Supersedes *Georgia Bar
Journal*, CtY-L, DLC, FU, NcD-L,
NjR

Georgia Stockman, Athens, Ga.,
Mar. 1964-?   GU

Hollins Critic, Hillsville, Va., Feb.
1964-current, CtY, DLC, NcD,
NcU, NN, TxHR

Ideafile, Dallas, Tex., 1964-?

Impact Magazine, Nashville, Tenn.,
1964-?   DLC

Journal of Bank Reserve, Troy,
Ala., Autumn 1964-current, DLC

Journal of Employment Counseling,
Columbia, Mo.; Falls Church,
Va., 1964-current, FU, KyU, LU,
MoU, NcRS

Journal of Leukocyte Biology --
See *RES: Reticuloendothelial
Society Journal*

Kentucky Farm & Ranch, Nashville,
Tenn., Jan. 1964-?

Kentucky Golfer, Louisville, Ky.,
May 1964-?   KyU

Kentucky Poetry Review, Louisville,
Ky., 1964-current. Formerly as
*Approaches; A Periodical of
Poems by Kentuckians*, KyU

Last Harass, Augusta, Ga., 1964-?

Latinamericanist, Gainesville, Fla.,
Feb. 3, 1964-?   FU

Louisiana Farmer, Alexandria, La.;
Nashville, Tenn., 1964-Dec. 1965,
LU

Mirror of the Valley, Staunton,
Va., 1964-?

Music City News, Nashville, Tenn.,
1964-current, DLC

NSDJA Digest, Memphis, Tenn.,
1964-current.   Currently as
*Shelter; Magazine for
Distribution and Marketing of
Products for Building and Home
Improvements*, WaU

North Carolina Farm and Ranch,
Raleigh, N.C.; Nashville, Tenn.,
Jan. 1964-?   NcRS

North Carolina Profile, Lincolnton,
N.C., Apr. 1964-?   NcRS

North Texas Retailer -- See
Retailer and Marketing News

Oceanic Abstracts, Louisville, Ky.;
Bethesda, Md., 1964-current.
Supersedes *Oceanic Index* and
Oceanic Citation Journal, DNLM,
MiEM, NN, ScCleU

Old West, Austin, Tex.; Iola, Wis.,
Fall 1964-current, DLC, NN, TxU

Our Heritage, Frankfort, Ky.,
1964-?   DLC, KyU-ASC, NcRS

Panhandle Magazine, Kansas City,
Mo.; Houston, Tex.,
1964-current, MoKL, NN

Pension World, Atlanta, Ga.,
1964-current

Physical Therapy, Alexandria, Va.,
Jan. 1964-current.   Continues
*American Physical Therapy
Association Journal*, DLC, TxU

Pecan Poetry Series, Deland, Fla.,
1964-?   DLC, KyU, MH

Poetry Review, Tampa, Fla., 1964-?
DLC, IaU, MoU

*Quinto Lingo; Multi-Lingual
Magazine*, Emmaus, Pa.;
Alexandria, Va., 1964-current,
DLC, LNHT, NSoaS

Rayito; Edicion Para Consejeras,
El Paso, Tex., 1964-current

Red Clay Reader, Charlotte, N.C.,
1964-? DLC, KyU, MH, NcD, NcU,
NN

Refrigerated Transporter,
Houston, Tex., 1964-current

Retailer and Marketing News,
Dallas, Tex., 1964-current.
Formerly as *North Texas
Retailer*

*RES; Reticuloendothelial Society
Journal*, Winston-Salem, N.C.;
New York, N.Y., 1964-current.
Currently as *Journal of
Leukocyte Biology*, CtY-M, DLC,
MiU, NcU-H, ViBlbV

Riverside Quarterly, Gainesville,
Fla., 1964-? CtY, KyU, MH, OU

Roanoke Historical Society Journal
-- See *Roanoke Valley Historical
Society Journal*

*Roanoke Valley Historical Society
Journal*, Roanoke, Va., Summer
1964-78. Formerly as *Roanoke
Historical Society Journal*, KU,
NN, Vi, ViBlbV, ViU

Scout Memorabilia, Sarasota, Fla.,
1964-current

Seminars in Hematology, Orlando,
Fla., 1964-current

Senior Golfer, Clearwater, Fla.,
1964-current

*Shelter: Magazine for Distribution
and Marketing of Products for
Building and Home Improvements*
-- See *NSDJA Digest*

South Carolina Farm and Ranch,
Raleigh, N.C.; Nashville, Tenn.,
Jan. 1964-? ScCleU

South Carolina Farmer-Grower,
Atlanta, Ga., 1964-?

Southern Dog Lover's Digest,
Shreveport, La., Fall 1964-?
DLC

Southern Host, Wilton Manors, Fla.,
1964-?

Southern Motoracing,
Winston-Salem, N.C.,
1964-current

Southern Veterinarian, Birmingham,
Ala., Jan. 1964-? AAP, GU,
KyU-ASC

*Southwest Business & Economic
Review* -- See *El Paso Business
Review*

Super Stock & Drag Illustrated,
Alexandria, Va., 1964-current

Tactics, Arlington, Va., Jan. 1964-?
DLC, NN

Tennessee Philological Bulletin,
Memphis, Tenn., Apr. 1964-?
AAP, GASU, MH, MsU, TU, ViBlbV

Texas Catholic Herald of Austin,
Austin, Tex., 1964-?

Texas Concho Register, San Angelo,
Tex., 1964-current

*Texas Dental Hygienists'
Association Journal*, Houston,
Tex., 1964-?

Texas Farm and Ranch, Dallas,
Tex., Jan.-Nov. 1964

*Texas Journal on Mental
Retardation*, Austin, Tex., June
1964-? DLC, TxHMC

Total Energy, Downers Grove, Ill.;
San Antonio, Tex., Oct. 1964-?
CSt

Trends in Parks and Recreation
-- See *Trends-Park Practice*

Trends-Park Practice, Arlington,
Va., July 1964-?   Formerly as
*Trends in Parks and
Recreation*, DLC, GU, MiU, NcRS,
ScCleU

Vine, Nashville, Tenn., 1964-?

Virginia Aviation, Richmond, Va.,
1964-?   DLC, Vi, ViU

Virginia Farm & Ranch, Nashville,
Tenn., Jan. 1964-?

Vue South, Orangeburg, S.C.,
1964-?

Wake Forest Law Review,
Winston-Salem, N.C.,
1964-current.   Continues
*Intramural Law Review of Wake
Forest College*, CtY-L, DLC,
NcU-L, NcWsW

Wee Lambs, Crockett, Ky.,
1964-current

West Texas Angelus, San Angelo,
Tex., 1964-current

Woman Constitutionalist, Summit,
Miss., 1964-current

ASMT News, Bellaire, Tex.,
1965-current, DLC

Actinomycetes -- See *Biology of the
Actinomycetes and Related
Organisms*

Adept -- See *Adept Quarterly*

Adept Quarterly, Houston, Tex.,
1965-?   Formerly as *Adept*, MH,
TxHR

Alabama Architect, Montgomery,
Ala. 1965-?   AAP

Alabama Baptist Historian,
Birmingham, Ala., 1965-current,
AAP, ViU

*Alabama Defense Lawyer's
Journal*, Birmingham, Ala., Apr.
1965-?   AU

Alabama Junior College Librarian,
Fayette, Decatur, Ala., Nov.
1965-73.   Since 1973 as *Alabama
Junior College Library
Association Newsletter*, AAP

Alabama M.D., Montgomery, Ala.,
1965-?   AAP

*Arkansas Archeological Society
Field Notes*, Fayetteville, Ark.,
Jan. 1965-current, ArU, FU,
MH-P

Arkansas Cattle Business, Little
Rock, Ark., 1965-current, ArU

Baptist History and Heritage,
Nashville, Tenn., Aug.
1965-current, DLC, NcD

Batting the Breeze, Fort Myers,
Fla., 1965-current

*Biology of the Actinomycetes and
Related Organisms*, Richmond,
Va., 1965-current.   Formerly as
Nocardial Biology.   Currently
as *Actinomycetes*.

*Bluebonnets and Silver Shoes of
Texas*, Brownwood, Tex., 1965-?

Brief of the School of Law, Dallas,
Tex., Dec. 1965-current, ViU-L

Bulletin Baudelairien, Nashville,
Tenn., Aug. 1965-current, CtY,
DLC, FU, MH, NcU, TxHR, ViU

Burley Tobacco Farmer, Raleigh,
N.C., 1965-?   KyU-ASC, NcRS

*Business and Economic Dimensions
Magazine*, Gainesville, Fla., Apr.
1965-current, DLC, FMU, FTaSU,
FU, NcU, NN

Charolais Banner, Shawnee Mission,
Kan.; Houston, Tex., Apr. 1965-?
IU, LU, TxCM

Chemical Engineering Education,
Storrs, Conn.; Gainesville, Fla.,
1965-current, FU, IU, NcRS, NN,
ScU, ViU

Choc-Talk, New York, N.Y.; McLean,
Va., 1965-? AAP, KyU-ASC

Command Magazine -- See *Command
Policy*

Command Policy, Arlington, Va.,
Nov. 1965-? Formerly as
Command Magazine, as
Commanders Digest, and as *For
Commanders-This Changing
World*, DLC

Commanders Digest -- See *Command
Policy*

Convenience Store Journal,
Atlanta, Ga., 1965-? DLC, NN

Cumberlands -- See *Twigs*

*East Central Florida Public
Broadcasting Monthly*, Winter
Park, Fla., 1965-current

English in Texas, Alpine,
Commerce, Tex., 1965-current,
DLC

Fine Arts Monthly, Amarillo, Tex.,
1965-?

Florida Conservation News,
Tallahassee, Fla., Oct. 1965-?
DLC, FMU, FTaSU

Florida Geographer, Tallahassee,
Boca Raton, Fla., 1965-? FU

Florida Restauranteur, Miami, Fla.,
1965-current

Florida Teacher, Jacksonville,
Fla., Oct. 1965-? FU, PPiU

Folio, Birmingham, Ala.,
1965-current, AAP, DLC

*For Commanders - This Changing
World* -- See *Command Policy*

Foundation Facts, Houston, Tex.,
1965-?

Georgia, Atlanta, Ga., 1965-?
Formerly as *Georgia Progress*,
DLC, GU, MH

Georgia Progress -- See *Georgia*

*Georgia's Agriculture; Management
& Marketing*, Athens, Ga., July
1965-? DLC, GU, NIC

Gold Coast of Florida, Fort
Lauderdale, Fla., 1965-current.
Also as *Gold Coast Pictorial;
The Magazine of Florida's Gold
Coast*

*Gold Coast Pictorial; The Magazine
of Florida's Gold Coast* -- See
Gold Coast of Florida

Great Outdoors Magazine, Saint
Petersburg, Fla., 1965-? FM

IMSA Journal, Fort Worth, Tex.,
1965-current

I.M.S.A. Signal Magazine, Houston,
Tex., 1965-?

Illuminations, San Francisco,
Calif.; Austin, Tex., 1965-71.
Incorporated into *Gar*, CU, MH,
NcD, ViU

Inside Arkansas -- See *This is
Arkansas*

International Odd Fellow, Dallas,
Tex., 1965-current

*Intramural Law Review of Wake
Forest College*, Winston-Salem,
N.C., 1965-? CtY-L, DLC, NcU-L,
ViU-L

Investment Sales, Miami, Fla.,
1965-?

Islander, Hilton Head Island, S.C.,
1965-current

Journal of Applied Behavior Science, New York, N.Y.; Arlington, Va., 1965-current, CtY, DLC, MH, NcD, NN, ViBlbV

Journal of Public Health Dentistry, Raleigh, N.C., Winter 1965-current. Continues *Public Health Dentistry*, DLC, InU

Journal of the University of Texas International Law Society -- See *Texas International Law Forum*

Kentucky Ancestors, Frankfort, Ky., July 1965-current, DLC, FU, KyU, LNHT, MH, NcU, NN

Labor Reporter, San Antonio, Tex., 1965-?

Latin American Research Review, Austin, Tex., 1965-current, CtY, DLC, NcD, NcU, TxHR, TxU

Medical College of Virginia Quarterly, Richmond, Va., Spring 1965-? DLC, MiU, Vi, ViU-M

Medical University Review, Charleston, S.C., 1965-76?

Mergers & Acquisitions, McLean, Va., Fall 1965-current, CtY, DLC, MCM, TxU, ViU

Mississippi Kite, Jackson, Miss., May 1965-? CoFS, MsSM

Mississippi Valley Journal of Business and Economics, New Orleans, La., Fall 1965-current. Currently as *Review of Business and Economic Research*, DLC, FU, GU, LNHT, LU, NcD, NjR

Model Car Raceways, Atlanta, Ga., 1965-?

NOVA: University of Texas at El Paso Magazine, El Paso, Tex., 1965-current

Nocardial Biology -- See *Biology of the Actinomycetes and Related Organisms*

North Carolina Journal of Mental Health, Raleigh, N.C., 1965-? DLC, NcD, NcRS, NcU-H

Open Door, Raleigh, N.C., 1965-? DLC, NcD, NcRS

Peanut Farmer, Raleigh, N.C., 1965-current, GU, NcRS

Quixote, Austin, Tex., 1965-? DLC, NN

Review of Business and Economic Research -- See *Mississippi Valley Journal of Business and Economics*

South Carolina Veterinarian, Columbia, S.C., 1965-? KMK

South's Illustrated, Birmingham, Ala., Sept. 1965-? AAP

Southern Literary Studies, Baton Rouge, La., 1965-? CtY, MA, MH, TxHR, ViU

Southern Markets/Media, Atlanta, Ga., 1965-? DLC

Southern Waterways, Fort Myers, Fla., 1965-? AAP, DLC, MH-BA, NjP

Southwestern Profiles, Austin, Tex., 1965-? CtY, DLC, FU, TxDaM

Spoke Wheels, Beaumont, Tex., 1965-?

Sunday School Senior Adults, Nashville, Tenn., 1965-current

Tennessee Bar Journal, Nashville, Tenn., Feb. 1965-current, DLC, NjR, TNJ

Tennessee Pharmacist, Nashville, Tenn., Feb. 1965-? DNLM, TU-M, ViRCU-H

Tennessee Survey of Business,
Knoxville, Tenn., Sept. 1965-?
DLC, FU, GU, MH-BA, NN, TNJ

Tennessee Valley Socialist,
Nashville, Tenn., 1965-?   WHi

*Texas Engineering & Science
Magazine*, Austin, Tex., Apr.
1965-?   TxHR

*Texas Gulf Historical and
Biographical Record*, Beaumont,
Tex., Nov. 1965-?   DLC, MH, NN

Texas International Law Forum,
Austin, Tex., Jan. 1965-current.
v.1 as *Journal of the University
of Texas International Law
Society*.   Currently as *Texas
International Law Journal*,
CtY-L, DLC, NcD-L, NcU-L, TNJ,
TxCM

Texas International Law Journal
-- See *Texas International Law
Forum*

*Texas Metro; Magazine of Texas
Living*, Arlington, Fort Worth,
Tex., 1965-current

*Texas Parks and Wildlife
Magazine*, Austin, Tex., Apr.
1965-current.   Continues *Texas
Game and Fish*, TxU

Texas Transportation Researcher,
College Station, Tex., Jan.
1965-current, DLC, MiU, NcRS,
TxCM

This is Arkansas, Little Rock,
Ark., Jan. 1965-current.   As
Inside Arkansas since 1976,
ArU, WHi

Tracor Today, Austin, Tex., 1965-?

Turf-Grass Times, Jacksonville
Beach, Fla., Oct. 1965-?   Merged
with *Landscape Industry* to
form *Landscape & Turf
Industry*, IU, MsSM, VtU

Twigs, Pikeville, Ky., 1965-current.
Currently as *Cumberlands*

*Voices: The Art and Science of
Psychotherapy*, Fair Lawn, N.J.;
Orlando, Fla.; New York, N.Y.,
Fall 1965-current, CtY-M, DLC,
FU, NcD, NcRS, ScU

*World Dredging & Marine
Construction*, Conroe, Tex.,
Summer 1965-current, MoU, NjP,
NN

Affirmation, Richmond, Va., Nov.
1966-?   FU, KyU, NcRS, Vi, ViU

American Way, Dallas, Tex.,
1966-current

Ancestry, West Palm Beach, Fla.,
Jan. 1966-current, DLC, IU, MH

Ancla, El Paso, Tex., 1966-current

Antique Outboarder, Richardson,
Tex.; Britt, Iowa, 1966-current,
DLC

Anubis, Arlington, Va., Fall 1966-?
DLC

*Arkansas Genealogical Research
Aid*, North Little Rock, Ark.,
Mar. 1966-?   In, MoS, NN

*Arkansas Journal of Health,
Physical Education and
Recreation*, _____, Ark., Spring
1966-?   ArU

Arkansas State, Little Rock, Ark.,
Fall 1966-?   DLC

*Art Insight/Southwest;   A Journal
Devoted to Recognition of the
Arts in the West and Southwest*,
Austin, Tex., 1966-current.
Formerly as *Southwestern Art*,
DLC, MH, TxCM, TxHR

Attakapas Gazette, Lafayette, La.,
1966-current, DLC, LNHT, TxHR

Augusta Magazine, Augusta, Ga.,
Winter 1966-current, GU

Basketball Mentor, Austin, Tex.,
Nov. 1966-? MnU

Bluegrass Unlimited, Wheaton, Md.;
Broad Run, Va., 1966-current,
DLC

Car Collector and Car Classics,
Atlanta, Ga., 1966-current.
Formed by the merger of *Car
Classics* and *Car Collector*,
1979, NcRS, NN

Children's Music Leader -- See
Music Leader

Childrens World, Athens, Ga.,
1966-?

Container News, New York, N.Y.;
Atlanta, Ga., 1966-current, DLC,
IU, MoRM

Criminal Law Monthly, Houston,
Tex., 1966-?

Cultured Dairy Products Journal,
Clemson, S.C., 1966-current, IaAS

*Current Concepts of
Cerebrovascular Disease:
Stroke*, New York, N.Y.; Dallas,
Tex., Winter 1966-? DLC,
TNJ-M, ViRCU-H

Dealerscope/Southeast, Atlanta,
Ga., 1966-?

DeKalb Literary Arts Journal,
Clarkston, Ga., 1966-current,
CU, DLC, NN

*Dialogue: A Journal of Mormon
Thought*, Stanford, Calif.;
Arlington, Va., Spring
1966-current, CtY, DLC, NcD,
NNC

Dimensions, Little Rock, Ark.,
1966-? ArU

*Education & Training of the
Mentally Retarded*, Reston,
Arlington, Va., Feb.
1966-current, CLU, DLC, MH,
NcRS

Entre Nous Houston, Houston, Tex.,
1966-? DLC

Fathom, Gainesville, Ga., 1966-?
GU

Florida Journal -- See *Florida
Profile: Sunshine State
Panorama*

*Florida Profile; Sunshine State
Panorama*, Fort Lauderdale,
Fla., 1966-? Formerly as
Florida Journal, DLC

Florida Journal, Fort Lauderdale,
Fla., Nov. 1966-? FMU

Focus on the Dallas Economy,
Dallas, Tex., 1966-? Supersedes
Dallas Economy

Foreign Language Beacon, Atlanta,
Ga., Spring 1966-current, GU

FUN Magazine, Houston, Tex.,
1966-?

*Georgia Alert; A Look at
Education's Role Today*, Atlanta,
Ga., 1966-current, GU

*Georgia Entomological Society
Journal*, Tifton, Ga., Jan.
1966-current, GU, KU, LU, NcRS

Georgia Golf, Atlanta, Ga., Mar.
1966-? GU

Georgia Impression, Athens, Ga.,
Fall 1966-? GU

Georgia Law Review, Athens, Ga.,
Fall 1966-current, CtY-L, DLC,
NcD-L, ViU-L

*Georgia Speech and Hearing
Association Journal*, Cave
Spring, Ga., Fall 1966-? GU

The Green Tree, Tuscaloosa, Ala.,
1966-?

Greensboro Review, Greensboro,
N.C., May 1966-current, DLC, MH,
NcGU, NcRS

Gulf Review, College Station,
Houston, Tex., Sept. 1966-71, IU,
N

HTA Contact, Houston, Tex., 1966-?
Superseded by *HTA Today*

HortScience, Saint Joseph, Mich.;
Alexandria, Va., Winter
1966-current, ICU, LU, NcRS, NjR

Human Mosaic, New Orleans, La.,
Spring 1966-current. Formerly
as *Mosaic*, CtY, LNHT, LU, MsSM

*INFO Journal; Science & The
Unknown*, Arlington, Va.,
1966-current

International Stewardess News --
See *Passenger & In-Flight
Service*

Irrigation Age, Hereford, Dallas,
Tex., Aug. 1966-current, KMK,
NbU

Journal of Business Research,
Athens, Ga., Jan. 1966-current.
Formerly as *Southern Journal
of Business*, DLC, GAT, GU,
MH-BA, NcU, NN

*Journal of Library History,
Philosophy and Comparative
Librarianship*, Austin, Tex.,
Jan. 1966-current, CtY, DeU, MH,
NcD, NN, TxHR, TxU-L

Journal of Thought, Warrensburg,
Mo.; Fayetteville, Ark.,
1966-current, ArU, DLC, FU, GU,
NN

*Kentucky Commentator; a
Socio-Legal Journal*, Lexington,
Ky., Oct. 1966-? C, ViU-L

Lone Star Sierran, Austin, Tex.,
1966-? TxU

Lost Treasure -- See *True
Treasure*

Louisiana Horizons, Baton Rouge,
La., 1966-? DLC

Louisiana LP-Gas News, Monroe,
La., 1966-current

*Lyrica Germanica; A Journal for
German Lyric Poetry*,
Lexington, Ky., May 1966-75?
GU, InU, KyU, NjR

Mosaic -- See *Human Mosaic*

Multivariate Behavioral Research,
Fort Worth, Tex., Jan. 1966-?
CtY, DLC, MH, NcD, NN, TxHR,
TxU

Music for Primaries, Nashville,
Tenn., 1966-? DLC

Music Leader, Nashville, Tenn.,
1966-current. Formerly as
Children's Music Leader, DLC

New Orleans Magazine, New Orleans,
La., Oct. 1966-current, DLC,
LNL, LU

New Products in Construction,
Lakeland, Fla., 1966-?

Newspaper Collector's Gazette, Fort
Lauderdale, Fla., 1966-75, DLC,
GU, N

North Texas Pioneer, Wichita Falls,
Tex., 1966-? MoS, NN, TxU

*North West Georgia Historical and
Genealogical Society Quarterly*,
Rome, Ga., 1966-current

Les Nouvelles, Richmond, Va.,
1966-?

Ocean Industry, Houston, Tex.,
1966-current, DLC, FU, MiU, NcD,
TxU

Omnis, Houston, Tex., 1966-? DLC

Paint Horse Journal, Fort Worth,
Tex., 1966-current, LU

Passenger & In Flight Service,
Miami, Fla., 1966-current.
Formerly as *Stewardess and
Flight Service* and as
International Stewardess News

Perception & Psychophysics,
Golteta, Calif.; Austin, Tex.,
Jan. 1966-current, CtY-M, DLC,
NcD, NN, TxHR, TxU

*Reality Magazine; A National
Monthly of Christian Belief and
Opinion*, Alexandria, Va., 1966-?

The Redskin, Memphis, Tenn.; East
Saint Louis, Mo.; Angola,
Franklin, Ind., 1966-79, DLC,
OkU, WHi

*Resumen; Bimestral de Arte y
Cultura*, Miami, Fla., 1966-?
DLC

*Revista Interamricana De
Radiologia*, Miami, Fla., 1966-?

Rice University Review, Houston,
Tex., 1966-? TxHR

*South Texas Genealogical &
Historical Society Quarterly*,
Gonzales, Tex., July/Sept.
1966-current, DLC

*Southeastern College Art
Conference Review and
Newsletter*, Columbia, S.C., Dec.
1966-? DLC, KyU, ScU

Southeastern Dairy Review,
Orlando, Fla., 1966-current

Southern Journal of Business --
See *Journal of Business
Research*

Southern Living, Birmingham, Ala.,
Feb. 1966-current, AAP, DLC,
GU, LNHT, LU, NcD, ViU

Southern Office, Atlanta, Ga.,
1966-? DLC

Southwest Heritage, Amarillo, Tex.,
Winter 1966-69, DLC, MiEM, OrU

*Southwestern Art; A Journal
Devoted to Recognition of the
Arts in the West and Southwest*
-- See *Art Insight/Southwest*

Specialty Advertising News,
Hallendale, Fla., 1966-?

Stewardess & Flight Service News
-- See *Passenger & In-Flight
Service*

Stock Car Racing, Alexandria, Va.,
1966-current

TSTA Texas Schools, Austin, Tex.,
Jan. 1966-Aug./Sept. 1979. Also
as *Texas Schools*, CaAEU, MnU,
TxSaT

Taxation for Accountants,
Paterson, N.J.; Tampa, Fla., Mar.
1966-current, DLC, FU, KU,
ViBlbV

Teen Talk, Valdosta, Ga.,
1966-current

Tejas, Barry, Tex., 1966-75

Tennessee Tech Journal,
Cookeville, Tenn., 1966-? DLC,
IU, LU, N, NcD, TNJ

Tennessee Vo-Tech News,
Murfreesboro, Tenn., 1966-?

Texas Business & Industry,
Houston, Tex., 1966-?

Texas Longhorn, Kerrville, Tex.,
1966-? OkU

Texas Schools -- See *TSTA Texas
Schools*

*Texas University Studies in
Accounting*, Austin, Tex., 1966-?
CtY, DLC, NcD, TxU

*Texas University Studies in
Insurance and Actuarial
Science*, Austin, Tex., 1966-?
DLC, GU, IU

TOPS, Atlanta, Ga., 1966-current,
GU

Treasure World -- See *True
Treasure, Lost Mines and
Buried or Sunken Treasures*

Triumph, Warrenton, Va., 1966-?

*True Treasure; Lost Mines and
Buried or Sunken Treasures*,
Conroe, Tex., Fall 1966-current.
Also as *Treasure World*.
Currently as *Lost Treasure*,
DLC, TxU

U. S. Glass, Metal & Glazing,
Memphis, Tenn., 1966-current,
DLC

VICA Journal, Leesburg, Va.,
1966-current. Also as *VICA
Magazine*, DLC

VICA Magazine -- See *VICA Journal*

Virginia Geographer,
Fredericksburg, Va., Nov.
1966-current, DLC, IU, LU, Vi,
ViU

Virginia Social Science Journal,
Blacksburg, Va., Apr. 1966-?
DLC, GU, NN, Vi, ViU

Virginia Town & City, Richmond,
Va., 1966-current. Supersedes
Virginia Municipal Review, DLC,
Vi, ViU

*Voices International; A South and
West Publication*, Fort Smith,
Little Rock, Ark. 1966-current,
ArU, RPB, UU

Wofford Bibliopolist, Spartanburg,
S.C., 1966-?

Young People Training for Action,
Nashville, Tenn., 1966-?

*Zygon: Journal of Religion &
Science*, Chicago, Ill.; Winter
Park, Fla., 1966-current, C,
CtY-D, DLC, FU, NcD, NjR, ViU

APBA Journal, Durham, N.C.,
1967-current

*Alabama Genealogical Society
Magazine*, _____, Ala., 1967-?
AAP, AU, DLC, NN

Alabama Law Reporter, University,
Ala., Nov. 1967-? WaU-L

Alive, Harrisonburg, Va., 1967-Feb.
1982

American Building Supplies,
Nashville, Tenn.; Atlanta, Ga.,
Jan. 1967-current. Supersedes
Southern Building Supplies, DLC

American Harp Journal, New York,
N.Y.; Lubbock, Tex., Spring
1967-current. Formerly as *Harp
News*, DLC, InU, IU, MB, MiU

American Literary Review,
Arlington, Tex., Fall
1967-current, CtY, DLC, NcD,
NcU, TxU, ViU

Antique Monthly, Tuscaloosa, Ala.,
1967-current. Formerly as
Antique Quarterly, DLC, ViBlbV

Antique Quarterly -- See *Antique
Monthly*

*Antitrust Law and Economics
Review*, McLean, Va.,
1967-current, CU, DLC, IU, LU,
MiU, NcRS, TxHR

*Arkansas Department of Education
Library Bulletin*, Little Rock,
Ark., 1967-current, ArU

Arkansas Lawyer, Little Rock,
Ark., June 1967-? ArU, DLC,
NcD-L, NjR, ViU-L

*Arlington Quarterly; a Journal of
Literature, Comment and
Opinion*, Arlington, Tex.,
Autumn 1967-? CtY, DLC, IU,
MH, NcD, TxHR, TxLT, ViU

Biblical Viewpoint, Greenville, S.C., Apr. 1967-current, CtY-D, DLC

Biophysics, Bioengineering, and Medical Instrumentation -- See *Medical Instrumentation*

Clemson University College of Architecture Semester Review; A Journal of Educational Thought, Clemson, S.C., 1967-current, ScCleU

Cost Reduction Journal -- See *Defense Management Journal*

Cost Reduction Report -- See *Defense Management Journal*

Crime Control Digest, Annandale, Va., 1967-current, CtY-L, TU, N

Defense Management Journal, Alexandria, Va., 1967-current. Also as *Cost Reduction Report* and as *Cost Reduction Journal*, DLC

Dixie Golf, Atlanta, Ga., Feb. 1967-? GU

Electronics Digest, Fort Worth, Tex., 1967-? DLC

Elementary School Guidance & Counseling, Falls Church, Va., Jan. 1967-current, CCC, DLC, GU, MsU, NcRS, ViBlbV

F.I.; Forum Italicum, Austin, Tex., 1967-? CtY, DLC, NcRS, NjR, TxLT

Federation of American Hospitals Review, Little Rock, Ark., 1967-current

The Florida Genealogist's Journal, Tampa, Fla., Feb. 1967-77. Continues *Florida Genealogist's Newsletter.* Continued by *Florida Genealogical Journal*, 1978, DLC

Florida Magazine, Coral Gables, Fla., 1967-?

Florida Quarterly, Gainesville, Fla., Summer 1967-? CtY, FMU, FU, ViU

Form, Alexandria, Va., 1967-current

Foxfire, Rabun Gap, Ga., Mar. 1967-current, CtY, DLC, GU, MH, PU

Franchising Around the World Magazine, New York, N.Y.; Miami, Fla., 1967-current. Currently as *Franchising Investments Around the World*, DLC

Franchising Investments Around the World -- See *Franchising Around the World Magazine*

Georgia Conservancy Magazine, Atlanta, Ga., 1967-?

Harbinger; A Magazine of Media Arts, Crystal City, Tex., 1967-?

Harp News -- See *American Harp Journal*

Hays County Historical and Genealogical Society Quarterly, San Marcos, Tex., 1967-?

Health For Life, Austell, Ga., 1967-current

Independent Republic Quarterly, Conway, S.C., 1967-current

Investments/Opportunities Around the World, Miami, Fla., 1967-?

The Investor-Owned Hospital Review, Little Rock, Ark., 1967-?

Journal of Research and Development in Education, Atlanta, Ga., Fall 1967-current, DLC, GASU

Kentucky Elementary School Principal, Louisville, Ky., 1967-?

Kentucky Review, Lexington, Ky., 1967-current, KyU, TxHR

Lillabulero: Being a Periodical of Literature and the Arts, Chapel Hill, N.C., Winter 1967-? CtY, DLC, MH, NcD, NcRS

Logistics Spectrum, Huntsville, Ala., 1967-current

Man About Town, Chattanooga, Tenn., Apr. 1967-? DLC

Medical Instrumentation, New York, N.Y.; Arlington, Va., 1967-current. Formerly as *Biophysics, Bioengineering, and Medical Instrumentation*, CtY-M, DLC, N, TxHP, ViU-M

Miami Malacological Society Quarterly, Miami, Fla., 1967-? DLC, TxCM

Mission, Irving, Austin, Abilene, Tex.; Chapel Hill, N.C.; Springfield, Mo., 1967-current. Currently as *Mission Journal*, DLC

Mission Journal -- See *Mission*

Mississippi Folklore Register, Decatur, Miss., 1967-current

Mufon UFO Journal, Sequin, Tex., 1967-current. Formerly as *Skylook*

Mundus Artium; A Journal of International Literature and the Arts, Athens, Ohio; Richardson, Tex., 1967-current, CtY, CU, DLC, GU, MH, NN, TxDaM, TxHR, ViU

Music At Georgia, Athens, Ga., 1967-? GU

North Carolina Anvil, Durham, N.C., Apr. 1967-current, CU, NcWsW, WHi

North Carolina Grower, Charlotte, Raleigh, N.C., 1967-? NcRS

Oak Ridge National Laboratory Review, Oak Ridge, Tenn., 1967-current

Open Road & the Professional Driver, Fort Worth, Tex., 1967-current

Pecan Quarterly, College Station, Tex., 1967-current

Poem, Huntsville, Ala., Nov. 1967-current, AAP, CtY, DLC, GU, IU, MiU, ViU

Poetic License - International, Saint Petersburg, Fla., Mar. 1967-? RPB

Relics; A Link With Our Pioneer Heritage, Austin Tex., Summer 1967-? AzU, DLC

The Review, Little Rock, Ark., 1967-?

Revista De Estudios Hispanicos, University, Ala., May 1967-current, AAP, CtY, DLC, ICU, NcD, TxU

Rice Farming, Memphis, Tenn., 1967-current. Later as *Rice Farming & Rice Industry News*, CU-A

Rice Farming & Rice Industry News -- See *Rice Farming*

Roanoke Review, Salem, Va., 1967-current, DLC, ViBlbV

San Antonio Magazine, San Antonio, Tex., 1967-current, NN, TxU

Skylook -- See *Mufon UFO Journal*

Soul Force, Atlanta, Ga., 1967-? MH, PPiU

South Texas Retailer, Houston, Tex., 1967-?

Southern Humanities Review, Auburn, Ala., Spring 1967-current, AAP, DLC, InU, LU, NcD, NcU, ScU, ViBlbV, ViU

The Southern Journal of Educational Research, Hattiesburg, Miss., Jan. 1967-current. Continued by *Educational and Psychological Research*, DLC, LNHT, MoU, ViBlbV, ViU

Soybean Farmer, Raleigh, N.C., 1967-? ArU, NcRS

Space Biology and Aerospace Medicine, Arlington, Va., 1967-? Continues *Space Biology and Medicine*

Spanish Today -- See *Spanish Today: The Bilingual Magazine*

Spanish Today; the Bilingual Magazine, Homestead, Miami, Fla., 1967-current. Currently as *Spanish Today*

Star of Hope, Crockett, Ky., 1967-current

Style, Fayetteville, Ark., Winter 1967-current, AAP, AU, DLC, GU, LU, NN, NcU, ViU

Sued-Florida Nachrichten, Hollywood, Fla., 1967-?

Sword & Trowel, Port Credit, Ont.; Clinton, Miss., 1967-? CaOONL

Tenneco, Houston, Tex., 1967-current

Tennessee Poetry Journal, Martin, Tenn., Fall 1967-? DLC, GU, IU, LU, MH, NcU, NN, ScU

Texas Cousins, Dallas, Tex., Nov. 1967-? NN, WHi

Texas Study of Secondary Education Research Journal, Austin, Tex., Fall 1967-? MiDW

Textile Equipment, Charlotte, N.C., 1967-?

Therapeutic Recreation Journal, Arlington, Va., 1967-?

University of Miami Center for Theoretical Studies Quarterly Bulletin, Coral Gables, Fla., 1967-current

UpDate, Gainesville, Fla., 1967-current

The Vanderbilt International, Nashville, Tenn., Winter 1967-Spring 1971. Continued by *Vanderbilt Journal of Transnational Law*, DLC, MH-L

Vanderbilt Journal of Transnational Law -- See *The Vanderbilt International*

Virginia Outdoors, Richmond, Va., 1967-?

Whispering Wind Magazine, New Orleans, La., 1967-current, DLC, NjP, OkU, ScU

White Power; the Revolutionary Voice of National Socialism, Dallas, Tex.; Arlington, Va., Sept. 1967-current. Supersedes *Storm Trooper*, MH, PPiU

Your Region, Arlington, Tex., 1967-current. Formerly as *Your Region In Action*

Your Region in Action -- See *Your Region*

A.C. Flyer, New Orleans, La., 1968-77

AHME Journal, Arlington, Va., 1968-current, DNLM, ArU-M

A.S.; Architectural Student, Baton
Rouge, La., Oct. 1968-78, KyU,
MCM, NIC

Above Ground Review, Arden, N.C.,
Nov. 1968-? DLC, MH, NcGU

Adventures in Poetry Magazine,
New York, N.Y.; Junction, Tex.,
Mar. 1968-current, RPB

Afro-American, Key Colony Beach,
Fla., 1968-?

Alabama Family Physician,
Montgomery, Ala., Jan. 1968-?
DNLM

Alabama Hospitality, Little Rock,
Ark., 1968-? ArU

Aloft, Miami, Fla., 1968-?

*Amazing Grace; Was Blind But Now
I See*, Tallahassee, Fla., 1968-?

*American Journal of Agricultural
Economics*, Gainesville, Fla.,
1968-current

Aquarian Messenger, Fort
Lauderdale, Fla., 1968-?

Ark/Ozark, Eureka Springs, Ark.,
Fall 1968-? ArU

*Arkansas Business and Economic
Review*, Fayetteville, Ark., Aug.
1968-current. Supersedes
Arkansas Economist and
Arkansas Business Bulletin,
DLC, FU, IU, LU, MnU, TxDaM

Arkansas Game and Fish, Little
Rock, Ark., 1968-current, DLC

Arrowhead, Fort Belvoir, Va., Aug.
1968-Mar. 1973, DLC, KMK, MoKL,
NN

*Association for Recorded Sound
Collections Journal*, Manassas,
Va., 1968-current, DLC, IU, MB,
MiU

Atlanta Arts, Atlanta, Ga., 1968-?
GU, NN

Bassmaster Magazine, Montgomery,
Ala., 1968-current, DLC

Beer Wholesaler, Delray Beach,
Fla., 1968-current

*Behavior Research Methods &
Instrumentation*, Austin, Tex.,
Sept. 1968-current, CtY, DLC,
MH, NcGU, NjP, TxHR, TxLT,
ViBlbV

La Bobina, Columbia, S.C.,
1968-current

Burning Spear, Louisville, Ky.,
1968-Aug. 1971

CAP Times -- See *Civil Air Patrol
News*

Carolina Financial Times, Chapel
Hill, N.C., 1968-? NcGU, NcWsW

Catfish Farmer Magazine, Little
Rock, Ark., 1968-? DLC

Central European History, Atlanta,
Ga., Mar. 1968-current, CtY,
DLC, GEU, GU, MB, NcRS, NN, ViU

Charlotte Magazine, Charlotte,
N.C., 1968-current

Chess Digest, Dallas, Tex., Jan.
1968-? NjP, OkS

Chieftain, Fulton, Miss., 1968-?

Christian Home, Nashville, Tenn.,
Sept. 1968-current, DLC

Civil Air Patrol News, Montgomery,
Ala., 1968-current. Formerly as
CAP Times, DLC

Computer Age--Software Digest --
See *Software Digest*

Conradiana, College Park, Md.;
Lubbock, Tex., Summer
1968-current, DeU, FU, MH,
NcGU, TxHR, TxLT

Continental Trailways, Dallas, Tex., 1968-73

DelMarVa Farmer, Richmond, Va.; Nashville, Tenn., 1968-? DNAL

D. H. Lawrence Review, Fayetteville, Ark., Spring 1968-current, AAP, DLC, FU, MH, NcU, NN

Dimension; Contemporary German Arts and Letters, Austin, Tex., 1968-current, CtY, DLC, NcU, NN, TxHR, TxLT, ViBlbV

Doors; Seminole Junior College Literary Magazine, Sanford, Fla., 1968-?

Education Trends -- See *Outlook in Education*

El Paso Archaeology, El Paso, Tex., 1968-current, CU, MH-P, NjP

Estrella de Esperanza, Crockett, Ky., 1968-current

Excerpta; A Summary for Science and Education Writers, Atlanta, Ga., 1968-?

EXXON Chemicals Magazine, New York, N.Y.; Houston, Tex., Spring 1968-current. Formerly as *Enjay Magazine*, currently as *Chemisphere Americas*, DP, PPiU

Fertilizer Abstracts, Muscle Shoals, Ala., 1968-?

Film Collectors Registry, Knoxville, Tenn., 1968-?

Florida & Tropic Sportsman -- See *The Florida Sportsman*

Florida Golfer, Miami, Fla., 1968-?

The Florida Sportsman, Tallahassee, Miami, Fla., 1968-current. Formerly as *Gulf Coast Florida Sportsman* and as *Florida & Tropic Sportsman*

Florida Turf, Jacksonville, Fla., 1968-? GU, KMK

GAHPER Journal, _____, Ga., Fall 1968-? GU

Georgia Government Review, Athens, Ga., 1968-current. Continued by *State and Local Government Review*, DLC, GASU, GEU, GU, ICU

Ginger, Memphis, Tenn., 1968-? DLC

Graphic Communications World, Tallahassee, Fla., 1968-current

Green River Review, Owensboro, Ky., Nov. 1968-current, DLC, GU, KyU, MH

Griffin Report of the Southeast, Atlanta, Ga., 1968-?

Gulf Coast Florida -- See *The Florida Sportsman*

Impact; Technical Education in South Carolina, Columbia, S.C., 1968-current, DLC

Jet Cargo News, Houston, Tex., May 1968-current, DLC

Journal of Consulting and Clinical Psychology, Arlington, Va., Feb. 1968-current. Continues *Journal of Consulting Psychology*, CtHT, DLC, TxDaM

The Kentucky City, Lexington, Ky., 1968-current, DLC, FU, KyU, NjP, NN, ViU

Kentucky Pioneer, Richmond, Ky., Oct. 1968-? KyU, WHi

Louisiana Corrections, Baton Rouge, La., June 1968-? DLC

Louisiana Economy, _____, La.,
Apr. 1968-?   DLC, LU, NcGU

Louisiana Heritage, Alexandria,
La., June 1968-?   LNHT, LU,
ScU, TxU

Lynchburg, Lynchburg, Va., Oct.
1968-current, ViBlbV

Material Culture -- See *Pioneer
American*

*Measurement and Evaluation in
Guidance*, Falls Church, Va.,
Spring 1968-current, CSt, DLC,
FU, IU, NcRS, ViBlbV

Metro Atlanta Builder, Atlanta,
Ga., 1968-?

Metrolina, Charlotte, N.C., 1968-?

Modern Images, El Dorado, Ark.;
Mattoon, Ill., 1968-current

New Orleans Review, New Orleans,
La., Fall 1968-current, CU, DLC,
FU, LNHT, LU, NcU, TxHR

*North Carolina Journal of Speech
Communications*, Chapel Hill,
N.C., 1968-?   Continues *North
Carolina Journal of Speech and
Drama*, AAP, GU, NcRS, TxArU

North Carolina Law Record, Chapel
Hill, N.C., Dec. 1968-?   GU-L,
NcD-L

Notes on Mississippi Writers,
Hattiesburg, Miss., Spring
1968-current, CtY, GEU, InU, MH,
MsU, ScCleU

Opera Journal, University, Miss.,
Winter 1968-current, DLC, IU,
KyU, LU, MiU, ScU, ViU

Outdoor Times, Dallas, Tex., 1968-?

Outdoor World, Atlanta, Ga., 1968-?
DLC, GAT, IU, N, Vi

Outlook in Education, Arlington,
Va., Jan. 1968-current.   As
Education Trends until 1976,
CU, GAT, IaU

*Paso Del Rio Showboat; About San
Antonio, One of America's Four
Unique Cities*, San Antonio,
Tex., 1968-?

Pennzoil Log, Houston, Tex., 1968-?
Formerly as *United Log*

Pioneer American, Falls Church,
Va.; Middletown, Pa.,
1968-current.   As *Material
Culture* since 1984, DLC, IU,
NjP, ViU

The Professional Engineer,
Raleigh, N.C., Nov.
1968-current, NcD, NcRS

Purpose, Charlotte, N.C., 1968-?

Raven Speaks, Dallas, Tex., 1968-?
OkU

Re: Artes Liberales, Nacogdoches,
Tex., Spring 1968-current.
Supersedes *Arts and Letters*, IU

Resources, Houston, Tex., 1968-?

Resplandor, El Paso, Tex.,
1968-current

Retailers & Marketing News, Dallas,
Tex., 1968-current

River Pilot, North Little Rock,
Ark., Oct. 1968-?   ArU

Rural America, Arlington, Va.,
1968-?   DLC, DNAL

*Sandlapper; The Magazine of South
Carolina*, Columbia, S.C., Jan.
1968-Mar. 1982, DLC, GU, KyU,
NcD, NcRS, NcU, ScCleU

School Administrator, Arlington,
Va., 1968-current

Shelby Report of the Southeast,
Atlanta, Ga., 1968-current

Sociological Symposium, Bowling Green, Ky.; Blacksburg, Va., Fall 1968-80. Merged with *Sociological Forum* to form *Sociological Spectrum*, CtY, DLC, KyU, MH, NcRS, PU

Software Digest, Annandale, Va., 1968-current. Currently as *Computer Age--Software Digest*

Soundings; An Interdisciplinary Journal, New York, N.Y.; Nashville, Tenn., 1968-current, ViU

South Asian Book News, Durham, N.C., 1968-?

South Carolina Review, Clemson, S.C., Nov. 1968-June 1973, DLC, NcRS, TxLT, UU

Southern Business & Realty, Atlanta, Ga., 1968-?

Southern Literary Journal, Chapel Hill, N.C., Autumn 1968-current, DLC, FU, KyU, MH, NcRS, PU, ViU

Southern Scene, Atlanta, Ga., Spring 1968-? DLC, GU

Southern Sociologist, Blacksburg, Va.; Gainesville, Fla.; Atlanta, Ga., 1968-current

Southern Supermarketing, Birmingham, Ala., 1968-current

Southwestern Studies: Humanities Series, Lafayette, La., 1968-? IU

State and Local Government Review, Athens, Ga., 1968-current. Supersedes *Georgia Government Review*

Statecraft; A Journal of Political Education, Alexandria, Va., 1968-? DLC, MH

Studies in the Literary Imagination, Atlanta, Ga., Apr. 1968-current, CU, FU, GASU, GU, MH, NcU, ScU, ViU

Talent News and Views, Dallas, Tex., 1968-current. Currently as *Whitmark News & Views*

Teaching Exceptional Children, Reston, Va., Nov. 1968-current, DLC, FU, GU, MB, NjR, TxLT

Texas Conchologist, Houston, Tex., 1968-? ICF, NNM, TxCM

Texas Outdoor Guide Magazine, Houston, Tex., 1968-current

USJ, Arlington, Va., 1968-current

Whitmark News & Views -- See *Talent News and Views*

AAS Photo-Bulletin, Gainesville, Fla., 1969-current

Acadiana Profile, Lafayette, La., 1969-current, DLC, LU

Achievement; The National Voice of the Disabled, Miami, Fla., 1969-current

Action, Abilene, Tex., 1969-76. Also as *Communicating on the West Central Texas Region*

The Advocate, Falls Church, Va., Mar. 1969-current, DLC, MH-L

Air Defense Magazine, Fort Bliss, Tex., 1969-? Formerly as *Air Defense Trends*, DLC, ULA

Air Defense Trends -- See *Air Defense Magazine*

Alabama Geographer, University, Ala., 1969-current, AAP, GU, IU

American Collector, Kermit, Tex., Sept. 1969-83. Also as *Collector* and as *Collector's Weekly*, CoU, DLC

American Fish Farmer, Little Rock, Ark., Dec. 1969-? DNLM, IU, KyU, LU, NjR, ScU

Annals of Ophthalmology, Chicago, Ill.; Birmingham, Ala., 1969-current. Supersedes *Journal of Experimental and Clinical Ophthalmology*, CtY-M, DLC, ICU, N

Appalachia Medicine, Harlan, Ky., Apr. 1969-June 1973, KyLoU-M, KyU-M, N, NcU-H, TxU-M, ViU-M

Arkansas Report, Little Rock, Ark., Jan. 1969-? ArU

Army Logistician; the Official Magazine of the United States Army Logistics, Fort Lee, Va., 1969-current, DLC, KMK, MsSM

Arts in Mississippi, University, Miss., 1969-?

Astrograph, Arlington, Va., 1969-current

Athletic Director, Reston, Va., 1969-current

Bath & Domestics, Delray Beach, Fla., 1969-current. Formerly as *Bath Products Merchandising*

Bath Products Merchandising -- See *Bath & Domestics*

Birding, Austin, Tex., 1969-current, CtY, GU, NIC, TxArU

Black Experience; A Southern University Journal, Baton Rouge, La., June 1969-? DLC, LU, MH

Caribbean Journal of Science and Mathematics, Cullowhee, N.C., Jan. 1969-72, DLC

Caribbean Review; A Books-Oriented Quarterly Dealing with Caribbean-Latin American Affairs, Miami, Fla., Spring 1969-current. Supersedes *San Juan Review*, CLU, DLC, FMU, FU, MH, NjR, TNJ, TxLT

Catholic Currents, Washington, D.C.; Warrenton, Va., 1969-? DLC

Christian School Builder, Crockett, Ky., 1969-current

Civil War Round Table Digest, Little Rock, Ark., 1969-current, DLC, IU

Clan McLaren Society, USA Quarterly, Dallas, Tex., Mar. 1969-current

Collector -- See *American Collector*

Collector's Weekly -- See *American Collector*

Communicating on the West Central Texas Region -- See *Action*

Corn Farmer, Raleigh, N.C., 1969-?

Dairyman's Digest: Southern Region Ed. Arlington, Tex., 1969-current

Dallas Natural Science Association Quarterly, Dallas, Tex., 1969-? CaOONM

Design Journal, McLean, Va., 1969-?

Dialogue, Birmingham, Ala., 1969-74. Also as *Today*

Discovery, Richmond, Va., 1969-?

Education in Mississippi, Jackson, Miss., 1969-current

Education of the Visually Handicapped, Louisville, Ky., Mar. 1969-current. Supersedes *International Journal for the Education of the Blind*, CLU, DLC, KMK, KyU, P

Educational Media, Fort Worth, Tex., 1969-? DLC, FU, LU, NcGU

Electric Florida, Tampa, Fla., 1969-76

Facets, Houston, Tex., June 1969-? TxDaM

Father Joe's Handy Homilies, Tampa, Fla., 1969-? DLC

Fathom; Surface Ship and Submarine Safety Review, Norfolk, Va., 1969-current, DLC

Financial Quarterly, North Palm Beach, Fla., 1969-current

Flamingo, Miami, Fla., 1969-?

Florida Economic Indicators, Gainesville, Fla., Jan. 1969-current, DLC, FU, NjP

Florida State Magazine, Winter Haven, Fla., 1969-? FU

Florida Veterinary Journal, Ocala, Fla., 1969-? Supersedes *Florida Veterinary Bulletin*, AAP

Franklin County Historical Review, Winchester, Tenn., 1969-current, CtY, DLC

Furman Review, Greenville, S.C., 1969-? DLC

Georgia Business Lawyer, Macon, Ga., Summer 1969-? C, GU-L, TxU-L

Georgia Reporter -- See *Georgia Social Science Journal*

Georgia Social Science Journal, Atlanta, Ga., 1969-? Formerly as *Georgia Reporter*, ICarbS

Good News, Nashville, Tenn., 1969-?

Great Issues, Troy, Ala., 1969-? DLC

Gridweek, New Orleans, La., 1969-?

Heart-O-Gram, Fort Lauderdale, Fla., 1969-?

History of Political Economy, Durham, N.C., Spring 1969-current, CtY-E, DLC, NcD, NcRS, NjP, NjP, TxU, ViBlbV

Houston Journalism Review, Houston, Tex., June 1969-Apr. 1974, WHi

Houston Teens, Houston, Tex., 1969-current

Hyperion; A Poetry Journal, Cedar Grove, N.C.; Austin, Tex., 1969-current

Industrial Engineering, Norcross, Ga., 1969-current. Supersedes *Journal of Industrial Engineering*

International Journal for the Education of the Blind -- See *Education of the Visually Handicapped*

International Journal of Symbology, Atlanta, Ga., Aug. 1969-? Supersedes *The International Journal of Symbols*, DLC, GASU, IU, ViU

The Journal, Shreveport, La., 1969-current

Journal of the Association for the Advancement of Medical Instrumentation, Arlington, Va., 1969-?

Journal of Leisure Research, Arlington, Va., Winter 1969-? CtY, DLC, MH, NcU, ScU, ViBlbV

Journal of Nematology, Athens, Ga., Jan. 1969-current, DLC, GASU, GU, NcD, TxU, ViBlbV

Journal of Reading Behavior, Athens, Ga.; Clemson, S.C., 1969-current, CtY, DLC, GEU, GU, NcRS, ScCleU

Journal of Undergraduate Mathematics, Greensboro, N.C., Mar. 1969-current, DLC, NcGU, NcRS, TNJ, TxLT

Kentucky Pork Producer's News, Louisville, Ky., 1969-current

Language Problems and Language Planning, Austin, Tex., 1969-current. As *Mondo Lingvo Problemo* until 1977

Lawyer of the Americas, Coral Gables, Fla., Feb. 1969-current, DLC, MH-L

Mississippi Freelance, Greenville, Miss., Apr. 1969-? DLC, MsSM, MsU

Mississippi Genealogy and Local History, Shreveport, La., 1969-? DLC, MsSM

Mississippi State Engineer, State College, Miss., 1969-? MsSM

Mondo Lingvo Problemo -- See *Language Problems and Language Planning*

Mountain Living, Franklin, N.C., 1969-?

Muleskinner News -- See *Music Country: A Magazine of Blue Grass and Old Time Music*

Music Country; A Magazine of Blue Grass and Old Time Music, Ruffin, N.C., 1969-? Formerly as *Muleskinner News*

New Literary History; A Journal of Theory and Interpretation, Charlottesville, Va.; Baltimore, Md., Oct. 1969-current, CU, DLC, FU, GU, MdBJ, MH, NcU, ViU

New Pictorialist, Ellenboro, N.C., 1969-? InLP, TxU

New River, Dallas, Tex., 1969-? DLC, IEN, TxDaM

New Wine Magazine, Mobile, Ala., 1969-current

Newman Genealogical Journal, Kennedy, Ala., 1969-? DLC

North Carolina Central Law Journal, Durham, N.C., Spring 1969-? Also as *North Carolina College Law Journal*, CtY-L, DLC, NcD-L, NjR

North Carolina College Law Journal -- See *North Carolina Central Law Journal*

Okra Press, Houston, Tex., 1969-?

Orangeburg Historical and Genealogical Record, Orangeburg, S.C., 1969-? DLC, NIC

Owl's Breath, Nashville, Tenn., 1969-?

Palmetto Licensed Practical Nurse, Cayce, S.C., 1969-?

Pembroke Magazine, Pembroke, N.C., 1969-? CtY, FU, MH, NN, NcD, TxU

Prim-Aid; The Magazine of Creative Ideas for Kindergarten and Primary Grade Teachers, Columbia, S.C., 1969-? ArU

Professional Sanitation Management, Clearwater, Fla., Spring 1969-current, DLC

Psychiatric Forum, Columbia, S.C., Winter 1969-current, DLC, MiU, TxU-M

Raleigh, Raleigh, N.C., Spring 1969-? NcD, NcRS

Richmond County History, Augusta, Ga., 1969-?

Rotorways, Fort Worth, Tex., 1969-?

Salt Lick, Austin, Tex., 1969-current

Savannah Magazine, Savannah, Ga., July 1969-79, GU

Shawensis, Raleigh, N.C., 1969-73?

Singing News, Pensacola, Fla., 1969-current

South, Deland, Fla., 1969-? IU

South Carolina Education Journal, Columbia, S.C., Fall 1969-? DLC

South Carolina Journal of Political Science, Columbia, S.C., 1969-? GASU

South Today, Atlanta, Ga., July 1969-? FU, GASU, GU, MH, NcGU, ViU

Southern Journal of Agricultural Economics, Lexington, Ky.; Fayetteville, Ark., 1969-current, DLC

Sports Merchandiser, Atlanta, Ga., 1969-current, DLC

Studies in the Novel, Denton, Tex., Spring 1969-current, DLC, LU, MH, MiU, NjP, PU, TxCM, TxHR, ViU

TEA News, Nashville, Tenn., 1969-current

Tampa, Tampa, Fla., Mar. 1969-? DLC

Tennis Guide, Fargo, Fla., 1969-?

Texas Journal of Alcoholism, Austin, Tex., 1969-? DLC

Texas Tech Law Review, Lubbock, Tex., Mar. 1969-current, IU, MnU-L

Textile Chemist & Colorist, Research Triangle Park, N.C., Jan. 1969-current, DLC, TxU

Tolar Creek Syndicate, Dell City, Tex., 1969-?

Tulane Medicine -- See *Tulane Medicine: Faculty and Alumni*

Tulane Medicine: Faculty and Alumni, New Orleans, La., 1969-current. Currently as *Tulane Medicine*

Underwater Reporter, West Palm Beach, Fla., 1969-current

University of Florida Magazine, Gainesville, Fla., Fall 1969-? FU

Verdict, Gainesville, Fla., Jan. 1969-? Formerly as *Shuffle*, C, CU

Virginia Phoenix, Norfolk, Va., 1969-? DLC

Western Carolina University Journal of Education, Cullowhee, N.C., Spring 1969-? CtY, DLC, NcD, NcRS, PU

Western Outfitter, Houston, Tex., 1969-current

Wild West Stars; Cowboy Film Corral, Knoxville, Tenn., 1969-?

Active Handicapped, Metairie, La., Feb. 1970-? DLC

African World, Greensboro, N.C., 1970-? DLC, CLU, NIC

Aim, Charlotte, N.C., 1970-? MiU

*Alabama & Gulf Coast Retailing
News*, Decatur, Ga., 1970-current

Alabama Development News,
Montgomery, Ala., Feb.
1970-current, DLC

*American Digest of Foreign
Orthopaedic Literature*, Tomball,
Tex., 1970-73, DLC, FU-HC, MiU,
TxU-M

Arete, Columbia, S.C., Spring
1970-current, DLC, FTaSU, GU,
TxU

Art Teacher, Reston, Va., 1970-?
Absorbed by *Art Education*, FU,
GU, KyU, NcCU

Atlanta Phoenix, Atlanta, Ga.,
Winter 1970-?   GASU, GU

Banc, Nashville, Tenn., 1970-?
IEN, IU, TNJ

Bible Searchers, Nashville, Tenn.,
1970-current

Biomedical News, Falls Church, Va.,
Jan. 1970-?   IU

Bio-Medical Insight, Arcadia,
Calif.; Miami, Fla., 1970-current,
DLC, DNLM, ViRCU-H

The Black Collegian Magazine, New
Orleans, La., 1970-current, DLC,
InU, LU, MH, NcD, NjP, ViBlbV

Book Business Mart, Clearwater,
Fla., 1970-current

Bottle News, Kermit, Tex., 1970-?

Broadside, Houston, Tex., 1970-?

Burning Spear, Saint Petersburg,
Fla., 1970-?   IEN, WHi

CEA Forum, College Station, Tex.,
Oct. 1970-current, CtY, DLC, FU,
IU, NjR, TxDaM, TxHR, ViBlbV

*CRC Critical Reviews in Analytical
Chemistry*, Boca Raton, Fla.,
Mar. 1970-current, CtY-M, DLC,
FTaSU, FU, MiU, NcU, ViBlbV

*CRC Critical Reviews in Food
Service and Nutrition* Boca
Raton, Fla., 1970-current.
Formerly as *CRC Critical
Reviews in Food Technology*,
DLC, GU, IU, TxU, ViBlbV

*CRC Critical Reviews in Food
Technology* -- See *CRC Critical
Reviews in Food Service and
Nutrition*

*CRC Critical Reviews in Solid State
& Materials Sciences*, Boca
Raton, Fla., Mar. 1970-current,
DLC, FTaSU, GU, MiU, MnU, TxHR

*Cadence of the Clinical
Laboratory*, Houston, Bellaire,
Tex., Jan. 1970-?   DNLM, GASU,
FU-HC

Chambless Quarterly, Morrow, Ga.,
1970-?   NN, WHi

Choctaw Community News,
Philadelphia, Miss., 1970-current

Church Training, Nashville, Tenn.,
1970-current

Coin Wholesaler, Atlanta, Ga.,
1970-?

Computer Age, Annandale, Va.,
1970-current, DLC, ViBlbV

*Contempora; A Literary Art
Magazine*, Atlanta, Ga., Mar.
1970-?   DLC, GASU, GU, KyU, LU,
MH, ViBlbV

Crusader, Memphis, Tenn.,
1970-current

Cumberland Law Review -- See
Cumberland-Samford Law Review

Cumberland-Samford Law Review,
Birmingham, Ala., Spring
1970-current.   Currently as
Cumberland Law Review, CtY-L,
GU-L, TNJ, TxU-L

Dave's Friends, Nocatee, Fla.,
1970-current

David, Jacksonville, Fla., 1970-?

Deacon, Nashville, Tenn.,
1970-current, DLC

Decision Sciences, Cincinnati, Ohio;
Atlanta, Ga., 1970-current, GU,
IU, KyU, NIC, ScU, ViBlbV

Decorating & Craft Ideas, Fort
Worth, Tex.; Birmingham, Ala.,
Oct. 1970-current.   Formerly as
*Decorating & Craft Ideas Made
Easy,* DLC

*Decorating & Craft Ideas Made
Easy* -- See *Decorating & Craft
Ideas*

Drummer, Orlando, Fla., 1970-?

Ecclesia, Knoxville, Tenn.;
Greenville, S.C., 1970-?   CtHC

Echoes of History, Falls Church,
Va., Nov. 1970-?   DLC, IU, GU,
NN, Vi, ViU

English Plug, Abilene, Tex., 1970-?

Event, Nashville, Tenn.,
1970-current.   Supersedes
Upward

Farm and Ranch, Mexia, Tex.,
1970-current

*Feminary; A Feminist Journal for
the South, Emphasizing the
Lesbian Vision,* Chapel Hill,
N.C., 1970-?   IEN, NcD

Filmograph, Alexandria, Orlean,
Va., 1970-?   CLSU, DLC, IaU

*Financial Trend; the Newsweekly
of Southwestern Industry and
Investments,* Dallas, Tex.,
1970-current, DLC, ICU, TxLT

Florida Probe, Gainesville, Fla.,
April 1970-?   FU

Forensic Science Gazette, Dallas,
Tex., Feb. 1970-current, IU-M,
DNLM, MBU-M

Foss, Edinburg, Tex., 1970-?

Georgia Advocate, Athens, Atlanta,
Ga., 1970-current.   Formerly as
*Georgia Advocate Advance
Sheet,* DLC, WaU-L

Georgia Advocate Advance Sheet
-- See *Georgia Advocate*

Georgia Educator, Decatur, Ga.,
Sept. 1970-?   Supersedes
Georgia Education Journal, DLC,
GAT, GU

*The Georgia Journal of
International and Comparative
Law,* Athens, Ga., Fall
1970-current, DLC, MH-L

Georgia Retailing News, Decatur,
Ga., 1970-current

Georgia's Health, Atlanta, Ga.,
1970-72

Germanic Notes, Lexington, Ky.,
1970-current, DLC, GU, KyU, LU,
MH, MiU, NcRS, ViU

*Graphic Antiquarian; the Magazine
for Collectors of
Photographica,* Wilmington, N.C.,
1970-76, DLC

Gulfshore Life Magazine, Naples,
Fla., 1970-current

Health Education, Reston, Va.,
1970-current, CLU, DLC, NcU,
TxU

Hi-Riser, Fort Lauderdale, Fla.,
1970-current

Horse World, Shelbyville, Tenn.,
1970-current

Indigo Forest of the Night,
Parsons, Tex., 1970-?

Infection and Immunity, Bethesda,
Md.; Birmingham, Ala., Jan.
1970-current, CtY-M, DLC, GU,
MnU, NcRS, NcU-H, ViBlbV

*Journal for Research in
Mathematics Education*, Herndon,
Va., Jan. 1970-current, DLC, FU,
GU, NcRS, TxCM

*Journal of Applied Rehabilitation
Counseling*, Austin, Tex.,
1970-current, AAP, DLC, MU,
NcWsW

*Journal of Clinical Hematology and
Oncology*, Dallas, Tex., Oct.
1970-current. As *Wadley
Medical Bulletin* until 1977,
DLC, ICJ, MiU, TxHMC

*Journal of International Business
Studies*, Atlanta, Ga., Spring
1970-current, DLC, GASU, GAT,
GU, NN, NcU, ViBlbV

Journal of Social Philosophy,
Columbia, Mo.; Augusta, Ga.;
Villanova, Pa., Fall
1970-current, DLC, FU, GAT, NN,
ViBlbV

*Journal of the Southern
Confederacy; the Magazine of
the Old South*, Plantation,
Jasper, Fla., 1970-? DLC, FU,
GU, NN, Vi

Journal of Zoo Animal Medicine,
Washington, D.C.; Atlanta, Ga.,
Sept. 1970-current, AAP, DNAL,
MnU-A, TxCM

Kentucky Agri-Business Quarterly,
Lexington, Ky., 1970-? DNAL,
KyU-ASC, GU, NN

Kentucky Herpetologist, Louisville,
Ky., 1970-? KyU-ASC

*Kentucky Journal of Communication
Arts*, Georgetown, Ky.,
1970-current, AAP, KyU

Liquified Natural Gas, Boulder,
Colo.; Arlington, Va., 1970-?
DLC

Living Blues, Chicago, Ill.;
University, Miss., Spring
1970-current, DLC, InU, IU, MB,
NcGU

Louisiana Senior Citizen, Baton
Rouge, La., 1970-? DLC, LU

Media: Library Services Journal,
Nashville, Tenn., 1970-current.
Supersedes *Church Library
Magazine*, LU, IU, NcWsW

*Memphis State University Law
Review*, Memphis, Tenn., Fall
1970-current, CtY-L, DLC, GU-L,
TNJ, TU

Meteor News, Jacksonville, Fla.,
1970-current

The Mother Earth News, North
Madison, Ohio; Hendersonville,
N.C., 1970-current, CtY, DLC,
FU, IEN, KyU, NcD, NcRS, ViBlbV

NOPA Industry Report, Alexandria,
Va., 1970-current

Northwest Orient, North Miami
Beach, Fla., 1970-current

Outreach, Nashville, Tenn.,
1970-current. Currently as
Sunday School Leadership

Pan American Review, Edinburg,
Tex., 1970-? ICU, KyU, NNC,
ScU, TxHR

*Performance; the International
Talent Weekly*, Fort Worth, Tex.,
1970-current

Pioneer News-Observer, San Angelo,
Tex., June 1970-? DLC

Poetry Towers, Parsons, Tenn.,
1970-?

Pollution Abstracts, La Jolla,
Calif.; Louisville, Ky.;
Bethesda, Md., 1970-current,
DLC, FU, GU, KyU, MH, MdU, NcU,
ViBlbV

Quetzal, Abilene, El Paso, Tex.,
1970-?   DLC, IU, MH, TxHR, ViU

Quorum Quotes, Oakton, Va.,
1970-current

Race Relations Reporter, Nashville,
Tenn., Feb. 1970-74, CLU, GU,
InU, MH, NcU, NN, NjP

*Representative Research in Social
Psychology*, Chapel Hill, N.C.,
July 1970-current, CtY, FU,
GAT, InU, MH, NcD, NcRS, NcU,
NN, ScU

Research in African Literatures,
Austin, Tex., Spring
1970-current, CtY, IU, LU, MH,
NjP, TxHR, TxU, ViBlbV

*The Review of Black Political
Economy*, Atlanta, Ga.; New
Brunswick, N.J., Spring/Summer
1970-current, DLC, MH-PA

Review of Regional Studies,
Blacksburg, Va.; Birmingham,
Ala., 1970-current, AAP, KyU,
MoU, NcD, NcRS, ViBlbV

SRDG, Tallahassee, Fla.,
1970-current

Sea Grant Seventies, College
Station, Tex.; Blacksburg, Va.,
Sept. 1970-83.   Later as *Sea
Grant Today*, DLC, LU, MoU, NcU

Sea Grant Today -- See *Sea Grant
Seventies*

*Social Theory and Practice; An
International and
Interdisciplinary Journal of
Social Philosophy*, Tallahassee,
Fla., Spring 1970-current, CU,
DLC, FTaSU, FU, GU, KyU, MH,
NcD, NcRS, TxU

Soul Confessions, Fort Worth, Tex.,
1970-?

Soul Teen, Fort Worth, Tex.,
1970-83

*South Carolina History
Illustrated*, Columbia, S.C., Feb.
1970-?   DLC

*Southeast Farm and Livestock
Weekly*, Knoxville, Tenn., 1970-?
DNAL, IU

Southern Cooperator, Epes, Ala.,
1970-?

Southern Hog Producer, Nashville,
Tenn., 1970-current, AAP,
ViBlbV

Southern Purchasor, Greensboro,
N.C., 1970-current

Southern Sailing, _____, Fla.,
Oct. 1970-?   FTaSU

Southwest Airlines Magazine, San
Antonio, Tex., 1970-current, TxU

*Southwestern Journal of Social
Education*, Denton, Tex., Fall
1970-current, CLU, TxCM, TxU

St. Andrews Review, Laurinburg,
N.C., 1970-current, CtY, GASU,
ICU, KyU, NcD

St. Mary's Law Journal, San
Antonio, Tex., 1970-current,
CtY-L, DLC, IU, NcD-L, TNJ, TxU

Statistical Journal, Raleigh, N.C.,
1970-?

Stroke: A Journal of Cerebral Circulation, New York, N.Y.; Dallas, Tex., 1970-current, CtY-M, DLC, ICU, MiU, NcU-H, TxHMC, TxU-M

Studies in Black Literature, Fredericksburg, Va., Spring 1970-77, DLC, GASU, MH, NcD, NcU, NjR

Sunday School Leadership -- See *Outreach*

Systems Building News, Atlanta, Ga., 1970-current. Combined with *Automation in Housing* to form *Automation in Housing/Systems Building News*, DLC, GU, NjP, TxCM, TxU

TEPSA Journal, Austin, Tex., 1970-current

Tennessee Realtor, Nashville, Tenn., 1970-? TNJ

Tennessee Valley Perspective, Knoxville, Tenn., Fall 1970-80, DLC, GU, KMK, NjP, TU

Texas Traveler, Bryan, Tex., 1970-current

Texas Wildcat Roundup, Austin, Tex., 1970-?

This Issue, Atlanta, Ga., 1970-? GASU, GU, NcRS

Today's Family, Denison, Tex., 1970-Jan. 1977

University Medical, Galveston, Tex., 1970-current, DLC, NN

Virginia Tidewater Genealogy, Hampton, Va., 1970-current

Wadley Medical Bulletin -- See *Journal of Clinical Hematology and Oncology*

Wig & Hairgoods Business, Port Lavaca, Tex., 1970-?

Woman Activist, Falls Church, Va., Jan. 1970-current, IEN, GEU, NmU, NjR

Woman Executive, Fort Lauderdale, Fla., Jan. 1970-? DLC

Women's Army Corps Journal, Birmingham, Ala., 1970-? DLC

ARC Action, Atlanta, Ga., 1971-current

Accident Reporter, Raleigh, Chapel Hill, N.C., 1971-75, NcRS

American Legislator, Lexington, Ky., Feb. 1971-75, CtY-L, DLC, GU, MH, NjR, Vi

Antiques Observer, Fairfax, Va., 1971-?

Arkansas Genealogical Register, Newport, Ark., Mar. 1971-?

Armadillo, Sarasota, Fla., 1971-? GASU, IU, MH, NcD, NN, ScU

The Army Lawyer, Charlottesville, Va., Aug. 1971-current, DLC, MH-L

Baptist Reformation Review, Nashville, Tenn., 1971-current. As *Searching Together* since 1981

Basketball Guide, Fargo, Fla., 1971-? Also as *Pro Basketball Guide*

Boating News, Virginia Beach, Va., 1971-?

The Bureaucrat, Arlington, Va., 1971-current

Central Kentucky Researcher, Campbellsville, Ky., Jan. 1971-current, DLC

Custom Applicator, Memphis, Tenn., Feb. 1971-current, DNAL

Dog Ears, Athens, Ga., Mar. 1971-?
GU

Engineering Horizons, Durham,
N.C., 1971-?

*Environmental Control News for
Southern Industry*, Memphis,
Tenn., Feb. 1971-current, DLC

Experimental Study of Politics,
Madison, N.J.; Boca Raton, Fla.,
Feb. 1971-current, CtY, DGW,
FU, GASC, MiU, NjP, TU, ViBlbV

Exploring, Irving, Tex.,
1971-current, DLC

Family Pet, Tampa, Fla.,
1971-current

The Film Journal, Hollins College,
Va., Spring, 1971-?   AU, DLC,
OCl, TxU, Vi

Financial Daily -- See *M/G
Financial Weekly*

Fotonovela Pimienta, Miami, Fla.,
1971-current

Furniture News Journal, Dallas,
Tex., 1971-?

Gar, Austin, Tex., 1971-current.
Absorbed *Illuminations*, IEN,
TxU

Gladio Grams, Bradenton, Fla.,
1971-current

Grain Sorghum News, Abernathy,
Tex., 1971-current

Graphic International, Margate
City, Fla., 1971-current

HTA Advocate, Houston, Tex.,
1971-current

Historical Highlights, Saint Simons
Island, Ga., June 1971-current,
GU, NjMD

Hoot Owl, Arlington, Tex., 1971-?

Houston Business Journal, Houston,
Tex., 1971-current

Houston Monthly, Houston, Tex.,
1971-current

Huntsville Historical Review,
Huntsville, Ala., Jan.
1971-current, AAP, NN

IBW Monthly Report, Atlanta, Ga.,
1971-current.   Formerly as
Inside the Black World

Inside the Black World -- See *IBW
Monthly Report*

International Barbed Wire Gazette,
Arlington, Sunset, Tex.,
1971-current, DLC, WyU

*Is: A Magazine of Popular
Literature and Popular
Culture*, Lakemont, Ga., 1971-?

Jewish Floridian & Shofar -- See
*Jewish Floridian of South
Broward*

*Jewish Floridian of South
Broward*, Hollywood, Fla.,
1971-current.   Also as *Jewish
Floridian & Shofar*

Journal of Drug Issues,
Tallahassee, Fla., Jan.
1971-current, DLC, FTaSU, FU,
MdU-H, NN, NjR, ScU

*Journal of Medieval and
Renaissance Studies*, Durham,
N.C., 1971-current, CtY, GU,
DGW, LU, NcD, NcRS, ViBlbV

Kentucky Nature Studies,
Lexington, Ky., 1971-?   AAP, IU,
NcD, NjP

LSU Journal of Sociology, Baton
Rouge, La., Mar. 1971-73, DLC,
FU, LU, GU, NN, ViU

Louisiana Woods & Water, Monroe,
La., 1971-?

M/G Financial Weekly, Richmond, Va., 1971-current. Formerly as *Financial Daily*, currently as *Media General Financial Weekly*, CPT

Magic and Spells Quarterly, Hollywood, Miami, Fla., 1971-? DLC

Media General Financial Weekly -- See *M/G Financial Weekly*

Metro Hampton Roads Magazine -- See *Metro, The Magazine of Southeastern Virginia*

Metro, the Magazine of Southeastern Virginia, Norfolk, Va., 1971-? Also as *Metro Hampton Roads Magazine*. Incorporated by *Commonwealth Magazine*

Mobile Air Conditioning, Dallas, Tex., 1971-?

Model Retailer, Clifton, Va., 1971-current

Narcotics Control Digest, Annandale, Va., Jan. 1971-current, IU, MdU-H, ScU

New Collage Magazine, Sarasota, Fla., 1971-? FU, GASU, MH, ViU

New Laurel Review, Onley, Va.; Chalmette, New Orleans, La., 1971-current. Supersedes *Laurel Review*

New Woman, Fort Lauderdale, Fla.; Fort Worth, Tex., June 1971-current, CtY, DLC, IU, InU, MH, NN, ViBlbV

North Carolina Foreign Language Teacher, Raleigh, N.C., Spring 1971-? DLC, KyU, NcGU, NcRS, ScU, ViU, ViBlbV

Northeast Texas Genealogical Society Quarterly, Mineola, Tex., 1971-?

Nostalgia News, Dallas, Tex., 1971-?

Nostros, El Paso, Tex., 1971-? AzTeS, TxArU

Notes on Contemporary Literature, Carrollton, Ga., 1971-current, GASU, GEU, GU, IEN, LNHT, NcGU, ViU

Onstage, University, Miss., Jan. 1971-? DLC, ICarbS

The Philatelic Journalist, Saint Augustine, Fla., 1971-current

Pro Basketball Guide -- See *Basketball Guide*

Radio 27, Indianapolis, Ind.; Wilmington, N.C., 1971-? DLC

Remember When, Dallas, Tex., 1971-?

Rockhound, Conroe, Tex., 1971-?

Searching Together -- See *Baptist Reformation Review*

Self-Reliance, Richmond, Va., 1971-?

Seventy Two; For the Discriminating Golfer, Orlando, Fla., 1971-?

Shutterbug Ads, Titusville, Fla., 1971-current

Southern Anthropologist, New Orleans, La., 1971-? MH-P

Southern Beef Producer, Nashville, Tenn., June 1971-current, DNAL, GU, TU

Southern Holstein News, Macon, Ga., April 1971-? GU

Southern Journal, Durham, N.C., 1971-? GU, ScU, ViBlbV

Southwest Airlines Magazine, San Antonio, Tex., 1971-current

Southwest Art -- See *Southwest Art Gallery Magazine*

Southwest Art Gallery Magazine, Houston, Tex., 1971-current. Currently as *Southwest Art*, OkU

Southwestern American Literature, Denton, Tex., Jan. 1971-? CtY, DLC, IU, MH, TxCM, TxLT, TxU

Sports Digest, Miami, Fla., 1971-?

Straight Talk, Jupiter, Fla., 1971-current

Tennessee Education, Knoxville, Tenn., Spring 1971-? GU, NcD, T

Texas Southern University Law Review, Houston, Tex., Fall 1971-81. Continues *Texas Southern Intramural Law Review*, continued by *Thurgood Marshall Law Review*, CtY-L, DLC, IU, N, NcU-L, ViU-L

Today's Chiropractic, Austell, Marietta, Ga., 1971-current

The Vineyard, Asheville, N.C., 1971-?

Vudoklak, Parsons, Tenn., 1971-?

Wake Forest Jurist, Winston-Salem, N.C., Spring 1971-? IU, WaU-L

Yard & Fruit, Nashville, Tenn., Sept. 1971-? DNAL, DeU, MH-A

Your School and the Law, Atlanta, Ga., 1971-current

AG Trucking News & Irregular Route Carrier, Austin, Tex., 1972-?

APLA Quarterly Journal, Arlington, Va., Dec. 1972-current, CtY-L, DLC, GU-L, MH-L, N, ViU-L

Accent West, Amarillo, Tex., 1972-current

Adelante; Al Servicio de la Comunidad Latinoamericana, Orlando, Fla., 1972-?

Aerophile -- See *Replica In Scale*

Ag Trucking News & Irregular Route Carrier, Austin, Tex., 1972-?

American Hiker; Magazine for Backpackers and Hikers, Houston, Tex., 1972-? DLC, NcWsW

American Journal of Criminal Law, Austin, Tex., Feb. 1972-current, CtY-L, DLC, FU-L, NcD-L, NcU-L, N, TU

Annals of Emergency Medicine, Dallas, Tex., 1972-current

Appalachian Journal: A Regional Studies Review, Boone, N.C., Autumn 1972-current, DLC, KyU, CtY, NcRS, NN, ScU, ViU, ViBlbV

Archaeological News, Tallahassee, Fla., Winter 1972-current, FU, FMU, FTaSU, ScU

Arkansas Advocate, Little Rock, Ark., 1972-78

Arkansas Journal of Sociology, Fayetteville, Ark., May 1972-? ArU, DLC

Backtracker, Rogers, Ark., 1972-current, ArU, DLC, NN

Bar, Austin, Tex., 1972-197?

Brown's Guide to Georgia, College Park, Ga., Dec. 1972-Oct. 1982, GEU, GU

Business Atlanta -- See *Real Estate Atlanta*

CRC Critical Reviews in Biochemistry, Boca Raton, Fla., Feb. 1972-current, CtY-M, DLC, FTaSU, NcRS, ViBlbV

Chasqui; Revista de Literatura Hispano Americana, Madison, Wis.; Williamsburg, Va., 1972-current, IU, KU, MH, NjR, TxHR, ViBlbV

Christian Review, Atlanta, Ga., 1972-current

Circle Comment, Denton, Tex., 1972-73, DLC, NN

Claudel Studies, Irving, Tex., 1972-current, CtY, DLC, IU, GU, MH, NN, ScU, TxU, ViU

ComeUnity, Saint Petersburg, Fla., 1972-current

Communities; A Journal of Cooperative Living, Louisa, Va., Dec. 1972-current. Supersedes *Modern Utopian*, as well as *Alternatives*, as well as *Newsmagazine*, as well as *Communitarian*, and *Communities*, CLU, CtY, MH, MU, NcRS, TxHR, ViBlbV, ViU

Construccion Pan-Americana, Miami, Fla., 1972-current

Consumer Educator, Reston, Va., Mar. 1972-74, IU, InU, MoU, TxLT

Cosmopolitan En Espanol, Virginia Gardens, Fla., 1972-current

Creative Moment -- See *Creative Moment: A Biannual of Creating Writing and Criticism*

Creative Moment; A Biannual of Creative Writing and Criticism, Sumter, S.C., Spring 1972-current. Formerly as *Creative Moment and Poetry East West* and as *Creative Moment*. Currently as *Creative Moment World Poetry and Criticism*, CtY, IU, NN, ScU, ScCleU

Creative Moment and Poetry East West -- See *Creative Moment: A Biannual of Creative Writing and Criticism*

Creative Moment World Poetry and Criticism -- See *Creative Moment: A Biannual of Creative Writing and Criticism*

Dalliance, New Orleans, La., 1972-? LU-NO

Dekalb Legend, Fort Payne, Ala., May 1972-? AAP, WHi

Delta Sky, Miami, Fla., 1972-current

Directions; Guide to the Southern Highlands, Asheville, N.C., 1972-?

Drag Review, Bristol, Tenn., 1972-current

E.H.P. Research Triangle Park, N.C., April 1972-current, CtY-M, DNLM, InU, KyU-M, TxU, ViBlbV

Ecolibrium, Houston, Tex., 1972-current, ArU, NcCU, NcGU, ScCleU

Explorer, Fort Lauderdale, Fla., 1972-?

Figaro, New Orleans, La., 1972-?

Financial Management, Albany, N.Y.; Chapel Hill, N.C., Spring 1972-current, CtY, DLC, MH-BA, NN, NcRS, NcU, NjR, ViU

The Financial Planner, Denver, Colo.; Atlanta, Ga., 1972-current, NN, NcGU, OrCS

Fireworks News, Lexington, Ky., 1972-?

Florida Horseman, Altamonte Springs, Fla., 1972-current

Food and Fiber Economics, College Station, Tex., 1972-?

Freshman English News, Fort Worth, Tex., 1972-current

Grassroots, Hollywood, Fla.,
1972-current

Heritage of Stone, Mountain View,
Ark., June 1972-? ArU, NN

*Historical Review & Antique
Digest*, Nashville, Tenn., 1972-?
Formerly as *Tennessee Valley
Historical Review*, NN, TNJ, Vi,
ViBlbV

Horn Speaker, Dallas, Tex.,
1972-current

Horse Facts, Chantilly, Va., 1972-?
DNAL

Houston Living, Houston, Tex.,
1972-current

Houston Scene, Houston, Tex.,
1972-?

Indian River Life, Vero Beach,
Fla., 1972-current

Informer, Atlanta, Ga., Summer
1972-? DLC, GEU, GU-L

Inside Kentucky Sports, Lexington,
Ky., 1972-? KyU

James Sprunt Review, Kenanville,
N.C., July 1972-? DLC

*Japanese Monthly Patent Data; A
Folio of Poets*, Coconut Grove,
Fla., 1972-?

Jazz Digest, McLean, Va., 1972-?
Formerly as *Hip: The Jazz
Record Digest*, DLC, NN

*Jewish Floridian of Greater Fort
Lauderdale*, Fort Lauderdale,
Fla., 1972-current

*Journal of Non-White Concerns in
Personnel and Guidance*, Falls
Church, Va., Oct. 1972-current,
DLC, ICU, MnU, N, NcRS, TxU,
ViBlbV

*Journal of the Roanoke Valley
Historical Society*, Roanoke, Va.,
Summer 1972-? Continues
*Journal of the Roanoke
Historical Society*, DLC

*Journal of the Southeastern Indian
Antiquities Survey*, Nashville,
Tenn., 1972-? MH-P, WHi

Konglomerati, Gulfport, Fla.,
1972-current

Language of Poems, Columbia, S.C.,
Jan. 1972-79, ArU, IU, NcCU,
NcGU

*Liberator: An Independent
Journal of Commentary on
Feminist Issues*, Fort Worth,
Tex., 1972-7?

Loggin' Times, Montgomery, Ala.,
1972-current. Currently as
Southern Loggin' Times, NcRS

MH, Arlington, Va., Summer 1972-?
Continues *Mental Hygiene*, DLC,
KMK, ViBlbV

Magazine of Bibliographies, Fort
Worth, Tex., Sept. 1972-? DLC,
KyU, MH, N, TxU

Mechanics, University Park, Pa.;
Blacksburg, Va.; Evanston, Ill.,
1972-current, LNHT, ScCleU,
ViBlbV

Mississippi Archaeologist,
University, Miss., 1972-? MH-P,
MsSM

Mississippi Review, Hattiesburg,
Miss., Jan. 1972-current, CtY,
DLC, NN, NcRS, ViU, ViBlbV

Music Power, Reston, Va., 1972-?
Formerly as *Up-Beat*

Musical Analysis, Denton, Tex.,
Winter 1972-74, DLC, IEN, IU,
NjP, NN, TxSaT

NADE Advocate, Frankfort, Ky.,
1972-current

Nashville Rag, Nashville, Tenn.,
Nov. 1972-? WHi

*New Banner. A Libertarian's
Journal*, Columbia, S.C., 1972-73,
CSt-H

New Pulpit Digest -- See *Pulpit
Digest*

*North Carolina Journal of Speech
and Drama*, Greensboro, N.C.,
Spring 1972-Fall 1978.
Continues *North Carolina
Journal of Speech*, continued
by *North Carolina Journal of
Speech Communication*, AzU,
ICRL, ICarbS, InLP

*Northwoods Journal; A Magazine
for Writers*, Meadows of Dan,
Va., 1972-?

Nuclear Materials Management,
Louisville, Ky., Apr.
1972-current, DLC, GAT, KMK,
NcRS

Old Mill News, Knoxville, Tenn.,
1972-current

Old Red Komono, Rome, Ga., Winter
1972-? GASC, GU

Outdoors in Georgia, Atlanta, Ga.,
July 1972-July 1979.
Supersedes *Georgia Game and
Fish*, LU, GU

*Over the Garden Fence; Natural
Living in North Texas*, Dallas,
Tex., 1972-current

Palmetto Economics, Clemson, S.C.,
1972-current

Panola Story, Batesville, Miss.,
Jan.-Mar. 1972-? DLC

The Paperworker, Flushing, N.Y.;
Nashville, Tenn., Oct.
1972-current, CLU, ICU, NN, NcU

Phoebe, Fairfax, Va., 1972-current

*Pilgrimage: The Journal of
Pastoral Psychotherapy*,
Atlanta, Ga., 1972-current,
MH-AH, NcCU, NcWsW, TxDaM-P,
ViRUT

Planetarian, Alexandria, Va., June
1972-current, DLC, KU, MiU, TNJ

The Plate Collector, Kermit, San
Marcos, Tex., 1972-current

Pleasure Boating Magazine, Miami,
Fla., 1972-current

Pro-Law, Houston, Tex., 1972-?

Proteus, Arlington, Va., Fall 1972-?
DLC, MdU

Pulpit Digest, Jackson, Miss.,
1972-current. Formerly as *New
Pulpit Digest*, NN

Reading in Virginia, Roanoke, Va.,
1972-current

Real Estate and Business Atlanta
-- See *Real Estate Atlanta*

Real Estate Atlanta, Atlanta, Ga.,
May 1972-current. Currently as
Business Atlanta. Formerly as
*Real Estate and Business
Atlanta*, GASU, GU

*Recollections: A Journal of the
Appalachian Oral History
Project of Lees Jr. College*,
Jackson, Ky., Dec. 1972-? DLC

Red Beans and Rice, New Orleans,
La., 1972-?

Replica In Scale, San Antonio,
Tex., Aug. 1972-current. As
Aerophile since 1976

Revista Chicano-Riquena, Houston,
Tex., 1972-current

La Revue de Louisiane, Lafayette,
La., 1972-82, DLC, InU, ViBlbV

Richmond Mercury Book Review,
Richmond, Va., 1972-?

Shopping Center World, Atlanta,
Ga., Feb. 1972-current, DLC,
GASU, MH-BA, NN

South Carolina Food Journal,
Columbia, S.C., 1972-current

Southeast Real Estate News,
Atlanta, Ga., 1972-current

Southern Antiques and Interiors,
High Point, N.C., Mar. 1972-?
DLC, NcD, NcGU, Vi

Southern Boating, Miami, Fla.,
1972-current

Southern Libertarian Messenger,
Florence, S.C., May
1972-current, CSt-H

Southern Loggin' Times -- See
Loggin' Times

Southern Presbyterian,
Centerville, Ala., 1972-? ViRUT

Spaceview Magazine, Beaumont,
Tex., 1972-?

Spanish River Papers, Boca Raton,
Fla., 1972-? NN

*Specialty Salesman & Business
Opportunities*, Atlanta, Ga., Mar.
1972-Feb. 1983. Continues
*Specialty Salesman and
Franchise Opportunities*.
Continued by *Selling Direct*,
DLC

The Speedy Bee, Jesup, Ga., Feb.
1972-current, DNAL, NIC

Stinktree, Memphis, Tenn. Feb.
1972-? DLC, ICU, KyU, NN, TU

Stone Drum, Huntsville, Ala.;
Dumes, Tex., 1972-74, NN

TPGA Journal, Austin, Tex.,
1972-current, TxU

*Tax Notes; The Journal of Policy
Relevant Tax Analysis*,
Arlington, Va., 1972-current,
CtY-L, IU, MiU-L, TxU, ViU-L,
ViBlbV

Tennessee Valley Historical Review
-- See *Historical Review &
Antique Digest*

Tennis Industry Magazine, Miami,
Fla., Sept. 1972-current, DLC

The Texas Flyer, Austin, Tex.,
1972-?

Texas Kin, Mesquite, Tex., Mar.
1972-current, NN

Texas League Savings Account,
Austin, Tex., 1972-current

Texas Rivers and Rapids, Pipe
Creek, Tex., 1972-? DLC

The Trumpeter, Borger, Tex.,
1972-current

U T Review, Tampa, Fla., 1972-?
GASU, IU, MH, NN, NcD

*Urban Health; The Journal of
Health Care in the Cities*,
Atlanta, East Point, Ga.,
1972-current, CtY-M, DNLM, MiU,
NjP, TU-M

VCU Magazine, Richmond, Va.,
1972-current, ViRCU-H

Vanderbilt Poetry Review,
Nashville, Tenn., 1972-current,
DLC, GU, KyU, MH, NIC

Virginair, Richmond, Va., 1972-?

Zoo World, Fort Lauderdale, Fla.,
1972-74

Africa News, Durham, N.C.,
1973-current

*Alabama Speech and Theatre
Journal*, Troy, Ala., 1973-? AAP

*American Blade; Magazine for
Cutlery*, New Orleans, La.; North
Hollywood, Calif., 1973-current.
Currently as *Blade Magazine*,
DLC, NN

American Firearms Industry, Fort
Lauderdale, Fla., 1973-current

Animal Learning & Behavior,
Austin, Tex., Feb. 1973-current.
Supersedes *Psychonomic Science*,
CtY-M, DLC, GU, MU, NcD, NcRS,
TxHR, ViBlbV

*Antique Price Report; A Monthly
Magazine of Antique Interests
and Markets*, Kermit, Tex.,
1973-?

Apalachee Quarterly, Tallahassee,
Fla., 1973-current

*Appalachian Heritage; A Magazine
of Southern Appalachian Life
and Culture*, Pippa Passes,
Hindman, Ky., Winter
1973-current, DLC, NN

Appalachian Notes, Lexington, Ky.,
1973-current, AU, GEU, MdU, NN,
Vi, ViBlbV

Arkansas Consumer, Little Rock,
Ark., 1973-?   ArU

Arkansas Criminal Justice Review,
Little Rock, Ark., 1973-?   ArU

Arkansas Nurse, Little Rock, Ark.,
Oct. 1973-?   PPiU-H

Asian Textile Journal, Atlanta,
Ga., 1973-?   Later as *Smith's
Asian Textile Journal*, GAT

Audubon Flyer, Chattanooga,
Tenn., 1973-?

Bank Note Reporter, Citra, Fla.,
1973-?

Beauty Culture Digest, Dallas,
Tex., 1973-?

Bluegrass Roots, Frankfort, Ky.,
Oct. 1973-?   NN, T

Border States, Highland Heights,
Ky., 1973-?   DLC

Central Florida Scene, Orlando,
Fla., 1973-current

Christian Educator, Cape
Canaveral, Orlando, Fla., May
1973-?   DLC

Clinical Engineering News,
Arlington, Va., May 1973-?
DNLM, GAT, TxCM, TxHMC,
ViRCU-H

Community College Review, Raleigh,
N.C., Apr. 1973-current, DLC,
FU, KyU, NcRS, NN, ScU, ViBlbV

Criminal Defense, Houston, Tex.,
Dec. 1973-current, CtY-L, DLC,
IU, MnU-L, ViU-L

Criminal Justice Digest, Annandale,
Va., 1973-76, CtY-L, GU, IU, N,
ScU

*The Crusader: The Voice of the
White Majority*, Metairie, La.,
Fall 1973-?   KU-S, MiEM, NcD

Dallas Bible College, Dallas, Tex.,
1973-?   Supersedes *Dallas Bible
College News*

Dallas Journalism Review, Dallas,
Tex., 1973-?   TxDaM

*Dekalb Business and Economic
Journal*, Decatur, Ga., 1973-?

Delta Scene Magazine, Clarksdale,
Cleveland, Miss., 1973-current,
MsSM

Dental Lab World, San Antonio,
Tex., 1973-current

Distaff, New Orleans, La., Feb.
1973-?   LU, LU-NO, WHi

Dynastat Report, Austin, Tex.,
1973-?

*Eric and the Elementary School
Principal*, Arlington, Va.,
Spring 1973-?   GU, MiDW, WM

Experimental Hematology, El Paso,
Tex., 1973-current, CtY-M,
DNLM, NNC-M, TxHMC

Faith for the Family, Greenville,
S.C., 1973-current

Fiber Producer, Atlanta, Ga.,
1973-current

Florida English Journal,
Plantation, Fla., 1973-?   FTaSU

Florida Field Naturalist, Maitland,
Fla., Spring 1973-current, CoFS,
FTaSU

Florida Life, Boca Raton, Fla.,
1973-?

Florida Out of Doors, West Palm
Beach, Fla., 1973-current

*Florida Speech Communication
Journal*, Tampa, Fla.,
1973-current, DLC, FTaSU, FU,
TxU

*Florida State University Law
Review*, Tallahassee, Fla., Winter
1973-current, DLC, GU-L, MiU-L,
NN, ViU-L

*Freshwater Ecosystem Pollution
Research Highlights*, Athens,
Ga., 1973-75

GPSA Journal, Atlanta, Ga.,
1973-current.   Currently as
Southeastern Political Review,
DLC, GAT, GU, NcGU, TNJ

*Genealogical Society of Old Tryon
County Bulletin*, Spindale, N.C.,
1973-current, DLC, In, NN

General Aviation Business, Snyder,
Tex., 1973-?

Georgia Cattleman, Macon, Ga., Feb.
1973-current, GU

*Georgia College Alumni News
Quarterly*, Milledgeville, Ga.,
1973-current

Graffiti, Hickory, N.C., 1973-?

Hip, Fort Worth, Tex., 1973-82.
Also as *Hep*

Human Dimensions Journal, Buffalo,
N.Y.; Columbus, N.C.,
1973-current.   Formerly as
Human Dimensions Magazine, KMK

Human Dimensions Magazine -- See
Human Dimensions Journal

Industrial Organization Review,
Blacksburg, Va., 1973-?   DLC,
FU, IU, MH-BA, NcRS, TxCM,
ViBlbV

IndustriScope, Richmond, Va.,
1973-current.   Supersedes
*Financial Industry
Industriscope*

Insect World Digest, Latham, N.Y.;
Gainesville, Fla., 1973-current,
CLU, DLC, GU, MiU, NcRS, TU,
ViBlbV

International Angler -- See
International Marine Angler

International Marine Angler, Fort
Lauderdale, Fla., 1973-current.
Also as *International Angler*

*Jacksonville Genealogical Society
Magazine* -- See *Jacksonville
Genealogical Society Quarterly*

*Jacksonville Genealogical Society
Quarterly*, Jacksonville, Fla.,
1973-current.   Formerly as
*Jacksonville Genealogical
Society Magazine*, DLC, NN, WHi

Jealous Mistress, Chapel Hill, N.C.,
1973-?   DLC, IU, ViU-L

*Jeffersonian Review; a Monthly
Journal of the Literary Arts*,
Charlottesville, Va., 1973-75,
DLC, NN, ViU

Journal of Applied Communication Research, Mississippi State, Miss., Winter/Spring 1973-current, DLC, FU, IaU, LU, MoU, NcRS

Journal of Biological Physics, Blacksburg, Va., 1973-? DLC, GAT, IEN, InU, TxCM, ViBlbV, ViU

Journal of Political Science, Clemson, S.C., 1973-current. Continues *South Carolina Journal of Political Science*, AU, DLC, LU, NN, NcCU, ViBlbV

Journal of Space Law, University, Miss., 1973-current

Journal of the Interdenominational Theological Center, Atlanta, Ga., Fall 1973-current, CtY-D, DLC, IU, NcCU, NjPT, TxDaM-P

Lost Generation Journal, Tulsa, Okla.; Little Rock, Ark.; Salem, Mo., May 1973-current, ArU, DLC, IU, MH, NN, TxHR

Memory & Cognition, Austin, Tex., Jan. 1973-current, CtY-M, DLC, MH, NcD, NcU, TxHR, TxLT, TxHMC

Mid-American Folklore -- See *Mid-South Folklore*

Mid-South Folklore, State University, Ark., Spring 1973-current. As *Mid-American Folklore* since 1979, ArU, DLC, GU, KyU, NcD, TxU

Mississippi Geographer, Hattiesburg, Miss., Spring 1973-? AAP, KyU, MsSM, ScU

Modern Spanish Teacher, Miami, Fla., 1973-?

Moonrigger, Gainesville, Fla., Fall 1973-? FU

Moral Majority Report, Richmond, Va., 1973-current

Mother Jones Gazette, Knoxville, Tenn., Jan. 1973-? IEN, WHi

Nanih Waiya, Philadelphia, Miss., 1973-78, CtY, LNU, MiU, WHi

Nashville! -- See *Nashville Magazine*

Nashville Magazine, Nashville, Tenn., Apr. 1973-current. Also as *Nashville!*, TNJ

National Defense, Arlington, Va., Sept./Oct. 1973-current. Continues *Ordnance*, DLC, KU, MnU, ULA

Needlepoint Bulletin, Juniper, Fla., 1973-current

New Atlantean Journal, Saint Petersburg, Fla., 1973-current

The New East, The Family Magazine of North Carolina, Greenville, N.C., 1973-77

Northern Kentucky Law Review -- See *Northern Kentucky State Law Forum*

Northern Kentucky State Law Forum, Covington, Highland Heights, Ky., 1973-current. Currently as *Northern Kentucky Law Review*, CtY-L, GU-L, IU, NjR

Notes on Teaching English, Statesboro, Ga., 1973-current

Obrero Christiano, El Paso, Tex., 1973-current. Supersedes *Pastor Evangelico*

Oilways, Houston, Tex., 1973-?

Old Friends; A New Arts Review, The Plains, Va., Spring 1973-? GASU, MH

Pace, Greensboro, N.C., 1973-current

Parapsychology -- See
*Parapsychology-Psychic Science
Reports; Magazine of Psychic
Phenomena*

*Parapsychology-Psychic Science
Journal* -- See
*Parapsychology-Psychic Science
Reports; Magazine of Psychic
Phenomena*

*Parapsychology-Psychic Science
Reports; Magazine of Psychic
Phenomena*, North Miami Beach,
Fla., 1973-current. Also as
*Parapsychology-Psychic Science
Journal*, and as *Parapsychology*

Parrott Talk, Sudan, Tex.,
1973-current, DLC, NN

*People: Human Resources in North
Carolina*, Raleigh, N.C., 1973-75,
AU, MdU-H, NcD, NcRS, NcWsW

Physiological Psychology, Austin,
Tex., Mar. 1973-current, CtY-M,
DLC, NcD, NjR, TU, TxHMC, TxU,
ViBlbV

Prolog, Dallas, Tex., May
1973-current, NN, NcWsW

Psychonomic Society Bulletin,
Austin, Tex., Jan. 1973-current,
CtY-M, DLC, MH, NcD, NcRS, NjP,
TxHR, TxU, ViBlbV

Retail Reporter, Gastonia, N.C.,
1973-current

Smith's Asian Textile Journal --
See *Asian Textile Journal*

*South Carolina Magazine of
Ancestral Research*, Kingstree,
Columbia, S.C., Winter
1973-current, In, NN

*South Central Kentucky Historical
and Genealogical Society, Inc.
Quarterly*, Glasgow, Ky., Apr.
1973-? T

Southeastern Political Review --
See *GPSA Journal*

*Southeastern Review, A Journal of
Sociology and Anthropology*,
Charlottesville, Va., Dec. 1973-?
DeU, FU, NcGU, NjR

Southern Exposure, Durham, N.C.,
Spring 1973-current, AU, CtY,
DLC, GU, MH, NN, NcD, NcRS,
TxU, ViBlbV

Southern Simmental, Dallas, Tex.,
1973-?

Southwest Real Estate News, Dallas,
Tex., 1973-current

*Studies in Browning and His
Circle*, Waco, Tex., Spring
1973-current, CtY, DGW, DLC,
GU, MiU, MH, NN, TxU, ViU

Surgical Neurology, Tryon, N.C.,
Jan. 1973-? CtY-M, DLC, DNLM,
ICJ, NcU-H, NjR, TxU-M

T.U.B.A. Journal, Denton, Tex.,
1973-current, DLC, GU, InU,
KyU, NcU, TxHR

Tejidos, Austin, Tex., Fall 1973-?
AzU, CtY, NN

Tennessee Reading Teacher,
Memphis, Tenn., Spring 1973-?
GU

Tennessee Thrusts, Nashville,
Tenn., Spring 1973-? DLC, TU

Texas Fiddler, Burleson, Millsap,
Tex., 1973-? DLC

*Texas Fisherman; Voice of the Lone
Star Angler*, Houston, Tex.,
1973-current

Texas Monthly, Austin, Tex., Feb.
1973-current, CtY, NN, TxCM,
TxHR, TxU

Titles Varies, Okemos, Mich.;
Chapel Hill, N.C., Dec. 1973-?
CLU, FMU, GU, NN, NcCU, TU

Today's Coins, Kermit, Tex., 1973-?

Truck Stop Management, Asheville, N.C., 1973-81

Turkey Call, Edgefield, S.C., 1973-current, ViBlbV

United Sisters, Tampa, Fla., 1973-?

Urology Times, Miami, Fla.; New York, N.Y., 1973-current

Virginia Legislative Researcher, Charlottesville, Va., 1973-? DLC, ViU-L

Virginia Phoenix Gazette, Richmond, Va., Mar. 1973-? ViU, ViW

Warrant Hedge Analysis, Denton, Tex., 1973-74

Accounting Historian -- See *Accounting Historians Journal*

Accounting Historians Journal, University, Ala.; Atlanta, Ga.; North Miami, Fla., 1974-current. As *Accounting Historian* until 1977, DLC, GASU, IU, KyU, MH-BA, NN, ViBlbV

Airline & Travel Food, Miami Springs, Fla., 1974-current. Formerly as *Airline Food & Flight Service* and as *Airline News*

Airline Food & Flight Service -- See *Airline & Travel Food*

Airline News -- See *Airline & Travel Food*

Alabama News Review University, Ala., Feb. 1974-? AAP

Alabama Personnel and Guidance Journal, Auburn, Ala., Sept. 1974-current, AAP

Alive and Well, Waco, Tex., 1974-?

American Indian Quarterly, Hurst, Tex.; Berkeley, Calif., 1974-current, DLC, ICN, NPotC, OkU, OrU, TxU, WHi

American Traveler, Atlanta, Ga., 1974-current

Aquaculture and the Fish Farmer, Little Rock, Ark., May 1974-? ArU, IU, KU, LU, NcRS, ScU

Ark, Memphis, Tenn., 1974-? CoFS

Arkansas Times, Little Rock, Ark., 1974-current

Aura Literary Arts Review, Birmingham, Ala., 1974-current, AAP, NN

Austin Living, Austin, Tex., 1974-current

Aviation Quarterly, Arlington, Va.; Plano, Tex., 1974-? DLC, InLP

Better Driving, Chapel Hill, N.C., 1974-75

Big Reel, Madison, N.C., 1974-current

Black Warrior Review, Birmingham, University, Ala., Fall 1974-current, AU, LNHT, MH, NN, NcD, NcU, ViBlbV

Blue Ridge Presbyterian, Lynchburg, Va., June 1974-? ViU

The Bookman, Galveston, Tex., Jan. 1974-current, CLU, TxU

Broward Life, Fort Lauderdale, Fla., 1974-? NN

Bull & Bear, Winter Park, Fla., 1974-current

Capital Magazine, Falls Church, Va., 1974-current

Cardiovascular Diseases, Houston,
Tex., Jan. 1974-current.
Currently as *Texas Heart
Institute Journal*, DNLM, ICJ,
N, TxHMC, TxU-M

*The Cass County Genealogical
Society*, Atlanta, Ga., 1974-?
DLC

Cathartic, Fort Lauderdale, Fla.,
1974-?   RPB

Cemetery Management, Falls Church,
Va., 1974-current

Clay Tablet, Morrow, Ga., Winter
1974-?   GASU

D, Dallas, Tex., Oct. 1974-current,
TxDaM

*Energy Abstracts for Policy
Analysis*, Oak Ridge, Tenn.,
Nov. 1974-current, ArU, NN,
TxHR, ViBlbV

Energy Week, Dallas, Tex., 1974-?
OkU

Family Line News, Jacksonville,
Fla., 1974-current, GU, T, TNJ,
ViU

Fiberarts, Albuquerque, N.M.;
Asheville, N.C., 1974-current,
AzU, DLC, KyU, MiU

Florida Banker, Orlando, Fla.,
Sept. 1974-current, FTaSU, FU

Florida Bar News, Tallahassee,
Fla., 1974-current, C, DLC

*Florida Food and Resource
Economics*, Gainesville, Fla.,
Nov. 1974-current, DNAL

Florida Libertarian, Miami, Fla.,
1974-?   CSt-H

Florida Shipper, Miami, Fla.,
1974-current

Gaiety, Memphis, Tenn., 1974-76

Georgia Legislative Review,
Atlanta, Ga., 1974-?   DLC, GASU

Georgia Life, Decatur, Ga., Summer
1974-Spring 1980, GASU, GAT,
GEU, NcD, NcWsW

Georgia State University Review,
Atlanta, Ga., 1974-?   GASU, GU

Gospel Choir, Nashville, Tenn.,
Oct. 1974-current, DLC

Helios, Lubbock, Tex.,
1974-current, KU, NjP, ScU,
TxLT

Hey Beatnik, Summertown, Tenn.,
1974

*The Hill Country Genealogical
Society Quarterly*, Llano, Tex.,
1974-?   DLC

Hopkins Quarterly, Columbia, S.C.,
Apr. 1974-current, CLU, DLC,
FU, LU, NcRS, NN, ScCleU, ScU

Hospital Infection Control, Atlanta,
Ga., Nov. 1974-current, DNLM

Houston Home & Garden, Houston,
Tex., Oct. 1974-current, DLC,
TxHR, TxU

Integrity Forum -- See *Integrity;
Gay Episcopal Forum*

Integrity; Gay Episcopal Forum,
Fort Valley, Ga., 1974-current.
Currently as *Integrity Forum*

*International Academy of
Preventive Medicine Journal*,
Houston, Tex., Spring
1974-current, CtY-M, DLC,
TxHMC, TxU-M, ViRCU-H

*Interstate; A Magazine of
Creative Acts*, Austin, Tex.,
Spring 1974-?   IaU, NN, TxCM,
TxU

Journal of Biocommunication, San Francisco, Calif.; Chapel Hill, N.C., June 1974-current, CLU, DLC, IU-M, NcU-H, TxHMC, TxU-M

Ky-Lar, Frankfort, Ky., Jan. 1974-? In, NNC

Magnolia LPN, Cayce, S.C., 1974-?

Materials for the Study of William Blake, Normal, Ill.; Memphis, Tenn., 1974-7? CtY, MnU, NcD, NcGU, NjR, ScU

Mecca; The Magazine of Traditional Jazz, New Orleans, La., 1974-? DLC, GU, KyU, LU, NN, NjP

Medal World, Kermit, Tex., Dec. 1974-Aug. 1975, WHi

Medical School Rounds, Concord, Mass.; Miami, Fla., Jan. 1974-current, WaU

Mississippi Pharmacist, University, Miss., 1974-current

Moonshadow, Miami Beach, Fla., 1974-? IEN

Mountain Review, Whitesburg, Ky., Sept. 1974-? CtY, DLC, KyLoU, MH, NcD, NcU, ViBlbV

New Broom; Journal of Witchcraft, Dallas, Tex., 1974-?

New Logic Notebook, Reston, Va., 1974-75

New Scripts Review, Dallas, Tex., 1974-?

North Carolina Review of Business and Economics, Greensboro, N.C., Oct. 1974-current, DLC, NcGU, NcRS

Peanut Science, Suffolk, Va.; Raleigh, N.C., Mar. 1974-current, AAP, DLC, IU, NcRS, ViBlbV

Pecan South, Atlanta, Ga., Jan. 1974-current, NcRS, ScCleU, TxLT

Perspectives In Religious Studies, Murfreesboro, N.C.; Macon, Ga., Spring 1974-current, CtY-D, NcWsW, NjPT, ViBlbV

Plants, Sites, & Parks, New York, N.Y.; Coral Springs, Fla., 1974-current, GASU, NNC

Play Meter Magazine, New Orleans, La., 1974-current

Pocket Poetry Monthly, Key West, Fla., June 1974-? NjP

Pointblank Times, Houston, Tex., 1974-?

Public Affairs Analyst, Lexington, Ky., 1974-? KyU, OkU

Puddingstone, Virginia Beach, Va., 1974-?

Pulpit Helps, Chattanooga, Tenn., 1974-current

RFD, Efland, Bakersville, N.C., 1974-current

Rice Literary Review, Houston, Tex., Spring 1974-? TxHR

Richmond Life Style Magazine, Richmond, Va., May 1974-? Absorbed by *Commonwealth Magazine*, NcD, ViRUT

The Roanoker Magazine, Roanoke, Va., 1974-current, NN, Vi

SNA Nursery Research Journal, Nashville, Tenn., May 1974-? DNAL, GU, TxCM, ViBlbV

Social Perspectives, Tuscaloosa, Ala., May 1974-current, AAP, AU, DLC, NN, TxU

The South Magazine, Tampa, Fla., 1974-? Also as *South; The Journal of Southern Business*

South Carolina Out-of-Doors,
Columbia, S.C., 1974-current

*South; The Journal of Southern
Business* -- See *The South
Magazine*

Southern University Law Review,
Baton Rouge, La., Fall
1974-current, CtY-L, DLC,
IEN-L, NNU-L

Southern Voices, Atlanta, Ga.,
1974-? DLC, KU, IU, FU, NN,
NjR, NcRS, ScU, ViU

Southwest Farm Press, Clarksdale,
Miss., 1974-current

*Stable & Kennel News of the
South*, Roswell, Ga., 1974-?

Strictly U.S. Dunedin, Fla., Oct.
1974-current, DLC

Studies in American Humor, San
Marcos, Tex., Apr. 1974-current.
Absorbed *American Humor*, ArU,
DLC, FU, MH, NN, NjP, TxCM,
TxHR

TASCD Journal, Murfreesboro,
Tenn., 1974-current, AAP, GU

Talk-Back, Falls Church, Va.,
1974-7?

*Tawte; A Journal of Texas
Culture*, Austin, Tex., June
1974-? TxHR, TxU

*Teaching English in the Two-Year
College*, Greenville, N.C., Fall
1974-current, DLC, ICarbS

Tennessee Liberty Bell, Nashville,
Tenn., Sept. 1974-current, CSt-H

Tennessee Stockman, Trenton,
Tenn., 1974-?

Tennessee's Business, Murfreesboro,
Tenn., Sept. 1974-? DLC, NN,
PSt

Texan Veteran News, Austin, Tex.,
1974-current

Texarkana U.S.A. Quarterly,
Texarkana, Ark.-Tex.,
1974-current, ArU, NN

Texas CPA News, Dallas, Tex., Aug.
1974-? Formed by merger of
Texas CPA and *Texas CPA News*,
ICU, NcWsW, TxU, ViBlbV

Texas Energy, College Station,
Tex., July 1974-? TxCM, TxLT

Texas Heart Institute Journal --
See *Cardiovascular Diseases*

Texas Horticulturist, College
Station, Tex., Spring 1974-?
TxCM, TxLT, TxU

Texas Literary Journal, Austin,
Tex., Spring 1974-? TxU

Texas Tech Journal of Education,
Lubbock, Tex., 1974-current,
DLC, LU, NIC, TxCM, TxDaM, TxU

Twins and Things, Austin, Tex.,
1974-?

United Methodists Today, Nashville,
Tenn., Jan. 1974-75. Supersedes
Christian Advocate and
Together, CtY-D, DLC, NcD,
TxDaM, ViRUT

Upshaw Family Journal, Marietta,
Ga., Winter 1974-current, DLC,
NN, T

Virginia Issues, Charlottesville,
Va., 1974-? IU, NIC, Vi

*The Arkansas Social Studies
Teacher*, _____, Ark., 1975-?
DLC

Austin Stone, Austin, Tex., 1975-?
WHi

B & E International, Houston, Tex.,
1975-?

Barbeque Planet, Nashville, Tenn., Fall 1975-79, DLC, WU

Barter Communique, Sarasota, Fla., 1975-current

Behavioral Disorders Journal, Reston, Va., Summer 1975-current, AU, IU, MdU, NcRS, PU

Bienvenidos A Miami Y A La Florida, Miami, Fla., 1975-current

Black Aging -- See *Minority Aging*

Blueboy, Miami, Fla., 1975-?

Bluegrass Reflections, Fort Worth, Tex., 1975-?   DLC

Carolina Planning, Chapel Hill, N.C., Summer 1975-current, DLC, IU, NcD, NcRS, NcU, ViBlbV

Cartoonews, Orlando, Fla., Apr. 1975-current, IC, MiEM

Charleston Magazine, Charleston, S.C., Aug. 1975-?   TxU

Coastal Magazine, Savannah, Ga., 1975-78. Also as *Coastal Quarterly*

Coastal Quarterly -- See *Coastal Magazine*

Concepts in Wood Design, McLean, Va., 1975-82. Supersedes *Wood Preserving*, ArU

Conservative Digest, Falls Church, Va., 1975-current, CtY, DLC, NN, NcD, ViW

Contemporary Administrator, Murfreesboro, Tenn., 1975-current

Dallas Fashion Retailer, Dallas, Tex., 1975-current. Currently as *Fashion Showcase Retailer*

Dulcimer Players News, Bangor, Me.; Front Royal, Winchester, Va., Jan. 1975-current, DLC

Encounter, Little Rock, Ark., 1975-?   ArU, ScU

Faith & Reason; the Journal of Christendom College, Front Royal, Triangle, Va., 1975-current, DLC, NjPT

Fashion Showcase Retailer -- See *Dallas Fashion Retailer*

Florida Administrative Reporter, Tallahassee, Fla., 1975-?   DLC

Florida Aviation Journal, Orlando, Fla., 1975-80

Florida Golfweek, Winter Park, Fla., 1975-current

Florida Media Quarterly, Orlando, Fla., Fall 1975-current, FTaSU, GASU

Florida Vocational Journal, Tallahassee, Fla., Oct. 1975-current, DLC, FU

Focal Points, Atlanta, Ga., Aug. 1975-current, InU

Gas Digest, Houston, Tex., 1975-current, DLC

Georgia Classicist, Athens, Ga., Oct. 1975-?   GU

Georgia Journal of Reading, Atlanta, Ga., Fall 1975-?   GU

Golf Industry, Miami, Fla., Oct. 1975-current, DLC

Gray Day, Athens, Ga., Summer 1975-?   GU, IaU, NN

"Gymnastics," Fort Worth, Tex., 1975-current

Houston Engineer, Houston, Tex., Sept. 1975-? Supersedes *The Slide Rule*, TxCM, TxLT

Houston Journal of Mathematics,
Houston, Tex., Oct.
1975-current, AAP, DLC, GU, NN,
NcRS, TU, TxHR, TxU, ViBlbV

Informer, Huntsville, Ala.;
Raleigh, N.C., June 1975-?   NNC,
WaU

Innkeeping World, Gainesville,
Fla., 1975-current

Instauration, Cape Canaveral, Fla.,
1975-current

International Poetry Review,
Greensboro, N.C.; University
Center, Mich., 1975-current.
Formerly as *Revista:*
International Poetry Review,
DLC, MiU, NcU, NN, ViBlbV

Jewish Floridian, Palm Beach, Fla.,
1975-?

Journal of Applied Photographic
Science and Engineering,
Springfield, Va., Fall
1975-current, DLC, GAT, NN,
NcRS, TxU, ViBlbV

Journal of Continuing Medical
Education International,
Lakeland, Fla., 1975-current

Journal of Education Finance,
Gainesville, Fla., Summer
1975-current, DLC, MoU, MsU, N,
TxU

Journal of Management, Lubbock,
Tex.; Auburn, Ala., Fall
1975-current, AAP, AU, IU,
MH-BA, TxArU, TxCM, ViU

Journal of Minority Aging -- See
Minority Aging

Journal of Physical Education and
Recreation, Reston, Va., Jan.
1975-Apr. 1981. Continues
Journal of Health, Physical
Education, Recreation.
Continued by *Journal of*
Physical Education, Recreation
& Dance, DLC, FU, MiU, NcRS,
ScU, TxU, ViBlbV, ViU

The Journal of the Linguistic
Association of the Southwest,
Austin, Tex., 1975-current.
Currently as *Southwest Journal*
of Linguistics, DLC, LU

Kentucky Coal Journal, Frankfort,
Ky., 1975-current

Lamar Journal of the Humanities,
Beaumont, Tex., 1975-current,
ICarbS, NcD, OkU

Language and Literature -- See
Linguistics In Literature

Law and Psychology Review,
University, Ala., 1975-?   CtY-L,
DLC, GU-L, NcGU, ViU-L

Legal Advocate, Houston, Tex.,
1975-?

Linguistics In Literature, San
Antonio, Tex., Fall
1975-current.   Currently as
Language and Literature, DLC,
GU, MH, NN, TxCM, TxSaT

Louisiana Schools, Baton Rouge,
La., Sept. 1975-?   GU, LNHT, LU

Louisville Law Examiner,
Louisville, Ky., May 1975-?
WaU-L

Loyola Lawyer, New Orleans, La.,
Spring 1975-?   CtY-L, DLC,
GU-L, NjR

Magazine of the Texas Commission
on Alcoholism, Austin, Tex.,
Aug. 1975-?   Formed by union
of *Texas Talks Alcoholism* and
Texas Journal on Alcoholism,
DLC

The Maritime Lawyer, New Orleans, La., Mar. 1975-current, DLC, MH-L

Martin Family Quarterly, Dallas, Tex., May 1975-current, DLC, NN, Vi

Mid-Hudson Genealogical Journal, Columbia, S.C., 1975-current

Minority Aging, Durham, N.C., Oct. 1975-current. Formerly as *Black Aging*. Currently as *Journal of Minority Aging*, NcD, NcGU, NcWsW, ViBlbV

Moondance, Memphis, Tenn., Fall 1975-? LU, NN, OrU

Movers Journal, Arlington, Va., 1975-current

NCAGT Quarterly Journal, _____, N.C., Winter 1975-? LNHT, NcGU

Nashville West: Austin's Own Country Music Magazine, Austin, Tex., Sept. 1975-? DLC

National Journal of Criminal Defense, Houston, Tex., Spring 1975-? CtY-L, GU-L, NN, ViU-L

Neighbors, Montgomery, Ala., Fall 1975-current, AAP

New River Review, Radford, Va., Fall 1975-? CtY, DLC, NN, TxU, ViBlbV

North Carolina Foreign Language Review, Raleigh, N.C., Fall 1975-? Continues *North Carolina Foreign Language Teacher*, MH, NcGU, ViBlbV, ViU

North Carolina Genealogical Society Journal, Raleigh, N.C., Jan. 1975-current, DLC, NN, NcD, Vi

Old Dominion Sierran, Emory, Va., 1975-?

Old Timer, Albany, Tex., 1975-? DLC

Older Texan, Austin, Tex., 1975-current. Formerly as *Encore*, TxCM

Perspective of Contemporary Literature, Louisville, Ky., 1975-?

Photo Artist USA, Winter Park, Fla., 1975-? Formerly as *Photohobby*

Photohobby -- See *Photo Artist USA*

Quarter Horse Track, Fort Worth, Tex., 1975-current

Revista: International Poetry Review -- See *International Poetry Review*

Riverrun, Saint Petersburg, Fla., 1975

Sarasota Town & Country Magazine, Sarasota, Fla., 1975-78

Schatzammer Der Deutschen Sprachlebre, Dichtung und Geschichte, Arlington, Tex., 1975-? InU, INS, TxArU

Scholia Satyrica, Tampa, Fla., Winter 1975-current. Supersedes *Pucred*, DLC, FU, GEU

School Student and the Courts -- See *Schools and the Courts*

Schools and the Courts, Asheville, N.C., Feb. 1975-current. As *School Student and the Courts* until Feb. 1979, ViBlbV, ViU

Service Shop, Fort Worth, Tex., 1975-current

Small Farm, Dandridge, Jefferson City, Tenn., Mar. 1975-? DLC, NN, T, TxU

South Texas, San Antonio, Tex.,
Sept. 1975-? Continues *South
Texan*, TxCM, TxLT

Southern Business Review,
Statesboro, Ga., Spring 1975-?
AAP, GU, ViBlbV

*Southern Journal of Criminal
Justice*, Columbia, S.C., Summer
1975-? NcCU

Southern Literary Messenger,
Mobile, Ala., Spring 1975-?
AAP, NN

Southern Media Messenger, Mobile,
Ala., Spring, 1975-? ArU

Southern School Law Digest,
Tuscaloosa, Ala., 1975-current,
DLC, ScCleU, TxCM

Southern Visions, Cedar Park,
Tex., 1975-? WU

Southwest Journal of Linguistics
-- See *The Journal of the
Linguistic Association of the
Southwest*

The Southwestern Bookman, Austin,
Tex., 1975-? Continues *Texas
Bibliographical Society*, AZ,
KyU, OrU, TxArU, TxCM, TxU,
ViU

The Space Gamer, Austin, Tex.,
1975-current

TDA Quarterly, Austin, Tex.,
Spring 1975-? TxArU, TxCM,
TxU

Telecourier, Palm City, Fla.,
1975-current

Tennessee Journal, Nashville,
Tenn., Jan. 1975-current, T

Tennessee Livestock, Smyrna,
Tenn., 1975-current

Tennessee Researcher,
Charlottesville, Va., 1975-? DLC

The Texas Business Executive,
College Station, Tex., Spring
1975-current, DLC, TxU

Texas Heritage, Fort Worth, Tex.,
June 1975-? DLC, T, TxArU

Texas Slough, El Paso, Austin,
Tex., 1975-? TxLT, WU

*Thanatos; Realistic Journal
Concerning Dying, Death &
Bereavement*, Saint Petersburg,
Fla., Sept. 1975-current, DLC,
NbU

Virginia Bar Association Journal,
Richmond, Va., Jan.
1975-current, DLC, NjR, Vi,
ViBlbV, ViU-L

*Virginia Educational Research
Journal*, Blacksburg, Va.,
Spring 1975-? ViBlbV

Voluntary Action Leadership,
Arlington, Va., 1975-current.
Absorbed *Voluntary Action
News*, DLC, NNC, TxU, ViBlbV

Winesburg Eagle, Richmond, Va.,
Nov. 1975-current, DLC, INS, MH,
NN, NcWsW, ViBlbV

Wings of Gold, Falls Church, Va.,
1975-current

Wood Ibis, Austin, Tex.,
1975-current, IEN, NN, TxU

Abba, A Journal of Prayer,
Austin, Tex., 1976-? DLC,
MH-AH

Aboard Inflight Magazine, Coral
Springs, Fla., 1976-current

Advisory Board Record, Chapel
Hill, N.C., 1976-current

Air Defense Magazine, Bliss, Tex.,
Jan./Mar. 1976-Fall 1983.
Continues *Air Defense Trends*,
continued by *Air Defense
Artillery*, DLC

Alabama Life, Opelika, Ala., Sept. 1976-? AAP

Allegorica, Arlington, Tex., Spring 1976-current, CtY, DLC, IU, MH, NN, NcD, TxArU, TxU, ViU

Anthropology and Humanism Quarterly, Tallahassee, Fla., Apr. 1976-current, CtY, DLC, FTaSU, MH, NcD, NcRS

Arlington Catholic Herald, Arlington, Va., Jan. 1976-current, DLC

Artifacts, Columbia, S.C., 1976-current

Birthin', Jackson, Miss., 1976-? IU-M

Broward Legacy, Fort Lauderdale, Fla., Oct. 1976-? DLC, MH

Confederate Air Force Dispatch, Houston, Tex., 1976-?

Continuing Inquiry, Midlothian, Tex., Aug. 1976-current, MH

Criminal Justice Review, Atlanta, Ga., Spring 1976-current, CtY-L, DLC, GAT, GU, NN, NcU-L, TU, ViBlbV

Cuban Topics, Miami, Fla., 1976-current

Dikta, Daytona Beach, Fla.; Huntsville, Ala.; Austin, Tex., Spring 1976-current, DLC, N, ScU, TxU

Directors & Boards, the Journal of Corporate America, McLean, Va., Spring 1976-? CtY-L, DLC, NN, NjR, TxU, ViBlbV, ViU

Electronic Warfare Digest, Annandale, Va., 1976-current

Energy Research Abstracts, Oak Ridge, Tenn., 1976-current, DLC, MnU, NcU, ViBlbV, ViU

Ensayistas, Athens, Ga., Mar. 1976-current, AAP, DGW, FMU, GU, NN, ScU, ViBlbV

Florida Gardening Companion, Largo, Fla., Sept. 1976-? FMU, FTaSU

The Florida Journal of Anthropology, Gainesville, Fla., Winter 1976-current, DLC, MH-P, TU

Format, Florissant, Mo.; Atlanta, Ga., 1976-? DLC

Fossil Energy Update, Oak Ridge, Tenn., 1976-current, DLC, IU, MCM

Fountain, Orlando, Fla., 1976-? WU

French-American Review; A Journal of the History of French and American Literary Relations, Fort Worth, Tex.; Charlotte, N.C., Winter 1976-current, CLU, CtY, DLC, MH, NcU, TU, ViBlbV, ViU

Fruit South, Atlanta, Ga., 1976-? ViBlbV

Furniture Today, High Point, N.C., 1976-current

Georgia Huguenot, _____, _____, Spring 1976-? GU

Georgia Sportsman, Marietta, Ga., 1976-current, GU

Geothermal Energy Technology -- See *Geothermal Energy Update*

Geothermal Energy Update, Oak Ridge, Tenn., Sept. 1976-current. Currently as *Geothermal Energy Technology*, DLC, NIC, ViBlbV

Gift Digest, Dallas, Tex., 1976-current

Glider Rider Magazine,
Chattanooga, Tenn.,
1976-current

Hospital Peer Review, Atlanta, Ga.,
Aug. 1976-current, NbU, WaU

Houston North Magazine, Houston,
Tex., 1976-?

*International School of Law - Law
Review* -- See *GMU Law Review*

The Jewish Star, Birmingham, Ala.,
1976-current

*Journal for Specialists in Group
Work,* Falls Church, Alexandria,
Va., 1976-current. Formerly as
Together, DLC, MnU, ViBlbV, ViU

Journal of Cherokee Studies,
Cherokee, N.C., 1976-?   ICN,
OkTU, OkU, WHi

*Journal of Childhood Communication
Disorders,* Reston, Va., 1976-?
DLC

*The Journal of Classroom
Interaction,* Houston, Tex., Dec.
1976-current.   Continues
*Classroom Interaction
Newsletter,* DGW, KyLoU, NcRS,
WvU

*Journal of Health Politics, Policy
& Law,* Durham, N.C., Spring
1976-current, CLU, CtY-L, DLC,
MH-BA, NcU-H, ViU-L

Journal of Hispanic Philology,
Tallahassee, Fla., Fall
1976-current, CLU, FTaSU, ICU,
IU, LU, NN, NcD, TxU, ViBlbV,
ViU

Kentucky Artist and Craftsmen,
Owensboro, Ky., Sept. 1976-?
KyU, KyLoU

Kentucky Business Ledger,
Louisville, Ky., 1976-current,
KyLoU

Kentucky Forestry News, Frankfort,
Ky., 1976-?   KyU-ASC

Klansman, Denham Springs, La.,
1976-current, CSt-H, LNU

Legal Malpractice Reporter,
Charlottesville, Va.,
1976-current, DLC, FU-L, IU,
NjR, ViU-L

Louisville Review, Louisville, Ky.,
Fall 1976-current, DLC, KyU,
LNHT, NN, NjP

Louisville Today, Louisville, Ky.,
Oct. 1976-?   KyLoU

Memphis Magazine, Memphis, Tenn.,
1976-current

Metropolitan Beaumont, Beaumont,
Tex., 1976-current

The Mississippi Educator, Jackson,
Miss., 1976-current

*Mumblepeg: The Voice of the
Bureaucrat,* Falls Church, Va.,
1976-current

Naples Now, Naples, Fla.,
1976-current

National Beauty News, Dallas, Tex.,
1976-?

*North Carolina Journal of
International Law and
Commercial Regulation,* Chapel
Hill, N.C., Spring 1976-current,
CtY-L, MnU-L, NjR, ViU-L

OEM Marine Digest, Fort
Lauderdale, Fla., 1976-?

Oil Patch, Lafayette, La.,
1976-current

Ophthalmology Times, Miami, Fla.;
New York, N.Y., 1976-?

Petroleum Production & Processing,
Houston, Tex., 1976-current

Pharmaceutical News Index,
Louisville, Ky., Jan.
1976-current, TxU, WU

Piedmont Literary Review, Danville,
Va., 1976-current

Producer News, Louisville, Ky.,
1976-current

Professional Carwashing,
Clearwater, Fla.; Latham, N.Y.,
1976-current

RV Industry, Dallas, Tex., 1976-?

Recaps, Fairfax, Springfield, Va.,
1976-current, CLU

Record of Exotics, Mountain Home,
Tex., 1976-? DLC, TxU

*Richmond Oral History Association
Journal*, Richmond, Va., 1976-?
ViRUT

*Rural Development Research and
Education*, Mississippi State,
Miss., Winter 1976-current, AAP,
DNAL, GU, NcRS, TU, ViBlbV

Sam Houston Literary Review -- See
Texas Review

Same-Day Surgery, Atlanta, Ga.,
1976-current

School Volunteer -- See *Volunteer
In Education*

Sarasota Magazine, Sarasota, Fla.,
1976-? Later as *Sarasota Town
& Country Magazine*

Sinister Wisdom, Charlotte, N.C.;
Amherst, Mass., 1976-current,
IEN, CoU, KU, NN, NcCU, WU

Solar Energy Update, Oak Ridge,
Tenn., 1976-current, DLC, KU,
InU, NjP

Solar Engineering & Contracting
-- See *Solar Engineering
Magazine*

Solar Engineering Magazine,
Dallas, Tex.; Troy, Mich., Jan.
1976-current. As *Solar
Engineering & Contracting* since
Jan. 1982, DLC, MiEM, MiU, NN,
TxU, ViBlbV

Southern Booklore, Atlanta, Ga.,
Dec. 1976-? GASU

Southwestern Entomologist, College
Station, Tex., Mar. 1976-current,
DNAL, GU, IU, NcRS, TU, TxCM,
TxU

Specialty Advertising Business,
Irving, Tex., 1976-current

Spray, Winter Park, Fla.,
1976-current. Currently as
Spray's Water Ski Magazine

Spray's Water Ski Magazine -- See
Spray

State & Local Government Review,
Athens, Ga., Jan. 1976-current.
Continues *Georgia Government
Review*, DLC, FU, MsU, NN, TxCM

Tarheel Cattleman, Raleigh, N.C.;
Macon, Ga., Jan. 1976-? DNAL,
NcRS

Tennessee Anthropologist,
Knoxville, Tenn., Spring
1976-current, ArU, GU, ICU,
LNHT, NN, NcD, T

Texas Business & Texas Parade,
Dallas, Tex., 1976-current.
Formed by merger of *Texas
Parade* and *Texas Business*.
As *Texas Business* since Nov.
1978, DLC, NN, TxArU, TxCM,
TxLT, TxU

Texas County Western Magazine,
_____, Tex., 1976-? DLC

Texas Review, Huntsville, Tex.,
1976-current. As *Sam Houston
Literary Review* until 1979,
ViBlbV

*Texas Speech and Hearing
Association Journal*, Abilene,
Tex., 1976-?   TxLT

*Texas Speech Communication
Journal*, Austin, Tex., 1976-?
DLC, TxLT

Texas Travel Guide, Dallas, Tex.,
1976-?

Timber Processing Industry,
Montgomery, Ala., 1976-current

Together -- See *Journal for
Specialists in Group Work*

TRIAD Magazine, Roanoke, Va.,
1976-?

VAST -- See *Volunteer In Education*

Van Nghe Tien Phong, Arlington,
Va., 1976-current

*Victimology; An International
Journal*, Arlington, Va., Spring
1976-current, CtY-L, DLC, MH,
NN, NcRS, NjP, ViBlbV, ViU-L

The Virginia Beachcomber,
Accomack, Va., 1976-current

Virginia Family Physician,
Richmond, Va., Jan. 1976-?
Continues *Virginia Family
Practice News* and *Virginia
General Practice News*, ViBlbV,
ViRCU-H

*Virginia Public Health Association
Journal*, Richmond, Va., 1976-?
ViU-M

Volunteer In Education,
Alexandria, Va., 1976-current.
Formerly as *School Volunteer*,
as *VAST*, and as *Volunteer Views*

Volunteer Views -- See *Volunteer
In Education*

AAR Times, Dallas, Tex.,
1977-current

AE, Airline Executive -- See
Airline Executive

Access, Tallahassee, Fla.,
Aug./Sept. 1977-Dec./Jan. 1982,
DLC, FU

*Adult Literacy and Basic
Education*, Auburn, Ala., Spring
1977-current, AAP, ArU, DLC,
NcRS, ViBlbV, ViU

Airline Executive, Atlanta, Ga.,
Oct. 1977-current. Formerly as
AE, Airline Executive, DLC

Alabama Education, Montgomery,
Ala., Sept. 1977-?   AAP, AU

*Alethia: An International Journal
of Philosophy*, Irving, Tex.,
June 1977-?   DLC, LU, MdU, NcU

*American Journal of Trial
Advocacy*, Birmingham, Ala., Fall
1977-current, CtY-L, DLC, GU-L,
NjR

American Preservation, Little
Rock, Ark., Oct. 1977-82, CtY,
DLC, MB, NN, TxU, ViBlbV, ViU

Art Happenings of Houston,
Houston, Tex., 1977-current

*Art Papers; Covering the Arts in
the Southeast* -- See
Contemporary Art-Southeast

Aventuras De Lo Sobrenatural,
Miami, Fla., 1977-?

Awards Specialist, Jacksonville,
Fla., 1977-current

Back Home in Kentucky, Bowling
Green, Ky., 1977-current

Black Heritage, Reston, Va.,
Sept./Oct. 1977-Mar./Apr. 1982.
Continues *Negro Heritage*, NN

Black Tennis Magazine, Dallas,
Tex., 1977-current

Boatmaster Magazine, Montgomery, Ala., 1977-79

Broadcast Equipment Exchange, Arlington, Va., 1977-?

The Carter Watch, Conyers, Ga., 1977-?   GU

Celestinesca; Boletin Informativo International, Athens, Ga., May 1977-current, DLC, GASU, GU, IU, NcGU, ViU

Censored, Bonita Spring, Fla., Spring/Summer 1977, DLC, TxU

The Comparatist, Martin, Tenn., 1977-?   DLC, TxU-Hu

Computer Parking, Atlanta, Ga., 1977-current

Contemporary Art-Southeast, Atlanta, Ga., Apr. 1977-current. Merged with *Atlanta Art Papers* to form *Art Papers; Covering the Arts in the Southeast*, DLC, GAT, GEU, GU, NcD, NcU, TxU, ViBlbV

Court Systems Digest, Annandale, Va., Jan. 1977-80, CtY-L, GASU

Dallas Jazz News -- See *Texas Jazz Magazine*

Data/Comm Industry Report, Annandale, Va., 1977-?

Dial, Dallas, Tex., 1977-current

EnviroSouth, Montgomery, Ala., Spring 1977-current

The Family Treebune, Dallas, Tex., 1977-current, DLC, NN

The Films of Yesterday, Clearwater, Fla., July 1977-?   DLC

Fine Dining, Miami, Fla., 1977-current

Fire & Movement, Austin, Tex., 1977-current

First World; An International Journal of Black Thought, Atlanta, Ga., Jan./Feb. 1977-? DLC, MdU, TxCM, Vi

Floral Underawl & Gazette Times, Chapel Hill, N.C., 1977-current

Florida Designers Quarterly, Miami, Fla., 1977-current

Florida Monthly, _____, Fla., 1977-?

Florida Police Informant, _____, Fla., Mar. 1977-?   DLC

Fusion Energy Update, Oak Ridge, Tenn., 1977-current, CU-A, WaU

GAMSP Journal, Athens, Ga., Spring 1977-?   GU

Genealogical Society of Okaloosa County Journal, Fort Walton Beach, Fla., Mar. 1977-current, DLC

GeoMundo, Virginia Gardens, Fla., July 1977-current, DLC, TxU

Georgia Community Banker, Atlanta, Ga., 1977-?   AAP, GU

Gospel Teacher, Sapphire, N.C., 1977-80

GRUB, Athens, Ga., Winter 1977-? AAP, GU

Gulf Coast Fisherman, Port O'Connor, Port Lavals, Tex., 1977-current. Also as *Harold Wells Gulf Coast Fisherman*

Harold Wells Gulf Coast Fisherman -- See *Gulf Coast Fisherman*

Heavy Duty Aftermarket Exchange, Longwood, Fla.; Akron, Ohio, 1977-current. Currently as *Heavyduty Marketing*

Heavyduty Marketing -- See *Heavy Duty Aftermarket Exchange*

Houston Arts Magazine, Houston,
Tex., 1977-?

Hudsoniana, Longview, Tex., Oct.
1977-current, DLC, NN

Impressions, Dallas, Tex.,
1977-current

In Houston, Houston, Tex.,
1977-Mar. 1978. Continued by
Houston City Magazine, TxHR,
TxU

*Inside Running; The Tabloid
Magazine That Runs Texas*,
Houston, Tex., 1977-current

Intersearch, El Paso, Tex., 1977-?

Journal of Humanistic Education,
Carrollton, Ga., Jan./Feb. 1977-?
CLU

*Journal of International
Relations*, Boston, Va., Spring
1977-Fall 1978. Continued by
International Security Review,
DLC, LU, MH, ViU

Journal of Research in Singing,
Denton, Tex., July 1977-current,
INS, IU, MiU, OCU

*Journal of Social Studies
Research*, Athens, Ga., Winter
1977-current, AU, ViU, WvU

*Journal of the Society of Ethnic
and Social Studies*, Burlington,
N.C., Jan. 1977-? AzU, MH-Ed,
NNC, NjR

Kentucky Cattleman, Macon, Ga.,
Oct. 1977-? KyU-ASC

*Kentucky Economy: Review and
Perspective*, Lexington, Ky.,
Dec. 1977-current, GASU, KyU,
InU, NN

Kudzu; A Poetry Magazine, Cayce,
Columbia, S.C., 1977-? DLC

LAE News, Baton Rouge, La.,
1977-current. Supersedes
Louisiana Teachers' Tabloid,
LNHT, LU

Licht des Lebens, Crockett, Ky.,
1977-current

Lithic Technology, San Antonio,
Tex., 1977-current. Continues
Newsletter of Lithic Technology,
TxU

Mature Living, Nashville, Tenn.,
1977-?

Mid-America Theological Journal,
Memphis, Tenn., 1977-? DLC

Mississippi Magazine, Edwards,
Miss., 1977-current

Morgan Migrations, Tomball, Tex.,
Jan. 1977-? NN

National Utility Contractor,
Arlington, Va., 1977-current

Nautilus Magazine, Independence,
Va., 1977-current

Off P'Tree, Atlanta, Ga., Nov.
1977-? GASU

Old Music News, Lexington, Ky.,
Nov. 1977-? KyU

PGA Magazine, Palm Beach Gardens,
Fla., Oct. 1977-current.
Continues *Professional Golfer*,
DLC

Performing Arts Magazine,
Houston, Tex., 1977-current

*Pizza Maker; The Pizza Industry's
Monthly Magazine*, Raleigh, N.C.,
1977-current

Practicing Midwife, Summertown,
Tenn., 1977-current

Public Administration Quarterly --
See *Southern Review of Public
Administration*

Purple Cow, Atlanta, Ga.,
1977–current

Quick Printing, Fort Pierce, Fla.,
1977–current

Racquetball Industry, Miami, Fla.,
Oct. 1977–current. Continued
by *Fitness Industry*, DLC

Radio World, Falls Church, Va.,
1977–current

Running Times, Woodbridge, Va.,
Jan. 1977–current, AAP, DLC,
InNd

SA, The Magazine of San Antonio,
San Antonio, Tex., Mar.
1977–June 1980, TxSaT

San Antonio Living, San Antonio,
Tex., 1977–current

*The Shelby Report of the
Southwest*, Refugio, Tex.,
1977–current

The Snowbird, Port Isabel, Tex.,
1977–?

South Atlantic Urban Studies,
Charleston, S.C., 1977–? DLC,
GU, MB, NcD, NN, ViBlbV, ViU

*South Texas Journal of Research
and the Humanities*, Brownsville,
Tex., Spring 1977–Fall 1979.
Continued by *Borderlands
Journal*, DLC, MH, NN, TxLT,
TxU

Southern Accents, Atlanta, Ga.,
1977–current, DLC, GAT, GU,
ScU, TxU, ViBlbV

*Southern Review of Public
Administration*, Montgomery,
Ala., June 1977–current.
Currently as *Public
Administration Quarterly*, CtY,
DGW, DLC, NcD, NcRS, T, ViBlbV

Southwest Journal, San Antonio,
Tex., 1977–? TxU

State Court Journal, Denver, Colo.;
Williamsburg, Va., Winter
1977–current, CtY-L, DLC, GU-L,
NjR, ViU-L

Strike; the Magazine for Bowlers,
Cocoa Beach, Fla., 1977–?

Tampa Bay Magazine, Tampa, Fla.,
1977–current. Continues *Tampa
Bay Life*. In 1982, continued
by *Tampa Bay*, FU, NN

*Tar Heel: The Magazine of North
Carolina*, Greenville, N.C., Sept.
1977–Feb. 1982. Merged into
Carolina Lifestyle, NcD, NcGU,
NcRS, NcWsW

Tennessee Judge, Nashville, Tenn.,
Aug. 1977–? T

Tennessee Legislative Digest,
Nashville, Tenn., Oct.
1977–current, T, TU

Tennessee Wildlife, Nashville,
Tenn., July/Aug. 1977–current,
CoFS, DLC

Texas Arts Journal, Dallas, Tex.,
1977–current, LNHT, MH, NN, TxU

Texas Books in Review, Dallas,
Tex., 1977–? TxArU, TxHR, TxU

Texas Child Care Quarterly,
Austin, Tex., Feb. 1977–current,
TxCM, TxLT

Texas Gardener, College Station,
Waco, Tex., 1977–current, TxCM,
TxLT

Texas Homes Magazine, Dallas,
Tex., Mar. 1977–current, DLC,
TxDaM, TxU

Texas Jazz Magazine, Dallas, Tex.,
1977–current. Formerly as
Dallas Jazz News. Currently
as *Texas Ragg*

Texas Ragg -- See *Texas Jazz
Magazine*

Texas Real Estate Research Center Quarterly, College Station, Tex., 1977-? TxLT

Tidewater Virginian, Norfolk, Va., June 1977-current. Supersedes *New Norfolk*, NN, Vi, ViU

Tierra Grande, College Station, Tex., 1977-current, TxLT

U.S. Journal of Drug & Alcohol Dependence, Hollywood, Fla., Feb. 1977-current, N, NN, TxU

Virginia Appalachian Notes, Roanoke, Va., 1977-current. Continues *Appalachian Notes*, DLC, ViBlbV

Virginia Business Education Journal, Richmond, Va., 1977-? GASU

Waterfowler's World, Memphis, Tenn., 1977-current

White Papers; The Research Aid for White, Whyte, etc. Families, Tomball, Tex., 1977-?

Advantage; The Nashville Business Magazine, Nashville, Tenn., May 1978-current, T

American Heart Quarterly, Dallas, Tex., Winter 1978-? Continues *American Heart News*, ICJ, MiDW-M, TU

American Journal of Clinical Biofeedback, Des Plaines, Ill.; Nashville, Tenn.; New York, N.Y., 1978-current, DLC, IEN-M, NNNAM

Arts Quarterly, New Orleans, La., Jan./Feb./Mar. 1978-? MdU, NjP, OO, TxDaM

Atlanta Business Chronicle, Atlanta, Ga., June 1978-current, GASU, GAT, GU

Bay Life Magazine, Tampa, Fla., 1978-?

Birding News Survey, Elizabethtown, Ky., Fall, 1978-? CoFS, KU

Blue Ridge Review, Charlottesville, Va., 1978-? RPB, ViU

Bluegrass Trucker, Pewee Valley, Ky., 1978-current

Callaloo: A Tri-Annual Black South Journal of Arts and Letters, Lexington, Ky., 1978-current, KMK, LU, MA, MU, NcU, NjP, T, ViBlbV

Central Georgia Genealogical Society Quarterly, Hartford, Ky.; Warner Robbins, Ga., 1978-current, DLC, NN

College Administrator and the Courts, Asheville, N.C., April 1978-current, ArU, DLC, ViU

Conservation Energy Update, Oak Ridge, Tenn., 1978-?

Corvette Fever Magazine, Triangle, Va., 1978-current

DFW People, Dallas, Tex., 1978-current

Dallas Civic Opera Magazine, Dallas, Tex., 1978-81. Continued by *The Dallas Opera Magazine*, DLC

Dallas-Fort Worth Home & Garden, Dallas, Tex., Oct. 1978-current, DLC

Dart News, Atlanta, Ga., 1978-current

Developing Country Courier; Concerning a New International Order and Reduction of the Development Gap, McLean, Va., 1978-current

The Editorial Eye, Alexandria, Va., 1978-current, DCU, OU, TxU

Fitness Industry Magazine, Miami, Fla., 1978-current

Florida Foliage Magazine/Digest, Apopka, Fla., 1978-current

Florida Genealogical Journal, Tampa, Fla., 1978-current. Continues *Journal, Florida Genealogical Society*. Continued by *Journal, Florida Genealogical Society*. Currently as *Florida Genealogist*, DLC, NN

Florida Genealogist -- See *Florida Genealogical Journal*

Florida Hotel & Motel News, Tallahassee, Fla., 1978-current

Florida Keys Magazine, Marathon, Fla., 1978-current, DLC

Focus on Alcohol & Drug Issues, Hollywood, Fla., 1978-current, OrU, Wa

Foliage Digest, Apopka, Fla., Feb. 1978-current, MdU, TxCM

G, Golden Triad, Greensboro, N.C., July 1978-?

G/C/T, Mobile, Ala., 1978-current, IaU, ViU

The GMU Law Review, Arlington, Va., Winter 1978-Spring 1980. Continues *ISL Law Review*. Continued by *George Mason University Law Review*, IU, MiDW-L

Golden Years, Melbourne, Fla., 1978-current

Governor's Journal, University, Ala., 1978-current

High Country Magazine, Helen, Ga., 1978-Nov./Dec. 1983. Also as *High Country Living: The Mountain Monthly*

High Country Living: The Mountain Monthly -- See *High Country Magazine*

Houston Career Digest, Houston, Tex., 1978-current

Houston City Magazine, Houston, Tex., Apr. 1978-current. Continues *In Houston*, TxHR, TxU

Houston Journal of International Law, Houston, Tex., Spring 1978-current, DLC, MH-L

Immunology Tribune, Houston, Tex., 1978-current

Impressions; The Magazine for the Imprinted Sportswear Industry, Richardson, Tex., 1978-?

The International Journal for Hybrid Microelectronics, Montgomery, Ala.; Silver Springs, Md., Jan. 1978-current, AAP, DLC

Jackson, The Mississippi Magazine, Jackson, Miss., 1978-? MsSM, NN

Journal for the Education of the Gifted, Reston, Va., Feb. 1978-? AzU, DLC, FU, NcRS, TxCM

The Journal of Clinical Psychiatry, Memphis, Tenn., Jan. 1978-current. Continues *Diseases of the Nervous System*, DLC, FU, ICJ

Journal of Crime & Justice, Jonesborough, Tenn., 1978-? DLC, IU

Journal of Developmental & Remedial Education, Boone, N.C., Spring 1978-current. Currently as *Journal of Developmental Education*, AzU, DGW, IU, MoU, ScU, VtU

Journal of Developmental Education
-- See *Journal of Developmental & Remedial Education*

The Journal of Financial Research, Lubbock, Tex., Winter 1978-?   AU, DLC, FU, IU, MoU, NcD, NcU, ViBlbV, ViU

Journal of Health and Human Resources Administration, Montgomery, Ala., Aug. 1978-current, AU, C, DLC, FU, LU, NW, NcRS, ViW

Journal of Sport Behavior, Mobile, Ala., 1978-current, AU, DLC, InU, KyLoU, MdU, NN, TxU

Journal of the Clan Campbell Society United States of America, Virginia Beach, Va., 1978-?   DLC, NN

Journal of the Division for Early Childhood, Reston, Va., 1978-?   DLC, IU, ViU

Journal of the Inter-American Foundation, Rosalyn, Va., Spring/Summer 1978-81. Continued by *Grassroots Development*, 1982, CtY, DLC, IU

Louisiana Association of Educators Journal, Baton Rouge, La., Feb. 1978-?   GU, LU

Louisiana Business, Baton Rouge, La., 1978-current. Also as *Louisiana, The State of Business*

Louisiana, The State of Business -- See *Louisiana Business*

Luz de la Vida, Crockett, Ky., 1978-current

Message, Nashville, Tenn., May/June 1978-?   Continues *Message Magazine*, DLC

Miniatures and Doll Dealer -- See *Miniatures Dealer*

Miniatures Dealer, Clifton, Va., 1978-current. Currently as *Miniatures and Doll Dealer*

Mini-Micro Computer Report, Annandale, Va., 1978-current

Mississippi College Law Review, Clinton, Miss., June 1978-current, DLC, MiDW-L, NjR, TU

Moonshine Review, Flowery Branch, Ga., 1978-?   WU

N.C. Insight, Raleigh, N.C., 1978-current, NcD, NcGU

National Energy Journal -- See *National Wood Stove & Fireplace Journal*

National Water Safety Congress Journal -- See *Water Safety Journal*

National Wood Stove & Fireplace Journal, Chesapeake, Va., 1978-current. Currently as *National Energy Journal*

Natso Trucker News, Alexandria, Va., 1978-current

Needlecraft for Today, Fort Worth, Tex., 1978-current

New Lazarus Review, Chapel Hill, N.C., 1978-?   IEN, NcU, WU

Oil & Gas Digest, Houston, Tex., 1978-current

Opiniones, Coral Gables, Fla., July 1978-current. As *Opiniones Latinoamericanas* until 1980, CtY, DLC, LNHT, NN, NcD, NcRS, ViBlbV

Opiniones Latinoamericanas -- See *Opiniones*

Paperback Quarterly, Brownwood, Tex., Spring 1978-?   MiEM, NN, TxU

Picturesque, Arlington, Va., 1978-?

Practical Law Books Review, Austin, Tex., Jan. 1978-current, DLC, NjR

Procurement Systems Digest, Annandale, Va., 1978-current

Professional Educator, Auburn, Ala., Spring 1978-current, AAP, IaU

Professional Woman, Dallas, Tex., 1978-?

Public Accounting Report, Atlanta, Ga., 1978-current

Review of Higher Education, Charlottesville, Va.; Washington, D.C., Fall 1978-current. Continues *Higher Education Review*, DLC, InU

Review of Southern Business Publications, Milledgeville, Ga., 1978-?

STTH, Melbourne, Fla., Winter 1978-current, DLC, KU, MH, NcD, NcU, TxCM, ViBlbV

Sarasota Town & County Business News, Sarasota, Fla., 1978-?

Snowbird Monthly, South Padre Island, Tex., 1978-?

Southern Changes, Atlanta, Ga., Sept. 1978-current, DLC, GASU, GU, NN, NcRS, TxU

Southern College Personnel Association Journal, Birmingham, Ala., Summer 1978-Fall 1981. Continued by *College Student Affairs Journal*, KyLoU, ViBlbV, ViU

The Southwest Virginian, Norton, Va., 1978-? DLC, NN, Vi

Spectator, Raleigh, N.C., 1978-current

Stetson Law Review, Saint Petersburg, Fla., Fall 1978-current. Continues *Stetson Intramural Law Review*, CLL, NNC-L, NjR, TU

Successful Business; the Magazine for Independent Business, Knoxville, Tenn., Winter 1978-79, IU, MH-BA, NN

Texas & Southern Quarterly Horse Journal, Fort Worth, Tex., 1978-?

The Texas Humanist, Arlington, Tex., Sept. 1978-current, NjP, TxArU, TxDaM

Texas Journal of Political Studies, Huntsville, Tex., Fall 1978-current, DLC, MH, NN, TxArU, TxU

Textile Products and Processes Sheetfed, Atlanta, Ga., Oct. 1978-current, DLC, NcRS, ViBlbV

Tidewater Life, Hampton, Va., 1978-?

Tree Talk, Jacksonville, Tex., July 1978-? DLC

Vegetarian Health Science, Tampa, Fla., 1978-current

Water Safety Journal, Burke, Va., 1978-current. Currently as *National Water Safety Congress Journal*

Water Technology, Clearwater, Fla.; Albany, N.Y., 1978-current

World Waterskiing Magazine, Winter Park, Fla., 1978-current

Alabama Genealogical Quarterly, Mobile, Ala., Jan. 1979-? AAP, AU, NN

The ALAN Review, Athens, Ga., Winter 1979-current. Continues *ALAN Newsletter*, TxU, ViBlbV, ViW

Annals of the History of Computing, Arlington, Va., July 1979-current, CPT, ScU, ViBlbV

Apparel South, Atlanta, Ga., 1979-current

Arena News; A Texas Journal of Horse Events, Austin, Tex., 1979-current

Arkansan, Little Rock, Ark., 1979-80, ArU

Arkansas Fisherman, Little Rock, Ark., 1979-?

Auditec; Advanced Auditing Technology Review, Altamonte Springs, Fla., 1979-?

Austin Arts & Leisure, Austin, Tex., May 1979-? TxU

The Best of Business, Knoxville, Tenn., Fall 1979-current, IaU, InU, ViU

Bluegrass Literary Review, Midway, Ky., 1979-current

Boats & Harbors, Crossville, Tenn., 1979-current

CRC Critical Reviews in Immunology, Boca Raton, Fla., 1979-current, AAP, DLC, IU, TxU-M

Campbell Law Review, Buies Creek, N.C., 1979-? DLC, IU, MH-L

Carolina: Inside Tar Heel Sports, Chapel Hill, N.C., 1979-?

Center for Southern Folklore Magazine, Memphis, Tenn., Spring 1979-Winter 1982. Continues *Center for Southern Folklore Newsletter*, InU, MsSM, NcD, T, ViBlbV

City Times Magazine, Knoxville, Tenn., 1979-current

Clubhouse Magazine, Sarasota, Fla., 1979-current

Continental Horseman, Weatherford, Tex., 1979-current

Critica Hispanica, Johnson City, Tenn., 1979-current, AU, CLU, DLC, KyU, ViBlbV, Vi

The Dallas Digest, Dallas, Tex., 1979-current

Dental Dealer -- See *Dental Dealer International Product News*

Dental Dealer International Product News, San Antonio, Tex., 1979-current. Also as *Dental Dealer*

Employee Health & Fitness, Atlanta, Ga., 1979-current, InU

Florida Gulf Coast Living, Tampa, Fla., 1979-current

Fort Worth Digest, Dallas, Tex., 1979-current

Georgia Pharmaceutical Journal, Atlanta, Ga., 1979-? PPP

Genealogical Gazette, Atlanta, Ga., 1979-?

Gospel Music, Nashville, Tenn., 1979-? DLC

Gothic; The Review of Supernatural Horror Fiction, Baton Rouge, La., June 1979-80, DLC, IU, PBL

Grass Roots Campaigning, Little Rock, Ark., 1979-current

Great Smokies Magazine, Gatlinburg, Tenn., 1979-?

The Houston Review: History and Culture of the Gulf Coast, Houston, Tex., Spring 1979-current, DLC, NN, NjP, TxCM, TxU

Hypertension, Dallas, Tex.,
Jan./Feb. 1979-current, DLC,
IU-M, MiU, ViBlbV

In Tech, Durham, N.C., Jan. 1979-?
Continues *Instrument
Technology*, DLC, FU, IU, MdU,
NcD, NcRS, TxU, UU

*Information World; News for the
Information Community*,
Arlington, Va., Feb. 1979-?
CLSU, MoU, PPiU, T

*Institute of Certified Financial
Planners Journal*, West Palm
Beach, Fla., Fall 1979-current,
DeU, IaU, MH-BA, NhD-BE

*The International Comet
Quarterly*, Boone, N.C., Jan.
1979-current. Supersedes *Comet
Quarterly*, MiU, ViU

*Journal for the Humanities and
Technology*, Marietta, Ga.,
1979-?   CSt, CtY, IaAS, NTR,
ScCleU

*Journal of Advanced
Transportation*, Durham, N.C.,
Spring 1979-current. Continues
*High Speed Ground
Transportation Journal*, DLC,
FU, KyU, MdU, NcD, NcU, TxU

*Journal of Educational and Social
Analysis*, Atlanta, Ga., Apr.
1979-?   CSt

*Journal of Information
Management*, Atlanta, Ga., Fall
1979-current, DLC

Journal of Southern Business --
See *South*

Journal of Virginia Education,
Richmond, Va., Sept. 1979-May
1980. Continues *Virginia
Journal of Education*.
Continued by *Virginia Journal
of Education*, MsSM, UU, Vi

Kentucky Constructor, Frankfort,
Ky., 1979-current

*Kentucky Pioneer Genealogy and
Records*, Hartford, Ky., Jan.
1979-?   NN, Vi, WM

*Latin American Music
Review/Revista De Musica
Latinoamericana*, Austin, Tex.,
1979-current

*Leisure Cooking; The Microwave
Method*, Richardson, Tex., 1979-?

The Ligand Review, Seguin, Tex.,
1979-current, IaU, TxCM, TxHMC,
ViRCU-H

Lone Star Book Review, Dallas,
Tex., June 1979-?   TxLT

Mid Cities Digest, Dallas, Tex.,
1979-?

Mississippi Libraries, Jackson,
Miss., Spring 1979-current.
Continues *Mississippi Library
News*, DLC, InU

Mississippi Outdoors, Jackson,
Miss., Nov./Dec. 1979-81.
Continues *Mississippi Game and
Fish*. Continued by *MS
Outdoors*, DLC, MoU, MsSM, NcD,
TxU

Mockingbird, Johnson City, Tenn.,
1979-?   NcD

National Tax Shelter Digest,
Dallas, Tex., July 1979-current,
DLC

Neurotoxicology, Little Rock, Ark.;
Park Forest South, Ill.,
1979-current, DGW, DLC, PPC,
ViU-H

*North Carolina Journal of Speech
Communications*, Chapel Hill,
N.C., Winter-Summer 1979.
Continues *North Carolina
Journal of Speech and Drama*,
AzU, IU, MdU, NmU, TxU

North Dallas Digest, Dallas, Tex.,
1979-?

Ocean Contractor Locator, Houston, Tex., 1979-current

Ornamentals South, Atlanta, Ga., 1979-current, GU

Palmetto Aviation, Columbia, S.C., Oct. 1979-? Continues *South Carolina Aviation News Letter*, DLC

Pandora, Murray, Ky., 1979-? Continues *Pandora, A Femzine*, CU-RiV, MiEM

Plantation Society in the Americas, New Orleans, La., Feb. 1979-current, DLC, FU, InU, LU, NcGU, ViU, ViW

Pool & Patio Life, Clearwater, Fla., 1979-current

Ports South, Beaufort, S.C., April 1979-80

The Price Family of America, Forest City, Ark., 1979-May 1980. Continued by *Prices of America*, DLC, NN

Producer Views, Louisville, Ky., 1979-current

Raleigh Journal, Raleigh, N.C., 1979

Review, Charlottesville, Va., 1979-? CtY, DLC, GU, NN, Vi, ViW

Richmond Lifestyle Magazine, Richmond, Va., Oct. 1979-? Resulting from the merger of *Richmond Magazine* and *Virginia Lifestyle Magazine*. Absorbed by *Commonwealth Magazine*, NcD, ViRCU-H

Shenandoah Valley Magazine -- See *The Virginian*

Shenandoah/Virginia Town and Country -- See *The Virginian*

Skydiving, Deltona, Fla., 1979-current

Sonshine Times, Springfield, Va., 1979-?

South, Mobile, Ala., Oct. 1979-Feb. 1980. Also as *Journal of Southern Business*, continues *South Magazine*, continued by *South Business*, GASU, NcD, NcRS, ScU, Vi

Southern Echoes, Augusta, Ga., Aug. 1979-current, DLC

The Southern Friend: Journal of the North Carolina Friends Historical Society, Greensboro, N.C., Spring 1979-current, NN, NcGU, NcWsW

Southern Partisan, McClellansville, S.C., 1979-? NcD, ViBlbV

Southern World, Hilton Head Island, S.C., Mar./Apr. 1979-May/June 1981, LU, NcRS, NcWsW, ScCleU, Vi

Southwest & Texas Water Works Journal, Temple, Tex., Oct. 1979-current. Continues *Water*, ICRL, NmLcU, TxArU

Subway, Arlington, Va., 1979-current

Tampa Bay History, Tampa, Fla., 1979-current, FMU, NIC

Texas Sports, Dallas, Tex., 1979-82

Texas Woman, Dallas, Tex., Feb. 1979-80, TxDaM, TxU

Thunder Mountain Review, Birmingham, Ala., Spring 1979-? IaU, KU, NN

Tiotis, Fort Myers, Fla., 1979-84, WU

Tyler Today, Tyler, Tex., 1979-current

Virginia Country, Middleburg, Va., 1979-current. Continues *Virginia Hunt Country*, DLC

The Virginian, Staunton, Va., 1979-current. Also as *Shenandoah/Virginia Town and Country* and as *Shenandoah Valley Magazine* until May-June 1984 issue, DLC, ViBlbV

Wealth Building, Dallas, Tex., 1979-current

Alabama Game & Fish, Marietta, Ga., 1980-current

Alabama School Boards, Montgomery, Ala., Jan. 1980-? AAP, AU

Atlanta Impressions, Atlanta, Ga., Spring 1980-Spring 1981, DLC

Austin Homes & Gardens, Austin, Tex., 1980-current

Baton Rouge Magazine, Baton Rouge, La., 1980-current

The Best of Lauderdale and the Gold Coast, Fort Lauderdale, Fla., 1980-current

Black Music Research Journal, Nashville, Tenn., 1980-? DLC, IaU, NN, NRU-Mus, NjR

Buffalo, Fayetteville, N.C., Nov. 1980-? InU, MH

Campaigns & Elections, McLean, Va., 1980-current

Complete Communication Coordination Monitor, Fort Worth, Tex., 1980-current

Confederate Historical Institute Journal, Little Rock, Ark., Winter 1980-current, ArU, MH

Corpus Christi Magazine, Corpus Christi, Tex., 1980-current, TxU

Country Magazine, Alexandria, Va., Oct. 1980-current, DLC

Criminal Justice Journal, Annandale, Va., 1980-current

Crop Dust, Bealeton, Va., Spring 1980-current, NN, WU

Dealer Communicator, Margate City, Fla., 1980-current

ETC. Magazine, McAllen, Tex., 1980-current

The Family Medicine Review, Chapel Hill, N.C., Winter 1980-? DNLM

The Fishing Tackle Retailer, Montgomery, Ala., 1980-current

The Florida B'nai B'rith Jewish News and Views, Miami, Fla., 1980-current

The Florida Specifier, Orlando, Fla., 1980-current

Focus on Latin America, Miami, Fla., Apr. 1980-? CSt-H, IU

For Your Eyes Only, Amarillo, Tex., 1980-current

Four Winds, Austin, Tex., 1980-? DLC, MH, OkU, TxU, WHi

Game Merchandising, Clifton, Va., 1980-?

Geojourney, Tallahassee, Fla., Aug. 1980-? Supersedes *Florida Conservation News*, CoFS, IU

George Mason University Law Review, Arlington, Va., Spring 1980-current. Continues *GMU Law Review*, MiDW-L, NjR

Georgia Journal of Accounting, Athens, Ga., Spring 1980-? DLC, GASU, GEU, NcD, ScU, TxU, ViBlbV, Vi

Gerontology & Geriatrics Education, Austin, Tex.; New York, N.Y., 1980-current

Inner View, Houston, Tex., 1980-current

The International Journal of Orofacial Myology, Nacogdoches, Tex., July 1980-? Continues *International Journal of Oral Myology*, CLSU, DNLM, TU-M, UU

The Jewish Floridian of Pinellas County St. Petersburg, Miami, Fla., 1980-current

Journal of Advanced Composition, Memphis, Tenn., 1980-? IaU, TxU

Journal of American Romanian Christian Literary Studies, Buies Creek, N.C., 1980-? DLC

Journal of Biological Photography, Durham, N.C., Jan. 1980-current. Continues *Journal of the Biological Photographic Association*, AzU, CtU, DLC, LU, N, NjP, TxCM

Journal of Caribbean Studies, Coral Gables, Fla., Winter 1980-current, CLU, DLC, IU, LU, NNC, NjP

Journal of Health Care Marketing, Boone, N.C., Winter 1980/81-? AU, DGW, IU, OCU, ViU

Journal of International Student Personnel, Normal, Ala., Fall 1980-? DLC, ICarbS

Journal of Labor Research, Fairfax, Va., Spring 1980-current, CLSU, CtY-L, DLC, FU, LU, NN, NcD, TxU, ViBlbV, ViU

Journal of Offender Counseling, Falls Church, Va., Nov. 1980-current, DLC

Journal of the Conductors' Guild, Vienna, Va., Winter 1980-current, CLU, DLC

Journal of the Virginia College Reading Educators, Williamsburg, Va., 1980-? ViBlbV, ViU

Keys to Early Childhood Education, Arlington, Va., 1980-Dec. 1981

Life Line Magazine, Orlando, Fla., 1980-?

Louisiana-Camera Ready, Baton Rouge, La., 1980-? Supersedes *Louisiana*

Medical Hypnoanalysis, Memphis, Tenn., Winter 1980-? DLC, MBCo

Memphis State Review, Memphis, Tenn., Fall 1980-current. Continues *Phoenix*, DLC

Miami Business Journal, Miami, Fla., 1980-current

Miami Mensual, Coral Gables, Fla., Dec. 1980/Jan. 1981-current, DLC

Mississippi Geology, Jackson, Miss., Sept. 1980-current, DLC, FU, IU, InU, MiEM, MsSM, NcRS, TxU, ViBlbV

New Orleans City Business, Metairie, La., 1980-current

Northwest Houston Business News, Houston, Tex., 1980-current

Ohio Builder, Frankfort, Ky., 1980-current

On Balance, Austin, Tex., May 1980-? TxU

Organized Crime Digest, Annandale, Va., 1980-current

Our Heritage, Wills Point, Tex., June 1980-current, DLC

The Prices of America, Forest City, Ark., June 1980-? DLC

Radio World International, Arlington, Va., 1980-?

Right Wing, Alexandria, Va., 1980-?

The Search; Journal for Arab-Islamic Studies, Miami, Fla., Winter 1980-current, DLC, FMU, MH

Sign Craft, Fort Myers, Fla., 1980-current

South Business, Tampa, Fla., Mar. 1980-current. Continues *South*, DLC, NN, NcD, NcRS, ScU, Vi

Southeastern Contractor, Darlington, S.C., 1980-current

Southern Exchange, Chapel Hill, N.C., 1980-?

Southern Garment Manufacturer, Atlanta, Ga., Feb.-Apr. 1980. Continued by *Southern Garment*, NN, ViBlbV

Southern Garment, Atlanta, Ga., May 1980-Dec. 1981. Continues *Southern Garment Manufacturer*, AAP, GASU, NcU, ViBlbV

Southwest Woman, San Antonio, Tex., 1980-?

Sports and the Courts, Winston-Salem, N.C., Winter 1980-? CLSU, DLC, InU, TxLT

Tampa Magazine, Tampa, Fla., 1980-?

Technology Watch; For the Graphic Arts and Information Industries, Springfield, Va., 1980-current

Tennessee Professional Builder, Frankfort, Ky., 1980-current

Tennessee Sportsman, Marietta, Ga., 1980-current

The Tentmaker's Journal, Lexington, Ky., 1980-current

Texas DO, Fort Worth, Tex., Aug. 1980-current. Continues *Texas Osteopathic Physicians Journal*, MBCo, MiEM, TxArU, TxCM, TxU

Texas Family Journal, Houston, Tex., 1980-? DLC

Texas Talk, Houston, Tex., 1980-? AzU, TxU

Tropical Retirement Magazine, Fort Lauderdale, Fla., 1980-?

Videodisc News, Arlington, Va., 1980-current

The Virginia Journal of Communication, Harrisonburg, Va., 1980-current

Xavier Review, New Orleans, La., 1980-current

American Journal of Kidney Diseases, Orlando, Fla., 1981-current

Auditing, Sarasota, Fla., Summer 1981-? DLC, FU, IU, NcRS, ViU

Austin Business Journal, Austin, Tex., Feb. 1981-? TxU

Auto Racing Magazine, Delray Beach, Fla., 1981-current

Beaux Arts, Louisville, Ky., Spring 1981-current, InU

Biotechnology Stocks, Fort Lauderdale, Fla., 1981-?

Braniff Flying Colors, Miami, Fla., 1981-current

Business, North Carolina, Charlotte, N.C., Oct. 1981-current, NcD, NcRS

Butler Skylite, Miami, Fla., 1981-current

CPA Marketing Report, Atlanta, Ga., 1981-current

Carolina Game and Fish, Marietta, Ga., 1981-?

The Carpenter and Related Family Historical Journal, Greer, Ky., Jan.-Mar. 1981-current. Continues *Carpenter and Related Family Paper*, DLC, NN

Cellular Radio News, Fairfax, Va., 1981-current

Church Music World, Grapevine, Tex., 1981-current

Communicator, Arlington, Va., Sept. 1981-?   Continues *NAESP Communicator*, IU, KyU, NjR, WvU

Connections Magazine, Palm City, Fla., 1981-current

Consulting Opportunities Journal, Leesburg, Va., 1981-current

Cumberland Poetry Review, Nashville, Tenn., Winter 1981-current, CtY, DLC, MH, WU

The Dallas Opera Magazine, Dallas, Tex., 1981-?   DLC

Drug Law Reporter, Houston, Tex., Aug. 1981-?   DLC

Educational and Psychological Research, Hattiesburg, Miss., Winter 1981-?   Continues *Southern Journal of Educational Research*, DLC, IU, LNU, MoU, MsSM, ViU

Electronic Education, Tallahassee, Fla., 1981-current

FFL Business News, Fort Lauderdale, Fla., 1981-current

Florida Racquet Journal, Jacksonville, Fla., 1981-?

Foodpeople, Atlanta, Ga., 1981-current

Genealogical Computing, Fairfax, Va., July 1981-current, NN, WM

Golden Age Living, Fort Lauderdale, Fla., 1981-current

Handmade, Asheville, N.C., 1981-current

Here to There, Port Richey, Fla., 1981-?

Independent Professional, Gainesville, Fla., 1981-current

Ink, Inc. Dallas, Tex., 1981-82

International Banjo, Kissimmee, Fla., 1981-current

It's Me, Fort Worth, Tex., 1981-current

Jack London Echoes, Chester, S.C., 1981-current, AzU, ULA

The Journal of Agent and Management Selection and Development, Dallas, Tex., Mar. 1981-?   DLC

Journal of Cash Management, Atlanta, Ga., Sept. 1981-current, DLC, MH-BA

The Journal of Computers in Mathematics and Science Teaching, Austin, Tex., Fall 1981-current, CLSU, DLC, LU, MH-Ed, MNS

Journal of Physical Education, Recreation & Dance, Reston, Va., May 1981-current. Continues *Journal of Physical Education and Recreation*, absorbed *Dance Dynamics*, DLC, IU, IaU, KyU, MdU, NcD, NcU, TxU, ViBlbV, ViU

Journal of Teaching in Physical Education, Blacksburg, Va., Fall 1981-?   DLC, InU, KyU, TxU, ViBlbV

Journal of the North Carolina Political Science Association, Boone, N.C., 1981-?   DLC

Journal of Urban Affairs,
Blacksburg, Va., Fall 1981-?
Formed by union of *Union
Interest* and *Urban Affairs
Papers*, CLU, InU, TxU, ViBlbV

*Journal of the World Mariculture
Society*, Baton Rouge, La.,
1981-?   Continues *World
Mariculture Society,
Proceedings*, CU-SB, OrCS, ScU

Louisiana Life, New Orleans, La.,
1981-current

Mainstream, Jackson, Miss., Spring
1981-current

Mid-South Business Journal,
Memphis, Tenn., Jan.
1981-current.   Supersedes
*Mid-South Quarterly Business
Review*, formerly *Memphis State
Business Review*, DLC, LU, NN,
NjR

Natchez Trace Traveler, Florence,
Ala., 1981-current, DLC, NN

Needle & Thread, Fort Worth, Tex.,
1981-current

Negative Capability, Mobile, Ala.,
July 1981-current, AAP, LNHT,
LU, NhD

New Florida, Tequesta, Jupiter,
Fla., July 1981-82, DLC

Ocean Realm, North Miami Beach,
Fla., Winter 1981-?   DLC

Palmetto, Winter Park, Fla.,
1981-current

Personal Selling Power,
Fredericksburg, Va.,
1981-current

Pest Management, Vienna, Va.,
1981-current

Pockets, Nashville, Tenn.,
1981-current

Post Script, Jacksonville, Fla.,
Fall 1981-current, CLSU, DLC,
LU, NIC

*PRO/VCOMM, The Professional
Communicator*, Austin, Tex.,
1981-current

*Production & Inventory Management
Review & APICS News*, Hollywood,
Fla., Jan. 1981-current, DLC,
GASU, MH-BA, NcRS, NcU, TxU

RDH, Waco, Tex., 1981-current,
ArU-M, InU, MiU, ViRCU-H

The Rainbow, Prospect, Ky.,
1981-current

Real Estate Humor of the World,
Houston, Tex., 1981-82

Research Perspectives, Raleigh,
N.C., Fall 1981-current.
Continues *Research and
Farming*, DLC, NIC, NcRS, TxCM

The Robotics Report, Annandale,
Va., 1981-current

The Roofer Magazine, Fort Myers,
Fla., Sept. 1981-current, DLC

San Antonio Monthly, San Antonio,
Tex., Oct. 1981-?

*The Second Century; A Journal of
Early Christian Studies*,
Abilene, Tex., Spring
1981-current, InU, MoU, PU, ViW

Seminars in Nephrology, Orlando,
Fla., 1981-current

South Atlantic Review, University,
Ala., Jan. 1981-current.
Continues *SAB, South Atlantic
Bulletin*, AU, CtY, DLC, KyU,
MoU, NcD, ScU, TU, ViBlbV, ViU

South Florida Living, Dade City,
Daytona Beach, Fla.,
1981-current

Southeastern Economic Insight, Atlanta, Ga., July 15, 1981-? InU, GASU, GEU, TxU

Sporting Classics, Camden, S.C., 1981-current

State Budget & Tax News, Arlington, Va., 1981-current

The Straight Line, Mississippi State, Miss., 1981-? MH-SD, MsSM

TSTA Advocate, Austin, Tex., 1981-current

Tampa Bay Business, Tampa, Fla., 1981-current

Third Coast: The Magazine of Contemporary Austin, Austin, Tex., 1981-current, TxU

Thurgood Marshall Law Review, Houston, Tex., Fall 1981-current. Continues *Texas Southern University Law Review*, CtY-L, IU, NIC, PU-L

Trade-A-Computer, North Miami Beach, Fla., 1981-?

Ultra Magazine, Houston, Tex., Sept. 1981-current, DLC, TxU

Virginia Contractor, Virginia Beach, Va., 1981-current

Wetlands: The Journal of the Society of the Wetlands Scientists, Wilmington, N.C., Sept. 1981-? DLC, NcRS

Windrider, Winter Park, Fla., 1981-current

Alabama Administration Monthly, Montgomery, Ala., Oct. 1982-? DLC

Amateur Golf Register, Hollywood, Fla., 1982-current

Attorneys Computer Report, Atlanta, Ga., 1982-current

Attorneys Marketing Report, Atlanta, Ga., 1982-current

Black New Orleans, New Orleans, La., 1982-current

The Blade Magazine, Chattanooga, Tenn., June 1982-current. Continues *American Blade*, DLC

Blue Chip Economic Worldscan, Arlington, Va., 1982-current

Blue Chip Financial Forecasts, Arlington, Va., 1982-current

Business Access Quarterly, Knoxville, Tenn., Spring-Fall 1982. Continued by *Top Line*, Winter 1983, DLC

Carolina Lifestyle, Norfolk, Va., Apr. 1982-Sept. 1983. The result of the merger of *Tar Heel* and *Sandlapper*, NcD, NcGU, NcRS, NcU, ScU

CPA Computer Report, Atlanta, Ga., 1982-current

CPA Personnel Report, Atlanta, Ga., 1982-current

Clinical Prosthetics & Orthotics, Alexandria, Va., Spring 1982-current. Continues *Newsletter, Prosthetics and Orthotics Clinic*, DNLM

Coastal Plains Farmer, Raleigh, N.C., 1982-current

Computer Crime Digest, Annandale, Va., 1982-current

Computerized Manufacturing, Conroe, Tex., 1982-current

Craftrends Magazine, Norcross, Ga., 1982-current

Dallasfed Energy Highlights, Dallas, Tex., 1982-? GASU, N, NcU, TxU

Educational Micro Review, Austin, Tex., Sept. 1982-? DLC

Engineers' Forum, Blacksburg, Va., 1982-current, ViBlbV

Florida Agricultural Research Gainesville, Fla., Fall 1982-current. Supersedes *Sunshine State Agricultural Research Report*, IU, KyU-ASC, NcRS, TU, TxCM

Fossils Quarterly, Charlotte, N.C., Spring 1982-? DLC

Free Lance Writer's Report, Port Saint Lucie, Fla., 1982-?

Fundamentalist Journal, Lynchburg, Va., Sept. 1982-? CLU, DLC

G. The Magazine of Gainesville, Gainesville, Fla., 1982-current

Garden Design, Louisville, Ky.; Washington, D.C., Spring 1982-current, MH-SD

Goodlife Magazine, Houston, Tex., 1982-current

Greenhouse Manager, Fort Worth, Tex., 1982-current

Greensboro Substitute, Greensboro, N.C., 1982-current

Hospital Admitting Monthly, Atlanta, Ga., July 1982-current, DNLM

Indian Nations of the Eastern United States, Maxton, N.C., 1982-?

Innovation: The Journal of the Industrial Designers Society of America, McLean, Va., Jan. 1982-? DLC, GAT, MiU

Interiorscope, Tampa, Fla., Jan./Feb. 1982-current, MH-SD, NcRS, ScCleU

Island Life, Sanibel, Fla., 1982-current

Journal of Accounting Literature, Gainesville, Fla., Spring 1982-? DLC, MH-BA, MoU, NcU, TxArU

Journal of Applied Gerontology, Tampa, Fla., June 1982-? DLC

The Journal of Cranio-Mandibular Practice, Chattanooga, Tenn., Dec. 1982-current, DNLM

Journal of Insurance Regulation, Tallahassee, Fla., Sept. 1982-? DLC

Kershner Kinfolk, Charlotte, N.C., Jan.-Mar. 1982-current, DLC

The Lawyer's Microcomputer, Lexington, S.C., 1982-current

Lone Star: A Magazine of Humor, San Antonio, Tex., 1982-?

Louisiana Industry Review, New Orleans, La., 1982-?

Medscope, Alexandria, Va., 1982-?

National Journal of Medicine & Medical Research, Altamonte Springs, Fla., 1982-? DNLM

New Business, Lafayette, La., 1982-current

Nuclear Fuel Cycle, Oak Ridge, Tenn., 1982-current

Oak Leaves, Bay City, Tex., Feb. 1982-current, DLC

Operations Management Review, Austin, Tex., Fall 1982-? DLC

Our Age, Arlington, Va., 1982-current

Parkway, Dallas, Tex., 1982-83?

Persons, Hattiesburg, Miss., Jan. 1982-84. Superseded by *Mississippi Arts and Letters*

*Propellants, Explosives,
Pyrotechnics*, Deerfield Beach,
Fla.; Weinheim, W. Germany, Feb.
1982-current.   Continues
Propellants and Explosives,
DLC, NN, TxCM

Public Fund Digest, Arlington, Va.,
1982-?   DLC

Rhetoric Review, Dallas, Tex., Sept.
1982-?   DLC, NhD, TxArU, TxDaM

Sea Shelters, Kill Devil Hills,
N.C., 1982-current

Seminars in Anesthesia, Orlando,
Fla., 1982-current

Southeastern Archaeology,
Gainesville, Fla., Summer 1982-?
MH-P

The Southside Virginian, Richmond,
Va., Oct. 1982-current, DLC

Stonepebbles, Jackson, Tenn.,
1982-?

Tennessee Business, Nashville,
Tenn., 1982-current

Texas Banker/Southwest Banker,
Tyler, Tex., 1982-current

Texas Lawyers' Civil Digest,
Austin, Tex., Jan. 4, 1982-?
Continues *Texas Lawyers'
Weekly Digest*, DLC, TxU

Virginia Historical Abstracts,
Orange, Va., Jan.-June 1982-?
DLC

Washington Business Journal,
McLean, Va., 1982-current

AES News, Greensboro, N.C., Spring
1983-?

Air Cargo World, Atlanta, Ga.,
Jan. 1983-current.   Continues
Air Cargo Magazine, DLC, MH-BA

Air Defense Artillery, Bliss, Tex.,
Winter 1983-?   Continues *Air
Defense Magazine*, DLC, ULA

American Malacological Bulletin,
Hattiesburg, Miss., July 1983-?
Continues *Bulletin of the
American Malacological Union*,
DLC, ViBlbV

Buildings Design Journal, Atlanta,
Ga., 1983-current

*Business View of Southwest
Florida*, Naples, Fla.,
1983-current

Cloverview, Blacksburg, Va.,
1983-current, ViBlbV

Crime Victims Digest, Annandale,
Va., 1983-current

Dinero, Miami, Fla., 1983-?

Fantasy Gamer, Austin, Tex.,
1983-current

Florida Leader, Gainesville, Fla.,
1983-current

Genealogy Today, Atlanta, Ga.,
Jan. 1, 1983-current, DLC, WM

HP Chronicle, Austin, Tex.,
1983-current

*Huckleberry: Magazine for the
New River Valley*,
Christiansburg, Va., Dec.
1983-current

Journal of Agribusiness, Athens,
Ga., Feb. 1983-?   DLC

Journal of Defense & Diplomacy,
McLean, Va., 1983-current

*The Journal of Equipment Lease
Financing*, Arlington, Va.,
Spring 1983-?   DLC

*The Journal of Health
Administration Education*,
Arlington, Va., Winter
1983-current, DLC

The Journalist, Columbia, S.C.,
1983-? ScU

Kentucky Trucker, Frankfort, Ky.,
1983-current

The Lawyer's PC, Lexington, S.C.,
1983-current

The Management of World Wastes,
Atlanta, Ga., Mar. 1983-current.
Continues *Solid Wastes
Management*, DLC

*Ministries: The Magazine for
Christian Leader*, Altamonte
Springs, Fla., 1983-current

Mississippi Armchair Researcher,
Hampton, Ga., Fall 1983-? DLC

New Business, Sarasota, Fla.,
1983-current

Office Guide to Miami, Miami, Fla.,
1983-current

The Opera Quarterly, Chapel Hill,
N.C., Spring 1983-current, DLC,
TxU, WaU

PCM, Prospect, Ky., 1983-current

Personal Communications Magazine,
Fairfax, Va., 1983-current

Physician Computing Monthly,
Atlanta, Ga., 1983-current

Pipe Smoker, Chattanooga, Tenn.,
1983-current

*Professional Psychology, Research
and Practice*, Arlington, Va.,
Feb. 1983-current. Continues
Professional Psychology, CtW,
DLC, NcD, NcU, TxU

Recreation News, Arlington, Va.,
1983-current

Resort Real Estate, Greensboro,
N.C., Spring 1983-?

Robotics World, Atlanta, Ga., Jan.
1983-current, DLC, MH-BA

SMR News, Fairfax, Va.,
1983-current

Selling Direct, Atlanta, Ga., Mar.
1983-current. Continues
*Specialty Salesman & Business
Opportunities*, DLC

Seminars in Urology, Orlando, Fla.,
1983-current

Shooting Sports Retailer,
Montgomery, Ala., 1983-current

*Spectrum: Journal of School
Research and Information*,
Arlington, Va., Spring 1983-?
DLC, ICU

Sun Belt Executive Magazine, New
Orleans, La., Jan. 1983-?

TV Technology, Falls Church, Va.,
1983-current

The Taylor Quarterly, Falls
Church, Va., Winter
1983-current, DLC

Texas Brangus, College Station,
Tex., 1983-current

Tom Mann's Junior Fisherman,
Eufaula, Ala., 1983-current

Torch Romances, McLean, Va.,
1983-current

Virginia Extension, Blacksburg,
Va., 1983-current, ViBlbV

Badger Builder, Frankfort, Ky.,
1984-current

Braniff, North Miami, Fla.,
1984-current

Builder Review, Frankfort, Ky.,
1984-current

Car Care News, Houston, Tex.,
1984-current

Clue, Richmond, Va., 1984-current

International Business Monthly Magazine, Houston, Tex., 1984-current

Mississippi Arts and Letters, Hattiesburg, Miss., 1984-current. Supersedes *Persons*

Paper Industry Equipment, Montgomery, Ala., 1984-current

Prestige, Lynchburg, Va., 1984-?

Pro Education ... the Magazine About Partnership With Education, Saint Petersburg, Fla., 1984-current

San Antonio Homes & Gardens, Austin, Tex., 1984-current

San Antonio Today, San Antonio, Tex., 1984-current

Soft Sector, Prospect, Ky., 1984-current

South Carolina Tennis, Hilton Head Island, S.C., 1984-current

South Florida Home & Garden, Miami, Fla., Oct. 1984-current

Stenciling Quarterly, Norcross, Ga., 1984-current

Wang Solutions, Vero Beach, Fla., 1984-current

Appendix A: Alphabetical List of Periodical Titles

K

V

Appendix B: List of Periodicals, Arranged by State

A

Alabama
1823
    Western Arminian 23
1825
    Christian Advocate 23
1833
    Flag of the Union 27
    Southern Evangelist 27
1835
    Alabama Baptist 28
1836
    Bachelor's Button 29
1837
    Mobile Monitor 30
1838
    Family Visitor 30
    Loafer's Journal 30
1839
    Mobile Literary Gazette 31
    Southron 31
1840
    Gallinipper 32
    Loco-Foco 32
    Southern Crisis 32
1842
    Messenger of Glad Tidings 34
1843
    Alabama Temperance 34
    Southern Educational Journal 35
1844
    Democratic Mentor 35
    Dollar Whig 35
    Harry of the West 35
1845
    Gospel Messenger 36
1846
    Alabama Planter 37
1848
    Old Zack 39
1849
    Alabama Baptist Advocate 39
    Crystal Fount 39
    Orion 40
    Social Messenger 40
    Universalist Herald 40
1850
    Southern Star 41
    Southwestern Baptist 41
1851

Southern Parlor Magazine 43
Spirit of the South 43
Sunny South 43
1852
    Southern Magazine 44
1853
    American Cotton Planter 44
1854
    Southern Military Gazette 45
    Southern Statesman 45
1855
    American Citizen 46
    Southern Times, A literary weekly 46
    Temperance Times 46
    Young America 47
1856
    Southern College Magazine 47
1857
    Alabama Educational Journal. Devoted to the Cause of Human Progress, Education, Science, . . . 48
    Educational Journal 48
    Southern Dial. A monthly magazine devoted mainly to a discussion of African slavery and the . . . 48
1858
    Howard College Magazine 48
1859
    Southern Teacher 50
1860
    Baptist Correspondent 50
    Southern Rural Magazine 51
    Young Lady's Mirror 51
1861
    Southern Visitor 52
1862
    Gulf City Home Journal 52
1863
    Confederate Spirit and Knapsack of Fun 52
1864
    Army and Navy Crisis 53
    Southern Observer 53
1865
    Christian Herald 53
    Jewell 53
    Literary Index 53
1866

M

Maryland
1792

1827
   *North American, or, Weekly
   Journal of Politics, Science
   and Literature* 24
1828
   Columbia Register 24
   *Emerald and Baltimore
   Literary Gazette* 24
   *Itinerant, or, Wesleyan
   Methodist Visitor* 24
1829
   *American Turf Register and
   Sporting Magazine* 25
   *Maryland Medical Recorder,
   Devoted to Medical Science
   in General* 25
   Minerva 25
1830
   *Baltimore Monthly Journal of
   Medicine and Surgery* 25
   *Metropolitan, or, Catholic
   Monthly Magazine* 25
   *Mt. Hope Literary
   Gazette* 25
   *National Magazine, or,
   Lady's Emporium* 26
   *Young Ladies' Journal of
   Literature and Science* 26
1831
   *Baltimore Southern Pioneer
   and Richmond Gospel
   Visiter* 26
   *Lutheran Observer and
   Weekly Religious Visitor* 26
   Methodist Protestant 26
1832
   Saturday Visitor 27
1833
   *Baltimore Medical and
   Surgical Journal and
   Review* 27
   Episcopal Methodist 27
1834
   Baltimore Athenaeum 27
   *Farmer and Gardener and
   Live Stock Breeder and
   Manager* 28
   *Lutheran Observer and
   Weekly Literary Religious
   Visitor* 28
   *Magazine of Gardening and
   Botany* 28
   *North American Archives of
   Medical and Surgical
   Science* 28
1835

*Baltimore Literary and
   Religious Magazine* 28
*Maryland Colonization
   Journal* 28
1836
   Christian Review 29
   *Covenant. A Monthly magazine
   devoted to the cause of
   Odd-Fellowship* 29
   *Universalist Circulating
   Family Library* 29
1838
   *American Museum of
   Literature and the Arts* 30
   *Annals of the Propagation
   of the Faith* 30
   *Baltimore Literary
   Monument* 30
   *Baltimore Monument. A Weekly
   Journal, Devoted to Polite
   Literature, Science, and the
   Fine Arts* 30
1839
   *American Journal of Dental
   Science* 31
   American Silk Society 31
   *Journal of American Silk
   Society and Rural
   Economist* 31
   *Maryland Medical and
   Surgical Journal, and
   Official Organ of the
   Medical Department of the
   Army and . . .* 31
1840
   *Farmer's Book; or, Western
   Maryland Farmer* 32
   Weekly Pilot 32
1841
   *Guardian of Health. A
   Monthly Journal of Domestic
   Hygiene* 32
1842
   Baltimore Monthly Visitor 33
   *Baltimore Phoenix and
   Budget* 33
   *Spirit of the XIX
   Century* 34
   *United States Catholic
   Magazine* 34
1843
   *Fackel. Literaturblatt zur
   Forderung Geistiger
   Freiheit* 35
1844
   *Reformer and People's
   Advocate* 36

*A.M.E. Zion Church
   Quarterly* 73
Asheville Medical Review 73
Southland 74
1891
   *North Carolina Journal of
   Education* 75
1892
   *Southern Medicine and
   Surgery* 76
1893
   Textile Manufacturer 77
   Wachovia Moravian 77
1894
   Desmos 78
   *Methodist Protestant
   Herald* 78
1895
   Coraddi 79
   St. Augustine's Record 80
1896
   *North Carolina White
   Ribbon* 81
1897
   Church Worker 81
   *North Carolina Home
   Journal* 82
   *Southland. A Journal of
   Patriotism. Devoted to
   History and the Cause of
   Confederate Veterans.* 82
1898
   Bryoloist 83
   Educator 83
   *North Carolina Journal of
   Education* 83
1899
   Cotton Mill News 84
   Journal of Tuberculosis 85
   Presbyterian 85
   Southern Medical Journal 85
1900
   *James Sprunt Studies in
   History and Political
   Science* 86
   *North Carolina Historical
   and Genealogical
   Register* 86
   *North Carolina Law
   Journal* 86
1901
   Furniture Merchandising 87
   *North Carolina Booklet.
   Great Events in North
   Carolina History.* 87

*Southern Furniture Journal;
   the Journal of the Southern
   Furniture Interests* 87
1902
   Harbinger 88
   South Atlantic Quarterly 88
1903
   *Southern Mills, a Monthly
   Devoted to the Industries
   of the South* 89
1904
   *American Cotton
   Manufacturer; Cotton and
   Cotton Textiles* 90
   *Merchants' Journal and
   Commerce* 90
   *North Carolina Journal of
   Law* 90
   *Southern Engineer, A
   Practical Southern Journal
   Devoted to the Operation of
   Steam, Electrical, Gas
   . . .* 91
1905
   Carolinas 92
1906
   *North Carolina Education; A
   Monthly Journal of
   Education, Rural Progress
   and Civic Betterment* 93
   Studies in Philology 94
1908
   Carolina Union Farmer 95
   Florida Grower 96
1909
   Carolina Churchman 97
   Down Homer 97
   North Carolina Review 97
1910
   *North Carolina
   Churchman* 99
   *North Carolina High School
   Bulletin* 99
   *Southern Good Roads. A
   monthly magazine devoted to
   highway and street
   improvement* 99
1911
   *Southern Textile
   Bulletin* 100
   Star and Lamp 100
1912
   Alumni Review 100
   Ensign 100
1913
   *Carolina and the Southern
   Cross* 101

*English, French, Spanish,
Italian, and German
. . .* 35
Rambler 35
*Southern Baptist
Advocate* 35
1844
*Carolina Planter. A Monthly
Register for the State and
Local Societies* 35
Farmers' Gazette 35
*Floral Wreath and Ladies
Monthly Magazine* 35
Polyglot 36
1845
Carolina Baptist 36
*Southern and Western
Monthly Magazine and
Review* 36
1846
*Charleston Medical Journal
and Review* 37
*Palmetto: A Temperance
Journal* 37
1847
Camden Miscellany 37
*Southern Harmony and
Musical Companion* 38
Southern Presbyterian 38
1848
*Journal of the South
Carolina Medical
Association* 39
*Southern Literary Gazette.
An illustrated weekly
journal of belles-lettres,
science, and the arts* 39
1849
*Schoolfellow: A Magazine for
Girls and Boys* 40
*Southern and Western
Masonic Miscellany* 40
1850
*Farmer and Planter
Monthly* 41
*Southern Eclectic
Magazine* 41
Sunday School Visitor 42
*Whitaker's Magazine: The
Rights of the South* 42
1851
Southern Home Journal 43
Southern Standard 43
1852
*Illustrated Family
Friend* 43

*Weekly News and Southern
Literary Gazette* 44
1853
People's Medical Gazette 44
*Self Instructor. A Monthly
Journal, Devoted to
Southern Education, and to
the Diffusion of a . . .* 44
1854
*College of Charleston
Magazine* 45
Southern Episcopalian 45
1855
*South Carolina Historical
and Genealogical
Magazine* 46
1856
Home Journal 47
*South Carolina
Agriculturist* 47
Southern Light 47
1857
*Journal of the Elliot Society
of Natural History* 48
Russell's Magazine 48
1858
*Erskine Collegiate
Recorder* 48
1859
*Courant. A Southern
Literary Journal* 49
Philidorian 50
1860
*Southern Insurance
Journal* 51
1861
*Portfolio: Devoted to Truth,
Virtue and Temperance* 52
Southern Lutheran 52
1862
New South 52
1864
Swamp Angel 53
1866
*Baptist Church and Sunday
School Messenger* 54
1867
*Our Monthly . . .A Monthly
Magazine of Christian
Thought and Work for the
Lord* 55
1868
Farm and Garden 56
Missionary 56
1869
Baptist Courier 56
Nineteenth Century 57

v

*Parks and Recreation; A
Journal of Park and
Recreation Management* 89
*Virginia Farm Journal, An
Illustrated Magazine for
Progressive Virginia
Farmers* 90
1904
*American Fruit and Nut
Journal* 90
Army 90
*Merchants' Journal and
Commerce* 90
1905
*National Shorthand
Reporter* 92
R-MWC Alumnae Bulletin 92
1906
Dollar Mark 93
Southern Magazine 94
Stained Glass 94
Virginia Masonic Herald 94
1907
*Horizon: A Journal of the
Color Line* 94
Musical Advance 94
*Virginia Journal of
Education* 95
1908
Mathematics Teacher 96
*Presbyterian of the
South* 96
*Southern Advertising
Journal* 96
Virginia Magazine 96
1909
American Motorist 97
*Jewish Record. A Weekly
Magazine for Jewish
Interests* 97
Presbyterian Outlook 97
Southwest Monthly 98
Virginia Farm Journal 98
1911
Presbyterian Survey 100
Southern Missioner 100
1912
Terrazzo Topics 101
*Virginia Federation of Labor
Journal* 101
1913
*University of Virginia
Alumni News* 102
*Virginia Folk-Lore Society
Bulletin* 102
Virginia Law Review 102

*Virginia State Horticultural
Society. Virginia Fruit* 102
1914
*Federal Reserve Bank of
Richmond Economic
Review* 102
*Music Educator's
Journal* 103
1915
American Fruit Grower 103
*Journal of the Association
of Official Analytical
Chemists* 104
*Quarterly Journal of
Speech* 104
*Richmond College Historical
Papers* 104
SI-DE-KA Magazine 104
*Virginia Education
Association Quarterly* 105
*Virginia State Teachers
Quarterly* 105
1916
Marine Corps Gazette 105
Virginia Pharmacist 106
1917
Automotive Executive 106
Cars & Trucks 107
Leatherneck Magazine 107
Mental Hygiene 107
NASSP Bulletin 107
1918
Appalachian Appeal 108
Extension News 108
*Head, Heart, Hands and
Health* 108
*Journal of the Patent Office
Society* 108
Virginia PTA Bulletin 108
1919
*American Gas Association
Monthly* 108
Military Engineer 109
*Southland Journal; In the
Interest of Farms, Schools
and Roads* 110
*Tyler's Quarterly Historical
and Genealogical
Magazine* 110
*Virginia Publisher and
Printer* 110
1920
Virginia Teacher 112
Virginia Wildlife 112
1921
*American Logistics
Association Review; Magazine*

About the Compiler

SAM G. RILEY is Professor of Communication Studies at Virginia Polytechnic Institute and State University. He specializes in mass media history and has written extensively on a variety of academic and popular subjects. His articles have appeared in *Journalism Quarterly, American Journalism,* the *Journal of Popular Culture, Journalism Educator,* and newspapers throughout the United States.